W9-AOM-115

IMPLEMENTING OPERATIONS RESEARCH/ MANAGEMENT SCIENCE

IMPLEMENTING OPERATIONS RESEARCH/ MANAGEMENT SCIENCE

Edited by

RANDALL L. SCHULTZ
Krannert Graduate School of Industrial Administration
Purdue University

DENNIS P. SLEVIN
Graduate School of Business
University of Pittsburgh

American Elsevier Publishing Company, Inc.
New York London Amsterdam

AMERICAN ELSEVIER PUBLISHING COMPANY, INC.
52 Vanderbilt Avenue, New York, N.Y. 10017

ELSEVIER PUBLISHING COMPANY
335 Jan Van Galenstraat, P.O. Box 211
Amsterdam, The Netherlands

Library of Congress Cataloging in Publication Data

Main entry under title:

Implementing operations research/management science.

Papers from a conference held Nov. 15-17, 1973 in Pittsburgh.
Includes bibliographies.
1. Operations research. I. Schultz, Randall L., ed.
II. Slevin, Dennis P., joint ed.
HD20.5.I45 658.4'034 74-14467
ISBN 0-444-00150-6

To Bobbi and Sue

Contents

Contributing Authors

N. R. BAKER	*University of Cincinnati*
RICHARD T. BARTH	*University of British Columbia*
ALDEN S. BEAN	*National Science Foundation*
C. WEST CHURCHMAN	*University of California, Berkeley*
CORNELIS A. DE KLUYVER	*Case Western Reserve University*
ROBERT DUNCAN	*Northwestern University*
CYRUS F. GIBSON	*Harvard University*
JAN H. B. M. HUYSMANS	*McKinsey & Company, The Netherlands*
HENRY C. LUCAS, JR.	*Stanford University*
P. M. MAHER	*University of Alberta*
JOHN H. MANLEY	*United States Air Force*
VANCE F. MITCHELL	*University of British Columbia*
IAN I. MITROFF	*University of Pittsburgh*
RODNEY D. NEAL	*University of Arkansas, Little Rock*
MICHAEL RADNOR	*Northwestern University*
ARNOLD REISMAN	*Case Western Reserve University*
A. H. RUBENSTEIN	*Northwestern University*
RANDALL L. SCHULTZ	*Purdue University*
C. R. SHUMWAY	*Texas A & M University*
DENNIS P. SLEVIN	*University of Pittsburgh*
RICHARD E. SORENSEN	*Appalachian State University*
WM. E. SOUDER	*University of Pittsburgh*
DAVID A. TANSIK	*University of Arizona*
ILAN VERTINSKY	*University of British Columbia*
GERALD ZALTMAN	*Northwestern University*
DALE E. ZAND	*New York University*

Foreword

Much has been written in recent years about ideas whose time has come. Mostly the comment is raised in connection with problems which have been with us for some time, but where solutions have either eluded society or where no one has taken on the challenge as their personal project. The subject material of this book is a response to that kind of problem.

The dual objectives of the conference producing the papers contained in this book were to move forward the frontiers of research on implementation, while at the same time communicating to practicing managers results that would be useful to them on their jobs. The conference attempted to bring together scholars from all over the world who were particularly concerned that the cascading number of OR/MS models being developed were put to good use, and tested in the industrial setting. The difficulties, both behavioral and technological, which were impeding this process, were the crucial foci of the conference.

One of the results of the conference has been to convince the Graduate School of Business at the University of Pittsburgh of the importance of developing a research thrust in the implementation area. We are in the process of focusing doctoral and faculty research on this topic. We hope that this will be but the beginning of a vast outpouring of facilitating literature, making it possible for models being developed to be more effectively and more quickly utilized in the industrial setting.

The University of Pittsburgh is grateful not only to the conference coordinators and their staffs, but also to the many scholars throughout the country who took time to contribute papers to the conference and to share with us the benefit of their current thinking. This book of readings bears dedication to the need for a continuing partnership between the academic and industrial segments of our society. To the extent that there are no barriers in moving from one segment to the other, to the extent that new knowledge generated in one segment can be transmitted effectively and quickly for use in the other segment, and to the extent that there is continuing dialogue between the industrial and scholarly communities, our society will be making maximum use of our resources. This book is dedicated to implementing that kind of partnership.

H. J. Zoffer
Dean, Graduate School of Business
University of Pittsburgh

Preface

Operations research/management science (OR/MS) has developed over the last three decades as a mature field of academic study and research. Important advances have been made in such areas as mathematical programming, stochastic modeling, and general systems analysis. The result of this work is an inventory of OR/MS models and systems that has great potential in solving management problems. Despite the promise of OR/MS as a problem-solving discipline, the current situation reveals a significant gap between management science theory and managerial application. Thus, the potential of OR/MS is largely unrealized. The current trend toward introspective looks at the practice of OR/MS has recently been augmented by research on the problems of OR/MS implementation. But until recently there had not been much empirical evidence on the process of implementation. Sue Slevin's 1973 bibliography on OR/MS implementation, for example, contains only about 30 references and most of these are nonempirical.

It was this lack of research on the implementation problem that motivated us to organize an international research conference. The conference, *The Implementation of OR/MS Models: Theory, Research and Application,* was held on November 15–17, 1973 in Pittsburgh, Pennsylvania. The purpose of the meeting was to critically examine the body of implementation research, to report on new research, and to identify avenues that will lead to a better utilization of OR/MS as a true problem-solving activity in the future. The conference was held as part of the fiftieth anniversary activities of the Graduate School of Business at the University of Pittsburgh and drew an international audience of OR/MS researchers and practitioners.

This volume includes most of the papers presented at the implementation conference. Since the conference was planned from an idea for a book, a set of invited papers was used to provide the basic structure of perspectives on implementation, research on implementation, and considerations for implementation management. A number of contributed papers were also received and then integrated into this basic framework. In this volume no distinction is made between the two types of papers.

Research on the implementation of OR/MS models generally falls into three categories: Implementation is seen as a process of organizational change, as a diffusion of innovations, and as a part of general systems analysis. These categories, of course, are not mutually exclusive. The implementation of an OR/MS model involves the diffusion of an innovation (the OR/MS project or model), the affecting of organizational change (use of the model), and the management of systems (the model-organizational interface). Various researchers have examined implementation problems from the point of view of operations research groups, from the model-building process, and from the dimensions of models themselves. New approaches have been developed that identify behavioral factors in the implementation process, such as attitudes of potential users toward the model, cognitive styles of decision making of managers, and organizational goals and constraints. The result of this research is a new inventory, not of models, but of findings that show how models can be used.

This book has the practical impact of about doubling the empirical literature on OR/MS implementation. We hope that it has an intellectual impact as well: to introduce the same rigor with which models are built into the study of how they are implemented. Implementation research is, by definition, management relevant. Thus, this book can be used in classes in business, management, industrial engineering, and operations research programs, and by practicing managers and professional management scientists where an emphasis is needed on *how* the results of OR/MS activity will be *used.*

ACKNOWLEDGMENTS

The research conference was made possible through the financial support of two organizations. We thank the Graduate School of Business at the University of Pittsburgh for sponsoring the conference and serving as its host. Dean H. J. Zoffer and Associate Dean Andrew R. Blair were instrumental in providing this initial support. In addition, we are grateful for a grant from the Organizational Effectiveness Research Programs of the Office of Naval Research. We appreciate the interest of Associate Director Bert T. King in the project and in his sponsorship of a number of the papers. Ms. Jean Leff deserves special thanks for help with the details of conference arrangements and publicity. Our greatest debt must undoubtedly be to our contributors, whose ideas are the main substance of this book. Finally, any sustained writing or editorial effort spills over into family life and, realizing this, we thank our families for their more subtle but nevertheless real support. We especially thank our wives, to whom this book is dedicated.

Randall L. Schultz
West Lafayette, Indiana
Dennis P. Slevin
Pittsburgh, Pennsylvania

PART ONE

INTRODUCTION

Chapter 1

Implementation and Management Innovation

Randall L. Schultz and Dennis P. Slevin

This book is about organizations, decision making, operations research, management science, and the process of implementing administrative innovation. It focuses on the problems associated with the utilization of decision-making technology in organizations. Of primary concern is the special management technology known as operations research or management science. The purpose of the volume is to lay a foundation of empirical research relevant to improving organizational decision making through successful management innovation.

Operations research/management science (OR/MS) is the name given to a wide range of activities of researchers and decision makers, all centered on the improvement of management through the application of formal and scientific methods such as systems analysis and mathematical model building. The formalization of decision making is intended to allow organizations to better achieve their goals and to better serve their publics. In the case of a business firm, for example, this may mean that OR/MS is utilized to increase customer satisfaction, increase sales, and maximize profit. For a government agency, the case may be one of delivering services in the most cost-efficient manner. A political party may use OR/MS to design an optimal media schedule. In all cases the goal is to bring OR/MS technology to bear on the process of organizational decision making.

The field of operations research/management science is quite well developed; there is a considerable inventory of OR/MS models and methods that can be used to improve decision making in organizations. The actual frequency of use of OR/MS, however, is quite low, especially with respect to its potential. This situation has resulted in an *implementation gap* between what has been developed and what is being used. To understand why this gap has occurred and how it can be closed is the main point of this book.

Thus, the central theme of the volume is the *process of implementation* of operations research/management science. The implementation process is generally treated as a special case of the process of management innovation and organizational change. This broad perspective seems particularly appropriate in the early stage of research on what is essentially a behavioral problem. In fact, if the results of the theoretical and empirical work can be anticipated, the major insight into the implementation problem will come from behavioral science as much as management science.

This initial chapter provides an overview of the work covered in the volume. The framework is spare by design. Empirical research and serious thinking about the implementation process is of recent vintage. It does not seem appropriate to foreclose yet on a single viewpoint, eliminating a richness that ought to characterize research in a new area. Instead, insight is sought through a diversity of ideas and through the juxtaposition of research methodologies. In this way the subsequent chapters become points of departure for a variety of new and exciting research questions.

THE IMPLEMENTATION PROBLEM

The problem of implementing operations research/management science is an old one: OR/MS is an applied field and, although the development of OR/MS methods may be thought of as basic research, the primary thrust of activity in this area has always been directed at application and implementation. The implementation problem is also a fundamental one precisely because of this *raison d'être.* Management decision making can only be improved through OR/MS if the methods and models are utilized in organizations. Finally, the implementation problem is a continuing one because future advances in OR/MS methods must be matched by new and useful applications. These are strong reasons for studying the implementation process in detail and with considerable rigor.

Another reason for studying the implementation process is the potential contribution of the research to the understanding of other fundamental processes of organizations, that is, for adding to organization theory, theories of change and knowledge of technological innovation. Indeed, most of the papers in this volume are rich with such behavioral and organizational implications.

The OR/MS Process

Implementation still means different things to different people. One way to clarify the issues surrounding the implementation problem is to consider the OR/MS process and the role of implementation in it. In Figure 1.1 a number of ingredients of OR/MS activity are identified and classified as inputs, agents, processors and outputs. How do they relate to the meaning of implementation?

OR/MS activity begins with the confluence of an organization and its

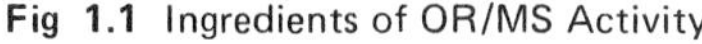

Fig 1.1 Ingredients of OR/MS Activity

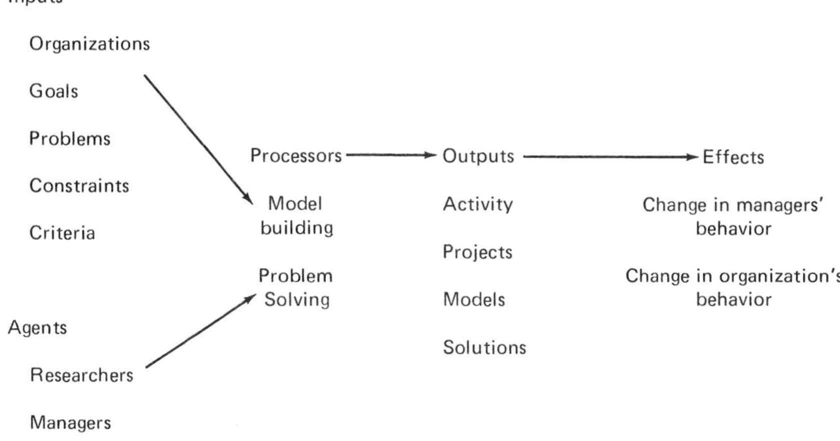

problems with the problem-solving skills of managers and researchers. The origin of the activity, then, is problem identification and the concomitant desire for a solution. The solution is sought with certain organizational goals and constraints in mind. In addition, decision criteria must be established to evaluate the acceptability of a proposed solution. The players or agents in the activity are managers and researchers. Their roles have traditionally been cast as manager/ decision maker and researcher/problem solver (the latter being the operations researcher or management scientist), although in principle and increasingly in practice, the roles are less distinct and may even be reversed or played jointly. In fact much of the confusion about implementation will be seen to stem from this apparent dichotomy. The manager of the OR/MS group (of researchers) might also be considered, but clearly this is also a role of dual function. In addition the ultimate user may be someone other than the manager. Those individuals have been termed the clients of the researcher and have been considered as a separate group by some (cf. Manley, Chapter 8). For simplicity in this discussion we are considering the manager and the researcher as the two chief players in the implementation process.

It is useful to distinguish between the objects of this research inquiry and the investigators themselves since the same terms apply to both. It has become traditional to refer to the manager/researcher interface where the latter is the OR/MS practitioner. The student of OR/MS implementation, however, is also a researcher, and the distinction between these two principals should be borne in mind. Similarly, the term model refers to both the output of an OR/MS practitioner and to the paradigm of a scholar of the implementation process. The

OR/MS process then, is something going on in organizations and something being studied by other investigators.

If a problem has been identified, organizational goals, constraints, and decision criteria specified, and a manager/researcher interaction established, then the model-building or problem-solving phase of OR/MS activity can begin. At this point, the researcher brings OR/MS methodology to bear on the problem. In other words, the researcher seeks a scientific solution to the problem. Because model building is central to OR/MS method, this step usually involves the development of some model of the problem and the solution offered is one to the model and hopefully the problem. Identification of the right problem and development of an appropriate model turn out to be crucial determinants of OR/MS success. Equally important, however, is the interaction and understanding of manager and researcher. When this relationship is good and when understanding is mutual, the chances that the manager will *use* the research results will be greatly enhanced.

The output of the OR/MS process is generally activity and specifically projects, models, and solutions. The projects and models can be regarded either as ends in themselves or as the means for influencing the organization's decision processes. The notion of influence provides a key to understanding the concept of implementation. The initial state of the organization was a set of decision processes (or procedures) and a problem. At the output stage of OR/MS activity, the organization has a solution to the problem. If the solution is *implemented,* then the final state of the organization is a revised set of decision processes incorporating the solution. Implementation, then, refers to the actual use of OR/MS output by managers that *influences* their decision processes. In this view, an OR/MS model or project that does not change decision making in some way would not be considered to be implemented. Changes in decision making will presumably lead to changes in the managers' and the organization's behavior. The degree to which actual change in the managers' or organization's behavior is required for a successful implementation may vary depending upon the researcher and the situation.

It is possible, of course, that organizational decision-making processes could be influenced without the *particular* OR/MS output being actually used. This situation could arise if, for example, an OR project was undertaken to create a decision model and the model was never used (i.e. for the purpose for which it was designed), but the OR *process* influenced management's way of thinking and, more importantly, their way of making decisions. This kind of indirect influence comes close to the notion that *any* OR/MS activity has some educational value for management. Still, since OR output has been broadly defined, the essence of implementation is in the direct influence of OR/MS on decision making.

Other interpretations of the OR/MS process and implementation are possible and it is, of course, the purpose of this volume to explore them. The institutionalization of OR/MS, for example, might be considered equivalent to implementing (or simply establishing) the OR/MS function itself in an organization. Institutionalization can be thought of in at least two ways: institutionalization of OR/MS groups in organizations or simply the institutionalization of the OR/MS concept. The former comes closest to the notion of mutual understanding and the latter to what might be called a mutual way of thinking. When manager and researcher are one, in the sense of mutual understanding and thinking, then institutionalization has certainly occurred, thus setting the stage for specific implementations of OR/MS projects and models. The highest phase in this process of utilization of OR/MS is perhaps when managers themselves initiate (or even conduct) the OR/MS work. Whether or not this is the "best" phase of implementation depends upon the tradeoff between understanding and efficiency in the sense of an optimal division of labor in a complex organization.

But what comes first, implementation or institutionalization? Successful implementations of OR/MS models, for example, are likely to create a favorable organizational climate for the institutionalization of the concept of OR/MS and the research group. On the other hand, an appropriate organizational milieu would seem to enhance the probability of successful implementations. The answer appears to be that these two things occur together; that is, the process is a simultaneous one, with significant feedback from one kind of implementation to the other. The main point to be made here is that (1) there is a system of organizational decision making and (2) reflection on the functioning of this system may lead to changes in it. The reflection that this book deals with is not of a casual sort, but of the rigorous methods of science. The organizational change and the management innovation are what implementation is all about.

OVERVIEW

The work presented in this volume is divided into four parts: introduction, perspectives on implementation, research on implementation, and considerations for implementation management. The analysis basically flows from theory to empirical research to practical issues. This section summarizes the major research approaches, implementation models, and research findings that are central to the study of implementing operations research/management science.

Research Approaches

The research approaches underlying studies of implementation are the principal methods of behavioral investigation. Case studies, survey research, experimentation, and theoretical and philosophical inquiries are all reported in the subsequent chapters. For a reader approaching this work with a background in organizational behavior, these designs are familiar and standard. For the operations researcher or professional management scientist, however, these methods contrast quite sharply with the usual tools of OR/MS research. The principal reason for this reliance on behavioral methodology is the fundamental nature of the implementation problem. It is, in any interpretation, a problem involving human participants, social interaction, organizational structure, and management change–in short, a complex behavioral process. The fact that the implementation problem brings operations researchers into contact with different methodologies and behavioral scientists into touch with a new problem area generates much of the excitement that runs through the various chapters.

The predominant research method seems to be survey research, in the sense that quite a few studies employ questionnaires and other data-gathering instruments to assess facts about implementation, attitudes toward implementation, and other behavioral implementation factors. Bean and others (Chapter 5) conducted a large-scale survey of U.S. business organizations in order to identify structural factors such as organizational size and management support related to the success or failure of OR/MS projects. Surveys of individual attitudes are integral to the work of Schultz and Slevin (Chapter 7), Manley (Chapter 8), Sorensen and Zand (Chapter 10), Vertinsky, Barth, and Mitchell (Chapter 12), and Duncan and Zaltman (Chapter 15). Attitude instruments are also used in several of the other studies. By obtaining information across organizations and individuals, survey research provides interesting insight into quantifiable factors that can be associated with measures of implementation success. As demonstrated below, these studies also lend themselves to theory building (essential at this stage of research) and to statistical data analysis.

Case studies are also important in implementation research because of their exceptional ability to provide in-depth and organizationally dependent analyses of implementation situations. The participant observation or action research employed by Gibson (Chapter 4) in his study of implementation in a bank is a case in point. A rich series of data that describes the cultural setting of implementation is collected including organizational business and social history. Mitroff (Chapter 11) uses the case study to reveal the psychology of moon scientists, and Reisman and de Kluyver (Chapter 14) forge a series of case studies into a systems view of the implementation process. Combining survey research and case method approaches, Souder and others (Chapter 6) and Lucas (Chapter 9) show how the two approaches can complement each other.

Experimentation, despite its significance as a method of causal research, plays a smaller part in implementation studies, at least at this time. Huysmans (Chapter 13) builds on his laboratory experiments of the effect of cognitive style on implementation. Manley's (Chapter 8) attitude instrument was used in a field experiment among school administrators and teachers. As models of the implementation process are developed and their organizational context explored, experimentation will be increasingly used to test theories of implementation.

No field of study can advance without a theoretical and philosophical framework, and, appropriately, the earliest writings on implementation reflect this kind of speculation. Churchman (Chapter 2) continues his exploration of "mutual understanding" and the philosophy of implementation, embedding it in the broader context of social change. A different approach is taken by Schultz and Slevin (Chapter 3) when they discuss implementation as a process of organizational change and describe a stepwise program of behavioral research. Gibson (Chapter 4), in discussing the bank study, also offers a world view for implementation research, contrasting his methodology with others in the behavioral sciences.

Throughout the book additional methodologies appear and are explained. Similarly, other perspectives emerge, such as social and managerial ones, that are not strictly philosophies of implementation. The common ground, then, is that most of the studies reported here are behavioral and most are empirical. This in itself represents a significant departure from earlier work.

Implementation Models

A number of models of the implementation process are suggested and several are built from empirically derived relationships. They should be evaluated from the perspective of exploratory research on a complex behavioral process. In no case does a model purport to explain the entire process of OR/MS development and utilization. On the other hand, all the models provide the means for testing specific hypotheses about implementation behavior. The form of these models contrasts with the form of earlier models in that such ideas as mutual understanding and selling OR/MS do not embody clear behavioral premises and thus cannot be operationalized in an empirical investigation. Thus, these models serve as a useful first approximation to a process that involves dynamic human and organizational relationships. The theory-building phase of implementation research is made possible by the bringing together of concepts such as these.

The general structure of the models is that some measure of implementation, a dependent variable, is explained by a set of so-called independent variables. In some cases the independent variables are intervening variables. For example, the quality of an OR model (an independent variable) may influence individual attitudes toward the model (an intervening variable) which in turn influence individual use (a dependent variable), as in Lucas' work. Thus, in general, the models have the form:

implementation = f(independent variables)

or

intervening variables = f(independent variables)
implementation = f(intervening variables).

A few of the models contain jointly dependent variables which imply simultaneous causality, viz.

implementation = f(explanatory variables)
explanatory variables = f(implementation).

Such a relationship holds between performance and payoffs in the Vertinsky, Barth and Mitchell model. As implementation models become more sophisticated (i.e. more behavioral), simultaneous-equation structures will be more common.

The models are summarized in Figure 1.2. Schultz and Slevin (A) posit a theory of behavioral model building in which the probability of success of an OR/MS model is dependent upon the organizational and technical validities of the model. The key concept is organizational validity, a multidimensional construct with variables that involve individuals, small groups, and organizations. They argue that when a model is capable of solving a problem and when a model is compatible with the user's organization, the probability of successful implementation is enhanced. In research on the individual dimension of organizational validity, Schultz and Slevin (E) derive several possible models from their empirical investigation of attitudes toward an OR/MS model. The simplest model describes the influence of attitudes on intended behavior. The more complex model relates a number of specific attitudes to actual model use.

In his case study, Gibson (B) implies that personality type, business history, and social history influence individual attitudes and, at the same time, the model-builder's knowledge of the company. These factors plus model characteristics then influence implementation. Although Bean and others (C) use a quite different methodology, their general model of the implementation process implies that the organizational implementation depends upon a set of structural and behavioral variables that are similar to Gibson's structural determinants. Souder and others (D) also develop a model with the same basic ingredients: model characteristics, organizational factors, and personal decision variables. Like Schultz and Slevin, their willingness to adopt dependent variables focuses on the individual rather than the organization.

Attitudes are the core of Manley's (F) model showing the relationship of client resistance (or acceptance) to probability of success. His attitude dimensions that influence client resistance are quite similar to some of Bean's structural factors, such as top management support. It is interesting to note that in this case, however, Bean uses an independent measure of support (percent of projects generated by top management), whereas Manley concentrates on perceived top management support.

Lucas (G) postulates that the quality of the OR/MS model influences attitudes and that attitudes, decision style, and situational and personal variables influence individual use. His use of decision or cognitive style and situational variables is similar to prior work on cognitive style by Huysmans and to the suggested influence of situational variables reported in Schultz and Slevin (Chapter 7). The position of these situational variables in the implementation process, however, is different in these and other cases.

Two quite different models are those of Sorensen and Zand (H) and Mitroff (I). In the former, OR/MS projects and (by implication) organizational and individual factors are seen to influence the organizational change process. The process itself involves unfreezing, changing, and refreezing phases corresponding to distinct behavioral changes. The change process then presumably determines implementation. In the latter, Mitroff implies that self-understanding is a precondition for mutual understanding, which Churchman had previously argued to be a necessary condition for implementation. Personal bias (or objectivity) in OR/MS scientific work can provide insight into the human participants in the implementation process.

In what is perhaps the most complex model, Vertinsky, Barth, and Mitchell (J) show how personal, group, and organizational factors are interrelated and influence use/implementation, which in turn influences individual performance and determines individual payoffs. The most important features of this model are its comprehensiveness (environmental factors are also mentioned as impinging on the process) and its recognition of feedback mechanisms. Another complex model, although at a conceptual and not empirical plane, is that of Huysmans (K). In this model, the environment, the manager, and the organization are linked with OR science, OR capability, and the problem and OR model. By implication, this complex interaction leads to OR success. Writing from his management viewpoint, Huysmans has provided a broad overlay with important reference points to empirical work.

The final model is one implied by Reisman and de Kluyver (L). In their systems approach to the implementation problem, they have uncovered many of the same variables included in other models. Beyond this, they suggest that these systems factors are related to the likelihood of successful implementation and that this probability can be assessed a priori and revised and updated as the process of implementation moves forward.

These models of implementation exhibit substantial similarities and important differences—points that should be the grist of future research. Such models and subsequent research are the building blocks of implementation theory and the more general theory of management innovation and organizational change.

Research Findings

The empirical research findings reported in this volume serve two purposes. First, they provide necessary tests of implementation hypotheses and important input for implementation models. Second, they offer useful and

Fig 1.2 Models of the Implementation Process

A. **Schultz and Slevin (I)**

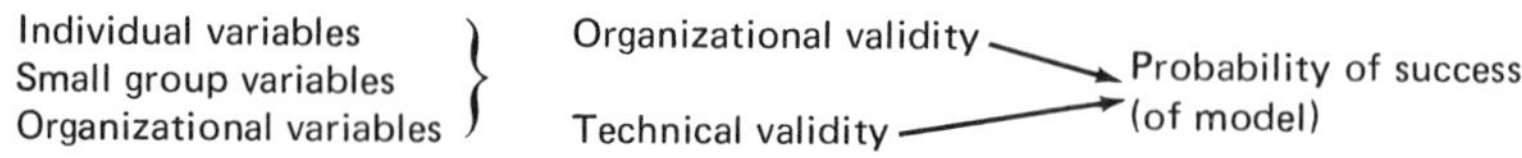

B. **Gibson** (implied)

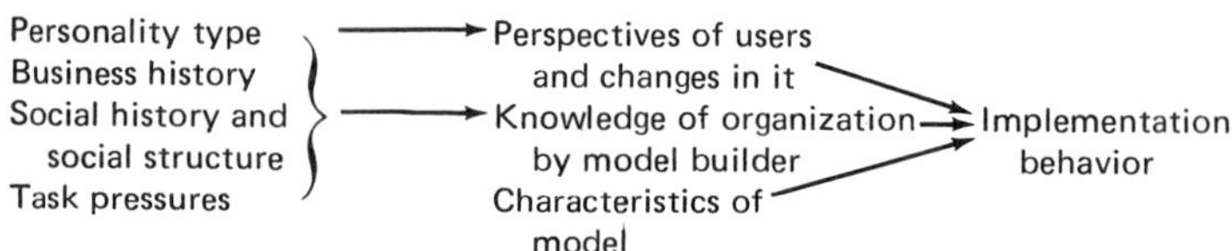

C. **Bean et al.**

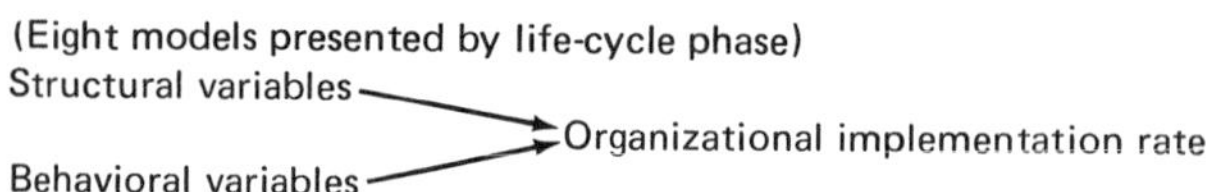

D. **Souder et al.**

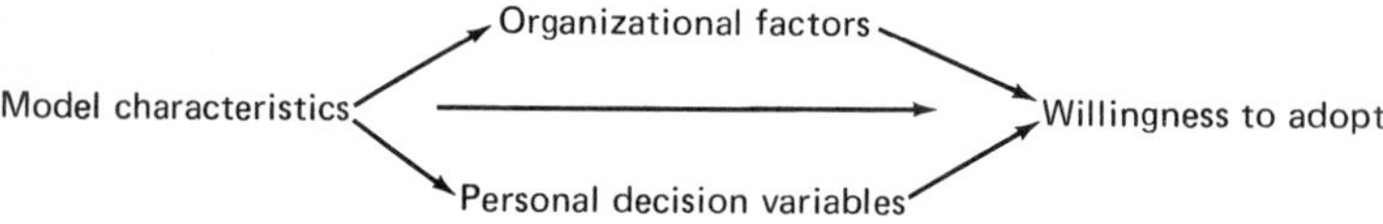

E. **Schultz and Slevin (II)**

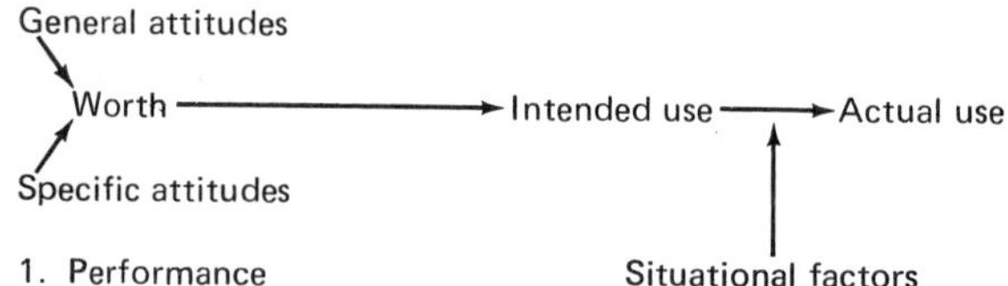

1. Performance
2. Interpersonal
3. Changes
4 Goals
5. Support/resistance
6. Client/researcher
7. Urgency

F. **Manley**

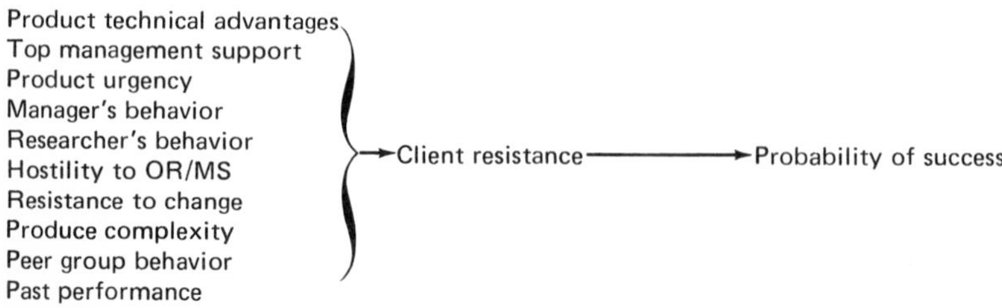

G. **Lucas**

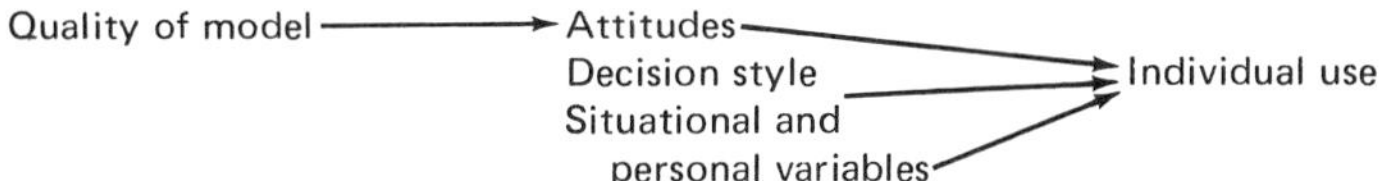

H. **Sorensen and Zand**

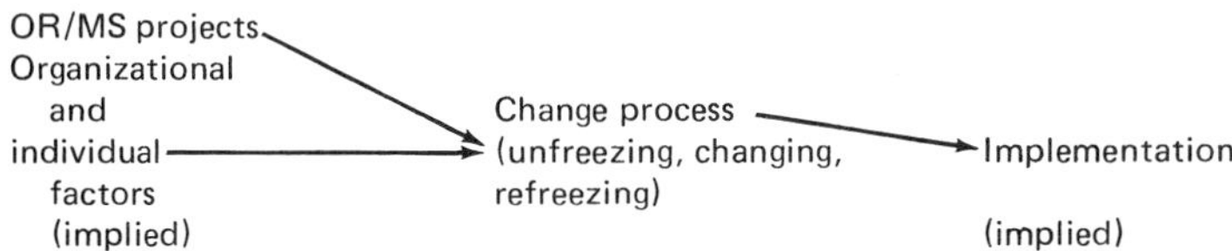

I. **Mitroff** (implied)

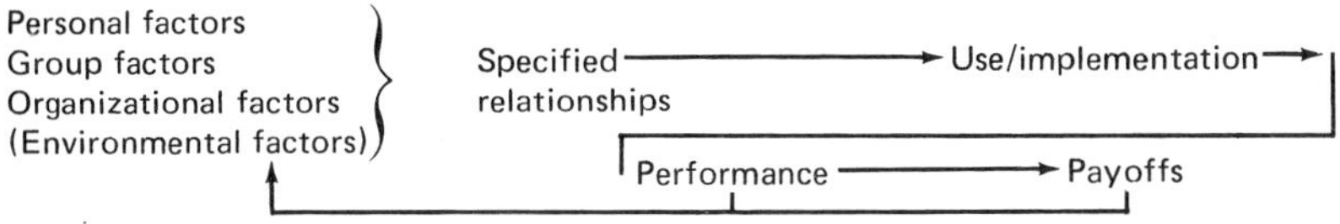

J. **Vertinsky, Barth, and Mitchell** (broad categories of a complex model)

K. **Huysmans**

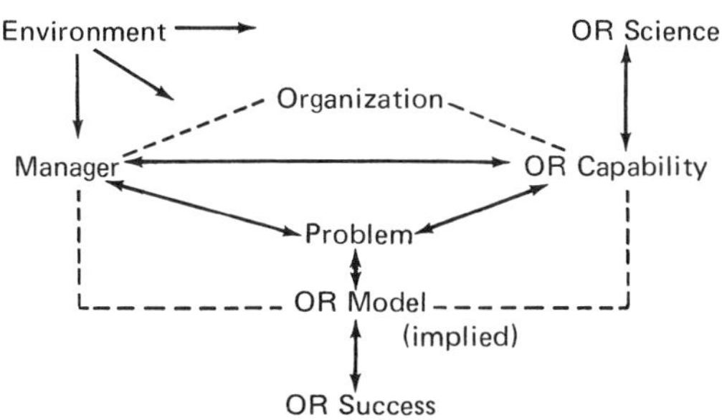

L. **Reisman and de Kluyver** (implied)

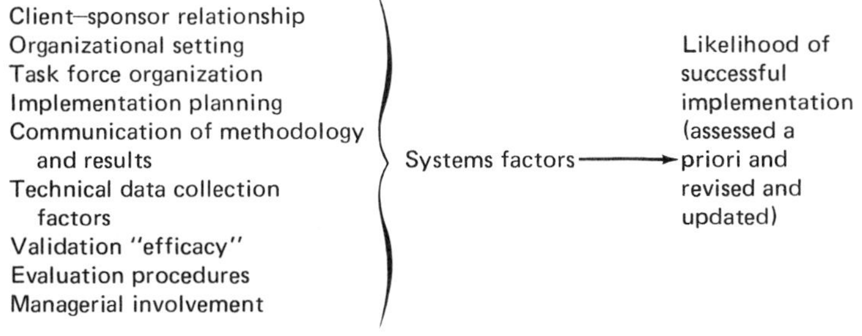

actionable implications for the management of organizational innovation. In this section some of the research considerations are pursued. In the following section the relationship of implementation studies to innovation and organizational change is explored.

The empirical studies of implementation are summarized in Table 1.1, which is largely self-explanatory. One of the features worth noting is the focus of the study. Several studies focus on an individual user and on an OR/MS model. These studies are concerned with factors related to individual behavior, such as attitudes, personality, and decision style. One study centers on implementation of OR/MS projects by organizations and thus deals with certain structural characteristics of organizations and with broadly-defined projects, some of which may be specific models. Another study focuses on clients as individual users and on the product of OR/MS activity, which may be models and/or projects. Other orientations include individual and project, individual and OR/MS, and the relationship between a researcher and his own methods of inquiry.

A second feature of the studies is choice of a dependent variable. Although the ultimate dependent variable of interest in all studies is implementation, a number of surrogates for this concept or intermediate stages in the implementation process have been employed. The dependent variables used generally fall into three categories; they are either attitudes, intentions, or behavior. The attitudes measured are those toward the OR/MS model, project, or product; toward the researcher; or even toward the OR/MS concept. Additional attitudes related to personal and situational factors were also sought in some studies. Intended use, rather than actual use, was the end point of several studies because of the difficulty in securing a record of actual use or implementation success. Actual behavior was the dependent variable in two studies, defined as percent of projects used in one case and various types of use in the other. The difficulty in defining actual use, let alone measuring it, stems from the ambiguity of implementation itself. If implementation is taken to be a change in a decision process resulting from the introduction of a model, for example, then an even more sophisticated measure of actual behavior would have to be obtained.

The independent or explanatory variables given in Table 1-1 are generally the findings of the empirical research. For example, Gibson suggests in his case study that personality type, business history, social history and current social structure and task pressures influence the perspectives of builders and users and that these in turn determine their behavior toward implementation. Bean and others identify a long list of structural and behavioral factors that correlate with implementation rate and with perceived success, as can be seen. Souder and others find that attitudes, and particularly the dimensions of model characteristics, organizational factors, and personal decision variables, are related to intended use. Similarly, Schultz and Slevin report that such attitude dimensions as performance, interpersonal relations, changes, goals, support/resistance, client/researcher relationship, and project urgency account for much of the variance in intended use, chance of success, model worth, and model accuracy. This attitude structure is quite consistent with the proposed models and other empirical research.

Using experimental data, Manley finds that top management support, personal involvement, and product relevance are related to probability of success due to client behavior. In addition, the effect of written communication (as used in the experiment) is suggested to be an important implementation consideration. Lucas and Vertinsky, Barth, and Mitchell find that a number of attitudinal, decision style, personal, and situational variables are related to actual or intended use. In the latter study, such concepts as self-esteem, need satisfaction, felt pressure, and cognitive dissonance add considerable behavioral sophistication to the implementation research tradition. The empirical work of Sorensen and Zand reveals that attitudes are related to perceived level of success. The process is explained in social change terms. In a study of ethical and value considerations in implementation, Duncan and Zaltman find interesting differences in attitudes for interventionists who are internal and external to the organization. Finally, Mitroff's study of moon scientists shows that a researcher's ideas and actions are to a considerable extent dependent upon his prior theories and ideas and upon social and personal relations.

These research findings support many of the implementation models and, in themselves, suggest the development of new or revised models of the implementation process. They set the stage for increased theoretical work on implementation and social change. They also support two propositions about implementation research. First, theories of implementation should be behavioral because the implementation process is behavioral. Second, theories of implementation should be cast in a form that makes their implications testable. Armed with behavioral theories of implementation that are falsifiable, implementation researchers—all operations researchers—will soon achieve second-approximation models that place in the hands of management the means of controlling their own organizational change.

INNOVATION AND ORGANIZATIONAL CHANGE

OR/MS implementation was initially defined and studied by operations researchers. Over time, however, their efforts have interfaced with those of behavioral scientists, and this has resulted in progress not only in the OR/MS implementation area, but also in our general understanding of organizational innovation. One reason for this mutual benefit is the fact that implementation is a special case of organizational innovation. Organizational innovation has been

TABLE 1.1
Empirical Studies of Implementation

Researchers	Focus	Dependent variables	Independent variables
Gibson	Individual user and builder/model	Behavior of users and attitudes toward model builders; ultimate model utilization	Personality types Business history Social history and Social structure Task pressures
Bean et al.	Organization/project	Implementation rate (Percent of projects used) Perceived success (Multiattribute attitude measure)	Structural factors Formalization of charter Quality and availability of data Size of budget Level in hierarchy Group size Life-cycle phase Total revenue Number of employees Decentralization Behavioral factors Top management interest Top management support Orientation of group leader % of leader's time selling % of leader's time "administering"
Souder et al.	Individual user/model	Intended use or willingness to adopt (Actual use reported but factors not related to it)	Attitude dimensions Model characteristics Organizational factors Personal decision variables
Schultz and Slevin (II)	Individual user/model	Intended use (Probability of *own* use and probability of *others'* use)	Attitude dimensions Performance Interpersonal relations Changes

		Chance of success Worth Accuracy	Goals Support/resistance Client/researcher Urgency
Manley	Client/product	Probability of success due to client behavior	Top management support Personal involvement Produce relevance (written communication)
Lucas	Individual user/model	Actual use (Various types of use)	Situational variables Personal variables Decision style variables Attitudinal variables
Sorensen and Zand	Individual/project	Level of success (Perception)	Level of unfreezing Level of changing Level of refreezing (Attitudes)
Mitroff	Researcher/methods	Objectivity of researcher (or bias) (Attitudes)	Prior theories and ideas Social and personal relations
Vertinsky, Barth, and Mitchell	Individual/(OR/MS)	Use/implementation Performance Payoffs (Attitude measures)	Performance expectancy Payoff expectancy Valence Self-esteem Prior experience Internal vs. external control Equity of outcome Need satisfaction Felt pressure Managerial style Manager's abilities Cognitive dissonance Social change
Duncan and Zaltman	Researcher/attitudes	Researcher attitudes and values	Location of researcher with respect to organization (Internal/external)

defined in a variety of ways. The simplest notion is that it consists of a number of people in an organization trying new things; i.e., individuals must try out new behaviors in order to implement any organization-wide innovation. The implementation problem fits this definition quite well. In order for an OR/MS model to be successful, new information inputs are sought, new decision-making rules are developed, changes are made in the locus of decision making, and a variety of similar changes that could well be classified as organizational innovation are required. As a result progress in the implementation area may lead to progress in our general understanding of organization change and innovation.

Implementation Research and Innovation

The literature on organizational change and innovation has been an important one for behavioral science for a number of years. However, it is probably safe to characterize much of this research as soft or lacking in rigorously defined conceptual models accompanied by empirical tests. A number of factors have led this research to develop in this way.

First, the organizational change literature is characterized by a great difficulty in defining appropriately the *criterion variable.* What is organizational change? How is it measured? Significant attention in the literature has been placed on attempts to define and conceptualize organizational change and innovation. As is common in other areas of behavioral science, when the criterion variable is difficult to define and measure, progress is slow in determining the factors that influence this variable. As a result, there is no real documented set of principles on organizational change and innovation.

Second, the development of methodology in the area of organizational change and innovation has been slow. Although a number of researchers have conducted interesting studies on the innovation process in recent years, a standard methodology approaching this problem has not yet gained acceptance. This "methodological shortfall" may be caused by many researchers who are generalists by nature and who are not committed to any particular approach of behavioral investigation. Another contributing factor is undoubtedly the difficult and complicated nature of the problem itself, i.e., organizational change and innovation, by their very nature, do not lend themselves to straightforward analytical interpretation.

Third, there is a tendency to focus on the process of organizational change as a rather organic, loosely defined, and unstructured activity. In many cases, the change process is regarded as equivalent to sensitivity approaches to personal relations, drawing upon interventions to accomplish a definite goal. The concepts of measuring the degree of change required in advance, establishing specific and quantifiable objectives, and studying the process in a scientifically rigorous manner have not permeated much of this literature.

Perhaps OR/MS implementation studies will help us to solve some of these problems in the organizational change research area and accelerate the progress of research. The implementation problem is characterized by a number of attributes that are both interesting and desirable from the standpoint of the study of organizational change and innovation. Implementation typically deals with a high-technology situation. It is often characterized by a model, by a computer system, and by the sophisticated use of mathematics and data analysis techniques. The field of organizational innovation has always been concerned with the problem of the development and implementation of new technology. Substantive changes are required to successfully implement a new OR/MS model in a social organization. Changes in decision-making style, formal and informal communications structures, etc., may be required. Some portions of the literature on organizational change have addressed problems of change in the "organizational climate" that are difficult to quantify and measure. However, the implementation problem inherently provides the researcher with a better-defined criterion variable.

Thus, the emphasis on implementation research seems to have come at a propitious time for both operations researchers and behavioral scientists who are studying organization change and innovation. There should be a strong felt need by OR/MS researchers for new implementation skills. Our historical failure to successfully implement more than a small percentage of potential models in social organizations has pointed out the need for improved implementation capabilities. It is also a time when the behavioral scientist studying the organizational change and innovation has been frustrated by the elusive nature of this process and may welcome the more concrete implementation situation. The net result should be that implementation research will benefit both the OR/MS practitioner and the behavioral scientist studying innovation and organizational change.

Future Developments

A number of future developments may occur that will benefit both the management scientist and the behavioral scientist. First, a methodology for conducting implementation research is being developed. A number of measurement techniques that have been used to study implementation are reported in this book and they are being used with increasing frequency by researchers in the field. Second, a number of conceptual models of implementation and consequently conceptual models of organizational innovation are being formulated. This theoretical work should lead to a better understanding of the process of organizational innovation in general. Third, there is a significant new tradition of empirical research on the implementation problem. In a field that was until recently characterized by a great emphasis upon casual reflection—from philosophical inquiries to accounts of management experiences—the movement to causal studies should lead to the establishment of linkages between key variables affecting implementation. Fourth, a rather accidental but quite significant benefit may be the greatly increased availability of research sites for the study of implementation and organizational innovation. Thousands of operations researchers throughout the world are attempting to implement models in social organizations on a daily basis. As they become increasingly concerned with the critical problem of implementation and as more people begin to study this problem, the locus of implementation research will be more evenly distributed among academic and professional management scientists. Although this may seem to be a minor benefit, it no doubt will have a strongly positive effect on the encouragement of research on implementation and innovation.

As knowledge of the processes of implementation and management innovation accumulates, the practice of operations research/management science will move toward the realization of its ultimate goal: the improvement of organizational decision making. By improving organizational decisions, the OR/MS community is presumably making organizations more responsive to their publics, whether these interests be owners, customers, or society at large. This broader perspective for the relevance of implementation research, where organizational implementation and change are regarded as means of social progress, makes the study of this phenomena not only more dramatic but also more crucial, precisely because of the link between the functioning of organizations and the welfare of individuals and society.

PART TWO

PERSPECTIVES ON IMPLEMENTATION

Chapter 2

Theories of Implementation*

C. West Churchman

Over the years of the history of planning and its many fields—operations research, urban planning, corporate planning—many of us have been struck by the enormously important contrast between the development of the intellectual base and the implementation of any of this development into social change. On the one hand, we have become far more sophisticated in our model building, in our understanding of social processes, and even in our understanding of the individual human being in these processes. On the other hand, we have come to understand very little at all about the implementation of any of this intellectual growth into social reality. To be sure, some of our planning has been accepted and put into use, but we have no sound basis for understanding *why* implementation occurred in the instances where it has occurred, or whether the implementation was a "good thing."

I should begin by warning the reader that this chapter does not attempt to explain the mystery of the implementation process. Rather, it is frankly a philosophical effort to do two things: attempt to clarify what is meant by the phenomenon of implementation and then make the situation far more confusing on the basis of this clarification. I make no apology for ending the chapter in confusion simply because I believe that at the present time, the implementation of planning and technology is largely confusing; i.e., it is largely a mystery.

So we begin our journey by asking the question: What is this phenomenon called implementation? As in all such journeys, we do well by beginning with a more or less common sense idea, namely, that implementation occurs when an organization has serious problems, and a group of "experts" examine the problems, who attempt through their examination to help the managers of the organization to make the best choices to gain the really important goals of the organization. The experts do this by the processes of observing and thinking, using their own intellectual backgrounds, whether they be mathematical model

---

*Preparation of this paper was supported by a grant from the Organizational Effectiveness Research Programs of the Office of Naval Research.

building, economics, social psychology, or political science. The implementation process, if it occurs at all, takes place when the managers of the organization are truly influenced by the experts' recommendations and put these recommendations into action. The implementation process undoubtedly also includes an evaluation of the actions once they have taken place.

This common sense can now be put into a set of necessary conditions for the phenomenon of implementation to occur.

1. There is a purposive mind, which may be a social mind like an organization. This mind is capable of making action choices, and the value of these action choices can be judged in terms of whether the choices do or do not bring about desirable goals of the organization.
2. There is a second purposive *and* observing mind that can scan the real choices (as opposed to the perceived choices). This second observing mind then evaluates the choices in terms of goals that the second mind deems to be the correct goals of the first mind. One of the second mind's goals is to influence the first mind to make the correct choice.

In this viewpoint, implementation is a very old process indeed. It certainly is as old as the history of technology. The process of technology consists of developing a choice, e.g., of the automobile or the radio, which did not exist before and which the technological expert deemed to be a better choice than those that were available. The implementation process consisted of his developing his product and selling it to the customers.

It is interesting to note that in the history of technology, there have been long periods where the obvious question about the implementation process was never seriously raised, namely, whether the second mind is "correct." Is it or is it not true that the offered technology really helps the individuals with respect to their true goals? Thus at this point in our journey there can be a parting of the ways. Some of the travelers may want to rest their heels and forget this obvious question by simply taking a common sense base that most technology, like most operations research and planning, is obviously to the good of the organization and that a little examination will show whether or not the second mind is correct. Once we have decided that it is indeed correct, then the problem of implementation becomes a problem of how to sell it and what is surely the correct prescription for the buyers. Thus the doctor examines the patient and tells him that he has a fever and needs to go to bed for a period of time. There doesn't appear to be any great need to judge whether the doctor is correct. One assumes that he is correct on the basis of his own expertise and experience.

Although this answer seems to have been popular in the 1950s and 1960s, we seem to have entered another era in which every responsible individual is raising questions about technology, and specifically about operations research, planning, and so on, and arguing that in many instances, and maybe a serious number of instances, the experts are not obviously correct and may even be obviously incorrect. These questioners point out that the simplistic answer rules the risk of immorality by trying to sell expert ideas to the innocent.

So to be timely we must complicate the picture of implementation with yet a third necessary condition, a third mind, which judges whether the second is correct.* Thus, implementation only occurs when the third mind judges that the second mind is correct and only when the second truly influences the first, i.e., only when the first would have chosen otherwise not so well.

All of this semiformalism has simply tried to clarify the common sense idea of the phenomenon of implementation. I am not interested in this chapter in whether these three minds constitute a sufficient set of conditions for the implementation phenomenon to occur, because I am far more interested in the implications of the conditions: They have landed us in the place the philosopher loves best of all, the paradox of the infinite regress or vicious circle. You can easily see that once we have introduced the third mind then there is nothing on earth to stop us from asking whether the third mind—which judges whether the second mind is making correct recommendations to the first mind—is itself correct. Do we need a fourth mind to judge whether the third mind is correct—and, ha ha! a fifth and a sixth? Or, if you are afraid of infinity, then you can take a trip around the circle and try to envision how the first mind eventually gets to be the judge of the other minds. In either event we are driven to paradox, i.e., to philosophy, because philosophy is essentially the discussion of paradox.

I feel urged to point out that the paradox is real enough in our present society. I was recently involved in a study of experimental schools (K–12) in Berkeley, California. The Office of Education had decided partially to fund the experimental schools in a number of cities, and Berkeley had been selected as one of them. The stipulation of the Office of Education was that each city had to have its own "inside" evaluation team. This team was in effect a third mind, because there had been people who had observed the Berkeley school system, decided that it was defective in various ways, and then decided to create a school that would better serve the educational purposes of the community. These people were in effect the second mind, who had observed the first mind, which was the school system itself. The Office of Education decided that an evaluation team within the school system might very well be biased and therefore stipulated that there should be an outside evaluation that would examine, from an outside point of view, how well the inner evaluation team was operating and thus examine the effectiveness of the experimental school itself. This outside evaluation team, of which I was a member, was therefore a fourth mind observing the inside third mind, which was observing the second mind, the experimental

*I won't pause here in the main text to point out the obvious, namely that all of these minds may exist in one individual, e.g., in one technological individual or one social organization.

school, which was, so to speak, the implementation of an idea with respect to the school system itself. But the process didn't stop there. There were a number of cities supported by the Office of Education, and therefore "obviously" the need to have another level of evaluation that would compare how well the different cities were doing, including how well the outside and inside evaluation teams were performing. Thus, there was created now a fifth mind observing the fourth mind, observing the third mind, etc. I am sorry to say that the process didn't stop there. There finally was a still higher sixth mind, which looked at the entire process of the experimental schools and the program of evaluation, and decided whether or not the whole effort was worth doing. So far as I know, a seventh mind may be in the process of creation that will decide in the negation, thus collapsing the whole process.

The same remarks apply to technological assessment, the label we use to refer to efforts to evaluate technological programs. For example, NASA sent up a satellite recently that takes images of sections of the earth's surface every 18 days. NASA has felt the need, perhaps prodded by the Office of Management and Budgets (OMB), to do a cost-benefit measure of this satellite. But the OMB has raised questions about whether those NASA-supported studies might not be biased because they were done under NASA contracts. Therefore studies are now being conducted by the Department of Interior to check on the studies being conducted by NASA—and so it goes. Consequently, the taxpayer is spending a modicum of money on the paradox of implementation, e.g., on the design of evaluating systems that rise in a hierarchical fashion.

But I want to leave the paradox for a moment and return to another aspect, namely the concept of "theory." According to the *Oxford English Dictionary,* theory originally means a "sight or a spectacle," and then a "mental view," i.e., a speculation. From this origin was developed the more familiar notion of a theory as a set of rules that would guide something that had to be done, and then ultimately an explanation of facts and phenomena. In logic there has been an emphasis on the logical structure of theory rather than on its philosophical base, so that logicians have been interested in questions about which sentences do or do not constitute theoretical sentences and the logical structure of an explanation.

I find none of this logical research to be particularly helpful in the context of the theory of implementation. To be sure implementation is a phenomenon, and it would be very useful—if we could understand the phenomenon—to develop generalizations to tell us when the phenomenon is most apt to occur. But because we don't understand the phenomenon itself very well, I think we are more or less obliged to turn to the second and obsolete meaning of theory, namely a mental view of speculation, and to say that a theory of implementation must at the present time be thought of as a mental view (weltanschauung) of how the third mind can be justified, i.e., be given the authority for its judgments on an ethically defensible basis.

The remainder of this chapter will examine some theories of implementation in this sense of "theory."

I'll begin with a theory that seems to be applied in much of U.S. federal funding but which seems to me to be absolutely indefensible. This consists of saying that in evaluating programs, evaluation becomes sounder as its viewpoint broadens. Thus the inside evaluation team for the Berkeley educational school program is the least justifiable according to this account, the outside evaluation team is a little more "objective," the next level that looks at a number of cities is even more objective, the team that judges all of the Office of Education projects is even more objective, and finally we land in the OMB, which looks at the many projects of the many departments of the federal government and is the most objective.

This theory of implementation can only receive the grade of "R" standing for ridiculous. There certainly is no reason to say that OMB is in a specifically good position with respect to its observation that enables us to say that it should be given the authority for the ultimate judgment on an ethically defensible basis. One might try to save this weltanschauung by saying that above OMB and the Executive office stands the public, which must therefore be regarded as ultimate third mind. Now this may very well be the desirable answer, but at the present time we have no concept of what it really means. For example, in the case of operations research, the public doesn't seem to be in a specifically good position to judge whether or not an operations researcher's model is the appropriate one because most of the public doesn't understand linear programming, nonlinear feedback systems, etc. Furthermore, the public can't possibly examine all of the multitude of programs that the federal, state, and local governments support.

Therefore leave this weltanschauung and turn to one that seems to be especially attractive to the technological community. This theory of implementation says that we need to establish a community of experts, what in I call a "Lockean community." We do this by first identifying those who are qualified to judge the study of a planning or operations research group. These would be other experts in the planning or operations research field who have a high degree of respect among their colleagues. We then select out of the Lockean community a subset to examine a specific study and to evaluate it. It is understood that there is to be debate among the members of the community on any issue that any member of the community wishes to raise. The weltanschauung implies, in more or less axiomatic form, that all such debates in principle can be resolved either by examining the issues carefully, or if such examination does not result in agreement, then by some kind of vote.

This idea of the justification of a third mind in terms of a Lockean community is exactly the justification for procedures used by the National Institutes of Health and the National Science Foundation in their study sections. The study sections are drawn from the specific research community (e.g., biochemistry, sociology, economics). The members of the study section have the reputation of being top notch researchers. They read the research proposal and often pay a site visit to discuss the proposal with its sponsors. They then meet together and discuss the virtues of the proposal, debate its pros and cons, and then eventually judge the proposal. The results of the study section are written up very carefully and presented for final check to an advisory council that makes the ultimate decision. The advisory council is mainly made up again of individuals from the particular discipline together with a few outsiders.

The spirit of this weltanschauung is also contained in the famous or infamous ORSA "Guidelines" that appeared in *Operations Research,* September 1971. Evidently the writers of the Guidelines believe that it would be possible to interpret their Guidelines if one was familiar with operations research methods. The Guidelines were in effect an attempt to establish a Lockean community that could judge the performance of specific operations researchers. Indeed, those who wrote the Guidelines did exactly that. They formed themselves into a third mind that judged the expert testimony of operations researchers to a senate committee.

It is not difficult to recognize objections to this weltanschauung. Many of them are being voiced in *Science* in the Letters to the Editor section where there is a kind of ongoing debate about the NIH/NSF study section method of evaluating projects. The point that is being raised is pretty obvious. If one stays within a discipline and takes the criteria of the discipline as being unquestionably correct, then the study section method seems obviously to be justified because the members of the study section do represent the community of their own discipline. If one raises the question whether research in economics should really be funded, say, in comparison with research in biochemistry, or of whether any of them should be funded at all, then obviously study sections have a thoroughly biased viewpoint because each one stands not for a research of the community but for a constituency. So viewed each study section becomes in effect a political agent for the members of its own discipline. Much the same problem arises for operations research and planning. Whatever the technique of planning, be it based on models or on applied political science thoery or social psychology, the judgment as to whether or not the research has been well carried out should clearly not be done by the model builders or the political scientists or any of the specific disciplines.

You will see from these remarks that we really have entered a new stage in our understanding of implementation. Consider, for example, Stafford Beer's work in Chile. Beer is a great enthusiast for cybernetics and specifically for Ross Ashby's "Design for a Brain." Beer and his colleagues have set up what approximates a real time computer information system that emits signals informing managers of the economy whether things are working properly or not. There is no question that Beer has "implemented" something, in the sense that the second mind has observed how things were going in Chile, which is the first mind, and decided that there was a lack of control and therefore the economic system had to be redesigned so that adequate controls based on the theory of the brain could be instituted. Ten years ago we might have stopped the discussion there and simply marveled that Stafford Beer and his colleagues had been "successful" implementers in something as confusing as Chile. But the discussion that is now raging in the British journal *The New Scientist* shows the 1970s flavor of the implementation question. No one is seriously raising the issue as to whether Stafford Beer has implemented something in the old-fashioned sense, but a number of the letters appearing in *The New Scientist* raise very serious and strong questions about the true benefits that Beer's system is providing. Many of the writers feel that the new procedures in Chile are "immoral" or even economically disastrous. So we have come into an age where the expert is no longer expert.

In such an age, therefore, a different mental speculation is called for. A number of us have been suggesting a "dialectical" approach in which we envisage a fourth mind that observes the debate between at least two Lockean third minds with dramatically different perspectives. The theory of implementation here says if a fourth mind can tolerate absorbing two radically different viewpoints of what is going on, then that fourth mind will be in a far better position to judge the recommendations and therefore to form itself into an ethically defensible basis for passing judgment on the recommendations. We emphasize that the debate in this case needs to be well designed. It needs to be both dramatic and well thought out or else the fourth mind will simply find itself in an indefensible position.

A more general theory of implementation that encompasses the dialectical approach might be called the adaptive approach. Here it is emphasized that implementation is an educational process and that we should not judge programs partially but rather consider them as ongoing and very long processes of societal learning. Implementation is then more a history than an epic. An epic is a tale told of specific events as in Ulysses' journey around the Mediterranean, but history is a long process in which the events are all tied together in some kind of network. Implementation occurs when there is actual growth: development or progress. Progress, of course, must not be construed in a linear sense. Both the dialectical approach and the adaptive approach run into the extreme difficulty of identifying what constitutes real growth or progress, and even those who are enthusaistic about the two ideas have failed so far to provide us with any sound basis for such a judgment.

At the present time I am convinced that both the dialectical and the adaptive theories of implementation are still largely speculative. We are living in the Lockean age in terms of technology and its assessment, whether it be specific engineering technology, or operations research, or whatever. We have much to do ahead of us in terms of developing a sounder theory of implementation in the direction of the adaptive-dialectical approach.

But meanwhile there is a speculation that is even more "far out" that I think is worth using to close this discussion. This is the speculation or spectacle of the battle between two great giants: the socioeconomic giant and the psychological giant. I, of course, do not mean the battle between the midgets called economics and psychology as we know them today, both of which disciplines tend to be extremely narrow and small in their views of the world. But the first embryonic glimpses of the giants-to-be might be identified even today. On the socioeconomic side the embryos of the coming giants are people who struggling to "save the world" by vast generalizations of the disciplines to encompass the many interrelated facets of social complexity. Forester-Meadows at MIT, Beer's work in Chile, the Lindblom-like efforts at Harvard and the University of Washington and other places in ecological assessment, are all examples of what I have in mind. None of these efforts is in the least a "giant" as yet. All of them have taken on the heroic task of trying to battle the complexities in the entire world. The embryos of the psychological giant are people like Norman O. Brown and James Hillman who are bringing to bear concepts of depth psychology borrowed from Freud and Jung specifically in order to raise questions about the deeper aspects of what I have been calling the theory of implementation. Specifically, both Brown and Hillman raise the question about the posture of what I called the third mind. Scientific tradition would say that the third mind needs above all to be "objective," to stand at a distance, else it will be "biased." Hillman and Brown both characterize this posture as Apollonian and call for the need for a Dionysian science. Hillman specifically has challenged the whole notion of development, which includes the notion of progress, as being based on a certain kind of psychological archetype that needs to have its contrast psychologically in "no growth."

That battle of the theory of implementation is coming, I think, but it is still far off. Nevertheless, we could hasten its occurrence if we begin to understand in greater depth what we are talking about in theories of implementation based on the adaptive-dialectical approach.

Chapter 3

A Program of Research on Implementation

Randall L. Schultz and Dennis P. Slevin

Two facts stand out against the background of operations research/management science theory and practice: First, over two decades of developmental work has produced a large inventory of OR/MS models and systems that has great potential in solving management problems, and second, over the same period of time, there has been relatively little use of these techniques in organizations. Thus, there is a significant gap between model development and implementation and so the potential of OR/MS is largely unrealized. This imbalance has been examined from a number of viewpoints, ranging from casual interpretations of the problem to more rigorous analyses of the basis for implementation. Still, there is little *research evidence* on the *process* of implementation.

Implementation, and hence implementation research, has been viewed from a variety of perspectives including selling, involvement, mutual understanding, and organizational change [*6, 29*]. *Selling* implies that implementation is a marketing problem and that the product of operations research (e.g., models) must be skillfully made, packaged, and sold to potential users. *Involvement* suggests that implementation requires potential users to play an active role in the research process, becoming involved as participants in management science. *Mutual understanding* refers to a state where the researcher and manager each understands the other's stake in the project. *Organizational change* describes a view of implementation that focuses on behavioral changes that occur in the process of model acceptance. Each of these perspectives is important in identifying implementation problems and even suggesting practical solutions, but research on the process of implementation requires that these ideas be integrated in a scheme that recognizes their interdependence. The research should be designed to produce results leading to explanations of implementation success or failure and strategies for managing implementation.

The basic literature on implementation includes over 30 articles and papers [*48*], and it is not our purpose to review it here (we have listed many references that are not specifically referred to in this chapter). Discussions of the background for implementation research are given in references *16, 33,* and *41*. The empirical research findings can be summarized rather easily. In survey research, Radnor, Rubenstein, and associates have found that top management support and client-researcher relations are factors related to implementation success across different organizations [*32, 33, 36*]. In an experiment Huysmans has shown that the cognitive style of managers and the method of presentation of research results can be important determinants of successful implementation [*15, 16*]. In a field study Manley demonstrated how a measure of client resistance to OR/MS projects can be used to predict implementation success [*26*]. Beyond this, most of the work has centered on general pleas for implementation or specific thoughts on the nature of implementation. The philosophical papers by Churchman and Schainblatt [*6*] and Reisman and de Kluyver [*34*] are important, but methods for operationalizing the concepts (e.g., mutual understanding) and for investigating them in empirical research have not yet appeared. An interesting paper by Vertinsky [*53*] discusses the cultural factors in implementation. In addition to these basic works, a number of other papers and studies are germane, although some in an indirect way [*8, 24, 27, 38, 43*]. What is needed, then, is a program of research that can bridge the gap between the philosophy of implementation and the practical necessity to develop workable strategies for implementation.

Research on implementation needs some structure and the one that we suggest seems straightforward: We propose to examine the nature of organizations and of models in order to assess their congruence, positing that when capable models are compatible with the organization, there is a greater likelihood that they will be used. The human organization provides the setting for implementation; models, or more generally innovations, are the product of operations research. The research question, then, is: How are models successfully developed and implemented in organizations? The answer will involve knowledge of the process of model development and implementation and, in particular, the identification of both behavioral characteristics of the organization and dimensions of the models (i.e., behavioral requirements) that are related to implementation success. More importantly, the answer can only be obtained if measures can be developed to judge this fit between the model and the organization.

This chapter describes a program of research on the implementation of OR/MS models. The purpose of the program is to introduce the same rigor with which models are built into the study of how they are implemented. This scientific goal leads to a common interest of management, that is, how to *develop* and *use* models as effective decision-making tools. This program is described in four major parts: First, a number of model-building paradigms are discussed; second, a theory of behavioral model building is developed; third, strategies for implementation research are presented; and fourth, the prospects for future work are explored. Our orientation here is largely behavioral, stemming from our theory of the process of implementation as organizational change. A fitting prologue is the final paragraph in Wagner's classic text [55]:

> The time is past when an operations researcher can build a mathematical model and remain impervious to the behavioral characteristics of the individuals affected and the organizational milieu. Visionaries among operations research professionals are fully aware that new developments such as those described above exert tremendous strains on the managerial fabric of a corporate organization. To enhance the adoption of these technical and technological advances by industry and government, management and behavioral scientists together will have to find ways by which executives can deal effectively with computerized systems as beneficial change agents.

This is our point of departure.

MODEL-BUILDING PARADIGMS

Management decision models have been traditionally developed by researchers or management scientists working independently of model users and user organizations. The result has been that few models are actually implemented and used. Urban and Karash have recently urged that this traditional model building be replaced by evolutionary model building [52]. In the latter, some interaction between the model builder and user takes place and this supposedly increases the usefulness of the model. What we call behavioral model building is an extension of both the traditional and evolutionary concepts in that it provides for significant monitoring of individual and organization behavior as the model is being developed. This extended behavioral knowledge can aid in both model building and implementation. Each of these model-building paradigms is discussed in turn.

Traditional Model Building

The three major building paradigms are shown in Figure 3.1. Traditional model building (TMB) implies that the model is created independently from the user (or user group) and the organization. The user and organization are confronted with the model and this leads to some response. Most of the early management decision models were built under this paradigm. Some interaction

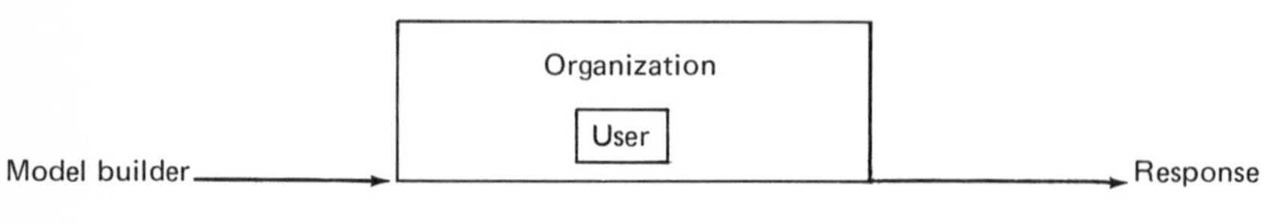

A. Traditional Model Building (TMB)

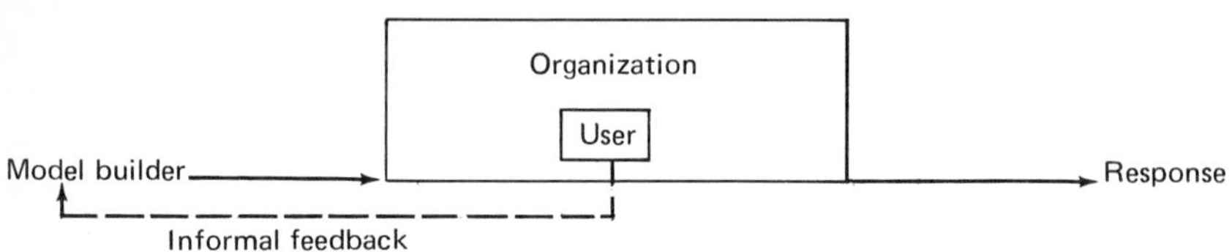

B. Evolutionary Model Building (EMB)

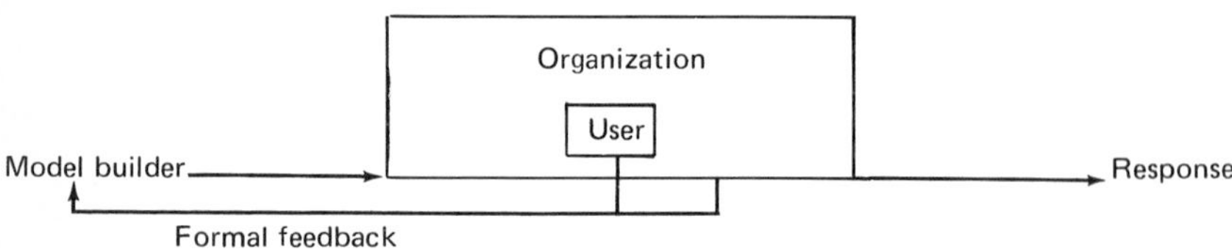

C. Behavioral Model Building (BMB)

Fig. 3.1 Model Building Paradigms

between model builder and user undoubtedly takes place under TMB, but it is largely for the benefit of the model builder himself. He understands his assignment better, which is not to say that he understands his user better or that his user better understands the model.

Evolutionary Model Building

In evolutionary model building (EMB), the model builder interacts with the user in an informal way, at least informal to the extent that the model builder is primarily concerned with the learning process of the user rather than with the user's behavior or organizational behavior. The premise is a good one: If the user better understands the model, by working with successively more complex versions of it, he will be more inclined to use it. The evolution of Urban's own SPRINTER model is an example of this approach. The approach is discussed in a broader context of normative model building by Little [*22*]. EMB increases the chance of developing a successful model.

Behavioral Model Building

The difference between behavioral model building (BMB) and EMB is one of both degree and kind. First, the degree of interaction between the model builder and user is greater. In BMB the model builder wants the user to learn not only about the model, but also about the process of building it. The feedback becomes a formal information flow. Second, the model builder studies the behavioral characteristics of his user and of the organization. This allows him to adjust the structure of the model so that it better represents the organization and enables him to plan for the implementation of the model. The feedback is significant and can change the development of the model. Thus, the behavioral approach is an evolution of EMB.

An Example

To illustrate the differences among these model-building paradigms, consider a normative marketing model for determining sales calls. The purpose of the model is to aid salesmen in planning their calls on customers. It includes a representation of the market (some sales response function) and, at least implicitly, a representation of the organization (including the users). Several prototypes of this kind of model are now available [*17*, pp. 380–403].

Under TMB the sales-call planning model is developed by a management scientist for a (generalized) salesman and delivered to the sales organization. Because the model addresses an important and practical problem, it has some chance of success. Its success depends upon how well the user thinks it represents the market (Is this the way the market works?) and how well it represents the organization (Is this the way we make decisions?). If company sales policy or an individual salesman's attitudes conflict sharply with the structure or output of the model, the model's chance of success is significantly reduced. A number of other individual, group, and organizational factors may preclude the successful application of the model, including the salesman's knowledge of it.

EMB would attempt to increase the chance of success by helping salesmen to learn about the model in stages. As they move from simple to more complex models, the salesmen would be expected to begin to appreciate the potential of the model. Of course, even under EMB, the model's technical and organizational validity are open questions.

Under BMB the management scientist would use inputs from both the organization and the user in developing the model. He would ask himself questions such as: Is the model threatening to the user? Does it call for a dramatic change in the way decisions are made in the organization? Is it compatible with the organizational structure? The use of behavioral inputs in the model-building process is intended to produce a model with high organizational validity, that is, compatibility with the user organization.

THEORY OF BEHAVIORAL MODEL BUILDING

The theory of behavioral model building rests on three basic concepts. The first concept is that of a successful model and what determines the probability of success of a model. The second concept is that of technical validity and the third, that of organizational validity. Each of these ideas is developed in turn.

Successful Models

A successful model is one that adequately represents the phenomenon being modeled and is used for the purpose for which it was designed. We are mostly concerned with decision models; a successful decision model is one which is used to *make* effective decisions. Any other use of the model makes it unsuccessful. A decision model can be helpful in a number of ways, but unless it has a direct and unambiguous influence on the decision-making process it is a failure. This definition probably makes most extant models failures, but this unhappy state motivates our discussion of behavioral model building.

The response in Figure 3.1 is, according to our definition, either a success (S) or a failure (F). The two factors determining the probability of success are technical validity and organizational validity, the former referring to the capability of the model in solving the problem and the latter to the compatibility of the model with the organization. Both of these factors are themselves multidimensional. In the simplest terms,

$$P(S) = f(TV, OV) \qquad (1)$$

where

$P(S)$ is the probability of success, $0 \leqslant P(S) \leqslant 1$
TV is technical validity
OV is organizational validity

We expect that a model that has greater technical and organizational validity will have a larger probability of success. Because perfect technical validity does not imply perfect organizational validity or vice versa, the two concepts must be examined separately, although they are not necessarily independent.

Technical Validity

The technical validity of a management decision model refers to its capability of providing some solution, usually an optimal one, to the stated problem. This notion of technical validity has considerable intuitive appeal for, as management scientists, we strive to develop models that can solve some problem in an optimal manner; in so doing, we like to think that, on a technical level at least, we have produced a model that *can* solve the problem if it is used. In other words, for any given definition of a problem, there is some possible technical solution to it, and, the better the technical solution, the more capable the model is in its role of a decision-making device.

Technical validity is usually measured by the degree to which the model optimizes and represents the decision situation. Measures of representativeness range from simple face validity and Turing tests to more complex measures of goodness of fit and methods for testing theories. Measures of optimization exist in the sense that a *model* can be solved optimally or not. This restricted view, however, does not consider whether or not the *problem* is solved optimally. Because solving the problem means that the problem has been correctly identified and the solution is implemented, these two additional factors must be taken into account in determining the success of a model.

If a model solves the wrong problem, then this involves both the technical and the organizational validity of the model. Technically, this is called a Type III error, and it means that the optimization is spurious because the problem has been incorrectly defined. The *process* of making an error of this kind, though, is a behavioral one. The management scientist has misread the situation or, perhaps, has been misled about it. In any event, the result is an error in model formulation stemming from behavioral as much as technical factors. This overlap in the two concepts is illustrated in Figure 3.2. The final type of error that we consider might be termed a Type IV error, that is, the error of developing a model that solves the right problem but is not used. Much of our argument

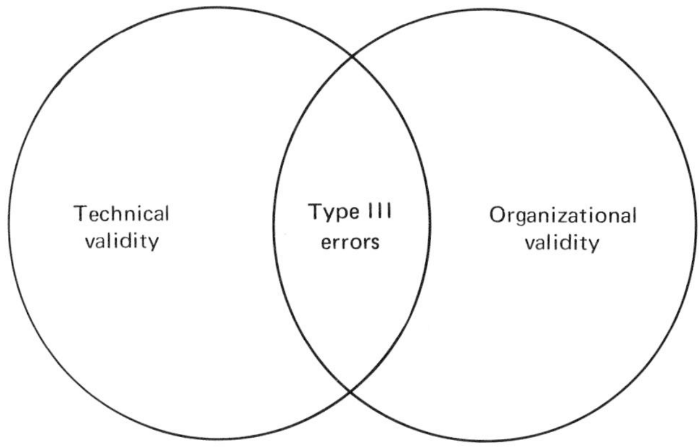

Fig. 3.2 Technical and Organizational Validity

revolves around models that can be technically valid but still not be used. We posit that the answer lies in a consideration of organizational validity.

Organizational Validity

The organizational validity of a management decision model refers to its compatibility with the user organization. The concept involves the behavioral congruence of the model and the organization. Because organizational behavior includes individual, small group, and (total) organizational factors, it is multidimensional and may be difficult to measure. Before considering these issues, however, let us consider an applied area, such as marketing, to show the relationship between technical and organizational validity.

The market is the external environment of a marketing model, whereas the human organization is its internal environment. A model with perfect technical validity would still have a finite probability of failure (perhaps large) if it failed to account for human behavioral factors. The organizational validity of a marketing decision model is its fit to the organization in terms of structure and behavior. This is based on the compatibility of the model with the organization. The parallel with technical validity, however, is not perfect. Although the firm has no control over market structure and little over market behavior, the firm can control its organizational behavior and help to shape the attitudes of its employees. In other words, if a model does not represent the market, the market cannot be changed to represent the model, although an organization can be changed if the model requires it. Thus, organizational validity can be achieved through model building and/or organizational change.

To further illuminate this idea, let us return to the sales call planning model. The behavioral model-building approach would require attention to both the model's technical and organizational validity before and during the model-building process. The model builder would measure technical validity using traditional instruments or tests. Armed with new instruments for measuring organizational validity, he would seek to develop his model in such a way that its probability of success was significantly enhanced. This would probably require the model builder to study the user's attitudes toward models and innovations and his background for using the model, the user group and its dynamics, and the factors of organizational behavior bearing on the use of the model. The concept of organizational validity can address some simple but important questions, such as: Will the salesmen use a computer model? Who will use it? Depending upon their attitudes and backgrounds, how can they be introduced to the call model? Will the organization permit them to make independent decisions with the model? How will their group dynamics affect acceptance of the model? All of these questions and others can be answered through an explicit focus on human organizational factors.

Consider a more tangible example of organizational validity. In a recent model developed by one of the authors [*37*], a method was offered for airlines to make scheduling and advertising decisions. The normative model was based on a positive description of market behavior. The technical validity of the model was judged to be high, but this did not ensure its future success as a decision-making tool. The model requires, for example, a close coordination between marketing management and the advertising and scheduling departments of airlines. If this coordination does not exist or cannot be made to exist (because of organizational inflexibility), the chance of the model being successful is decreased. In this example, the behavioral model building approach could have changed the structure of the decision model and would almost certainly have changed the structure of the organization interfacing with the model.

Before organizational validity can be shown to be an important factor in building and implementing management science models, a program of research must be undertaken that identifies critical organizational factors and develops measures of critical factors (instruments). In the following section, a number of methods are discussed that can lead to measures of the fit between models and human organizations.

RESEARCH ON ORGANIZATIONAL VALIDITY

Although the problem of implementing management science models is critical to their success, it has only recently gained the attention of management researchers and practitioners. In 1957 Churchman, Ackoff, and Arnoff [*5*] argued for such research by observing that no well-formulated methodology for implementation was then available and yet the implementation problem was one of the most significant ones facing management scientists. During the next decade, programs of research were carried out at the University of California at Berkeley, Northwestern University, and other centers. Progress in understanding the problem has been slow, however, and recent literature reviews [*16, 33, 41*] show few studies devoted specifically to implementation with many of these being highly speculative. Our conclusion is that even today there is still no well-formulated methodology for implementation.

The following discussion proposes a way in which such a methodology could be developed within the framework of behavioral model building. We specifically deal with the concept of organizational validity, that is, the fit between the model and the organization. Because organizational validity is multidimensional, the concept of fit consists of a variety of factors such as attitudes of users, group dynamics of the informal organization, and communications and authority structures of the formal organization. These factors seem to fall within three levels of aggregation: individual, small group, and organizational. For this reason, we propose an approach to implementation research that measures fits at each level and combines them in an overall measure of organizational validity.

A Measure of Organizational Validity

A quantitative measure of the fit between a model and an organization is the degree of organizational change required to implement the model. This degree of change could be measured by the distance between the initial and final states of each variable. One possible representation of this distance could be:

$$\text{Change} = [(X_1 - X_0)^2 + (Y_1 - Y_0)^2 + (Z_1 - Z_0)^2]^{1/2} \tag{2}$$

where

X_1 is the required state of individual variables
X_0 is the actual state of individual variables
Y_1 is the required state of small group variables
Y_0 is the actual state of small group variables
Z_1 is the required state of organizational variables
Z_0 is the actual state of organizational variables

The total change required is a function of the changes needed at individual, small group, and organizational levels. By measuring these variables it may be possible to determine the total amount of change required *before* the implementation is begun. The model builder can use this diagnostic information in deciding on the appropriate mix of two alternative courses of action: (1) change the model to improve its organizational validity and (2) change the behavioral variables to improve this fit. The appropriate implementation steps will be a function of the costs and benefits of each strategy.

Individual, Small Group, and Organizational Factors

One of the first requirements for the successful implementation of a model is acceptance on the part of the user, i.e., the *individual.* The individuals affected by the model must have a favorable, open attitude in order to be motivated to accept the model. Although several well-developed methodologies have been offered by behavioral scientists for attitude scaling [*10, 11, 50*], few have been applied to the problem of implementation. Some authors have measured attitudes in doing implementation research [*9, 18, 53*]; most of these efforts, however, have been directed at measuring a small component of user attitudes. Manley [*26*] constructed a multiplicative attitude model using the paired comparison technique of Metfessel [*28*] and the semantic differential technique as developed by Osgood and others [*31*]. To this date, though, a research effort designed to measure a broad spectrum of user attitudes in a general, replicative fashion has not been presented, and yet it seems to be a necessary step in implementation research. An instrument that could be used by a number of OR practitioners in a variety of settings would be valuable in generating research data on this topic. Efforts to develop such an instrument are described in a later section.

The importance of *small group* variables on the implementation of change has been known since the classic Coch and French study [*7*]. Since that time a large body of evidence about small group behavior has been accumulated (see for example [*4, 14, 35*]). Such variables as cohesion, group norms, pressures to conform, and group composition have been known to be important for some time. It is difficult to select from this large array which variables and which research findings are most appropriate to implementation. One fact does seem to stand out clearly: The implementation of a management science decision model may often change the communication pattern of the small group. For example, if one member of the group is the primary model user he may become a communication focus in the group. For this reason the communication net experiments initiated by Bavelas and continued by Leavitt, Shaw, and others appear particularly important [*3, 21, 46*]. A measurement instrument that determines the required changes in communication structure would give insight into the scope of the implementation problem.

Although the small group area is very important to the practitioner (most managers recognize the tremendous power of the small group to accept or reject innovation), it is also the most difficult for the researcher. First, it may be difficult to identify the real "informal" groups without spending considerable time in the organization. Second, so many variables are important that it is difficult to select a starting point for measurement. For these reasons, the small group variables are considered in the later phases of this implementation research program.

We would like a methodology that might be used to measure the fit between a model and the *organization* to possess two properties. First, it should be general, focusing on the systemic properties of organizations and applicable to a wide variety of organizational types. Second, it should focus on variables that are important and will predict the probable success of the model. We would like to be able to focus on structural variables that can be changed both in the organization and in the model. Instruments that measure organizational climate, trust, etc., may be of little value because we may not know how the model affects these variables even after we have measured them. Fortunately, a methodology for measuring organizational structure exists and has been reasonably well tested.

Lawrence and Lorsch [*19*] have developed and tested instruments for measuring two systemic properties of organizations: differentiation and integration. Differentiation is defined as the difference in cognitive and emotional orientation among managers in different functional departments. Differentiation is measured on four dimensions: orientation toward goals, time orientation, interpersonal orientation, and formality of structure. Highly differentiated organizational subunits would have managers that are quite different, whereas organizational subunits that are slightly differentiated would have managers that are similar in these four attributes.

On the other hand, every system that is highly differentiated must have some degree of integration in order to have the unity of purpose necessary to accomplish its objectives. Integration is defined as the quality of the state of collaboration that exists among departments that are required to achieve unity of effort by the demands of the environment. Integration is necessary to resolve subunit conflicts and to provide the necessary coordination. It is measured by soliciting management opinion on the amount of coordination that exists between various departments.

The Lawrence and Lorsch concepts of differentiation and integration appear well suited to organizational validity research. They have developed instruments that are standardized and can be used in a variety of settings. They have spearheaded a program of research that has resulted in the measurement of these attributes in a variety of organizational settings, from highly diversified companies [*1*] to individual plants [*56*]. A primary finding has been that the organization-environment match is a crucial one in determining the effectiveness of the organization. In a dynamic environment, for example, high levels of both differentiation and integration are needed. This has significant implications for the study of organizational validity. If the model requires a change in integration or differentiation for an organization that is well matched to its environment, the model must be changed. If the model requires a change in integration and differentiation that would result in a better match between the organization and its environment, then the model builder must concentrate on ways to change the organization. Lawrence and Lorsch have used their instruments in organization development work [*20*] to point out the need for and ways to accomplish needed change. Hence the measurement of integration and differentiation might not only lead to problem diagnosis, but also help in problem solution.

A number of research questions might be asked concerning these concepts. Are models more easily implemented in highly differentiated organizations? What is the role of integration in model implementation? Can models be easily changed so they have varying effects on differentiation and integration? Once some research data are accumulated, it may be possible to measure the integration and differentiation of an organization and then to comment on the likelihood of success of a particular model.

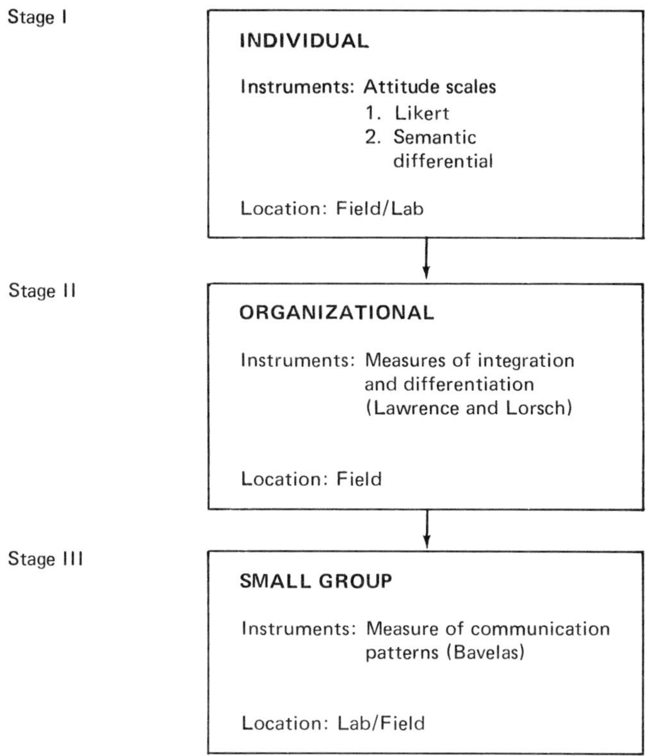

Fig. 3.3 Stages of Implementation Research

Stages of Research

Programmatic research naturally progresses through various stages in terms of the topic of study, the location of the research, and the type of data collection used. This proposed program is seen as moving through three stages corresponding to the different behavioral variables being considered (Figure 3.3). The initial stage is the measurement of individual attitudes. This stage is currently in progress and a brief review of its current status is given in the next section. Stages II and III represent the organizational and small group levels, respectively. The progress from Stage I to II is made easier by the fact that the research setting (field) and the data collection instruments are reasonably similar. Progress to Stage III (small group) will be more difficult.

Attitudes and Implementation

Some progress has been made in an attempt to monitor individual attitudes toward implementation. An attempt was made to develop an attitude instrument to measure user attitudes toward an OR/MS implementation. In developing an instrument there were two key objectives: First, the instrument should be sufficiently generic to be applicable to a variety of populations and a variety of innovations; second, it should be scorable yielding quantitative measures of key attitudinal dimensions. Such an instrument has been developed, pilot tested, and recently field tested [*42, 47*]. The empirical results are discussed in this volume in Chapter 7.

DIMENSIONS OF MODELS AND IMPLEMENTATION

A number of interesting but difficult research questions are raised by the theory of behavioral model building. One of the most important is how can hypotheses regarding the nature of models and organizations be developed that lead to empirically verifiable tests of organizational validity. A promising approach seems to be an investigation of the dimensions of models that lead to behavioral considerations of implementation [*39*]. The dimensions of organizations are equally important factors as we have noted above. Once again, we choose marketing as our substantive setting.

Analyzing Dimensions

The number of marketing decision models developed in recent years has grown dramatically, although the use of decision models has been less than spectacular. Models have appeared that deal with advertising budgeting decisions, media selection decisions, sales call planning decisions, distribution size, location decisions, and many others. What are some of the dimensions of these models that have behavioral implications?

Table 3.1 lists a number of dimensions of marketing decision models together with their logical ranges. A multidimensional analysis of the characteristics of models should be as complete as possible. But because our objective here is more modest—to identify leading behavioral hypotheses—we will concentrate on the two major dimensions of use of data and use of computers. This focus seems to be quite consistent with the features of many new marketing decision models.

Figure 3.4 is a simple two-dimensional diagram that shows the data-computer space of a marketing decision model. The use of data in models ranges from those requiring only subjective inputs of marketing executives to those requiring only empirical inputs of actual market data. Models that fall in

TABLE 3.1
Some Dimensions of Marketing Decision Models

Dimension	Range
Number of variables	Univariate–multivariate
Use of data	Subjective–empirical
Use of computer	Noninteractive–interactive
Handling of uncertainty	Stochastic–deterministic
Method of solution	Algorithmic–heuristic
Character of system	Steady state–transient
Relationships among variables	Linear–nonlinear
System boundary	Open–closed
Variation over time	Static–dynamic
Level of aggregation	Macroanalytic–microanalytic

between combine subjective and empirical data in some appropriate fashion. The use of computers in models ranges from those that require the computer for data processing and/or analysis without the direct interaction of the user to those that require the user to interact with the computer via conversional-type programs. Of course, some models may not use the computer at all, but we have not considered this case. The behavioral implications of these two dimensions can be analyzed at the individual, small group, and organizational levels. An analysis of some extant marketing models that fit into this scheme is given in Reference *39*.

Behavioral Hypotheses

Consider the two-dimensional scheme in Figure 3.4. The following hypotheses are made with respect to organizational change necessary for successful implementation of marketing decision models.

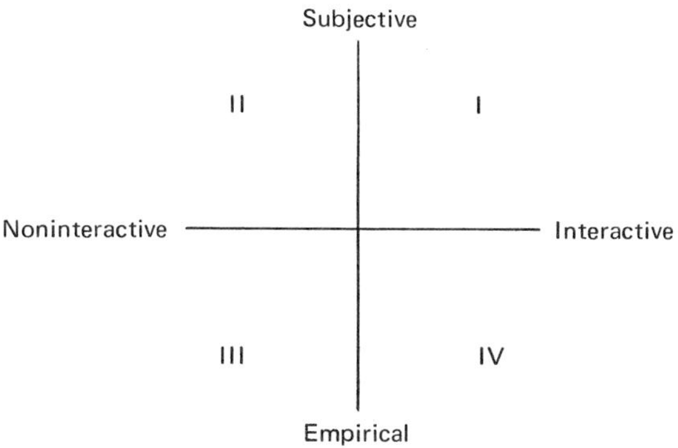

Fig. 3.4 Behavioral Factors In Two Dimensions

$$(X_1 - X_0) \textit{ increases} \text{ as models become more interactive.} \qquad \text{(H1)}$$

It seems reasonable to assume that traditional marketing decision making involves the analysis of historical data that are assembled in some report format. The use of an interactive model is going to require that the decision maker relegate some of this analysis to the computer while he is in the process of making a decision. The use of the interactive console and the change in decision-making style is going to require substantial learning and substantial attitude change on the part of the individual decision maker.

$$(X_1 - X_0) \textit{ decreases} \text{ as models become more empirical.} \qquad \text{(H2)}$$

An a priori argument can be made either for or against this hypothesis. On the one hand, one could argue that the decision maker is accustomed to analyzing empirical data and that having the computer perform part of this function represents only a small change from the status quo. On the other hand, one could maintain that a model using the decision maker's subjective inputs is less threatening because it still requires his judgment as input and therefore less attitude change is needed.

$$(Y_1 - Y_0) \textit{ increases} \text{ as models become more interactive.} \qquad \text{(H3)}$$

$$(Y_1 - Y_0) \textit{ increases} \text{ as models become more empirical.} \qquad \text{(H4)}$$

There are no good a priori arguments either in favor or against these hypotheses. The degree of change needed in the group in each case will depend on the details of the situation and the interaction between the group and the model. Empirical research is needed to gain more insight into the effect of model dimensions on group change.

$$(Z_1 - Z_0) \textit{ increases} \text{ as models become more interactive.} \qquad \text{(H5)}$$

The use of interactive models requires that certain members of the organization become specialists in their use. This requires an increase in organizational differentiation (differences in cognitive and emotional orientation among managers in different functional departments) [*19*]. At the same time, the interactive specialist must coordinate his activities with other members of the organization. This requires an increase in integration (quality of the state of collaboration that exists among departments). Both of these increases (differentiation and integration) will require an increase in organizational change needed $(Z_1 - Z_0)$.

$$(Z_1 - Z_0) \textit{ increases} \text{ as models become more empirical.} \qquad \text{(H6)}$$

If a subjective model is used, the role of the decision maker using the model changes little in the organization. Previously he made subjective decisions; now he makes computer-aided subjective decisions. However, if an empirical computer model is used, it requires a new reliance on empirical computer output. This requires that individuals who previously made decisions themselves rely more heavily on empirical computer output. This may result in changes in the differentiation and integration of the organization and hence an increase in $(Z_1 - Z_0)$.

All of the above hypotheses are made on *plausible* rather than empirically based arguments. It is important that data be collected to determine the relationship between these two model dimensions and the organizational change required. Moreover, hypotheses can be made about the other dimensions of models and research conducted to discover the required (i.e., by the model) state of relevant behavioral variables. When combined with measures of actual states of the same variables, there is a basis for analyzing the degree of organizational change necessary to implement a model.

Costs of Organizational Change

In all cases the final determination of whether an organization is changed to fit a model should depend on whether the *benefits* from the model outweigh the *costs* of model development and organizational change. The quantitative measurement of change presented in this chapter is felt to be representative of the *total organizational energy* required to implement the model. The formal accounting system of the organization may not reflect the total costs of the change required; nevertheless, the organization will use up resources in terms of human energy that are proportionate to the change required.

Some models, although requiring substantial change, may be implemented quickly because their benefits are substantial. The methodology proposed here for measuring the change will help the model builder to think in terms of the total energy of the organizational system required to implement the models. Changes in the model may reduce the amount of energy required, or prior knowledge of the energy required may enable the implementation process to go more smoothly.

FUTURE ACTIVITY

The concept of behavioral model building has implications for both management and behavioral science research. First, from the operations research standpoint BMB implies that the implementation process can be managed. Under

BMB the model builder takes into account behavioral data as he constructs his model. Thus, the model evolves in such a way that it not only fills the decision makers needs, but also fits the organization in which it is to be used.

Second, in the behavioral science area, BMB proposes that the extent of organizational change required by a model be measured before it occurs. The model builder can either alter the model or prepare to modify the organization in such a way that it has a better fit with the model. The methodology enabling one to measure such a priori organizational change must be developed to make BMB a success. If it can be developed, it may be useful for the more general problem of introducing organizational change, whether it is in the form of a model or not.

New Research

The lack of successful management science models can be traced to inadequacies of the models, the process of implementation, or both. This chapter presented a theory for unifying model building and implementation and methods for creating better models and managing implementation. The theory and methods, however appealing, are yet untested. A program of research is necessary to build upon these ideas and develop the ' well-formulated methodology" that was called for many years ago.

Real progress in this area will occur only through an organized, sequential research program, hopefully supported by the users who, after all, have the most to gain. Instruments need to be further selected and refined. An environment must be found for collecting data and testing hypotheses. Key causal relationships between the aspects of a model, its fit with the organization, and its acceptance must be found. Finally, this program must lead to applications of behavioral concepts in the design and implementation of management science models.

In particular, behavioral model building requires a program of research to discover:

1. Critical factors that determine the organizational validity of models.
2. How these factors can be measured:
   a. the required state implied by the model
   b. the actual state of the organization
3. Given critical factors and instruments to measure them, how can behavioral model building be used to:
   a. anticipate organizational change
   b. manage the implementation process

Points 1 and 2 above can include a multidimensional research effort consisting of field studies using interviews and survey research instruments, field experiments in which variables such as model type are varied in the field, and laboratory experiments. The first goal will be to develop the instruments appropriate to the measurement of change required at the individual, small group, and organizational levels. The second goal will be to empirically test hypotheses relating model dimensions to the organizational change required. Progress is being made in a number of these areas, but much work remains to be done.

The future, then, promises to be a time when OR/MS returns to its original mission: to build models that will be used to make better decisions in organizations.

References

1. Allen, Stephen A., III, "Corporate-Divisional Relationship in Highly Diversified Firms" in Jay W. Lorsch and Paul R. Lawrence (Eds.), *Studies in Organizational Design,* Homewood, Ill.: Richard D. Irwin, 1970.
2. Argyris, Chris, "Management Information Systems: The Challenge to Rationality and Emotionality," *Management Science,* **17,** no. 6, B275–292 (February 1971).
3. Bavelas, Alex, "Communication Patterns in Task-Oriented Groups," *Journal of the Acoustical Society of America,* **22,** 725–730 (1950).
4. Cartwright, Dorwin, and Zander, Alvin, *Group Dynamics: Research and Theory,* New York: Harper & Row, 1968.
5. Churchman, C. West, Ackoff, Russell L., and Arnoff, E. Leonard, *Introduction to Operations Research,* New York: Wiley, 1957.
6. Churchman, C. W., and Schainblatt, A. H., "The Researcher and the Manager: A Dialectic of Implementation," *Management Science,* **11,** no. 4, B69–B87 (February 1965).
7. Coch, L., and French, Jr., J.R.P., "Overcoming Resistance to Change," *Human Relations,* p. 512–532 (1948).
8. Drake, John W., *The Administration of Transportation Modeling Projects,* Lexington, Mass.: Heath, 1973.
9. Dyckman, Thomas R., "Management Implementation of Scientific Research: An Attitudinal Study," *Management Science,* **13,** no. 10, B612–B620 (June 1967).
10. Fishbein, M. (Ed.), *Readings in Attitude Theory and Measurement,* New York: Wiley, 1967.
11. Guilford, J. P., *Psychometric Methods,* New York: McGraw-Hill, 1954.
12. Harvey, Allan, "Factors Making for Implementation Success and Failure," *Management Science,* **16,** no. 6, B312–B321 (February 1970).
13. Hertz, David B., "Implementing an Operations Research Program," *Banking,* **58,** 47–49 (March 1966).
14. Hopkins, Terrence K., *The Exercise of Influence in Small Groups,* Totowa, N.J.: Redminster Press, 1964.
15. Huysmans, Jan H. B. M., "The Effectiveness of the Cognitive-Style Constraint in Implementing Operations Research Proposals," *Management Science,* **17,** no. 1, 92–104 (September 1970).
16. Huysmans, Jan H. B. M., *The Implementation of Operations Research: An Approach to the Joint Consideration of Social and Technological Aspects,* New York: Wiley, 1970.

17. Kotler, Philip, *Marketing Decision Making: A Model Building Approach,* New York: Holt, Rinehart and Winston, 1971.
18. Ladd, D. E., "Report on a Group's Reaction to 'The Researcher and the Manager: A Dialectic of Implementation,' " *Management Science,* **12,** no. 2, B24–25 (October 1965).
19. Lawrence, Paul R., and Lorsch, Jay W., *Organization and Environment,* Division of Research, Graduate School of Business Administration, Harvard University, Boston, 1967.
20. Lawrence, Paul R., and Lorsch, Jay W., *Developing Organizations: Diagnosis and Action,* Reading, Mass.: Addison-Wesley, 1969.
21. Leavitt, H. J., "Some Effects of Certain Communication Patterns on Group Performance," *Journal of Abnormal and Social Psychology,* **46,** 38–50 (1951).
22. Little, John D., "Models and Managers: The Concept of a Decision Calculus," *Management Science,* **16**, no. 8, 466–B485 (April 1970).
23. Malcolm, Donald G. "On the Need for Improvement in Implementation of O.R.," *Management Science,* **11,** no. 4, B48–B58 (February 1965).
24. Malone, David W., "System Implementation and Evaluation." Paper presented at the International Symposium on Systems Engineering and Analysis, Purdue University, October 23–27, 1972.
25. *Management Science,* "Commentary on the Researcher and the Manager: A Dialetic of Implementation" (series of comments), **12,** no. 2 (October 1965).
26. Manley, John H. "A Measure of the Probability of Success for OR/MS Projects Due to Client Behavior," unpublished doctoral dissertation, University of Pittsburgh, 1971.
27. Mason, Richard O. and Mitroff, Ian, "A Program for Research on Management Information Systems," *Management Science,* **19,** no. 5, 475–487 (January 1973).
28. Metfessel, M., "A Proposal for Quantitative Reporting of Comparative Judgments," *Journal of Psychology,* **24,** 229–235 (1947).
29. Morris, William, *Management Science: A Bayesian Introduction,* Englewood-Cliffs, N.J.: Prentice-Hall, 1968.
30. O'Reilly, Francis J., "Why Operations Research Doesn't Always Work," *Management Review,* **56,** no. 4, 53–56 (April 1967).
31. Osgood, E. E., Suci, G. J., and Tannenbaum, P. H., *The Measurement of Meaning,* Urbana, Ill.: University of Illinois Press, 1957.
32. Radnor, Michael, Rubenstein, A. H., and Bean, A. S. "Integration and Utilization of Management Science Activities in Organizations," *Operational Research Quarterly,* **19,** no. 2, 117–141 (June 1968).
33. Radnor, Michael, Rubenstein, Albert H., and Tansik, David A., "Implementation in Operations Research and R&D in Government and Business Organizations," *Operations Research,* **18,** 967–991 (November–December 1970).
34. Reisman, Arnold and de Kluyver, C. A., "Evaluation and Implementation of Systems Studies: Some Philosophical Comments." Paper presented at the International Symposium on Systems Engineering and Analysis, Purdue University, October 23–27, 1972.
35. Roby, Thornton B., *Small Group Performance,* Chicago: Rand McNally, 1968.
36. Rubenstein, Albert H., Radnor, Michael, Baker, Norman R., Heimen, David R., and McColly, John B., "Some Organizational Factors Related to the Effectiveness of Management Science Groups in Industry," *Management Science,* **13,** no. 8, B508–B518 (April 1967).
37. Schultz, Randall L., "Market Measurement and Planning with a Simultaneous-Equation Model," *Journal of Marketing Research,* **8,** 153–164 (May 1971).

38. Schultz, Randall L., "Methods of Handling Competition in Dynamic Market Models," *European Journal of Marketing,* 7, 18–27 (Spring 1973).
39. Schultz, Randall L., and Slevin, Dennis P., "Behavioral Considerations in the Implementation of Marketing Decision Models," *Combined Proceedings,* Spring and Fall Conferences, American Marketing Association, 494–498, 1972.
40. Schultz, Randall L., and Slevin, Dennis P., "Behavioral Model Building," Paper no. 376, Institute for Research in the Behavioral, Economic and Management Sciences, Krannert Graduate School of Industrial Administration, Purdue University, September, 1972.
41. Schultz, Randall L., and Slevin, Dennis P., this volume, Chapter 1.
42. Schultz, Randall L., and Slevin, Dennis P., this volume, Chapter 7.
43. Scott Morton, Michael S., *Management Organization Systems: Computer-Based Support for Decision Making,* Division of Research, Graduate School of Business Administration, Harvard University, Boston, 1971.
44. Shakun, M. F. "Developments in Comparative Operations Research," *Management Science,* **15**, no. 2, 11–12 (October 1969).
45. Shakun, Melvin F., "Management Science and Management: Implementing Management Science Via Situational Normativism," *Management Science,* **18**, no. 8, B367–377 (April 1972).
46. Shaw, Marvin E., *Group Dynamics: The Psychology of Small Group Behavior,* New York: McGraw Hill, 1971.
47. Slevin, Dennis P., Baxter, Graham R., Keim, Robert T., and Schultz, Randall L., "Implementation Attitudes Questionnaire," September, 1972.
48. Slevin, Susan M. "An Annotated Bibliography on the Implementation of Operations Research/Management Science Techniques," unpublished, May, 1973.
49. Stillson, Paul, "Implementations of Problems in OR" *Operations Research,* **11**, no. 1, 140–147 (January–February 1963).
50. Torgerson, W., *Theory and Methods of Scaling,* New York: Wiley, 1958.
51. Turban, Efraim, "They're Planning OR at the Top," *Industrial Engineering,* **1**, no. 12, 16–20 (December 1969).
52. Urban, Glen L., and Karash, Richard, "Evolutionary Model Building," *Journal of Marketing Research,* **8**, 62–66 (February 1971).
53. Vertinsky, Ilan, "OR/MS Implementation in Valle, Columbia, S. A.: A Profile of a Developing Region," *Management Science,* **18**, no. 6, B314–B327 (February 1972).
54. Wagner, N. M., "Practical Slants on Operations Research," *Harvard Business Review,* 61–70 (May 1963).
55. Wagner, Harvey H., *Principles of Operation Research,* Englewood Cliffs, N.J.: Prentice-Hall, 1969.
56. Walker, Arthur H., and Lorsch, Jay W., "Organizational Choice: Product versus Function," *Harvard Business Review,* (November–December 1968).

Chapter 4

A Methodology for Implementation Research*

Cyrus F. Gibson

For a period of nearly two years from 1972 to 1973, I worked with a team of management scientists on the implementation of computer-based models into several organizations. Since 1967 the head of the team had been working on a "base" model that was a simulation of the demographic and economic characteristics of a New England region. Although such a model was useful in and of itself as a tool for urban planning and research, one objective that the builder had was to adapt it for use for planning by different organizations. These adaptation projects were undertaken with a commercial bank, a town government, and a gas utility company. In each case the implementation consisted of the development of a "translator" model by the team working with personnel in the organization.

My role and that of a research colleague working with me in these implementation projects might be described as participant observation or action research.† As such our involvement had two purposes. On the one hand, we sought to observe, record, and interpret behavior and events longitudinally on a case-by-case, exploratory basis. Our aim here was to develop concepts and relationships and to test working hypotheses toward the building of a theory that would be closely grounded in the data [*10*] and that would yield immediately useful findings for practitioners concerned with the implementation of models. On the other hand, we were committed to assisting and facilitating the implementations. In this respect we worked closely with and between the model builders and the users and undertook to exert influence on the parties as it seemed appropriate.

---

*This chapter is based upon research supported by funding from the Division of Research of the Harvard Business School and from the National Science Foundation, Grant GI-38977. I wish to thank my colleagues David Birch, John Hammond, William Earner, and Richard Miller for their collaboration and suggestions during the course of this work. I am particularly indebted to the officers of "Northville National Bank" for their time and contributions to the research.

†For an outstanding example of the participant observation methodology see Dalton [*7*]. For discussions of the methodologies, see Hammond [*11*] and Foster [*9*].

In this chapter I shall illustrate this dual role, especially aspects of the research methodology, by describing the project in the commercial bank. I shall argue that the advantages of this research approach far outweigh the disadvantages for the state of knowledge and practical needs that currently exist in the implementation of models into organizations.

THE PLAYERS: MODELERS, BANKERS, AND RESEARCHERS

In 1972 a research colleague and I joined with the principal model builder, an academic colleague, whom I shall refer to as Davison, to participate in the implementation of the base model into a medium-sized commercial bank located in the Standard Metropolitan Statistical Area (SMSA), which the model simulated. By any standards the promise of the potential value of the output of the base model was impressive. Input to the model were data from the U.S. census tapes for three separate censuses and economic and commercial data from a number of other sources. When fully operating, the output would consist of yearly projections of such variables as population, distributions by age, income, and race, and the numbers and types of business establishments. The unusual feature of the projected data was to be their volume and detail. Some 560 variables could be projected for each of the 61 census traits in the region; values for these and an additional 400 variables could be projected for the region as a whole.

On several occasions Davison had worked with officers in the bank in gathering and structuring input data for the base model. There had been an implicit understanding that when the model was up and running the bank would be the first to make use of the output. In early 1972 Davison judged that the model was sufficiently complete so that work on the translator and on the implementation research could begin. The design and technical work on the translator was to be done as a doctoral thesis by a student working under Davison.

At the outset we judged from our discussions and involvement that the model builders had three goals in their total perspective toward their work. The first and most explicit was to demonstrate the practical use of the base model, so many years in development within academic walls, and in particular its value as a tool for long-range planning by the top management of the bank. The second goal was to document the work that had gone into building the base model, work that could represent significant advances in the theory of urban development as well as computer modeling. The pertinent audience for this was the more scholarly one, which Davison knew would be more interested in reports on the theory underlying the modules of code within the base model and less concerned with the immediate practical utility. The third goal, particularly salient to the doctoral student, was to produce an acceptable thesis within one to one and a half years.

The bank that was to be the target of the implementation effort will be called Northville National. It was a very old and respected institution with assets of about $350 million, a total employment of some 300 people, and 22 branch offices, all located within the SMSA. In the 1950s Northville National had been the largest bank in the region, conducting over 40 percent of all the commercial bank business. During the 1960s this position was undermined by competition from larger banks from other parts of the state. In 1972 share of market had slipped to 35 percent, and for two years running there had been a decline in earnings per share. To increase its asset base and reverse the decline in earnings, Northville National had initiated negotiations for a merger with a bank of equal size in an adjacent region in 1970. In the midst of negotiation, however, the Department of Justice filed suit against the merger as an alleged violation of the antitrust laws. In early 1972 the special burden of these problems was occupying much of the time of the bank's president, many of the directors, and several other officers, who were working on backup material for the bank's law firm in preparing the case for trial.

These more or less public facts were about all we knew of the perspective of the top officers of the bank at the outset of the project. We shared with Davison some early concern that the bank's top management might be too preoccupied with problems of declining performance and the contested merger to give adequate attention to model implementation. Nevertheless, Davison's strong credibility with several officers, particularly Mr. Graves, senior vice president of marketing and former head of operations, encouraged us to proceed with the project. Moreover, by the time we learned of the possible untimeliness of the project from the point of view of bank management, the research funding and time commitments for the builders and researchers had been established.

For our part, my research colleague and I set as a first objective the completion of his thesis on the research by June 1973. As our roles evolved his responsibilities in the research came to be an emphasis on data collection, analysis, and documentation. We worked together on interpretation, conceptualization, and development of working hypotheses, and I took primary responsibility for informing and influencing the model builders and the bank officers in ways that we perceived would facilitate the implementation. It was anticipated that our research would consist of three phases. We would conduct interviews and possibly a survey of attitudes in the bank by June 1972, prior to the introduction of the translator. From June to October we expected to be heavily involved in observations and facilitation of the translator development and introduction, work that would bring the builders and users in close contact. The period from October 1972 to February 1973, was for postintroduction in which we would monitor the use of the model and the translator and assess their

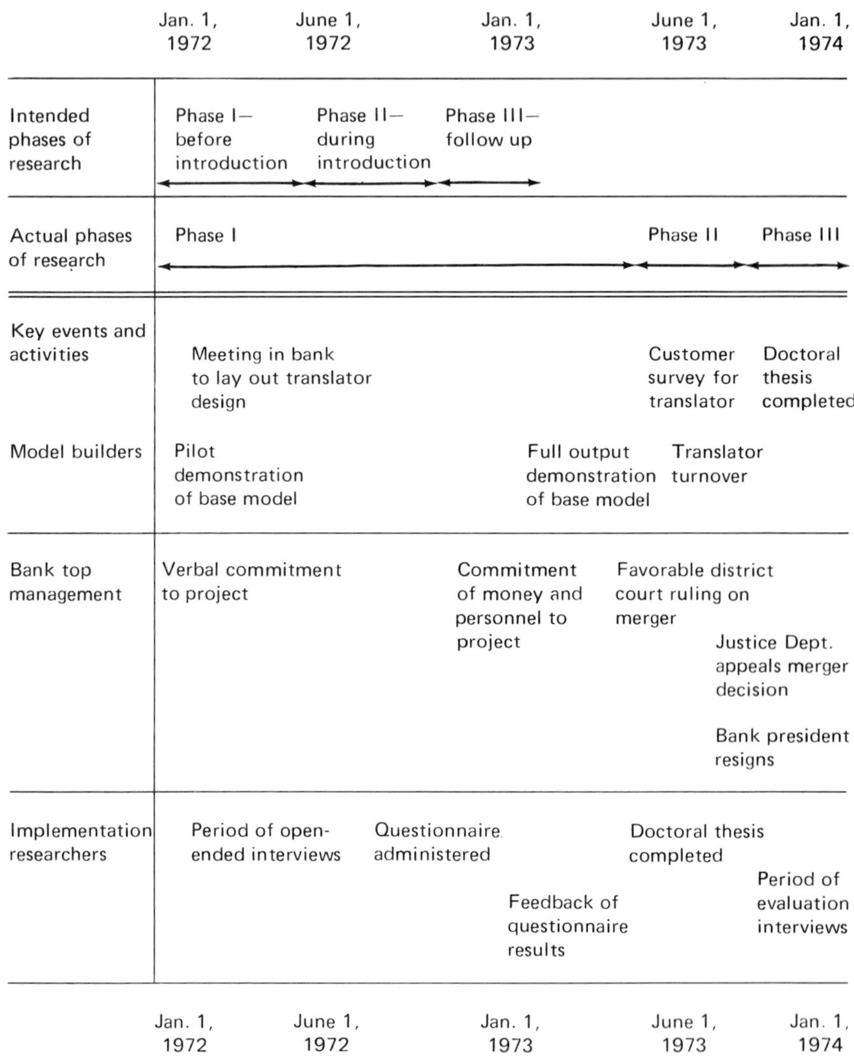

Jan. 1, 1972
June 1, 1972
Jan. 1, 1973
June 1, 1973
Jan. 1, 1974
Intended phases of research
Phase I—before introduction
Phase II—during introduction
Phase III—follow up
Actual phases of research
Phase I
Phase II
Phase III
Key events and activities
Meeting in bank to lay out translator design
Customer survey for translator
Doctoral thesis completed
Model builders
Pilot demonstration of base model
Full output demonstration of base model
Translator turnover
Bank top management
Verbal commitment to project
Commitment of money and personnel to project
Favorable district court ruling on merger
Justice Dept. appeals merger decision
Bank president resigns
Implementation researchers
Period of open-ended interviews
Questionnaire administered
Feedback of questionnaire results
Doctoral thesis completed
Period of evaluation interviews
Jan. 1, 1972
June 1, 1972
Jan. 1, 1973
June 1, 1973
Jan. 1, 1974

Fig. 4.1 Research Phases and Key Events

impact on planning and decision making in the bank. These planned phases are shown along the top row of Figure 4.1, followed in the second row by the phases as they actually occurred. The remaining three rows show relevant events and activities that occurred to affect the perspectives of the model builders, the bank management, and the implementation researchers over the period of the project.

PHASE I: INITIAL INVOLVEMENT, FINDINGS, AND STRATEGIES

In January 1972 we began our field research by attending a pilot demonstration of an abridged and preliminary version of the base model by Davison and his team before several officers of the bank. Significantly, neither the president, the executive vice president, nor Mr. Graves, Davison's earlier contact, were able to attend the demonstration. This left Davison in the position of having to work first with second-level officers. Nevertheless, these men showed considerable interest in the project. In a subsequent meeting with the president, we obtained verbal commitment to proceed with the project and conduct open-ended interviews as the first part of our implementation research (Figure 4.1). In March, Davison and the doctoral student who would build the translator met with essentially the same group of second-level officers, with Graves, and with us. In this meeting it was decided that the basic thrust of the translator would be to provide information to assist in selecting sites for branch location. A possible secondary use would be to provide standards by which branch manager performance could be measured. With the scope of the project narrowed in this way we were better able to focus our interviews on those officers whose work would be most affected by model utilization.

During the first phase we interviewed the president, the executive vice president, the four senior vice presidents, and seven other officers, most of whom were in the branch administration department or the marketing department. (See Figure 4.2, an organization chart of the bank at the time of the interviews.) From these interview data we documented the decision-making processes involved in branch site selection and performance appraisal of branch managers, accumulated qualitative information on characteristics of key individual officers, and noted differences in attitudes toward the banking business, bank strategy in a competitive environment, and the use of computers and simulation models. Using these interviews, file documents, and published research done previously by social scientists in the bank, we were able to develop a fairly comprehensive picture of the history of social relationships over the previous twenty years in the organization. Two important discoveries resulted from this exploratory and time-consuming phase, which illustrate the value of the methodology.

The first of these discoveries concerned the difference between the formal or official decision-making process for branch site selection and the actual process. In one of our interviews we learned in considerable detail from Tom, a staff officer in marketing, how he went about searching for potential branch sites, gathering information on alternative sites, deciding whether to open a new branch or to try to buy an existing small bank, and finally making a recommendation to the executive vice president. We were able to draw a flowchart of the decision process just as he had laid it out, and we noted that it fit a rational

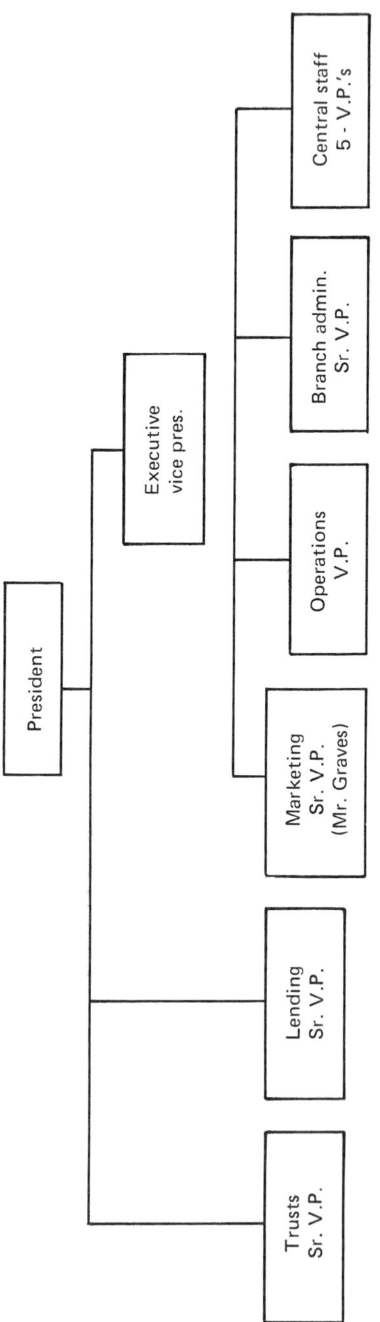

Fig. 4.2 Abbreviated Bank Organization in 1972

decision-making model quite well. Sometime later in an interview with the executive vice president we asked somewhat routinely, "How does the bank go about getting new branches?" Here are some excerpts from his reply:

> Well, we pretty much open them were ever and when ever we can. . . .
>
> I heard the other day the president of the little Bridgeville bank had died. I got on the phone and called his son, offering my condolences, and saying I hoped he wouldn't feel I was overstepping the bounds of decency if I asked if he had considered putting his bank up for sale. . . .
>
> The pitch for one bank we are taking a look at came from a member of one of our advisory boards for one of our branches. He happens to be a personal friend of the president of a small bank in his town, and he put the bee in the bonnet of this gentleman to think about a merger. . . .

Our next question was what Tom, down in marketing, does. The executive vice president's answer was, "Well, he checks out our prospects, works up the numbers, and satisfies the regulatory requirements for us."

In other words, what had appeared to be a straightforward decision process of intelligence, design, and choice by a middle-level staff man in fact turned out to be a somewhat opportunistic, almost random initial process. We later confirmed that the process of deliberation was equally affected by such nonrational elements within the board of directors itself. We would have had very little chance of discovering the actual branch selection process had we sought a description only through a questionnaire or on the basis of the description by Tom, the officer with formal delegated responsibility.

This knowledge led us to caution the model builders against a straightforward modeling of the formal decision process. As a result of this discovery and other forces, the translator model that eventually emerged did not directly simulate the organizational process of site selection. Rather, the model is a simulation of branch operations and market size throughout the region. It permits the user to experiment with simulated openings by his own bank and by competitive banks and to see the results in terms of performance. As such, the model becomes an interactive tool for checking out the effects of prospective mergers and new branches in a short time and comparing the projected results against intuition. It is a more readily acceptable and usable aid to a decision process, which is in effect initiated by stochastic events and characterized by a series of negotiations within the bank and with external parties.

The second discovery from the first phase of research was the existence of two distinct informal coalitions within the officer corps of the bank. The first clue to this was the considerable variation we got in answers to standard questions in interviews, particularly questions relating to how the banking business should be conducted, the utility of computers and models in bank management, and the advisability of continuing with the pursuit of the contested merger. Not only was the variation of interest in itself, but the diversity of attitude and opinion represented a change from published descriptions of this same organization in the 1950s [*2, 3*].

As a result of extensive interviews with employees, Argyris had noted a strong homogeneity of attitudes and personalities and characterized the prevailing type of employee as the "right type." Based on the data from our small sample of interviews, we hypothesized that there were correlations among opinions for each respondent (i.e., there were patterns of attitude clusters such that if an officer held, say, a conservative view on bank strategy he would also be conservative in the use of computers). We also hypothesized that the biographical data would be predictive of attitude clusters and that the different groupings of officers emerging from this analysis would not be perfectly aligned with departmental assignments (i.e., the groups crossed departmental lines). We tentatively decided to call the more conservative group the bankers and the more risk-prone group the marketers, using words that had in fact been used by an employee in an interview when describing his colleagues.

Our strategy at this point, in June 1972, was to go back to several bank employees, particularly a young officer in the controller's department who had shown interest in our research, and test our hypotheses about coalitions by questioning them. Just at this time, however, we learned from Davison that unforeseen problems had arisen in the running of the base model that would delay the demonstration of it and the development of the translator for at least three months. This slip in schedule necessitated a total revision in our research plan and raised a dilemma with respect to our involvement in the bank. It became clear that it would be impossible for my research colleague to complete a thesis on all three phases of implementation by June 1973. Moreover, by virtue of our extensive and confidential interviews with key bank officers, we were aware that we had contributed to raising their expectations about the eventual payoff of the entire project. If we withdrew for three months those expectations might well be replaced with the cynicism of subjects who feel exploited without due return. We found ourselves somewhat trapped by having involved ourselves and not in fact having the power to directly influence the model implementation itself. In short we had become part of the process and therefore were responsible for some of it.

The solution we reached was to pursue in more detail the hypotheses regarding the political coalitions and social structure of the bank by means of a formal questionnaire survey. After obtaining approval for this from the president, we administered a 12-page questionnaire to a stratified random sample of

52 officers (out of a population of 130) in October 1972. The results were presented to an officer's meeting in February 1973. The net outcome of this unexpected change in the research appears to have been to strengthen rather than weaken the relationship that the model builders and we as researchers had with the key officers in the bank. Moreover, the documentation that resulted from the analysis of questionnaire data yielded a successful thesis [*8*] and gave us additional insights on the organization that would prove useful for model implementation.

Nevertheless, it should be noted that this change in research strategy was at best a holding action with some side benefits. Among some officers in the bank there seemed to be mild frustration with the delay in model implementation. At times it became difficult and a delicate matter for us to continue our research in the bank and at the same time encourage the acceptance of a model that was not available. Finally, by virtue of our explanations to our bank confidants of the problems and efforts to alleviate them, we had destroyed any prospects of testing for changes in attitudes toward the modelers and their models that might have resulted had we not intervened. The "participant" and "action" aspects of our methodology had quite clearly interfered with the longitudinal hypothesis testing of the "observation" and "research" aspects. Whatever research results we would produce would not be tests of formal hypotheses or unobtrusive tracking of variables.

FURTHER FINDINGS AND IMPLICATIONS FOR ACTION

The results of the analysis of the questionnaire survey, although somewhat tangential to our primary interest in model implementation, provided a means for maintaining our communications with key officers in the Northville National Bank during the delay in model development. By sharing with them our conclusions about the informal social camps of "bankers" and "marketers," we learned more about the social system, how it had developed, and how it related to what turned out to be a state of organizational crisis in the bank in 1973. This information had important—and negative—implications for the prospects of entirely successful implementation of the model as a tool for top management planning.

In his thesis, Earner [*8*] describes the development, administration, and analysis of results of the questionnaire. It included sections dealing with personal and work history, sociometric choices, and attitudes and opinions toward banking and the use of computers and models in the bank. From a methodological point of view it should be emphasized that the questionnaire was highly organization specific. Many of the items were modified quotes of statements from senior officers in the open-ended interviews, items that we expected would yield variance among the larger sample of surveyed officers and would help to differentiate informal coalitions. Its purposes were to help us understand the system we were working in and to help us maintain relationships in that system. The purpose was not to generate an instrument for a survey across a sample of organizations, although some items could be used in that way.

An encouraging result of the questionnaire was the confirmation of our prior impressions that there were distinct clusters of attitudes among officers and that these could be predicted on the basis of biographical data. We established an index of a banker-marketer dimension by assigning weights to variables that we expected to predict attitudes toward banking, computers, models, and the bank as a place to work. The best such independent variables turned out to be department worked in, age, years experience in the bank, whether or not the respondent held a college degree, and whether or not he had participated in the bank's orientation program for potential officers. Respondents in the sample were ranked according to their index scores. The top eleven in the list were operationally labeled marketers, the bottom ten bankers, and the remaining thirty-one were called "middle." Our hypotheses about the relationships between type of officer and attitudes were explicitly predicted for each of eleven questionnaire items. In all, six of the eleven were confirmed in the three-part order predicted, i.e., either bankers > middle > marketers, or marketers > middle > bankers. (The probability of obtaining six or more confirmations in eleven trials, where each is viewed as a binomial trial with a probability of success of 1/6, is less than .01.) Table 4.1 contains four of the questionnaire

Table 4.1
Illustrative Items Related to Attitudes of Coalitions[a]

Item	Predicted	Mean scores of groups		
		"Bankers" n = 10	Middle n = 31	"Marketers" n = 11
When it comes to using computers in this bank, a little knowledge is a dangerous thing.	B > Mid > Mkt	5.0	4.5	3.0
Computers are at their best when used for routine operations.	B > Mid > Mkt	4.1	3.5	2.6
In the face of competition from other banks, we should expect considerable loyalty from our commercial customers.	B > Mid > Mkt	4.8	3.0	2.6
This organization is not a good place to work.	Mkt > Mid > B	1.5	2.0	2.4

[a]Each item was rated on a scale from 1, "strongly disagree," to 7, "strongly agree".

Table 4.2
Sociometric Choices by Marketers and Bankers on the question: "If you had to name one person who now works in the bank whom you would most like to work on a special project with, whom would it be?"

Choices from \ Choices to	Marketers	Bankers
Marketers	3	0
Bankers	0	3

$p = .05$, Fisher exact test

items for which the predicted order was confirmed, to provide an illustration of the type of items used and the general flavor of attitude differences between bankers and marketers.

At the same time, it was not so clear from results of the questionnaire that these coalitions also formed groups in which members were explicitly aware of a group identity, or that these groups in fact crossed departmental lines. On the one hand, some limited data available from the sociometric section suggested that when given the choice of a colleague with whom they wished to work, officers who held the more conservative banker attitudes tended to choose bankers, and marketers to choose marketers (Table 4.2). On the other hand, one of the best variables for predicting attitude scores was departmental affiliation, with the bankers being clustered in the lending department and in some branch offices and the marketers in marketing and other branch offices. We turned to our confidants in the bank to help us understand the social system, with a feeling that such understanding would be useful in our effort to implement the model.

The two or three most articulate officers in this subject each took a historical perspective in explaining the nature of the current social system. We learned that in the 1960s there had been a close and productive rivalry between two senior vice presidents for the presidency of Northville National. The man who was president during our research had won out over his rival in 1967 after a prolonged and apparently bitter debate within the board of directors. In what appears to have been a move to compromise this unusual (for the bank) degree of conflict, the board reorganized the bank and gave the loser the new title of executive vice president. The resulting organization (Figure 4.2) had the trusts and lending departments reporting directly to the president, and the branches, marketing, operations, and other staff groups reporting to the executive vice president. We surmised that this structure might have actually resulted in a prolongation of the rivalry between the two men, a lessening of necessary interdepartmental communications (especially between lending and the branches and staff groups), and an increasing rigidity, with submersion of conflict and indecision by the top management.

It appeared to us and to some of our informants that the bank's recent decline in performance was largely due to an inadequate early response by top management to competitive pressures, a problem arising from the rivalry and its nonresolution, and that the plan to merge with another bank was a belated attempt to make up for lost opportunities. Whatever the background, it was evident that the Justice Department suit had prolonged the negotiations and was a frustrating drain on time and funds for the management. The bank's lawyers had advised that there be no new branches added while the suit was being contested.

The sapping of resources, the halting of growth, and the lack of conflict resolution in the rigid structure seemed to have reopened the old wounds of the rivalry between the two men at the top. Although their offices were next to each other and they could be seen regularly having coffee in the cafeteria, from what we learned and from a review of our data, it seemed that the attitudes of the two men toward a variety of issues were polarized. The president was the more conservative, prototype banker and the executive vice president was the prototype marketer. One informant told us the president intended that the executive vice president be given only a relatively minor position in the merged bank.

Cycling back to our questionnaire data, we found that it could be used to test one aspect of these discussions. If there was more structural rigidity and less interdepartmental communications after the succession of the current president in 1967 than there had been before, we hypothesized that the career paths of the officers in the sample would show a decline in the proportion of promotions and transfers across departmental lines. The results, given in Table 4.3, confirmed the predicted trend.

Clearly our initial concept of bankers and marketers forming informal, cross-departmental coalitions needed elaboration. There had indeed been an evolution of a dichotomy of opinions and management styles among the officers. But the people holding similar views had not become explicit groups, nor had their diversity contributed to organizational vitality. Rather, it seemed that their differences were personified in the two top men of the organization, leaders whom they had respected and with whom they came into frequent contact. The lack of communication and norms of putting a gentlemanly lid on long-seething rivalries seemed to have inhibited managers throughout the bank from facing their differences openly and constructively and from identifying

Table 4.3
Officer Promotions and Transfers before and after 1967

	Before 1967		1967 to 1972	
	number	%	number	%
Within same department	46	56	51	76
Across departments	36	44	16	24
	82	100	67	100

with one group or the other. The largely uncontrollable forces of competition and the prolonged merger trial had both exacerbated the polarity of these differences and driven them further from explicit attention by these men. The result was that responses to business problems were less than adequate and apparently affected more by political motivation than with organizational objectives in mind.

Adding to the unproductive climate of this social evolution was the necessary preoccupation with the merger and short-run business performance. In an organization that had never developed sophisticated procedures for long-range planning, the prospects for a long-term view in 1973 were even less given the prohibition on branch expansion and emphasis on cost-cutting programs that would improve the operating statement for that very year. For any individual officer, the prospect of merger with another bank had to present a threat of change and job uncertainty. The situation among the senior officers at Northville National could truly be described as one of crisis.

With this new and sobering view of the context into which we were attempting to implement a model for coordinated long-range planning and branch site selection by top managers, we asked ourselves two questions. First, how might the model and its development be adapted and employed to fit with or help resolve current problems in the organization and immediate concerns of the officers themselves? Second, what power did we have to see that such changes in implementation strategy were brought about?

Several potential steps and actions were contemplated. At the suggestion of a social scientist who had done work in the bank, and who agreed with our analysis of the social system, we considered using the base model as a device to break down barriers of communication between the president and the executive vice president. As such a device, the model might serve as wedge to get us involved in what could turn out to be discussions of interpersonal relationships akin to "T-group" sessions. We saw little prospect of being qualified or able to do this within any reasonable time period. Another option was to provide information from the model that would be useful in the merger itself. An issue in the case before the court was the possible need for one or the other of the two banks to divest itself of some branches, which were in overlapping trading areas. We asked the model builders if a simulation could be run showing future relative share of market of these branches, as an aid to decide which would be best to keep. Unfortunately, it seemed that the translator had not been developed sufficiently for such a run. Moreover, the model builders felt that because the tracts in question were at the boundaries of the region covered by the main model, the reliability of projections was less and the risks of poor results were higher than would be the case for branches farther within the region. With more technical knowledge we might have contested these arguments; without it and with limited influence over the design of the models we had no choice but to accept them.

The option that we followed in early 1973 was essentially to hedge on the initial objective that the model could become a tool for top management planning in the near future. We shared with the model builders our interpretations of the organizational crisis and its implications for top management preoccupation. The doctoral student who was building the translator was initiating his contacts with middle-level managers in the marketing department in developing the model. We all recognized the importance of aligning our efforts with marketers in the bank, in view of their more positive attitudes toward computers and models in general. Despite their frustration over the virtual paralysis in top management action, several of these officers understood the project and wanted to make use of the model when and if they could. Our explicit approach was to demonstrate the value of the model to lower-level managers first and to wait for appropriate opportunities or changes in the climate of receptivity at the top before going higher. In retrospect we saw how untimely the implementation effort was for Northville National. Ironically, it was doubtful that we could have seen the gravity of the organizational crisis without having pushed the project to a point of no return.

PHASES II AND III: THE EVOLVED IMPLEMENTATION STRATEGY

In April 1973 Davison and his team produced a file of output projections from the base model and conducted a demonstration at the bank for three middle-level officers using an on-line, remote-access terminal. The extended slip in schedule had resulted in a base model that Davison felt was significantly improved. From the perspective of the bank management, however, the delay had caused some embarrassment by those who had advocated the value of the project. One manifestation of this was a meeting held in January 1973 in which Thomas, the doctoral student working on the translator, ran into resistance when he asked for the commitment of funds from the bank that had been informally agreed upon in the previous year. Davison's intervention cleared this up, however. Coincident with the April demonstration thc bank agreed to a total commitment of some $10 to $15 thousand in support of the project, including the time of a young officer in marketing. Thomas now went to work in earnest to obtain information from the bank and to work mutually to develop assumptions and specifications for the translator model for branch site selection.

Within a very few weeks Thomas began to find his work in the bank time consuming and unproductive, and he increasingly worked on his own to gather data and develop the model. The difficulties in communications and interpersonal relationships appear to have led Thomas to place more emphasis on the goal of completing a significant piece of management science research by the fall deadline for his thesis and less on continual involvement of potential users in model development. During the spring and early summer, Thomas was finding it increasingly difficult to get information from or to explain to Walker, the officer who had been assigned to work with him, his approach to model building. At the same time, his counterpart in the bank was increasingly unsure where the whole project was leading.

In his thesis on these phases of the implementation, Miller [*14*] explored the multiple causes for the lack of development of effective working relationships among Thomas, Walker, and other officers. The contributing causes included differences in personality, cognitive style, and social and task reference groups, and different requirements of the separate insitutional systems of which Thomas and the officers were members. In his work Miller made use of two interesting measurement techniques for implementation research. One was the administration of standardized psychological tests to the key players, the data from which enriched and clarified understanding of the qualitative data on working relationships. In addition, Miller monitored the record of log-on time for model running by bank users, giving an unobtrusive indicator of utilization. Miller's research provided essentially a structural socio-technical framework of variables for our view of the interpersonal relationships during the developmental phases of the implementation.

By virtue of our longitudinal involvement, we were also able to track the dynamics or changes in these structural variables. Apart from this, we were able to witness critical events external to these relationships that had significant impact on the evolving character of the implementation process. In May 1973 the vice president of personnel of the bank died suddenly. In a larger organization this might have had no effect on a distant project involving middle management in a different department. At Northville National, however, it resulted in the promotion of a young marketing officer to personnel and an increase in responsibilities for Walker, Thomas' counterpart on the model. In particular, Walker became involved in routine problems of branch renovations and was forced to cut down on his involvement in the model-development project. The second occurrence was that Walker got married and took an extended vacation, leaving Thomas virtually no one familiar enough with the project to provide information and with whom to share design concepts.

The third event was a ruling by the court in favor of the contested merger. Although we anticipated this would bring relief to the tense managerial climate in the bank, it actually increased the tension. For one thing, the closer prospect of the merger raised more prominently the career concerns of officers. A senior vice president stopped us in the hall about this time, very agitated, and openly expressed his feeling that his career was virtually at an end. In addition, most officers felt quite sure that the Justice Department would appeal the ruling to a higher court.

The net effect of these events was to further diminish the joint concerns and perspectives on the implementation project by Thomas and Walker. For Thomas, the approaching thesis deadline made it increasingly attractive to develop his model independently. For Walker, the urgent demands of his seniors and the lack of any productive results from the project diminished his interest. On both sides, at about this time, we noticed an increase in good-natured but derogatory comments about the other, a new phenomenon that signaled to us that each side would find it difficult to return to a fully shared implementation approach between Thomas and Walker.

In August we huddled with Davison and intervened again. We decided with him that a necessary condition for model implementation by the bank was some degree of involvement by a bank officer. We reasoned that if this person were familiar with Fortran programming and branch banking it might even be possible for him to make up for lost time by understanding the translator and sharing in its final development. On the other hand, if he were familiar either with programming or branch banking, he could learn to use the model and some of the basic assumptions of its construction, enabling him to become its "keeper" if not its designer. We presented these arguments to our most trusted higher officer, who agreed with them and went immediately to work. Within two weeks he had brought about the assignment of Jackson, a bright, young, recent college graduate who had just completed the orientation program and seemed ideal for the keeper role. Most important, he obtained his assignment to the project on a full time basis.

As Thomas' new counterpart, Jackson took on his assignment zealously. Instead of waiting for Thomas to come to the bank, he came to the university and went out of his way to learn all he could about the all but completed translator. We later learned that Jackson had become somewhat bored with his training assignments and perceived the chance to work on the model project as an important career opportunity. This was reinforced by the fact that he was assigned to report on the model's capabilities to two senior officers, the controller, and Mr. Graves, the senior vice president of marketing. Despite the fact that Thomas had by then completed the translator and was ready to turn it over to the bank and write up his thesis, Jackson learned enough to take the model under his wing.

In September the model was turned over, marking the end of the development effort. What had been planned as a phase of joint development between builders and users evolved into a virtual turnkey project.

Also in September another sudden series of events occurred affecting model utilization. This time, however, the effects were to be largely beneficial. One morning, representatives of the Justice Department filed an appeal to the ruling in favor of the merger, signaling a further prolonged court battle. That same afternoon, the president of the bank submitted his resignation to the board of directors, and the executive vice president was named to replace him. The improvement in the social atmosphere was immediate and very noticeable to us. Despite the fact that the merger was still pending, the new president moved quickly to carry out the board's mandate to "improve morale and cut costs." At last report he was succeeding on both counts. Within weeks a reorganization was announced, which included the promotion of Mr. Graves to executive vice president, the former controller to a position of long-range financial planning, and the creation of two cross-departmental committees.

For his part, Jackson took an explicitly tactical approach to the use of the model in his work as staff assistant to the new planner. His intent was to integrate model output with other data whenever his assignments made that possible. Although hardly being used consistently by top management, the model at least became integrated into the bank through this key individual.

SUBSTANTIVE AND METHODOLOGICAL CONCLUSIONS

This research is suggestive of several substantive conclusions for researchers and practitioners of implementation. At the most general level, it would be impossible to underestimate the importance of organizational and behavioral forces in affecting the outcome of the implementation in the Northville National Bank. It is difficult for me to imagine that any model implementation or similar technical innovation potentially affecting middle and upper levels of administration in any organization would not be equally affected by such forces. Clearly, the implementation researchers in this case emphasized these aspects in part because they were applied social scientists themselves. The reader may judge whether the inferences about these forces and the importance placed on them have validity.

In more operational terms, others have documented the essentially political nature of organizational decision making, particularly at the higher levels and for significant decisions [*1, 4, 6*]. The study of Northville National has indicated that a history of key social relationships and organizational performance is essential to fully understand the nature of organizational politics and organizational decision making that would be impacted by model implementation. Further, the idea of the total *perspective* of individuals proved useful to us as a concept for focusing the organizational and other forces acting on individual players and ultimately causing their behavior [*5, 14*]. Such a concept is worthy of wider use. It was Jackson's *perception* of the opportunity that the model project afforded for his career prospects, in contrast to his previous work in the bank, that was largely responsible for his high motivation and desire to learn. It was Thomas' *view* of the project as a research opportunity to be completed in a short time that propelled him to work independently in the face of problems of sharing the development effort with Walker. The *preoccupation* of the two top officers with the highly pressing merger, trial, and declining performance tended to focus their attention on short-run issues rather than tools to assist in long-range planning.

The political and even idiosyncratic nature of many high level decisions, such as the actual process of acquiring branches as opposed to the ostensible one in Northville National, has direct implications for the design and content of models that would aid those decisions. Such models clearly need to be what Scott Morton [*16*] refers to as "decision support systems" rather than direct or complete analogs of the full decision-making process.

The research on this implementation project suggests that we be very cautious with generalizations about a list of factors or attributes that insure or contribute to implementation success from one situation or organization to another. For example, there is a tendency in the literature to advocate mutual involvement and participation of builders and users in model development. In the case of Thomas at Northville National, the context in which he was working made this virtually impossible. Had he pursued a path of heavy mutual involvement with Walker in the face of the crisis climate in the organization, their divergent goals and perspectives, and their lack of knowledge of each other's expertise, the result would surely have been a much prolonged and probably totally unsuccessful effort. As it was, Thomas was able to turn over a finished product to Jackson, who eagerly learned what he needed to make use of the model. In short, normative generalizations about model implementation need to be made contingent on factors deriving out of the organizational, social, and task context of the situation.

As a final substantive point, this project indicates the value of conceiving of implementation as a *process of influence* in organizations. That is, successful implementation of models with significant potential for bringing about organizational change of either a structural or process kind [*13,* chapter 13] requires the exercise of influence, which in turn requires a basis of power for changing behavior. Such a conception is implicit in the dictum that a successful implementation requires top management backing. However, this more general conceptualization opens prospects for influence other than hierarchical authority.

With respect to methodology, it is clear that a major disadvantage of the longitudinal, action-research approach is the difficulty of replication of results. Although some parts of questionnaires and some instruments could be used in a variety of settings or for survey research, the critical parts of those instruments and those data that place those measures in context are highly organization-specific. Rather than a single research project yielding broad results, this methodology requires multiple case studies and tailoring of results from one site to the working hypotheses and instruments for the next. Theory building and testing are slowed by this approach.

Another limitation has to do with the interference of researcher action with researcher observation. As we noted with respect to our efforts to maintain bank interest during the delay in model development, we lost the opportunity to test our hypothesis and that delay could have soured expectations. Nevertheless, in this type of research we do attempt to maintain a distinction between what is object and what is subject, and to examine the results of interventions and acts of influence in a manner that makes it possible to infer what might have happened had they not taken place.* Another way of expressing this problem with the methodology is to state the difficulty of conducting the research such that meaningful and useful results come out.

Against these disadvantages, this methodology has the basic strength of being congruent with the process of implementation itself. At least to the extent that implementation is indeed best conceived as a *process,* taking place over time, and as a complex, multivariate process of interpersonal *influence,* then the longitudinal, case-by-case, action research methodology is most appropriate. Moreover, if one believes as I do that the state of implementation theory leaves much to be desired, the exploratory and grounded-theory nature of this methodology is more likely to yield valid constructs and relationships for eventual theory.

Although I have illustrated that intraorganizational surveys and the use of standardized tests are helpful as part of this methodology, the basic research approach is one that conceives of inference and even data collection itself as processes of mental construction by the researcher. The methodology is true to this conception by its application of cycling back and forth from hard to qualitative data toward the end of obtaining valid models of the process under study. The sources of data that are admissable include the wide range of observed behavior in the actual organizational context, as well as subjects' responses to a questionnaire.

---

*These problems are explored elsewhere in Holton [*12*] and Mitroff [*15*].

The account of implementation at Northville National reveals how unexpected and sometimes unpredictable events outside the scope of the implementation project had effects on the process. The sensitivity of the project to these events may have been greater than would be the case in organizations where the OR/MS function was more accepted by managers, or where more of a base of OR/MS expertise existed, or in which greater size and number of personnel provided more of a buffer around the project, or in which a state of crisis did not exist. Nevertheless, I suspect that for long-term projects in any organization, the impact of these kinds of events plays a much greater role in determining implementation than we have acknowledged. To the extent this is true, a longitudinal methodology which puts the implementation researcher in close touch with the users and builders and their total set of concerns is more appropriate for documenting these events and their effects on implementation. It is only when we have faced the fact that these events threaten to make messy our hoped-for clean models of the implementation process, and documented the events and their impacts, that we can build more valid models and provide more useful help to managers and OR/MS practitioners.

Finally, this methodology seems to have a high potential payoff for practical purposes of improving the skills of operations researchers and management scientists in achieving implementation of models which are worthy and would benefit their clients. For the most part, the test of validity of the results was the opinion of the people being researched. Those of us who reach these conclusions and conduct this research should as a result be much more attuned to the problems these practitioners face. If we work out of an academic institution, we should be in a better position to help them understand the problems and barriers through our writing and teaching than if we conducted our research using other research methods.

References

1. Allison, G. T., *Essence of Decision,* Boston: Little, Brown, 1971.
2. Argyris, Chris, *Organization of a Bank,* Labor and Management Center, Yale University, New Haven, Conn. (Mimeograph), 1954.
3. Argyris, Chris, "Human Relations in a Bank," *Harvard Business Review,* 32, no. 5, 63–72 (September–October 1954).
4. Bauer, R. A., and Gergen, K. J., *The Study of Policy Formation,* New York: The Free Press, 1968.
5. Becker, H. S., Geer, Blanche, Hughes, E. C., and Strauss, A. L., *Boys in White,* Chicago: Univeristy of Chicago Press, 1961.
6. Bower, J. L., *Managing the Resource Allocation Process,* Boston: Division of Research, Harvard Business School, 1970.
7. Dalton, M., *Men Who Manage,* New York: Wiley, 1959.
8. Earner, W. A., "An Assessment of Organizational Elements That Affect the Introduction of a Computer-Based Simulation Into Some Organizational Decision Processes," unpublished doctoral dissertation, Harvard Business School, Boston, 1973.

9. Foster, M., "An Introduction to the Theory and Practice of Action Research in Work Organizations," *Human Relations,* **25**, 529–556 (1972).
10. Glaser, B. G., and Strauss, A. L., *The Discovery of Grounded Theory,* Chicago: Aldine, 1967.
11. Hammond, P. E., (Ed.), *Sociologists at Work,* New York: Basic Books, 1964.
12. Holton, G., "The Roots of Complementarity," *Daedalus,* pp. 1015–1055 (1970).
13. Katz, D., and Kahn, R. L., *The Social Psychology of Organizations,* New York: Wiley, 1966.
14. Miller, R. D., "Multidimensional Processes of Implementing Computer Based Models," unpublished doctoral dissertation, Harvard Business School, Boston, 1974.
15. Mitroff, I. I., "The Mythology of Methodology: An Essay on the Nature of Feeling Science," *Theory and Decision,* **2**, 274–290 (1972).
16. Scott Morton, M. S., "Decision Support Systems: The Design Process," Sloan School of Management, M.I.T., Working Paper #686–73, 1973.

PART THREE

RESEARCH ON IMPLEMENTATION

Chapter 5

Structural and Behavioral Correlates of Implementation in U.S. Business Organizations*

Alden S. Bean
Rodney D. Neal
Michael Radnor
and David A. Tansik

Studies on OR/MS implementation often begin with a complaint of low implementation rates. Following some discussion of what is meant by implementation, it is suggested that an important mechanism or strategy to increase implementation is the improvement of the management science/client relationship through better communications, increased understanding, improved attitudes, modified value systems, etc. We too believe that improving understanding will often help. An increase in enlightened trust between expert and client (and even ultimate service beneficiaries) will lead to better outcomes and seems to carry considerable face validity. But, from the admittedly limited perspective of the practitioner who may be concerned with achieving implementation under a variety of conditions, we are left with a number of important and very practical issues. How directly manipulatable are these attitudinal variables, as compared to others that might be considered for change? How much of the variance between differential implementation experiences can be accounted for by the "understanding" type of variable, independent of other conditions? How much change can we reasonably expect to achieve from attempts to alter the understanding and attitudes of the expert, client, management, and other involved parties? These questions implicitly call for a comparison between the direct understanding strategies and alternative strategies based on the manipulation of structural, process, and technological variables. We hasten to add that we recognize that structural and similar changes may indirectly lead to changes in learning, values, etc. We do, however, differentiate such strategies from the head-on confrontation with attitudes, values, and language.

Therefore, we attempt to examine the role of the many other variables

*Funds for this study were provided under NASA Grant NGL14-007-058

(e.g., budgets and administrative procedures) that may influence rates of implementation—variables that tend to be accepted as parameters of implementation and are seldom mentioned in discussions of the problem. Particularly, we are interested in considering the manipulatability of these variables and their differential impact. Such an analysis could contribute to much needed multivariate or systems theory of implementation. A more comprehensive theory is needed, either in its normative form as a guide to the experts and professional purveyors of new ideas and improvements or in its descriptive form to researchers and analysts concerned with understanding the phenomenon of differential implementation rates.

The data for this study come from our extensive research on the activities of OR/MS practitioners (the experts) in U.S. business firms, and their attempts to implement their programs with line and staff groups (the clients) at various management levels. (These data are drawn from the same sample of companies reported upon in References *1* and *2*.)

CONCEPTUAL FRAMEWORK

Although the recent studies on implementation that have focused primarily on social psychological-behavioral variables provide results that indicate behavioral factors do indeed influence implementation, there is enough unexplained variance to suggest that the other factors we have mentioned may also play a significant role. Radnor, Rubenstein, and Tansik [*3*] developed a multivariable model of behavioral influences on implementation that has been used to generate a number of propositions relating to implementation success and failure. Our intent here is to propose several systems-related variables useful in augmenting the behaviorally based models. The concepts of interest in this study relate to the operating environment of the firm and the operating procedures of OR/MS within the firm as they relate to measures of OR/MS success and implementation.

Organizational Environment

Typically, an OR/MS group is a technical support or staff activity in the organization. The environment in which the organization operates acts as an influence on many functions that might be performed by the OR/MS activity. Specifically, industry competitiveness, organization size, profitability, organization structure, and similar variables may create opportunities and hinderances for OR/MS functioning. For example, a small organization with low profitability in a competitive industry may well benefit from an OR/MS activity but may be unable to support it adequately. Successful OR/MS functioning will very likely be difficult to attain under such conditions even in the presence of numerous other positive behavioral factors such as top management support, client interest, and understanding.

OR/MS Operating Procedures

The internal organization and procedures of the OR/MS group also are believed to influence its functioning and success. Factors such an organizational location and the internal administrative and technical procedures of OR/MS are of special interest. These factors may influence communications patterns, authority levels, structural interrelationships with clients, etc. Our purpose is to determine the degree to which factors such as these influence the implementation process.

Implementation and Success

For our purposes implementation is considered to be the utilization by a client of the results of OR/MS work, particularly formal projects. Implementation differs from the overall concept of success. Implementation as defined makes no judgment concerning the quality of OR/MS work beyond the technical evaluation of the practitioner, nor does it consider unused work that has been shelved for extenuating reasons. Neither does it deal with the effect of unused projects and general education activity on organizational decision makers' thinking. A project that leads to a better understanding of a work environment or confirms the appropriateness of traditional decision policies often produces client satisfaction. Although the result might not lead to implementation, it very likely would leave feelings of success relative to the effort. Such changes in thinking may be potentially more valuable than the project itself. Thus, success in general terms is a nebulous, highly subjective concept. There does not *necessarily* need to be a strong relationship between success and implementation.

Life Cycles

An attenuating factor in the functioning of an OR/MS activity is the stage of development it has attained at any given time. Several papers have been written describing the life-cycle concept as it relates to the integration and institutionalization of OR/MS activities within organizations [*4–6*]. Our analysis here focuses on the life cycle as a modifier of the system-related variables described above. The several phases that are considered in the analysis are discussed below. Within each of these phases there may be important differences in the conditions necessary for effective OR/MS functioning.

Prebirth

Forces from both within and outside the organization usually combine to provide an entry for OR/MS in an organization. Changes in organizational environment, advances made by other organizations, or pressures by organizational members can, for example, provide forces that may lead to a new technology being introduced. Prebirth is the phase during which the pressures build that may eventually lead to the formation of an OR/MS activity or a recognized organizational function.

Missionary

Upon the birth of the activity there typically will be a nucleus of persons desiring to apply this new technology in the organization. A primary need is to convince other organizational members that they should support and utilize the new function. During this phase there tends to be a concerted selling effort by the OR/MS proponents (missionaries) as they attempt to make other organizational members aware of their existence and capabilities; in other words, "convert the natives."

Organizational development

If the missionary efforts are at least partially successful in gaining clients, a new phase of development typically occurs. In many cases the new OR/MS activity does not meet with the full and unequivocable acceptance and support of many organizational members. Thus, some resistance to the new activity may occur. This resistance is usually met by what may be termed bargaining. This bargaining essentially revolves around attempts by the OR/MS activity to show what they can and desire to do in the organization and attempts by other organizational members to prevent the activity from overly impinging upon their actions. Generally an aura of practicality prevails. The OR/MS activity is viewed in terms of its obvious tangible contributions to the organization.

Very often the result of this give and take is that members of the OR/MS activity go through a period of deprofessionalization, i.e., the level of technical sophistication becomes something less than originally intended by the OR/MS staff. This may be accomplished by removing a highly professional leader from the group or by various "accommodations" made by the OR/MS activity during the bargaining process.

Reprofessionalization

The result of the organizationalizing process is not always determinable on an a priori basis. The activity could emerge as a routine technical service function severely compromised by the bargaining process. Alternatively, little resistance may have been encountered resulting in little or no deprofessionalization. In either case, given that the OR/MS activity is able to perform reasonably well and is able to show some organizational benefits, it will acquire a degree of legitimacy. As organization members become familiar with OR/MS, they may well come to demand the services of the activity in an improved or reprofessionalized form.

Maturity

Given that an OR/MS activity progresses through the above phases it may reach a point where it is routinely accepted as an ongoing organizational component. It has become institutionalized [5].

Diffusion

Often associated with maturity is an interest in establishing OR/MS activities in varying parts of the organization. This diffusion allows for local control of the technology and its ready availability for unique problems. Diffusion is most frequently encountered in the maturity phase—when the technology is accepted and used as a routine function.

METHODOLOGY

The initial intent of this study was to identify the structural and behavioral factors that might affect the success of OR/MS activities and then to suggest strategies that might be helpful in accentuating the favorable influences and neutralizing those that were inhibiting. A literature search was conducted prior to the investigation in order to compile a list of likely influencing factors and useful procedures for pursuing OR/MS endeavors. The list was then expanded through discussions among the various members of the research team. A pilot survey of 13 companies resulted in some revisions to the research instrument and some additions to the areas of interest.

The objective of the plan was to visit 10 companies in each of 10 industrial sectors. To allow for the possibility of nonresponses and dropouts, we initially contacted 130 firms. All of the firms were included in *Fortune* magazine's "500" list of large U.S. corporations. The average company revenue was $1.74

Table 5.1

Industry code no.	Sector	No. of firms
1	Automotive	10
2	Engineered products	10
3	Electrical	10
4	Materials processing	5
5	Chemical/pharmaceutical	4
6	Petroleum/chemical	10
7	Chemical/synthetic	8
8	Transportation	10
9	Food processing	10
10	Finance	10
11	Merchandising	10
12	Utilities	11
		108

billion per year. The average employment for each firm was 47,000. It became evident early in the study that the presence of OR/MS activities was closely associated with the size of the firm. Of the 108 companies contacted whose annual revenues exceed $500 million, 104 had OR/MS groups. Of the 22 firms below $500 million, only 13 had OR/MS groups and of these 8 had revenues of about $400 million. Although a total of 117 of the 130 firms agreed to participate in the study, scheduling problems limited our final sample to 108. (See Table 5.1.)

Entrance to the firm was generally through the OR/MS manager, and the manager was the principal source of information. The interview instruments and procedures were designed to cross check all of the key areas of investigation. Inconsistencies in responses did occur, but in many cases the inconsistencies were helpful in furthering our understanding of the OR/MS manager and how he perceived and responded to his environment. In addition to the 109* OR/MS managers visited, 32 OR/MS practitioners and 37 liaison and client personnel were interviewed to check the validity of the managers' data. In 13 firms these validation interviews were conducted without going through the OR/MS manager. In general the managers' reports were upheld, this was particularly true in extreme cases, such as instances where failure and success seem to be readily identified by both practitioners and users. There were some minor differences over the middle ratings of the various factors surveyed.

Occasionally, as the study proceeded, new insights were gained that suggested other areas worthy of investigation. The methodology was adjusted to accommodate the related factors. Because of this some data were not developed

*In one firm we interviewed both the incumbent manager and his predecessor.

for all 108 of the firms. On the other hand, the number of firms sampled for each extension of the data base was sufficient to allow for considerable analysis.

On occasion the researcher had to make judgments about the data to be used in developing the company profiles. Two examples are: (1) classifying the OR/MS manager as either a professional or organizational and (2) determining the life-cycle phase of the OR/MS group. In each instance there was considerable supporting information. For example, data on professional experience, frequency of moves, educational emphasis, and future aspirations aided in the decision to classify OR/MS leaders as organizationals or professionals. In most of the decisions the categorization was unambiguous. In the borderline situations the final decision was more subjective. The decisions were made before the analysis commenced and were not changed thereafter. The rigid adherence was maintained even though occasionally it appeared that a shift would lend increased significance to a relationship. Regarding precision of measurement, some factors, such as group age, could be properly treated as ratio scales. Other factors, such as the perceived success of the group, have either a nominal or ordinal character. Whenever any doubts existed, the approach was to code the data "conservatively."

FINDINGS

Industrial Adoption of OR/MS

Before moving to an analysis of the structural and behavioral correlates of implementation, it is interesting to note the variations in OR/MS adoption patterns in our sample across industries. As Table 5.2 indicates, industries that contained the most innovative firms, as indicated by date of adoption (industries #9, 12, and 3), were not uniformly innovative within the industry. Compare, for example, the food processing industry (#9) to the electrical industry (#3). One firm in each industry adopted OR/MS in 1954, however, the median date of adoption for all firms in the food processing industry sample was 1960, and no firms adopted later than 1965. In the electrical industry, on the other hand, the median adoption period was 1964 to 1967, but 3 firms adopted in 1969. Thus, for this sample, the earliest date of adoption within the industry was not a good indicator of a general industry trend. Based on skewness of adoption patterns within industries, it appears that the in petroleum, automotive, and synthetic chemical industries (#6, 1, and 7) innovative firms were followed rather rapidly by a second wave of adopters, whereas in the electrical, transportation, and merchandising industries (#3, 8, and 11) early adoptors did not precipitate an immediate bandwagon effect. The other industries display more symmetrical patterns of adoption.

Table 5.2
Frequency of Adoption of OR/MS by Industry and Year of Adoption (Ranked by Median Adoption Date)

Year of adoption	Industry code no. 6	9	7	12	1	4	10	5	3	11	2	8	*N*
1954	0	1	0	1	0	0	0	0	1	0	0	0	3
1955	0	0	0	0	0	0	0	0	0	0	0	0	0
1956	2	0	2	2	0	0	0	0	0	0	0	1	7
1957	***3**	0	1	0	1	0	0	0	0	0	0	0	5
1958	**0**	1	0	0	0	1	0	0	0	0	0	0	2
1959	**0**	1	0	0	3	1	0	0	1	0	0	0	6
1960	**1**	**4**	**2**	2	0	0	2	1	0	1	0	0	13
1961	0	0	0	**1**	**2**	0	0	0	2	0	0	0	5
1962	1	0	1	2	0	0	0	**1**	0	0	1	0	6
1963	0	1	0	0	0	0	1	**0**	0	0	0	1	3
1964	1	0	0	0	1	**1**	1	**0**	**1**	2	1	0	**8**
1965	1	2	2	2	1	1	**4**	**0**	**0**	1	1	1	16
1966	0	0	0	0	1	1	0	**0**	**0**	**1**	1	1	5
1967	1	0	0	0	0	0	2	**0**	**1**	**1**	**4**	**2**	11
1968	0	0	0	1	0	0	0	**2**	1	1	1	2	8
1969	0	0	0	0	1	0	0	0	3	3	1	1	9
	10	10	8	11	10	5	10	4	10	10	10	9†	107†

Index to Industry Codes

1 = Automotive
2 = Engineered products
3 = Electrical
4 = Materials processing
5 = Pharmaceuticals and chemicals
6 = Petroleum
7 = Synthetic chemicals
8 = Transportation
9 = Food processing
10 = Financial
11 = Merchandising
12 = Utilities

*Median period is enclosed in the box.
†Data not available in one case.

The reasons for these differences are not clear at this time, and it is not our purpose to explain them. However, it is interesting to note that such differences exist in this sample and to think of their possible implications for the organizational development of OR/MS groups within individual firms. Specifically, we suggest that OR/MS groups that were begun at an early date and were unique within their industry would find it difficult to obtain satisfactory evaluations of their performance relative to the accomplishments of other

OR/MS groups. This might result in a greater felt need to strive for security by organizationalizing their activities. Pursuing this idea for a moment, it is interesting to note that of the six industries with the highest proportion of mature OR/MS units (see Table 5.3) only one (#4) contains a firm that was unique in its early adoption. Thus the industries in which OR/MS was most mature (#4, 5, 6, 7, 9, and 10) were made up primarily of cases where innovative firms within the industry were followed rather rapidly by a substantial number of firms in the same industry (see Table 5.2). This finding could be viewed as an artifact caused by the correlation between stage of development and age of the groups. However, note that industries 4, 5, and 10 were rather late adoptors (first adoption in 1958 to 1960), whereas industries 6, 7, and 9 were rather early adoptors (first adoption in 1954 to 1956). This tends to refute the contention that stage of development is simply a function of age.

The above issues are suggestive of researchable questions that should be explored further through a different sampling procedure than the one used here.

Table 5.3
Current (1969) Life-Cycle Phase by Industry

		Group Life-Cycle Phases						
No.	Industry	Pre-Birth	Group missionary	Org.	Reprof.	Maturity	Diffusion	*N*
6	Petroleum	0	0	1	0	9	0	10
9	Food processing	0	0	0	1	9	2	10
7	Synthetic chem.	0	0	1	0	7	0	8
12	Utilities	0	1	5	0	5	0	11
1	Automotive	0	1	5	0	3	1	10
4	Materials processing	0	0	0	1	3	1	5
10	Financial	0	2	2	0	6	0	10
5	Pharm/chem.	0	1	0	0	1	2	4
3	Electrical	2	3	1	0	3	1	10
11	Merch.	0	4	2	0	4	0	10
2	Eng. prod.	1	1	4	0	4	0	10
8	Transp.	0	4	2	0	2	1	9*
	N	3	17	23	2	54	8	107*

Note: Box denotes median frequency.

*Data not available in one case.

Patterns of Implementation and Success

Two success variables have been developed. One is an implementation variable, referring to the percentage of all formal projects completed by the OR/MS group within the 2–3 year period preceeding our interviews, and that were actually used for decision-making purposes by the intended user. This figure was developed by identifying the set of all projects worked on during the period, dividing it into projects completed and not completed, and further dividing it into projects implemented and not implemented. Thus the only projects that were considered implemented were those that the OR/MS manager felt had been satisfactorily completed from a technical point of view and that were also utilized as intended by a client. The number of projects considered in each firm averaged about 12. Thus some 1300 formal projects in the sample of 108 firms were considered in this study.

The second success variable is a composite of five ratings, all of which represent perceptions of the OR/MS manager about his group's overall success, its level of support from top management, its level of client support, its project backlog, and the proportion of projects in the portfolio generated by persons external to the OR/MS group. Thus an appropriate name for this variable is overall index of perceived success. It is referred to throughout this chapter as both overall success and perceived success. The reader will note that it probably reflects the satisfaction or dissatisfaction of the OR/MS manager with the organizational environment rather than accounting for the contributions of OR/MS to corporate profits.

These two variables are used throughout this chapter to aid in our understanding of implementation problems. By using them together, we are able to highlight the extent to which the OR/MS managers' perceptions of organizational success are consistent with the concept of implementation as defined above. It is important to do so, because the correlation between implementation rate and success for the entire sample was only .32.* Thus variations in the implementation rate explain only 10 percent of the variation in success scores in our sample.

Implementation and Success across Industries

Tables 5.4 and 5.5 illustrate the relationships between type of industry, the median implementation rates, and general success ratings of OR/MS groups in those industries. These figures indicate first that perceived success and implementation rates are not highly correlated within industries, except in very extreme cases (#2, 12, 9, 6, and 4). The correlation between implementation and success across the entire sample was .32; the relation is weak in general, but

*Rank correlation coefficient between "success" and "implementation" after transformation of variables to ordinal values. $p = .3199$, $n = 103$, significance level >.999.

Table 5.4
Implementation Rates and General Success of OR/MS Activities by Industry

		Implementation Score			Success Score		
No.	**Industry**	**Median**	**Range**	**Rank**	**Median**	**Range**	**Rank**
1	Auto	2.75	3	5–6T	2.75	1	5–6T
2	Eng. prod.	3.00	2	1	2.83	3	3
3	Elec.	2.90	3	2	2.38	3	9
4	Mat. proc.	1.33	2	12	1.25	2	12
5	Pharm.	2.50	3	7–8T	2.75	1	5–6T
6	Pet.	2.16	2	11	2.67	1	7
7	Synth. chem.	2.83	3	4	2.30	1	10
8	Transp.	2.75	3	5–6T	3.00	2	2
9	Food	2.25	3	10	2.16	3	11
10	Fin.	2.33	2	9	2.78	2	4
11	Merch.	2.50	3	7–8T	2.50	3	8
12	Util.	2.86	3	3	3.50	3	1

Note: Implementation rates and success scores were assigned in terms of standard deviations above and below the mean. A score of 1 was assigned if the observed value was more than 1 standard deviation below the mean, a score of 2 was assigned if the observed value was less than 1 standard deviation below the mean, 3 if it was less than 1 standard deviation above the mean, and 4 if it was more than one standard deviation above the mean.

Table 5.5
Scatter Diagram of Industry Implementation and Success Rankings by Industry Code Number

		Implementation (Rank Order)											
Perceived Success		**(Highest)**											**(Lowest)**
(Rank Order)		**1**	**2**	**3**	**4**	**5**	**6**	**7**	**8**	**9**	**10**	**11**	**12**
(Highest)	1			12									
	2					8							
	3	2											
	4									10			
	5						1	5					
	6												
	7											6	
	8							11					
	9	3											
	10				7								
	11										9		
(Lowest)	12												4

it does appear that some additional explanatory power is gained when the data are grouped by industry. One interpretation is that the norms for perceived OR/MS success differ across industries. It is also plausible to argue that differences in life-cycles phases of groups within industries influence actual implementation rates and perceived success. Because this study focuses primarily on the implementation of formal projects, it is difficult to investigate the first issue. Thus in the remainder of this chapter we analyze the data according to life-cycle phases, but we do not attempt to explore variations due to industry differences beyond those reported above. The reader is asked to recognize that additional data on each industry are needed to help resolve the industry differences issue.

Implementation and Success in the Total Sample

Implementation rate data were obtained from 104 firms. The mean implementation rate was 71.9 percent of all projects that had reached technical completion. The standard deviation was 22.2 percent. Success score data were available for 103 firms, with a mean score of 13.35 and a standard deviation of 3.6 on a scale ranging from 0 to 18 points. Table 5.6 contains the Pearson

Table 5.6
Pearson Correlations between Explanatory Variables and Scaled* Implementation and Success Variables

Explanatory variables	Implementation rate	Success score
I. Firm's operating environment industry type	(See text)	(See text)
II. Firm's characteristics		
A. Total revenue	−.25[1]	−.06
B. No. of employees	−.18[2]	−.02
C. Return on assets	.08	.14[3]
D. Return on revenue	.10	.00
E. Decentralization	.00	−.15[3]
F. Innovativeness re OR/MS	−.11	−.05
III. Organizational environment of the OR/MS group		
A. Functional location	−.10	.10
B. Levels below top of the hierarchy	−.18[3]	−.16[3]
C. Access to computer	−.01	.08

*The scaling procedure results in a four-point ordinal scale for both implementation and success. The resulting correlations are either rank order or point-biserial correlations, depending on the measurement of the second variable (see Appendix I). Because it has been shown that Pearson's *r*, Spearman's *ρ*, and point-biserial correlations are computationally identical and thus comparable for descriptive purposes [*7*, page 371], the term "Pearson correlations" accurately reflects the computational method. All calculations were done using SPSS [*8*].

D. Formality of charter	.30[1]	.27[2]
E. Availability of data	.12[3]	.16[3]
F. Size of budget	–.14[2]	.00
G. Formalization of liaison	.09	.12
IV. Transactions between OR/MS and the organization		
A. Sources of project ideas		
1. % generated by OR/MS	–.04	–.37[1] †
2. % generated by TM	–.03	.26[2]
3. % generated by CL	.07	.10
B. Influences over project selection		
1. % selected by OR/MS	.10	–.18[3]
2. % selected by TM	–.09	.10
3. % selected by CL	.05	.05
C. Involvement of OR/MS in formal committees	.08	–.06
D. Top management support of OR/MS	.21[3]	.66[1]
E. Top management interest in OR/MS	.20[3]	.47[1]
V. Characteristics of the OR/MS group		
A. Structural characteristics		
1. Formal group size	–.06	–.07
2. Group size as % of total no. of employees	.16[3]	.24[2]
3. Diffusion ratio	–.05	–.10
B. Attributes of group leader		
1. Orientation	–.21[3]	–.09
2. Age	.00	.09
3. Education	–.07	.04
C. Allocation of leader's time	.07	–.24[2]
1. Time spent selling	.07	–.24[2]
2. Time spent administering	.09	.12
3. Time spent innovating	–.24[2]	.00
4. Time spent implementing	.14[3]	.14[3]
D. Administrative Procedures		
1. Number of procedures	–.02	.34[1]
2. Cost-benefit analysis	.09	.06
3. Project evaluation	.34	.05
4. Sophistication of procedures	*X*	*X*
E. Project portfolio characteristics		
1. Project mix-size	.07	.10
2. Project mix-time frame	.07	.10
3. Variety of OR techniques	.22[2]	.06
4. Variety of functional areas	.13[3]	.11
5. Method of project cost allocation	.03	–.15
VI. Theoretical parameters		
A. Life cycle phase of the OR/MS group in the organization	–.20[3]	–.03

1 = significant at $P \leqslant .001$
2 = significant at $P \leqslant .01$
3 = significant at $P \leqslant .1$

†These correlations are spuriously high due to the construction of the success index. See Appendix I for details.

correlation coefficients of all the data in the study with the two dependent variables, the implementation rate, and the success score.

Analysis of Structural and Behavioral Correlates of Implementation and Success

Implementation can be viewed as a possible outcome of a transaction or a series of exchanges of project related ideas, information, reports, etc., between OR/MS, the client, and others in the organization. If implementation rates are strongly correlated with frequency and nature of these transactions, it seems appropriate to view these as behavioral correlates of implementation (where behavioral has the meaning given above). The variables listed in sections IV and V of Table 5.6 are the most appropriate to consider as behavioral, and only those in section IV and group D of section V involve direct interaction between management scientists and clients. It is apparent from Table 5.6 that the only behavioral variables correlated with implementation to a significant degree and that involve direct management science/client transactions are related to the allocation of time by the OR/MS leader among selling, administering, innovating, and implementing projects. The strongest correlations appear among the non-behavioral variables!

Before accepting these observations as conclusive, it is important to consider the limitations of the data and reflect on what they are likely to hide as well as what they may reveal. First of all, there are conditions under which a zero correlation coefficient may emerge even though a strong relation exists among variables.

1. When the relationship is curvilinear, the correlation coefficient may be small and disguise the existence of a relationship.
2. When the value taken on by one variable does not change, no correlation will appear. Thus an important factor influencing implementation could be overlooked in an analysis strictly dependent on correlation coefficients. (Appendix II contains descriptive statistics on all variables included in this study.)
3. When variations in other relevant variables intervene to offset or mask the relationship to be measured, an incorrect correlation may be obtained.

Our analysis at the time of this writing has not proceeded far enough to reveal significant nonlinear relationships, except in those cases where the non-linearities are covariants of the life-cycle-phase variable. (Those findings are discussed below.) Thus the only relationships that we intend to investigate here are straightforward linear relationships across the entire sample (Table 5.6) or within each life-cycle phase (Tables 5.9 through 5.19), as reflected by simple correlation coefficients. Our analysis does not reveal relationships between implementation and success, or variables that did not exhibit variation in this study, but that might influence implementation and success if their values were manipulated experimentally or were in some way changed. Finally, we have yet to conduct partial correlation analysis to control for other covariates of implementation and success.

To summarize, only two of the direct OR/MS-client transaction variables exhibited a significant linear relationship with implementation across the entire sample:

1. Time spent innovating (trying to change the clients' way of doing things to the management science way), $r = -.24$,
2. Time spent implementing (adjusting and adapting the results of the project to the operating style and parameters of the clients' environment), $r = +.14$.

However, several other transaction variables involving OR/MS and nonclient personnel were correlated with implementation. For example, top management support ($r = +.21$) and top management interest in OR/MS ($r = +.20$) are apparently important across the entire sample. This suggests that the interactions between OR/MS personnel and top management might be an important but indirect influence on client behavior. Thus it might be useful to analyze the extent to which factors within the control of the OR/MS manager, regardless of whether they are directly associated with OR/MS-client interactions and transactions, are associated with implementation and success. We can thus obtain a general idea of the extent to which the OR/MS manager can activate and control variables that may enhance implementation and success regardless of whether they involve direct interaction with clients.

The data have been reorganized to enable us to explore this possibility. Tables 5.7 and 5.8 display only those variables that were correlated beyond the .1 level with the two success variables. The variables have been assigned to four categories according to their manipulability by the OR/MS group leader:

1. Directly controllable variables: within the normal discretion of the OR/MS leader without obtaining approval of anyone outside his group.
2. Directly influenced variables: can be accomplished through direct cooperation between the OR/MS group leader and at least one member outside his group.
3. Indirectly influenced variables: a process leading to the desired condition can be initiated by the OR/MS group leader through interaction outside the group, but group members do not participate directly in the process once it has been initiated.
4. Exogenous variables: conditions are created by events lying outside the sphere of influence of the OR/MS group leader and its members.

Table 5.7
Significant Correlates of Project Implementation Rates Grouped According to Controllability

Category and variable	r	Sig.	Type of relationship
1. Directly controllable variables			
% of leader's time allocated to innovating	.24	.01	Inverse
% of leader's time allocated to implementing	[.14*]	.1	Direct
Variety of OR techniques used	.22	.01	Direct
Variety of functional areas served	.13	.1	Direct
2. Directly influenced variables			
Formalization of charter	[.30]	.001	Direct
Quality and availability of data	[.12]	.1	Direct
Size of budget	.14	.01	Inverse
Orientations of group leader	.21	.1	Groups led by organizationally oriented leaders have better implementation rates than professionally oriented leaders.
3. Indirectly influenced variables			
Level in the hierarchy	[.18]	.1	The higher the reporting level, the greater the implementation rate.
Top management support	.21	.1	Direct
Group size as a % of organization size	.16	.1	Direct
Life-cycle phase	[.20]	.1	Inverse
Total revenue of the firm	.25	.001	Inverse
Top management interest	.20	.1	Direct
4. Exogenous variables			
Number of employees in the firm	.18	.01	Inverse

*Factors which are correlated with both "implementation" and "success" are enclosed in a box.

This way of organizaing the data (Tables 5.7 and 5.8) leads us to several tentative conclusions:

1. Implementation rate (Table 5.7) is linearly correlated with fifteen explanatory variables. Only two of these variables involve direct interaction between OR/MS and clients, and the two variables (% of leaders time allocated

Table 5.8
Significant Correlates of Overall Success Grouped According to Controllability

Category and Variable	*r*	Sig.	Type of Relationship
1. Directly controllable variables			
% of projects generated by OR/MS	.37	.001	Inverse
No. of admin. procedures	.34	.001	Direct
% of leaders time selling	.24	.01	Inverse
% of leaders time administering	.24	.01	Inverse
% of leaders time implementing	[.14*]	.1	Direct
2. Directly influenced variables			
Formality of charter	[.27]	.01	Direct
Quality and availability of data	[.16]	.1	Direct
% projects selected by OR/MS	.18	.1	Inverse
3. Indirectly influenced variables			
Return on assets	.14	.1	Direct
Level in hierarchy	[.16]	.1	The higher the reporting level, the greater the perceived success.
% of projects generated by top management	.26†	.01	Direct
Top management support	[.66†]	.001	Direct
Top management interest	[.47†]	.001	Direct
OR/MS group size as a % of total employees	[.24]	.01	Direct
4. Exogenous variables			
Decentralization	.15	.1	Inverse—the greater the degree of centralization, the greater the perceived success.

*Factors which are correlated with both implementation and success are enclosed in a box.

†Spuriously high due to construction of success index. See Appendix.

to innovating; and % of leader's time allocated to implementing) are interdependent by definition. The direction of the relationship suggests that leaders spending time trying to change the way the organization does things and trying to accommodate OR/MS models and outputs to the organization's operating environment will experience higher implementation rates. The other correlates of implementation rate include both structural variables, such as formalization of charter, size of budget, and level in the hierarchy, and behavioral variables, such as orientations of group leader and top management support. Thus the data indicate that both structural and behavioral variables are significant linear correlates of implementation and that, among the behavioral variables, direct transactions between OR/MS and the client group are important but do not explain a large proportion of the variation in implementation rates.

2. Success scores (Table 5.8) are more strongly correlated with direct transaction variables than was the implementation rate. The three "% of leaders time" variables are, of course, interdependent. Once again, the direction of the relationships suggest that leaders who spend a high percentage of their time accommodating OR/MS models and outputs to the organization's operating environment and a small percentage of their time in selling and administration will be leaders of more successful groups. Similarly, groups that are well organized in the sense that they have developed a set of administrative procedures to guide their operations and organizational relations are perceived to be successful groups. Finally, the fewer projects selected or generated by OR/MS, the greater the perceived success. Thus, in contrast to the correlates of implementation (Table 5.7), the correlates of success (Table 5.8) include a higher proportion of client transaction variables and a number of other behavioral variables that can be controlled or influenced by OR/MS. However, it is also important to note that structural variables, such as formality of charter, return on assets, level in the hierarchy, are also important linear correlates of overall success.

3. It is somewhat surprising to find that only seven variables appear on both lists. Three are subject to direct influence and control by OR/MS, whereas four are not. Interestingly, the relationships are in the same direction for these seven variables, i.e., each is associated with both implementation and success in the same direction. Yet there is no apparent reason to believe that a combined structural and behavioral approach to the problem of improving OR/MS acceptance and implementation would be contradictory. Closer examination of intercorrelations among explanatory variables might cause us to modify this impression, of course.

4. It appears that implementation may be less amenable to OR/MS control than success, because the levels of significance of the directly controllable and directly influenced variables tend to be higher in the success case (Table 5.8) than for implementation (Table 5.7). Our tentative interpretation of this finding is that the conditions that induce clients to implement project results are likely to be the product of the specific pressures and demands emanating from the client's working environment rather than from the direct influence attempts of OR/MS personnel. Similarly, a successful relationship to clients may be created, even under conditions of low implementation, if OR/MS groups can do work that is perceived as *potentially* relevant to client problems but, at the same time, avoid a hard-sell, innovative approach to client relations.

5. Finally, the implementation rate was found to be significantly related to the theoretical parameter, life-cycle phases. This suggested to us that the data should be broken down by life-cycle phases and examined in greater detail in order to gain insights into possible differences in relationships that might be discovered within each life-cycle phase.

Analysis of Implementation and Success by Life-Cycle Phases

Before proceeding to a detailed analysis of each variable, note in Table 5.9 that the average implementation rates and success scores *decline* after reaching their maximum values in the organizational phase! We will refer to this finding from time to time in our discussion. It is interesting to note, however, that an increasing implementation rate may not be a requirement for continuing group development beyond the organizational phase.

In the following section we discuss the results of our analysis in which each variable was systematically studied to determine the nature of its relation to implementation and success in each life-cycle phase.

Firm's Characteristics (II)

The following discussion is organized according to the major headings presented in Table 5.6, beginning with section II, Firm's Characteristics. For

Table 5.9
Descriptive Statistics on Implementation and Overall Success by Life-Cycle Phase of OR/MS in the Organization

	Implementation Rate			Success Score		
Life-cycle phase	*N*	Mean*	S.D.	*N*	Mean†	S.D.
1. Pre-birth	2	75.0	7.1	2	8.5	2.1
2. Missionary	17	72.1	23.1	17	13.6	3.6
3. Organizational	23	85.3	14.2	22	14.5	2.5
4. Reprofessionalization	2	66.0	8.5	2	8.0	0
5. Maturity	53	69.3	20.6	53	13.8	3.2
6. Diffusion	7	47.1	33.6	7	9.4	5.1
Overall	104	71.9	22.2	103	13.35	3.6

*Based on a scale of 0 to 100% (see Appendix I).
†Based on a scale of 0 to 18 (see Appendix I).

Table 5.10
Relation between Firm Characteristics (II), Implementation, and Success by Life-Cycle Phases

Relation between implementation and:	Life-cycle phases 1	2	3	4	5	6	Relation between overall success and:	Life-cycle phases 1	2	3	4	5	6
A. Total revenue	−1.00	−.31*	+11	−1.00	−.30	.27	A. Total revenue	−1.00	−.14	−.41	X	−.04	.10
B. No. of employees	−1.00	+.04	+.34	−1.00	−.06	.17	B. No. of employees	−1.00	+.16	−.25	X	+.01	+.18
C. Return on assets	X	−.10	+.33	X	.004	.22	C. Return on assets	X	−.32	.56	X	.14	.23
D. Return on revenue	X	−.14	−.13	X	+.33	+.51	D. Return on revenue	X	−.20	−.14	X	.23	.27
E. Decentralization	−1.00	−.08	+.10	−1.00	−.10	−.15	E. Decentralization	−1.00	.03	−.11	X	−.15	−.16
F. Innovativeness re OR/MS	X	−.43	+.31	−1.00	−.10	−.17	F. Innovativeness re OR/MS	X	−.05	.33	X	−.17	−.11
N =	2	17	23	2	53	7 = 104	*N* =	2	17	22	2	53	7 = 103

*Correlations that are significantly different from zero at the $p \leqslant .10$ level are enclosed in a box. *X* indicates that a correlation coefficient could not be calculated due to lack of data.

convenience, the same numerical and alphabetical characters used in Table 5.6 are used to identify the relevant sections of the following discussion.

Table 5.10 contains a summary of the correlation coefficients of the firm's characteristic variables by life-cycle phases. It is interesting to note the changes in direction of relationships in across the life-cycle phases, especially in the case where a large number of variables tend to change. For example, between the missionary and organizational phases, four of the six variables change from a negative to a positive correlation with implementation. A similar shift occurs between the organizational phase and maturity phase, when five of the six relationships change sign. These shifts suggest interesting questions about causality for investigation in logitudinal studies. One would not expect these firm characteristics to change drastically from year to year. Thus, an interesting question for further study is whether changes in implementation rates or success *cause* a movement from the missionary to the organizational stage of development. Given our definition of the organizational phase (see page 80), we would predict the opposite relationships.

It is interesting, furthermore, to speculate on the types of firms and phases in which OR/MS groups are most likely to be successful in implementing their projects. For example, missionary groups are likely to experience implementation problems in large, decentralized firms that were early adopters of OR/MS. The same statement would describe mature groups, but, in addition, low rates of return on revenue might increase implementation problems. Additional analysis and research is needed to clarify these questions.

Regarding success in general, it is interesting to note that perceptions of success tend to emerge as a correlate of firm characteristics in the organizational phase in somewhat centralized firms with high rates of return on assets and where firm size is relatively small. Different variables explain perceived success in maturity, however, with return on revenue being a positive correlate of success.

A brief discussion of each variable in the above table seems appropriate here.

A. TOTAL REVENUE. The only significant correlations between total revenue and implementation rates are negative, occurring in the missionary and maturity phases. This tendency indicates, at least, that the very largest firms, in terms of total revenue, tend to have the greatest difficulty with implementation. When taken together with the findings on the other rate of return (ROR) variables, it suggests that revenue-related projects, which tend to be implemented by mature groups in high ROR firms, are less successful in firms with high revenues and low returns on revenue. Once again, additional study might add to our understanding of this relationship.

B. NUMBER OF EMPLOYEES. If organizational size, in terms of members of employees, makes any difference in OR/MS success, it apparently does so only in the organizational phase, where it has a positive relation to implementation and a negative relation to perceived success. It may be determined that it is more difficult to implement a program to its full potential in a large, complex organization. The result could explain not only the lower implementation rate, but the lower success score as well. The time dimension also must be considered. A mature group in a large firm today may have a different operating environment than did a mature group five or ten years ago. Once again, additional study might add to our understanding of this relationship.

C. RETURN ON ASSETS. The only significant relationship between return on assets and success scores occurs in the organizational phase where the relationship is positive. Considering the dynamics of the organizational phase, this might indicate that implementation occurs most readily in firms that are already doing well from the financial standpoint. By contrast, even though the correlations are not significant, it is interesting to note that implementation and success scores in the missionary stage tend to be negatively correlated with financial performance. The data suggest that the missionary-to-organizational phase transition might consist of the conversion of high performance firms from nonusers of OR/MS to users. In a few cases it appeared that firms that were doing well were under less pressure to consider alternative management techniques.

D. RETURN ON REVENUE. The only significant correlations when using return on revenue as an explanatory variable is a positive relationship in the maturity phase and a marginally significant positive relationship when OR/MS operates in a diffused form. The general pattern of correlations here differs from that found when return on assets (ROA) was used as an explanatory variable, thus suggesting possible differences in implementation problems between firms that utilize their financial resources differently. Thus an analysis of the project implementation rates among firms with various combinations of ROAs and RORs might provide interesting insights. Without having performed that analysis, the data suggest a positive relation between implementation and the proportion of projects dealing with asset management problems during the organizational phase, and a positive relation between revenue management or revenue-generating projects during the maturity and diffusion phases. This further implies that organization respond favorably to financially oriented models before they implement marketing oriented models.

E. DECENTRALIZATION. There is a small but significant negative relationship between degree of corporate decentralization and implementation rate in the missionary, maturity and diffusion phases and a small positive relationship during the organizational phase. Intuitively, centralization would seem to facilitate most OR/MS endeavors with its central data sources and potential for economies of scale. On the other hand, it might encourage an effort into an area too large in scope and too complex for the group to pursue successfully under certain conditions. Thus during the early missionary phase where a strategy of small, quick payoff projects is seen as desirable, the advantages achieved through centralization may be less important and could even be dysfunctional if they lure the group into a commitment beyond its capability.

The evidence suggests that under present technical and behavioral constraints some centralized firms face environments that are not conducive to large OR/MS projects. This appears to be one influence on the diffusion process that moves practitioners into areas where the problems are generally smaller, more self-contained, and workable. Thus we possibly have several influences that are not considered jointly in this analysis that could work against each other to obscure correlations that might otherwise be observed.

F. INNOVATIVENESS RE OR/MS. These findings indicate that the older a group is, in terms of its date of establishment in the firm, the greater its implementation success during the organizational phase. This finding, coupled with the negative (but insignificant) finding regarding implementation success in the missionary phase (i.e., that the longer the group has been in the missionary stage, the lower its implementation rate) implies that a high implementation rate may be associated with a short missionary period and a long organizational period. The values of the variables lead us to define a short missionary period as less than three years and a long period as more than three years.

Organizational Environment (III)

As indicated by Table 5.11, an interesting shift in the relationship of formality of charter and of liaision with implementation rate occurs between phases 2 and 3. The data indicate that a formal charter and tight control over liaison contribute to implementation in phase 2, but just the opposite is true in phase 3. The situation reverses itself again between phase 3 and phases 5 and 6. This suggests that longitudinal studies of developing groups would reveal two relatively important changes in mission and methods of relating to clients in those cases where a stable implementation rate is maintained over the life cycle.

Interestingly, two variables (size of budget and formalization of liaison) are related to both implementation and success in the same phases. Unfortunately, it appears that formalization of liaison has the opposite relation to perceived success as it does to implementation in the missionary stage. Thus it appears that effective liaison arrangements may be somewhat difficult to develop in the early stages but tend to emerge as important factors in implementation and success for organizational and diffused groups.

Again, a brief discussion of each of the variables in Table 5.11 follows.

A. FUNCTIONAL LOCATION. The organizational location data indicate that finance remains the most popular location for OR/MS, with MIS/

Table 5.11
Summary of Relation between Organizational Environment of OR/MS and Implementation and Success by Life-Cycle Phases

Relation between implementation and:	Life-cycle phases						Relation between overall success and:	Life-cycle phases					
	1	2	3	4	5	6		1	2	3	4	5	6
III. Organizational environment													
A. Functional location	(See text)						A. Functional location	(See text)					
B. Reporting level (distance from top)	−.81	.05	.33	1.00	−.10	−.15	B. Reporting level (distance from top)	−1.00	[−.57]	−.14	*X*	−.03	−.40
C. Access to computer	*X*	.29	*X*	*X*	.05	*X*	C. Access to computer	*X*	.10	*X*	*X*	.05	*X*
D. Formality of charter	*X*	[.75]	[−.33]	*X*	[.24]	.36	D. Formality of charter	*X*	.18	.22	*X*	.15	.53
E. Availability of data	.82	.48	−.08	*X*	.05	.05	E. Availability of data	1.00	−.09	.09	*X*	[.20]	*X*
F. Size of budget	*X*	[.23]	.06	*X*	.05	[.94]	F. Size of budget	*X*	[.22]	−.16	*X*	−.02	[.81]
G. Formalization of liaison	−.81	[.46]	[−.24]	*X*	.07	[.43]	G. Formalization of liaison	*X*	[−.19]	[−.15]	*X*	.21	[.23]

Table 5.12
Organizational Location of Sample Group

	Finance		MIS and administration		Top management and planning		Operations	
Life-cycle phase	*N*	%	*N*	%	*N*	%	*N*	%
Prebirth	1	33.3	2	66.7	—	—	—	—
Missionary	7	41.2	4	23.5	4	23.5	2	11.8
Organizational	14	60.9	4	17.4	2	8.7	3	13.0
Reprofess.	2	100.0	—	—	—	—	—	—
Maturity	19	35.2	13	24.1	16	29.6	6	11.1
Diffusion	2	25.0	4	50.0	1	12.5	1	12.5
	45		27		23		12	

administration and top management/planning next in popularity, as shown in Table 5.12. Additional tables were constructed to investigate relationships between implementation success and organizational location across life-cycle phases, but none was found except in the case of highly diffused groups, where an operations location was apparently superior. Thus in contrast to our earlier findings [*11*] there was little difference in implementation rates across these locations.

B. NUMBER OF REPORTING LEVELS BETWEEN OR/MS AND CORPORATE TOP MANAGEMENT. The data (Appendix II) indicate that the median reporting level was three levels from the top of the hierarchy in all but the missionary stage, when it was two levels from the top. Success is strongly correlated with high reporting levels in the missionary stage, but implementation is very weakly related, if it is at all. This apparent halo effect involving perceived success and top management sponsorship in the missionary stage is further discussed by Radnor and Bean [*9*]. The only other finding of notable interest here is that mature groups may have better success and implementation records if the group reports relatively high in the organization.

C. ACCESS TO COMPUTER. This variable actually measures whether the OR/MS group has its own computer. The data show that few OR/MS groups do, in fact, have their own computers. The eleven groups that did found that it facilitated project work, particularly on small projects necessary for developing a recognized position in the firm. A slightly positive correlation with implementation in the missionary stage supports this proposition.

D. FORMALITY OF CHARTER. The data suggest that the existence of a formal charter was not strongly related to perceived success but was strongly related to implementation of formal projects in missionary groups and the more mature groups and that it was strongly related to nonimplementation in organizational-phase groups.

The first finding is interesting, because one would expect that unless having a formal charter was perceived to be a precondition of success, few groups would initiate the development of a charter, thus possibly hurting their early implementation record.

The second finding suggests that one aspect of the organizational phase may be the revision or rejection of previously unsatisfactory missions or work statements. In fact we found that the critical examination of the OR/MS group's purpose and structure as it related to the rest of the organization to be characteristic of the organizational stage. The practitioners seemed quite aware of the problems confronting them and were seeking ways to solve them.

E. AVAILABILITY OF DATA. Quality and accessability of data were weakly and positively related to implementation in all except the organizatioal phase. Thus, apparently data are always factors, but never of overriding importance in implementation. Generally, new groups without a data base see this as a critical issue. If they are having problems, particularly in the early phases, the difficulties are often related to a lack of adequate believable data. As the group matures and the data base and the groups linkages to information sources increases, emphasis is shifted away from the data question.

F. SIZE OF BUDGET. Apparently the only time a large budget makes a significant impact is in missionary groups and in highly diffused, mature groups. It apparently is related to both implementation and perceived success in a similar fashion. The differences in financial commitment between mature groups and the others is quite prominent. We can report that we also found a strong correlation between size of professional staff and size of budget ($r = .6, p \leqslant .011$), thus indicating that a great deal of budget increases go into professional staff salaries.

The data also suggest that some optimum level of staffing for an OR/MS group may exist. In its early phases, its capability is limited, and additional resources increase the likelihood of implementation and success. In its mature phase the marginal effect of new funds is less, probably because an optimum relative size has been achieved and possibly exceeded. The group begins to diffuse almost naturally during this stage, although a core group could continue to grow. The diffused practitioners initiate additional programs at other levels that may bring about a second incremental need for more services.

G. FORMALIZATION OF LIAISON. Formalized liaison is apparently an important positive correlate of implementation in missionary and highly diffuse groups but a negative factor in groups in the organizatinal stage. These findings would thus tend to indicate that intermediaries are most helpful to missionary and mature, diffused groups and would be most harmful to organizational groups. However, another study by Bean [*10*] indicated that the functional reporting area of the liaison person has a great deal to do with his effectiveness. Closer analysis of the data used for this chapter showed that *informal* liaison based on an individual's perceived need and interest in developing communication lines did facilitate implementation and success in the missionary and diffusion phases. On the other hand, formalized liaison in the middle phases often was viewed as a bureaucratic nuisance.

Transactions Between OR/MS and the Organization (IV)

In summarizing the transactions data in Table 5.13, we call the reader's attention to the fact that abrupt reversals in implementation relationships do not occur between adjacent phases as they did in earlier data. The importance of client participation in project selection and ingenerating project ideas is understandably strong in the diffusion stage. The trend appears to be away from self-generated projects in the early phases toward client generated projects in diffusion. In the middle stages, it doesn't seem to be very important who generates them. Top management support and interest is an important factor in implementation in the missionary, maturity, and diffused stages. The use of top management support ratings in the construction of the success index makes the success correlations appear stronger than they would otherwise be.

A. SOURCES OF PROJECT IDEAS. *1. Percentage of Projects Generated by OR/MS.* There are no strong relationships between the percentage of projects generated by the OR/MS group and the implementation rate. The relation to perceived success is spurious due to the construction of the success index. Thus it appears that a high proportion of self-generated projects may be viewed as unpopular or inappropriate project selection behavior, when it actually doesn't influence implementation enough to make a noticeable difference in implementation rate.

2. Percentage of Projects Generated by Top Management. Top managers as generators of projects apparently have no direct affect on implementation rate, except perhaps for highly diffused groups. Correlations with success scores are spurious due to the method of construction of the success index.

3. Percentage of Projects Generated by Clients. One of the most interesting findings in the study is that there is no relation between implementation rate and client generation of projects except in the diffused stage, where the relation is positive. This suggests that implemented projects result more significantly from what happens after initiation rather than who initiates them. The correlations with success score are spurious due to the method of constructing the success index. Thus although project initiation by clients apparently influences implementation in the diffused stage, it may be a negative influence in centralized groups in earlier phases of development, as determined by the subsequent action taken by OR/MS. The acceptance rate of client-generated

Table 5.13
(IV) Transactions between OR/MS and the Organization and Their Relation to Implementation and Success across Life-Cycle Phases

Relation between implementation and:	Life-cycle phases 1	2	3	4	5	6	Relation between overall success and:	Life-cycle phases 1	2	3	4	5	6
A. Sources of project ideas							A. Sources of project ideas						
1. % generated by OR/MS	−1.00	−.13	.03	−1.00	.09	−.23	1. % generated by OR/MS	−1.00	−.22	−.41	X	−.22	−.41
2. % generated by TM	X	.17	−.03	1.00	−.08	−.29	2. % generated by TM	X	.37	−.04	X	.23	.36
3. % generated by CI	1.00	.09	−.02	1.00	−.06	.62	3.% generated by CI	1.00	−.12	.37	X	−.12	.23
B. Influence over project Selection							B. Influence over project selection						
1. % selected by OR/MS	.33	.13	.10	X	.08	−.40	1. % selected by OR/MS	−1.00	.07	−.03	X	.23	.64
2. % selected by TM	X	−.17	−.09	X	−.17	.28	2. % selected by TM	1.00	−.05	.03	X	.19	.50
3. % selected by CI	−.33	–	−.11	X	.20	.45	3. % selected by CI	1.00	X	.26	X	.17	.48
C. OR/MS on committees	X	−.13	.05	X	.11	.46	C. OR/MS on committees	X	−.36	.25	X	−.13	.24
D. Top management support	X	.45	.04	X	.13	.08	D. Top management support	X	.54	.53	X	.71	.59
E. Top management interest	−1.00	.45	.07	X	.06	.47	E. Top management interest	−1.00	.49	.20	X	.36	.61

projects might clarify the relationship. These relationships are explored below.

B. INFLUENCE OVER PROJECT SELECTION. *1. Percentage of Projects selected by OR/MS.* When OR/MS groups are highly influential in project selection, a moderate positive relation to implementation appears in the prebirth stage and a relatively strong negative relation appears in highly diffused groups. The negative effect may be due to the greater likelihood of territorial infringements into areas now under the influence of previous members of the core group.

2. Percentage of Projects Selected by Top Management. The only instance in which top management involvement in project selection apparently influences implementation is in the diffused phase. Quite often a divisional manager will have a good experience with OR/MS and might desire to have his own capability. A strong manager with ideas that he wants executed will often acquire OR/MS talent from or outside the core group. He then will proceed to direct his own OR/MS activities and thus indirectly influence the efforts of the core group.

3. Percentage of Projects Selected by Client. The degree of client influence over project selection is negatively associated with prebirth implementation and positively associated with diffusion phase implementation and perceived success.

The combined findings from the project selection data seem to indicate that participative decision making involving OR/MS, top management, and the client is possibly important in the diffusion phase but not important in the other phases. It seems that a certain time interval is required to bring client interest to a level where it becomes a factor in project generation. Because of this, the significance of client influence may increase over time, as shown above.

C. OR/MS PARTICIPATION IN COMMITTEES. Committee participation apparently does not influence implementation rate nor perceived success in a direct manner. Although insignificant within phases, there is a trend for the use of committees to have an increasingly positive effect on implementation as the group matures.

D. TOP MANAGEMENT SUPPORT. The apparent correlation of top management support with success is spurious due to the method used to construct the success index. It is interesting to note that top management support is strongly associated with implementation success in the missionary phase but less important in other phases. At this phase the group generally does not have a reputation sufficient to justify many activities. This weakness appears to be compensated by an executive who actively sponsors its efforts. To some extent, the executive may be lending his reputation and position as a guarantee of the groups usefulness.

It is interesting to find that the proportion of top managers interested and involved in OR/MS is only related to implementation and perceived success in the missionary and diffusion stages. Although this indicates that a broad base of support may be important for success in these two phases, it also could mean that the support of a very few influential top managers may be sufficient to help OR/MS to survive the organizational phase and develop into maturity. Another possibility is that the operating environment changes for the group at each phase, as explained in the previous section. Initially top manager support is vital for the group's continuation. Successes lead to more and broader client support and involvement that reduces, somewhat, top management interest as a factor. Diffusion may produce a new multilevel environment that pushes OR/MS into new areas where top management support is again important.*

Characteristics of the OR/MS Group (V)

Because of the length of this section (see Table 5.6), the findings and discussion for each set of variables are presented separately.

A. Structure. *1. Size of the Formal OR/MS Group.* Table 5.14 reinforces the previous suggestion regarding the existence of an optimum group size. Initially the group is too small to contain the amount or variety of resources necessary to do the work. As it grows it may reach some optimum size. We feel that this occurs when the size encourages communications and relations within the group to the detriment of outside associations. This may be one reason for the evolution of the diffusion phase.

2. Group Size Relative to Organizational Size. Most OR/MS leaders who see themselves as being successful tend to have large groups (actually and relatively) across all phases of the life cycle. The perceptions of success coinciding with having a large group are particularly strong in the diffusion condition, which is understandable given the problems of operating across a diffused environment.

There is another aspect of group size that is related to the time of the group's birth. OR/MS groups tended to be established earliest in larger firms. The actual size of the older groups is considerably larger than that of the newer ones, but their relative size is often smaller because the newer groups are starting in smaller firms. There are probably several other factors that influence the relationship making interpretation difficult.

3. Diffusion Ratio. The importance of having a cohesive integrated group appears as an especially important factor when the OR/MS is operating in an environment in which nongroup OR/MS has been widely diffused. There are strong negative correlations between diffusion ratio and implementation during the diffused stage. There is a similar but weaker relation in the organizational phase—possibly related to the need to rebuild OR/MS on the basis of well-executed project activity.

*See Reference *9* for a further discussion of OR/MS-top management relations.

Table 5.14
OR/MS Group Structure, Implementation, and Success

Relation between implementation and:	Life-cycle phase 1	2	3	4	5	6	Relation of overall success and:	Life-cycle phase 1	2	3	4	5	6
A. Structural characteristics							A. Structure characteristics						
1. Size of the group	*X*	.39	.11	*X*	.04	−.14	1. Size of the group	*X*	.24	−.20	*X*	.12	.09
2. Group size/org. size	−1.00	.23	.17	*X*	.18	.66	2. Group size/org. size	1.00	.05	.39	*X*	.23	.69
3. Diffusion ratio	*X*	−.10	−.23	*X*	.02	−.79	3. Diffusion ratio	*X*	−.18	−.23	*X*	.07	−.81

Table 5.15

Group Leader Attributes, Implementation, and Success

Relation of implementation and:	Life-cycle phase 1	2	3	4	5	6	Relation of overall success and:	Life-cycle phase 1	2	3	4	5	6
B. Leader's attributes							B. Leader's attributes						
1. Professionalism	1.00	−.30	−.07	*X*	−.06	−.35	1. Professionalism	1.00	.13	.13	—	−.12	−.61
2. Age	*X*	−.17	[.38]	*X*	.03	.27	2. Age	*X*	−.21	[.33]	*X*	[.26]	.06
3. Education	.82	−.04	−.30	*X*	.03	.17	3. Education	*X*	.51	−.13	*X*	−.13	.40

There is also the possibility that diffusion occurs when members of the core group or divisional managers perceive that some programs can be done best if they are done outside the main OR/MS activity. As diffusion increases the implementation rate of the core group could very well be adversely effected with a corresponding lowering of the success score.

B. ATTRIBUTES OF OR/MS GROUP LEADERS. Changes in leadership were often associated with OR/MS group development in our earlier studies [*11*]. It was quite common to see a young OR/MS professional replaced by an older, experienced organization man as groups moved from the missionary into the organizational phase. The present data (Table 5.15) tend to agree with those earlier findings.

1. Orientations of Group Leaders. The organizational type of leader is genearlly the most successful. However, the relation is quite interesting. Implementation rates are highest in the missionary and organizational phases. By the time the maturity phase is reached (and in the diffused mode) the relationship between implementation and leader orientation disappears. In terms of the overall success of OR/MS leaders, there is *no* relation in the missionary and organizational phases, but there is in the maturity and diffused phases. The lag effect is very strong, i.e., there may be an inertia in organizations continuing to believe in their success beyond the facts. We also note that 70 percent of the leaders studied are organization men and only 30 percent are professionals.

2. Age. The mean age of OR/MS leaders is 38 (range: 27–55)–a relatively young group. Age (greater) is helpful in the organization phase. It does not seem to affect the implementation rate at maturity but appears helpful for those perceiving themselves successful.

3. Education. Most leaders have an MA or MS level of education (63 percent), 23 percent have a BA or BS, and only 13 percent have a PhD. There is a shift as follows between the major phases:

	High School	BS	MS	PhD
Missionary	–	12%	76%	12%
Organizational	4%	30%	65%	–
Maturity	–	21%	60%	20%

This trend closely follows the pattern of leadership changes we have observed in other studies [*11*]. It indicates that the BS and MS types are most useful in the missionary and organizational phases, whereas PhD's become more useful as OR/MS matures.

Overall it seems that a relatively large cohesive group led by an organizational type is most helpful in the missionary and organizational phases, but this becomes less important as the activity matures. Although our findings indicate that most groups could benefit by being larger during the early phases, we

Table 5.16
Allocation of Leader's Time, Implementation, and Success

Relation of implementation and:	Life-cycle phase 1	2	3	4	5	6	Relation of overall success and:	Life-cycle phase 1	2	3	4	5	6
C. Allocation of leader's time							C. Allocation of leader's time						
1. % selling	X	.52	.09	X	−.10	.35	1. % selling	X	.21	−.30	X	−.42	.18
2. % administering	X	.42	.04	X	.15	.73	2. % administering	X	.20	.27	X	.09	.27
3. % innovating	X	−.56	−.25	X	−.16	−.81	3. % innovating	X	−.32	−.02	X	.19	−.41
4. % implementing	X	.12	.06	X	.13	.27	4. % implementing	X	.30	.03	X	.17	.33

should emphasize that a group might grow too large, too fast. The data suggest that the firm has to be prepared for the extent and sophistication of any OR/MS effort for it to develop successfully.

C. ALLOCATION OF LEADER'S TIME. The data in Table 5.16 indicate that the negative relationship among innovation implementation, and success in the data overall (see Tables 5.6 to 5.8) is supported also by the life-cycle data. Thus OR/MS leaders who attempt to "change the way the organization is doing things" have consistently poor implementation records and are less successful overall (with the possible exception of the maturity phase) than leaders who adopt a strategy of finding a fit with the organization through a mixed strategy of effective administration, salesmanship, and implementation services and assistance.

The breakdown of the data into life-cycle phases reveals some interesting differences in leader influence over implementation and success. Although "innovating" is apparently to be avoided during the missionary phase, it appears that time spent selling and administering are positively related to implementation, but time spent implementing is not! If there is an explanation for this, it seems plausible that a client who has been converted in the missionary phase may proceed to implementation with a minimum of OR/MS assistance. Interestingly, in the missionary phase, perceived success seems to be associated with OR/MS leader involvement in implementation. Could it be that OR/MS leaders who spend considerable time on implementation perceive themselves to be relatively successful, when, in fact, their implementation record is no better than average?

Looking at patterns of relationships across phases, it appears that selling, which is an apparently useful activity in the missionary phase, is, together with innovating, anathema to perceived success in the organizational and mature phases. Thus selling may help with implementation in the missionary phase, and it may never hurt implementation rates; it appears to have a negative association with overall success in the organizational and missionary phases, however. This may provide a partial explanation for our earlier findings [*11*] of leader turnover. Hard sell professionals are many times responsible for the successful launching of an OR/MS group, but their reputation as salesmen or a continuation of their hard sell tactics in the organizational and maturity phases may inhibit group success or may inhibit group transition from the missionary to the organizational or maturity phases.

Thus, it appears that it almost *never hurts* implementation or success to spend time implementing and developing effective administrative procedures, it *seldom helps* to spend time trying to innovate, and selling is helpful in the early stages, but can be harmful later on. However, the reader is reminded that all of the above explanatory variables concern the allotment of time among competing activities by the OR/MS leader, not the total amount of time spent on each activity. Thus, all of these variables are interdependent in the values they can assume. See Appendix II for the actual percentage of time devoted to each activity by OR/MS leaders in our sample. It is interesting to note that, during the prebirth phase, innovation occupies a considerable proportion of the OR/MS practitioners' time. As potential projects are discovered, the need to sell them may increase and more time may be devoted to this endeavor. As the group grows, more time must be spent administering the group. Selling and administration reduce the time available for innovating. The result could be a decrease in the number of projects generated. The leader's available time may then be shifted to innovating once more. The decrease in group size during the diffusion phase also may decrease the administrative load and thus provide more time for other activities.

D. USE OF ADMINISTRATIVE PROCEDURES, IMPLEMENTATION, AND SUCCESS. The use of administrative procedures in OR/MS work is discussed extensively by Neal and Radnor in Reference 2. It is useful to note some of the differences in their use across life-cycle phases, as shown in Table 5.17.

1. Number of Procedures. In the missionary and organizational phases, using a large number of procedures aids implementation, although it is not strongly related to the success score, i.e., some groups who think they are doing well, but who actually are not, are using few procedures. The relation drops off in maturity, perhaps because effective informal relationships have been established and the need for a formal set of procedures is reduced. Some groups work with highly structured procedural guidelines that they see as an important basis of their success, and the data support this view. On the other hand, good informal relations may do much to compensate for a lack of structure [*10*].

2. Use of Cost/Benefit Procedures. A majority (59 percent) use cost/benefit procedures. These help considerably in the missionary period, but they drop off in succeeding phases even becoming possibly negative factor in the diffused mode. This may indicate a need for definitive proof of worth when legitimacy is not yet established, while becoming less necessary as OR/MS role as a researcher/consultant becomes established.

3. Use of Project Evaluation Procedures. Project evaluation seems helpful in missionary and maturity although seeming less so in the organizational phase. Evaluating projects early in the life cycle is one way of determining the group's contribution and developing a basis for new work. During the organizational phase less work is sought and undertaken, usually because of the emphasis on getting proeprly established. The group typically is carried through this period by work and good will resulting from the missionary phase. During the maturity phase project evaluation is used as one means of identifying new areas of opportunity as well as correcting problems in previous projects. Many OR/MS managers indicated that it was a great deal easier to build new programs onto

Table 5.17
Administrative Procedures, Implementation, and Success

Relation of implementation and:	Life Cycle Phase 1	2	3	4	5	6	Relation of overall success and:	Life-cycle phase 1	2	3	4	5	6
D. Administrative procedures							D. Administrative procedures						
1. Number of procedures	1.00	.36	.07	*X*	.19	.64	1. Number of procedures	1.00	.11	.34	*X*	.21	.58
2. Use of cost/benefit	*X*	.45	–.14	*X*	.00	–.18	2. Cost/benefit	*X*	.09	.16	*X*	.04	–.23
3. Use of project evaluation	*X*	.30	.27	*X*	.33	.70	3. Program evaluation	*X*	.00	.12	*X*	.05	.23
4. Sophistication of procedures	–.82	.23	.09	*X*	–.24	.40	4. Sophistication	*X*	.27	–.12	*X*	.00	.54

Table 5.18
Project Portfolio Characteristics Implementation and Success

Relation of implementation and:	Life-cycle phase 1	2	3	4	5	6	Relation of overall success and:	Life-cycle phase 1	2	3	4	5	6
E. Project portfolio characteristics							E. Project portfolio characteristics						
1. Project mix-size	–.81	.39	.31	*X*	–.13	.00	1. Project mix-size	*X*	.31	.35	*X*	–.04	0
2. Project mix-time frame	–.81	.39	.32	*X*	–.13	.00	2. Project mix-time frame	.00	.30	.34	*X*	–.04	0
3. Variety of OR tech.	*X*	.33	–.29	*X*	.16	.39	3. Variety of OR tech.	*X*	.10	–.07	*X*	.10	–.10
4. Variety of functional areas	.00	.25	–.43	*X*	.16	.41	4. Variety of functional areas	–1.00	.18	.13	*X*	.09	–.11
5. Project cost alloc. method	*X*	.10	.16	*X*	–.12	.40	5. Project cost alloc. method	*X*	.36	–.42	*X*	–.17	–.29

previous successes. During the diffusion phase more independent projects are usually undertaken, which may account for the lower correlation.

4. Sophistication of Procedures. The data weakly support the generality of a supposed trend we observed during the investigation. Relatively new groups usually are successful in obtaining interest and support on fairly simple general applications. Often the next step is to undertake a project in an area of highly visible need at a much higher but appropriate level of sophistication. The difficulty over time is that, although there is no limit to the number of highly sophisticated projects that could be undertaken, there may be a limit to the number the firm will accept over a given period. Shorter projects still need to be selected to raise and maintain interest and support. There seems to be an inclination toward successively larger projects that eventually lowers both the implementation rate and success scores. Generally most OR/MS groups seem to recognize the problem and shift to a mix that includes a variety of techniques and functional locations. Diffusion appears to renew the pattern begun during the missionary stage. The reason is not readily apparent. There were some instances where the diffused practitioners utilized the core group as a resource for dealing with larger, more sophisticated projects, while they personally worked on the shorter jobs. In this way the necessary balance between significant programs and continued reinforcement was achieved.

E. PROJECT PORTFOLIO CHARACTERISTICS. In our earlier study [*11*], a shift in proper portfolio characteristics was noted as groups matured. Missionary groups tended to work on large-scale, long-term projects, but then changed the mix to include short-term, small-scale tasks. The present data show that mixed portfolios are most common (Table 5.18).

1. Project Mix–Size. Most project portfolios are of the mixed variety (66 percent–as compared with 14 percent for small and 20 percent for large). In the missionary phase large projects appear to be helpful, but by the organizational and maturity phases this disappears as a factor with many portfolios being mixed and all doing better. OR/MS leaders with both large and mixed portfolios perceive themselves to be successful in the missionary period and the relation continues into the organizational phase, but then it disappears.

2. Project Mix–Time Frame. Again regarding project time frame, the mixed strategy is the most popular (66 percent) as compared to short (14 percent and long (20 percent). (Note these are the same as the size mix figures.) Again, long projects lead to success in the missionary phase. As before, those perceiving themselves as being successful also had long and mixed portfolios in both the missionary and the organizational phases. The effects disappear in the maturity phase.

3. Project Variation–Technical. Using a variety of OR/MS techniques had little impact except possibly in the missionary phase.

4. Project Variation–Functional. Most groups spread their project activities across several client groups (81 percent). Overall project mix strategies seem to be important in the missionary period but become less important over time. In the missionary period a portfolio of big, long projects in a variety of functions seems to be helpful. Interestingly, in the organizational phase implementation is high when the portfolio is concentrated in a few functional areas. The change from positive to negative correlations between the missionary and organizational phases suggests that the truly important, influential clients emerge in the organizational phase from the relatively large number contacted during the missionary period.

5. Allocation of Project Costs. Most groups do not charge (63 percent), 16 percent share, and 21 percent fully charge clients for project costs. Charging becomes more popular over time but there is no clear impact on success rates. It is interesting that those who perceive themselves to be less successful also charge—possibly a reflection of more difficult interpersonal relations influencing perceived success. Thus in the missionary phase, charging seems to be almost positively related to success, but in the organizational and maturity phases it is negative.

Summary of Correlates of Implementation and Success across Life Cycles Phases

Table 5.19 summarizes the findings regarding correlates of implementation and success by life-cycle phases. By scanning the columns and rows, the reader can gain insights into the degree to which variables are associated with implementation and success in the various phases. Variables found to be related to both implementation and success are boxed. The degree of control exercised by OR/MS over the explanatory variables is indicated by a code number ranging from 1 to 4. The number 1 signifies directly controllable by OR/MS, and 4 signifies exogeneous to OR/MS, as previously defined on page 1.

We have combined the prebirth and missionary phases; the organizational and exprofessional phases; and the maturity and diffusion phases in our summary discussion for the sake of brevity and because of the similarity of findings in these phases. Figures 20, 21 and 22 have been developed to aid our discussion of the similarities and differences in the types of variables which are correlated with implementation and success in the various phases, and to help us examine the extent to which the "behavioral" variables which are associated with OR/MS-client interaction patterns, explain variations in implementation and success within each phase.

1. PREBIRTH AND MISSIONARY PHASES. As indicated by Table 5.20, implementation and success in these phases appear to be heavily influenced

Table 5.19
Significant* Linear Correlates of Implementation and Success by Life-Cycle Phases

Explanatory variables	Implementation by phase						Degree of OR/MS control	Success by phase					
	1	2	3	4	5	6		1	2	3	4	5	6
I. Firm's operating environment			(See text)							(See text)			
II. Firm's characteristics													
A. Total revenue	—	−.31	—	—	−.30	—	3	—	—	—	—	—	—
B. Number of employees	—	—	.34	—	—	—	4	—	—	−.25	—	—	—
C. Return on assets	—	—	.33	—	—	—	3	—	—	.56	—	—	—
D. Return on revenue	—	—	—	—	.33	.51	3	—	—	—	—	.23	—
E. Decentralization	—	−.08	.10	—	−.10	−.15	4	—	—	−.11	—	—	−.16
F. Innovativeness re OR/MS	—	—	.31	—	—	−.17	3	—	−.05	—	—	−.17	−.11
III. Org. environment of OR/MS GP													
A. Functional location			(See text)				3			(See text)			
B. Level below top of hierarchy	—	—	—	—	—	—	3	—	−.57	—	—	—	—
C. Access to computer	—	—	—	—	—	—	2	—	—	—	—	—	—
D. Formality of charter	—	.75	−.33	—	.24	—	2	—	—	—	—	—	—
E. Availability of data	—	—	—	—	—	—	2	—	—	—	—	—	—
F. Size of budget	—	.23	—	—	—	.94	2	—	.22	—	—	—	.81
G. Formalization of liaison	—	.46	−.24	—	—	.43	2	—	−.19	−.15	—	—	.23
IV. Transactions between OR/MS and the organization													
A. Sources of project ideas													
1. % generated by OR/MS	—	—	—	—	—	—	1	—	—	—	—	—	—
2. % generated by top mgt.	—	—	—	—	—	—	2	—	.37	−.04	—	—	—
3. % generated by clients	—	—	—	—	—	.62	2	—	−.12	—	—	—	—
B. Influences over project selection													
1. % selected by OR/MS	.33	—	—	—	—	−.40	2	—	—	—	—	—	—
2. % selected by top mgt.	—	—	—	—	—	.28	2	—	—	—	—	—	—
3. % selected by clients	−.33	—	—	—	—	.45	2	—	—	—	—	—	—

C. OR/MS involvement in formal committees	—	—	—	—	—	—	2	—	—	—	—	—	—
D. Top management support for OR/MS	—	**.45**	—	—	**.13**	—	3	—	**.54**	.53	—	**.71**	.59
E. Top management interest in OR/MS	—	45	—	—	—	.47	3	—	—	—	—	—	—
V. Characteristics of the OR/MS group													
A. Structural characteristics													
1. Formal group	—	**.39**	—	—	—	—	2	—	**.24**	—	—	.12	—
2. Group size as % of total employees	—	.23	—	—	**.18**	**.66**	3	—	—	.39	—	**.23**	**.69**
3. OR/MS diffusion ratio	—	—	—	—	—	**−.79**	3	—	—	−.23	—	—	**−.81**
B. Attributes of group leader													
1. Orientation (professionalism)	—	—	—	—	—	—	2	—	—	—	—	—	—
2. Age	—	—	**.38**	—	—	—	3	—	—	**.33**	—	.26	—
3. Education	—	—	—	—	—	—	2	—	—	—	—	—	—
C. Allocation of leader's time													
1. % spent selling	—	.52	—	—	—	—	1	—	—	−.30	—	−.42	—
2. % spent administering	—	.42	—	—	.15	.73	1	—	—	.27	—	—	—
3. % spent innovating	—	**−.56**	**−.25**	—	**−.16**	**−.81**	1	—	**−.32**	**−.02**	—	**.19**	**−.41**
4. % spent implementing	—	—	—	—	**.13**	—	1	—	.30	—	—	**.17**	—
D. Administrative procedures													
1. Number of procedures	1.00	.36	.07	—	—	**.64**	1	—	—	—	—	**.21**	—
2. Cost-benefit analysis	—	**.45**	−.14	—	—	—	1	—	**.09**	—	—	—	—
3. Project evaluation	—	—	—	—	.33	.70	1	—	—	.12	—	—	—
4. Sophistication of procedures	—	—	—	—	—	—	1	—	—	—	—	—	—
E. Project portfolio characteristics	—	—	—	—	—	—	1	—	—	—	—	—	—
1. Project mix-size	—	**.39**	—	—	—	—	2	—	**.31**	—	—	—	—
2. Project mix-time frame	—	**.39**	—	—	—	—	2	—	**.30**	—	—	—	—
3. Variety of OR techniques	—	—	—	—	—	—	2	—	—	—	—	—	—
4. Variety of functional areas	—	—	−.43	—	—	—	2	—	—	—	—	—	—
5. Method of project cost allocation	—	.10	—	—	—	**.40**	2	—	—	−.42	—	**−.17**	—

*Level of significance is $p \leqslant .10$.

Relationships that are significant for both implementation and success in the same life-cycle phase are boxed for ease of identification.

Table 5.20
Prebirth and Missionary Phases

Potential degree of OR/MS control	Number of significant correlates: Of implementation	Of success	In common	With conflicting signs
1. Direct control	5	3	2	0
2. Direct influence	9	7	5	1
3. Indirect influence	4	3	1	0
4. Exogenous	1	0	0	0
N =	19	13	8	1
Direct control variables				
% time spent selling	+	0	0	0
% time spent administering	+	0	0	0
% time spent innovating	–	–	√	0
% time spent implementing	0	+	0	0
Number of procedures	+	0	0	0
Cost benefit analysis	+	+	√	0
Direct influence variables				
Formality of charter	+	0	0	0
Size of budget	+	+	√	0
Formalization of liaison	+	–	√	√
% projects generated by T.M.	0	+	0	0
% projects generated by client	0	–	0	0
% projects selected by OR/MS	+	0	0	0
% projects selected by clients	–	0	0	0
Formal group size	+	+	√	0
Project mix-size	+	+	√	0
Project mix-time	+	+	√	0
Method of project cost allocation	+	0	0	0
Indirect influence variables				
Total revenue	–	0	0	0
Firms innovativeness re adoption of OR/MS	0	–	0	0
Top management support	+	+	√	0
Top management interest	+	0	0	0
Group size vs. total employers	+	0	0	0
Level below top of hierarchy	0	–	0	0
Exogenous variables				
Decentralization	–	0	0	0

Key
+ signifies that a significant positive correlation exists.
– signifies that a significant negative correlation exists.
0 signifies no correlation; no commonality or no conflict in signs exists.
√ signifies that a commonness or a conflict in signs does exist.

by OR/MS control and influence variables. Clearly, with 14 of 19 implementation-related variables and 10 of 13 success-related variables classified as directly controlled or directly influenced by OR/MS, this interpretation is straightforward. Interestingly, however, when the specific variables of interest are noted, few of the important behavioral variables directly involve clients. Most OR/MS influence and control attempts that are associated with implementation and success seem directed toward top management or toward the things that top management controls (such as the OR/MS budget, formal charter, group size) or administrative procedures for the group itself (cost benefit analysis and makeup of the project portfolio). Thus, direct relations with clients does not appear to explain the major part of implementation success.

Successful groups with good implementation records in these phases are likely to be:

a. strongly supported by top management
b. relatively large in size (more than six professionals)
c. more than adequately funded
d. working on large-scale, long-term projects
e. spending very little time trying to promote innovative changes in the organization
f. placed relatively high in the hierarchy (one or two levels below the top level senior executives)
g. experiencing conflict over the design of effective liaison mechanisms
h. using cost/benefit analysis to aid in project selection decisions

Groups in these phases may be able to further enhance their overall perceptions of success or their implementation rates, but different strategies might have to be employed for each purpose. The relatively large number of common variables among the direct influence variables suggests that efficient success and implementation strategies might involve the formation of coalitions and interest groups who can deliver the support needed to influence these variables.

2. ORGANIZATIONAL AND REPROFESSIONALIZING PHASES. As indicated by Table 5.21, these phases are much different than the prebirth/missionary period. There are some basic conflicts over which the OR/MS group has no control. Groups in large, decentralized firms tend to have high implementation rates, but do not perceive themselves as successful. Conversely, groups in smaller, centralized firms apparently believe they are successful, but have relatively poor implementation rates. Thus, in the organizational phase, the basic structure of the organization apparently creates a dilemma for OR/MS.

All other things considered, the relatively successful OR/MS group with a good implementation record in this period is likely to:

a. have a somewhat older leader than most groups (45–55 range)
b. work in a firm where return on assets is relatively high

Table 5.21
Organizational and Reprofessionalization Phases

Potential degree of OR/MS control	Number of significant correlates: Of implementation	Of success	In common	With conflicting signs
1. Direct control	3	4	1	0
2. Direct influence	3	3	1	0
3. Indirect influence	3	5	2	0
4. Exogenous	2	2	2	2
$N =$	11	14	6	2
Direct control variables				
% leaders time selling	0	–	0	0
% leaders time administering	0	+	0	0
% leaders time innovating	–	–	√	0
No. of procedures used	+	0	0	0
Cost-benefit analysis	–	0	0	0
Project evaluation	0	+	0	0
Direct influence variables				
Formality of charter	–	0	0	0
Formalization of liaison	–	–	√	0
% projects generated by top management	0	–	0	0
Variety of functional areas served	–	0	0	0
Method of project cost allocation	0	–	0	0
Indirect influence variables				
Return on assets	+	+	√	0
Innovativeness re OR/MS	+	0	0	0
Top management support for OR/MS	0	+	0	0
Group size/total employment	0	+	0	0
OR/MS diffusion ratio	0	–	0	0
Leaders age	+	+	√	0
Exogenous variables				
Total number of employees in firm	+	–	√	√
Decentralization	+	–	√	√

Key
+ signifies that a significant positive correlation exists.
– signifies that a significant negative correlation exists.
0 signifies no correlation; no commonality or no conflict in signs exists.
√ signifies that a commonness or a conflict in signs does exist.

c. avoid the use of highly formalized liaison procedures and concentrate on the development of informal linkages to clients and support groups
d. avoid spending time on innovative activities

There are additional variables that are apparently associated with high implementation rates and high success ratings, but they involve different activities, and the OR/MS group has limited control over them. Factors outside the OR/MS-client sphere of influence, such as OR/MS diffusion ratio, formality of charter, and project cost allocation methods, play an important role in either implementation or success, but not in both. Thus the organizational/reprofessionalization period may be one in which the OR/MS group must learn to do many different things well in order to do well; even so, external factors may have more to do with its success than anything it can do itself. The weak intersection between implementation and success factors may indicate the need for separate strategies to maintain organizational viability during this period.

3. MATURITY AND DIFFUSION PHASES. During this period, as indicated by Table 5.22, successful OR/MS groups with good implementation records tend to emerge:

a. in the more highly centralized firms
b. in firms where OR/MS itself is relatively centralized and the group size is relatively large as a percentage of total employment
c. where top management is supportive
d. in firms where return on revenue is high
e. where OR/MS is a relatively new function in the firm
f. where a high proportion of projects are generated by clients, especially in diffused groups
g. in firms where liaison relations have been formalized
h. where a generous budget is provided
i. in firms where a large number of administrative procedures are used by OR/MS
j. where the OR/MS leader devotes a substantial amount of his time working on project implementation, and avoids spending time on innovative activites, except when his group's activities are highly diffused
k. where project cost allocation methods are likely to be a contentious issue, with groups who absorb project costs having poor implementation records, but perceiving themselves as relatively successful

Once again, implementation rates and perceived success are associated with variables other than those mentioned above, but none are commonly associated with both of them. However, this period has a greater number of variables commonly associated with implementation and success than either of the other periods, and they are evenly distributed among the nonexogenous control categories. This could be taken as a rather solid intersection between variables that are influenced and controlled by a wide variety of forces in the organiza-

Table 5.22
Maturity of Diffusion Phases

Potential Degree of OR/MS Control	Number of Significant Correlates: Of implementation	Of success	In common	With conflicting signs
1. Direct control	5	4	3	1
2. Direct influence	8	6	4	1
3. Indirect influence	7	6	5	0
4. Exogenous	1	1	1	0
N =	21	17	11	1
Direct control variables				
% leaders time selling	0	–	0	0
% leaders time administering	+	0	0	0
% leaders time innovating	–	+, –	√	√
% leaders time implementing	+	+	√	0
No. of procedures	+	+	√	0
Project evaluation	+	0	0	0
Direct influence variables				
Formality of charter	+	0	0	0
Availability of data	0	+	0	0
Size of budget	+	+	√	0
Formalization of liaison	+	+	√	0
% projects generated by clients	0	+	0	0
% projects selected by OR/MS	–	0	0	0
% projects selected by T.M.	+	0	0	0
% projects selected by clients	+	+	√	0
Formal group size	0	+	0	0
Project cost allocation method	+	–	√	√
Indirect influence variables				
Return on revenue	+	+	√	0
Innovativeness re OR/MS	–	–	√	0
Top management support	+	+	√	0
Top management interest	+	0	0	0
Group size as % all employees	+	+	√	0
OR/MS diffusion ratio	–	–	√	0
Leaders age	0	+	0	0
Total revenue	–	0	0	0
Exogenous variables				
Decentralization	–	–	√	0

Key
+ signifies that a significant positive correlation exists.
– signifies that a significant negative correlation exists.
0 signifies no correlation; no commonality or no conflict in signs exists.
√ signifies that a commonality or a conflict in signs does exist.

tion, thus reflecting the broad base of support one would expect for a mature, successful organizational function.

However, as one can see from scanning the phase 5 and 6 data in Table 5.19, the maturity and diffusion period is not entirely smooth sailing for OR/MS groups. Indeed, the data seem to indicate that the more highly diffused groups may have very different problems than do the more centralized groups and that different explanatory variables are operative. Thus "maturity" may take many forms. Perhaps there are even distinct stages of development beyond that which we have called maturity.

To conclude, it is tempting to discuss the between-phase differences in correlations as if they were events in a causal sequence. Indeed this may be so. In fact, some of our earlier comments do propose causal relationships of this type. Some of them we believe quite strongly, especially when they tend to confirm findings from our earlier, retrospective case histories of OR/MS groups [*9, 11*]. However, the data presented here are cross-sectional, not longitudinal, and thus it is not appropriate to assert that we have observed causal events.

One of the things we hope to do in the future is to pool the data analyzed here with those reported upon earlier [*9, 11*], so we may investigate possible causal chains more directly.

In this study, the most pervasive overall finding is that direct interaction between OR/MS group members and clients is pervasively important to implementation and success *only* when the OR/MS representative attempts to be an innovator, in which case his influence is strongly negative. Behavioral variables that are *not* directed at improved OR/MS-client transactions are important correlates of implementation and success in all phases of development, and structural and exogenous variables are also important factors throughout the development process.

CONCLUSIONS

1. The data clearly indicated that structural as well as behavioral variables are related to implementation and success, thus implying that structural change as well as attitudinal and behavioral change may go hand in hand in furthering the development of OR/MS in organizations.

2. The analysis has called our attention to several variables that are related to both implementation and success in various phases of the life cycle, thus suggesting the possibility that organizational development and change strategies can be developed to advance both causes simultaneously.

3. Areas for additional research seem to be emerging, such as the need to develop comparable samples of firms across industries so the industry differences can be analyzed more completely.

There are some things the study hasn't done that should be made clear.

1. The data are cross-sectional, not longitudinal; thus inferences about possible causal relations across life-cycle phases would not refer to a single organization in any case. This has both good and bad points. We can certainly say that our observations are not autocorrelated across life-cycle phases.

2. The study hasn't been carried far enough in the direction of multivariate analysis. We have done some cluster analysis, and we have made one brief attempt to develop a discriminant function for successful and unsuccessful implementors. More work needs to be done in this area.

References

1. Radnor, Michael, and Neal, Rodney, "The Progress of Management Science Activities in Large U.S. Industrial Organizations," *Operations Research,* **21**, no. 2 (March–April 1973).
2. Neal, Rodney, and Radnor, Michael, "The Relation between Formal Procedures for Pursuing OR/MS Activities and OR/MS Group Success" *Operations Research,* **21**, no. 2 (March–April 1973).
3. Radnor, Michael, Rubenstein, Albert H., and Tansik, David A., "Implementation in Operations Research and R&D in Government and Business Organizations,' *Operations Research,* 18 (1970).
4. Rubenstein, Albert H., Radnor, Michael, Baker, Norman, Heiman, David, and McColly, John B., "Some Organizational Factors Related to the Effectiveness of Management Science Groups in Industry," *Management Science,* **13** (1967).
5. Tansik, David A., and Radnor, Michael, "An Organization Theory Perspective on the Development of New Organizational Functions," *Public Administration Review,* no. 6 (November–December 1971).
6. Rubenstein, Albert H., "Integration of Operations Research into the Firm," *The Journal of Industrial Engineering,* **XI** (September–October, 1960).
7. Young, Robert K., and Veldman, Donald J., *Introductory Statistics for the Behavioral Sciences,* New York: Holt, Rinehart and Winston, 1965.
8. Nie, Norman H., Bent, Dale H., and Hadlai, C. Hull, *SPSS: Statistical Package for the Social Science,* New York: McGraw-Hill, 1970; and Nie, Norman H., and Hull, C. Hadlai, *SPSS Update Manual,* National Opinion Research Center, University of Chicago, 1972.
9. Radnor, Michael, and Bean, Alden S., "Top Management Support for Management Science," *Omega: The International Journal of Management Science,* **2**, no. 1 (1974).
10. Bean, Alden S., "Client Receptivity and the Structure of the MS-Client Interface," working paper presented at TIMS/ORSA/AIIE Conference in Atlantic City, New Jersey, November 1972; *Management Science,* in press.
11. Radnor, Michael, Rubenstein, Albert H., and Bean, Alden S., "Integration and Utilization of Management Science Activities in Organizations" *Operational Research Quarterly,* **19** (1968).

Appendix I

Definition of terms and explanation of scoring or classification:

1. **OR/MS Group**
   a. **Age.** The year in which a recognized OR/MS activity was initiated in the firm prior to a base data of 1970. If the age is 12, then the activity commenced in 1958. In

many instances the activity may have died, been reborn, or been shifted one or more times from one functional area to another. The age actually refers more to the amount of time that the organization has been exposed to OR/MS endeavors or ideas rather than the age of continuously existing group.

b. **Phase.** Prebirth, missionary, organizational, reprofessionalization, maturity/diffused. Established on the basis of an opinion regarding the classificatory fit of the group relative to the NU defined attributes of each phase.
c. **Function.** Operations top management/planning, MIS, finance. The functional assignment for the OR/MS group was made on the basis of the highest department or division reporting to the chief executive of the firm that contains the group.
d. **Level.** The level of the OR/MS manager below the chief executive. Level "1" would indicate that the head of the OR/MS group reports directly to the chief officer of the company.
e. **Size.** The number of OR/MS competent practitioners in the group.
f. **Relative Size.** The ratio of OR/MS practitioners in the group relative to the size of the company. The ratio was based on the number of practitioners to each $100 million of yearly revenue. If the firm did $1.2 billion in business in 1969 and there were 10 practitioners then the relative group size ratio would be

$$\frac{10}{12} = .85$$

g. **Diffusion.** The diffusion of OR/MS talent was based on a ratio between the total number of OR/MS practitioners estimated to be in the company by the OR/MS manager and the number in the core group. If there are 10 in the core group and 10 others, the diffusion ratio would be

$$\frac{20}{10} = 2.0$$

2. **Organizational Characteristics**
   a. **Industry.** Automotive, engineered products, electrical, material processing, chemical/pharmaceutical, chemical/synthetic, petroleum, food processing, merchandizing, financial utilities, transportation. The sector selection was based on the primary commercial interests of the firm.
   b. **Size ($).** Based on yearly revenue for 1969.
   c. **Size (No. of Employees).** Based on number of employees for 1969.
   d. **Profit/Revenue.** Based on profit as a percentage of revenue for 1969.
   e. **Profit/Assets.** Based on profit as a percentage of assets for 1969.
   f. **Centralization.** Scored on the basis of "0" if centralized, "1" if a combination, and "2" if decentralized. This is a matter of the interviewers opinion, based on the firms organizational chart, physical dispersion, comments on local autonomy, the MIS and control system, the size and function of the corporate office, and the respondent's opinion. In general there was an obvious trend from decentralization back to recentralization in the majority of companies visited.
   g. **Data Base.** Scored on the basis of "0" if poor, "1" if fair, and "2" if good. Based solely on the OR/MS managers perception. Verification was through questions dealing with specific problems and advantages.
   h. **Liaison.** Scored on the basis of "0" if none, "1" if some, and "2" if considerable. Some liaison effort would be the result of either an official or unofficial liaison effort between some of the client groups and the OR/MS activity. Considerable

liaison effort would be on the basis of officially established positions in most or all of the potential client groups.

i. **Computers/Own.** If the group had their own computer for their use only then it would be scored "1".

j. **Time Sharing.** If the group had access to a time-sharing capability then it would be scored "1".

k. **Computer/Access.** Scored on the basis of "0" if poor, "1" if fair, and "2" if good. Based on the OR/MS manager's perception, with supporting rationale.

l. **Charter.** Scored on the basis of "0" if there were no charter, "1" if there was a positional job description, and "2" if there existed a charter.

3. **OR/MS Manager**

a. **Orientation.** Scored on the basis of "1" if viewed as an organizational and "2" if a professional. The decision was a matter of the interviewer's opinion based on several tangible elements, such as education, experience, and aspirations, qualified by comments and attitudes expressed during the interview. An example would be an expression of loyalty to the company.

b. **Age.** The age of the OR/MS manager in years in 1970.

c. **Education.** Scored on the basis of "1" for high school, "2" for BS/BA, "3" for MS/MBA, and "4" for PhD.

4. **Procedures**

a. **Number of Procedures.** Scored from 0 to 11, based on the number of procedures used from a list based on suggestions in literature.

b. **Cost/Benefit Analysis.** Scored in the basis of "0" if no, "1" if yes.

c. **Post Evaluation.** Used to determine success of the project and its satisfactory implementation. Scored on the basis of "0" if no, "1" if yes.

5. **Projects Generated**

a. **OR/MS.** Percentage initiated by OR/MS activity.

b. **Top Management.** Percentage initiated by top management.

c. **Clients.** Percentage initiated by clients.

6. **Project Selection**

a. **OR/MS.** Scored on the basis of "0" if not influential, "1" if most influential, and "2" if influence is shared.

b. **Top Management.** Scored on the same basis as "a" above.

c. **Clients.** Scored on the same basis as "a" above.

7. **Use of Project Committees.** Scored on the basis of "0" if rarely or not at all, "1" if occasionally, and "2" if often.

8. **OR/MS Managers, Time Allocation**

a. **Selling/Educating.** Percentage of time spent by OR/MS manager.

b. **Administration.** Same as "a".

c. **Innovating.** Same as "a".

d. **Implementing.** Same as "a".

9. **Success Score**

a. **Implementation Rate.** Based on the percentage of projects that eventually were used out of all those seriously started as perceived by the OR/MS manager.

b. **Success Score.** Based on a composite of several indicators as perceived by the OR/MS manager. The factors were as follows:

1. Level of success of OR/MS group scored from "0" for low to "4" for high.
2. Top management support, scored same as above.
3. Client receptivity, scored same as above.

4. Project backlog, scored on the basis of "0" if service exceeds demand, "1" if the same and "2" if demand exceeds service.
5. Percentage of projects generated by non-OR/MS personnel, scored on the basis of "0" for none and then 1 additional for each quartile in the percentage ranking for each firm.

10. **Top Management Support**
   a. **Top Management Support.** See 9.b.2 above.
   b. **Top Management Involvement and Interest.** The percentage of all top managers interested and involved in OR/MS activities as seen by the OR/MS manager.

11. **Project Characteristics**
   a. **Mix/$.** Scored on the basis of "0" if the projects are generally low cost, "1" if the projects are a mixture, and "2" if they are generally high in cost.
   b. **Mix/Time.** Scored on the basis of "0" if the projects are generally short, "1" if they are a mixture, and "2" if they are generally long.
   c. **Technical.** Scored on the basis of "0" if the group concentrates on one quantitative approach, "2" if they utilize a few different algorithms, and "2" if they use several.
   d. **Functions.** Scored on the basis of "0" if the group concentrates in one functional area, "1" if they work in a few different areas, and "2" if they work in several different areas.

12. **Funding**
   a. **Budget.** The size in $ thousand of the annual budget.
   b. **Charge.** Scored on the basis of "0" if there is no charge, "1" if the costs are shared, and "2" if there is a full charge.

13. **Level of sophistication.** Scored on the basis of "0" if the OR/MS applications are simple, "1" if fairly sophisticated, and "2" if very sophisticated. This score was the opinion of the researcher based on the examples of OR/MS projects provided by the OR/MS manager.

Appendix II
Description of Data Base
Variables
I. Firm's Operating Environment (see text)
II. Firm's Characteristics

Life-cycle phase	A. Total revenue			B. Number of employees			C. Return on assets		
	N	Mean	S.D.	*N*	Mean	S.D.	*N*	Mean	S.D.
Prebirth	3	.73	.35	3	26.00	14.73	2	5.35	.78
Missionary	16	1.07	.68	15	32.87	24.92	13	4.62	3.22
Organizational	23	.92	.98	23	23.83	22.45	20	5.78	4.43
Professionalization	2	60	.14	2	18.50	3.54	2	8.20	0
Maturity	55	3.00	4.75	53	70.37	125.82	44	5.65	3.38
Diffusion	8	1.78	2.25	8	56.00	74.06	8	5.59	3.15

Explanatory variable: Life-cycle phase	D. Return on revenue			E. Decentralization			F. Innovativeness re OR/MS		
	N	Mean	S.D.	*N*	Median	Range	*N*	Median	Range
Prebirth	2	5.35	.78	2	1	2	2	2	0
Missionary	14	9.84	4.34	17	1	2	17	3	6
Organizational	20	9.28	4.63	23	1	2	23	6–7	14
Professionalization	2	15.90	5.66	2	1–2	1	2	10–11	1
Maturity	49	10.90	4.05	53	1	2	53	9	14
Diffusion	8	11.93	5.52	7	1	2	7	9	10

III. Org. Environment of OR/MS Group

Explanatory variable: Life-cycle phase		B. Level below top of hierarchy			C. Access to computer		
		N	Median	Range	*N*	Median	Range
Prebirth		3	3	1	3	0	0
Missionary		17	2	4	17	0	1
Organizational		23	3	4	23	0	0
Reprofessionalization	A. See text	3	3	2	2	0	0
Maturity		55	3	4	55	0	1
Diffusion		8	3	2	8	0	0

Explanatory variable: Life-cycle phase	D. Formality of charter			E. Availability of data			F. Size of Budget			G. Formalization of liaison		
	N	Median	Range	*N*	Mean	S.D.	*N*	Median	Range	*N*	Median	Range
Prebirth	3	0	0	3	1	1	2	30.0	0	3	1	2
Missionary	17	0	2	16	1	2	16	107.5	62.9	17	1	2
Organizational	23	2	2	23	1	2	23	162.0	127.6	23	0	2
Reprofessionalization	2	0	0	2	.5	1	1	80.0	—	2	0	0
Maturity	53	1	2	52	1	2	53	408.7	527.65	54	0	2
Diffusion	8	1	2	8	1	2	7	447.1	366.7	8	0	1

IV. Transactions between the OR/MS Group and Its Organizational Environment

Explanatory variable:	A. 1. % Generated by OR/MS			2. % Generated by top management			3. % Generated by clients		
Life-cycle phase	*N*	Median	Range	*N*	Median	Range	*N*	Median	Range
Prebirth	2	20–50	30	2	0	0	2	50–80	30
Missionary	17	40–50	90	17	35	100	17	30–45	75
Organizational	23	25	100	23	33	75	23	30–33	100
Professionalization	2	50–100	50	2	0–20	20	2	0–30	30
Maturity	53	33–40	90	53	33–40	90	53	40	100
Diffusion	7	50–60	75	7	20	95	7	30	60

Explanatory variable:	B. 1. % Selected by OR/MS			2. % Selected by top management			3. % Selected by clients		
Life-cycle phase	*N*	Median	Range	*N*	Median	Range	*N*	Median	Range
Prebirth	3	1	2	3	0	0	3	1	2
Missionary	17	2	2	17	0	2	17	0	0
Organizational	23	2	2	23	0	2	23	0–1	1
Professionalization	2	2	0	2	0	0	2	0	0
Maturity	55	2	2	55	0	2	55	0	2
Diffusion	8	2	2	8	0	2	8	0	2

Explanatory variable:	C. OR/MS involvement in formal committees			D. Top management support for OR/MS			E. Top management interest in OR/MS		
Life-cycle phase	*N*	Median	Range	*N*	Median	Range	*N*	Median	Range
Prebirth	2	2	0	2	0	0	2	7–10	3
Missionary	17	1	2	17	0–1	1	14	33	70
Organizational	23	1–2	1	23	0–1	1	20	20–30	100
Professionalization	2	2	0	2	0	0	1	—	—
Maturity	52	1–2	1	53	0–1	1	47	33–40	87
Diffusion	7	1	2	7	0–1	1	7	33	94

V. Structural Characteristics of the OR/MS Group

A. Explanatory variable: Life-cycle phase	1. Formal Group *N*	Mean	S.D.	2. Group size as % of total employees *N*	Mean	S.D.	3. OR/MS diffusion ratio *N*	Mean	S.D.
Prebirth	3	1.67	.57	3	3.83	5.34	3	3.99	5.19
Missionary	17	3.47	2.35	17	.84	.65	17	.79	.26
Organizational	23	5.13	3.08	23	1.95	2.51	23	.69	.31
Professionalization	2	5.00	2.82	2	1.37	1.09	2	.74	.37
Maturity	55	10.30	6.36	55	2.28	2.28	55	.96	1.80
Diffusion	8	4.00	4.20	8	2.32	3.21	8	1.60	3.40

B. Explanatory variable: Life-cycle phase	1. Orientation (Professionalism) *N*	Median	Range	2. Age *N*	Median	Range	3. Education *N*	Median	Range
Prebirth	2	1.5	1	2	38.0	9.8	3	3	1
Missionary	16	1	1	17	36.1	6.6	17	3	2
Organizational	23	1	1	23	36.0	5.8	23	3	2
Professionalization	2	1	0	2	50.0	7.1	2	2	0
Maturity	54	1	1	55	38.8	6.8	55	3	2
Diffusion	8	1.5	1	8	37.8	5.1	8	3	2

C. Explanatory variable: Life-cycle phase	1. % spent selling *N*	Mean	S.D.	2. % spent administering *N*	Mean	S.D.	3. % spent innovating *N*	Median	Range	4. % spent implementing *N*	Median	Range
Prebirth	2	12.5	17.67	2	2.5	3.5	2	62.5	24.7	2	22.5	3.5
Missionary	16	19.9	14.4	16	17.4	14.1	16	43.5	25.5	16	18.9	10.4
Organizational	23	22.6	15.4	23	24.8	19.5	23	32.2	15.7	23	18.9	12.9
Professionalization	2	37.5	17.7	2	47.5	31.8	2	13.5	16.3	2	1.5	2.1
Maturity	53	24.0	16.1	53	34.3	19.3	53	27.0	17.4	53	14.5	11.1
Diffusion	6	20.3	9.4	6	13.3	15.4	6	15.9	7.4	6	15.8	7.3

V. Structural Characteristics of the OR/MS Group—*Continued*

D. Explanatory variable: Life-cycle phase	1. Number of procedures			2. Cost/benefit analysis			3. Project evaluation			4. Sophistication of procedures		
	N	Median	Range	*N*	Median	Range	*N*	Median	Range	*N*	Median	Range
Prebirth	3	2	3	3	0	0	3	0	0	3	1	2
Missionary	17	4	10	17	0	1	17	0	1	16	1	2
Organizational	23	6.5	10	23	1	1	23	0	1	20	1	2
Professionalization	2	6.5	1	2	1	0	2	1.5	1	2	1.5	1
Maturity	55	7	11	54	1	1	54	0	1	47	2	2
Diffusion	8	6	9	8	0	1	8	1.5	1	8	2	2

E. Explanatory variable: Life-cycle phase	1. Project Mix—Size			2. Project Mix—Time Frame			3. Variety of OR techniques		
	N	Median	Range	*N*	Median	Range	*N*	Median	Range
Prebirth	3	1	1	3	1.5	1	3	1	0
Missionary	17	1	2	17	1	2	17	2	2
Organizational	23	1	2	23	1	2	23	1.5	1
Professionalization	2	1	0	2	1	0	2	2	0
Maturity	55	1	2	55	1	2	55	2	1
Diffusion	8	1.5	2	8	1.5	2	8	2	2

Explanatory variable: Life-cycle phase	4. Variety of functional areas			5. Method of project cost allocation		
	N	Meidan	Range	*N*	Median	Range
Prebirth	3	0	1	3	0	0
Missionary	17	1	2	17	0	2
Organizational	23	2	2	23	0	2
Professionalization	2	2	0	1	0	0
Maturity	55	2	2	54	0	2
Diffusion	8	2	2	8	0	2

Chapter 6

An Organizational Intervention Approach To the Design and Implementation of R&D Project Selection Models*

Wm. E. Souder, P. M. Maher, N. R. Baker,
C. R. Shumway, and A. H. Rubenstein

Countless project selection models of various forms have been developed. They range from the simple indexes of return, such as the Pacifico model [*12*], to the more complex mathematical programming model, such as the Atkinson and Bobis model [*1*] and the Souder model [*16*]. The literature literally contains descriptions of hundreds of such methods [*3, 4*].

Ostensibly, a project selection model is an aid to evaluating proposed projects and portfolios. That is, a "good" one helps managers make decisions about which of several alternative programs to start, which projects to kill, how much to spend, etc. Unfortunately, the promise of project selection models seems unfulfilled. Some of the models in the literature seem to have been generated as sophisticated and theoretical mathematical exercises by persons who are not adequately familiar with real R&D problems. Other models are so simplistic that their potential contributions are difficult to perceive.

Several cases are known where project selection models were used for some brief periods, e.g., a few budgetary cycles and a few evaluations, only to be abandoned later [*1, 6, 16, 20*]. A lack of management interest–probably because the models did not provide what management believed were benefits proportionate to the cost and trouble of maintaining them–seems to have been responsible for their abandonment. On the other hand, there are known and notable exceptions to the hypothesis that project selection models have not been adopted [*5, 10*]. Furthermore, it is highly likely that there may be proprietary project selection methods in use today within some firms, which have not been published and therefore are unknown to the general public. However, it is clear

*Work in this area has been supported by Office of Naval Research Grants Nonr-1228(38), NR 949-215, National Aeronautics and Space Administration Grant NGL 14-077-058, and Army Research Office Grants DA-ARO-D-31-124-G-1158 and 71-G123.

that the number of unacceptable models and unsuccessful attempts to use models far outnumber the acceptable models and successful uses.

Reasons for this absence of real applications are not difficult to find. The construction of useful R&D project selection models is a very perplexing problem for both managers and operations research (OR) analysts. In a recent study [*19*], it was found that over forty models in the literature generally were not highly useful, both by management's own standards and by other analytical approaches. A companion study [*22*] also found that the value of a project selection model as a decision aid was highly dependent not only upon the form of the model but also upon the decision-making climate and the adoption status of the individuals within that organization. Thus, given the right organizational conditions and people, several useful model forms appeared to exist [*18, 23*].

This chapter describes the use of a questionnaire-based method to design a project selection model that an organization would be willing to adopt. The word adopt here does not mean that the organization will use the model simply for a pilot study or on several different occasions. Rather it means to make a commitment to routine and frequent use over a long time period. The questionnaire-based method, which will be referred to simply as the design method, and three case studies of its application are described below.

THE DESIGN METHOD

Basic Variables and General Method

In general, studies by several investigators indicate that an individual's willingness to adopt (WTA) a new innovation may be influenced by a large number of factors. Rogers [*13*] has identified several such factors that appear to be important determinants of the adoption and diffusion of any innovation. For individuals in organizations, these determining variables fall into three categories: (1) characteristics of the thing being adopted, (2) factors pertinent to the nature and character of the organization, and (3) pertinent variables relevant to the individual doing the adoption.

Figure 6.1 shows this concept relative to project selection decision models. An R&D manager's willingness to adopt a model is viewed as determined by his perceptions of the impact of the model on certain organizational factors, the characteristics of the model itself, and the impact of the model on his personal decision variables. Thus, the model characteristics are the originating variables in a causal chain (Figure 6.1).

From the model builder's standpoint then, Figure 6.1 suggests a general design methodology. First, find out what *specific* variables constitute the *basic* variables sets that are shown in Figure 6.1 as organizational factors and personal

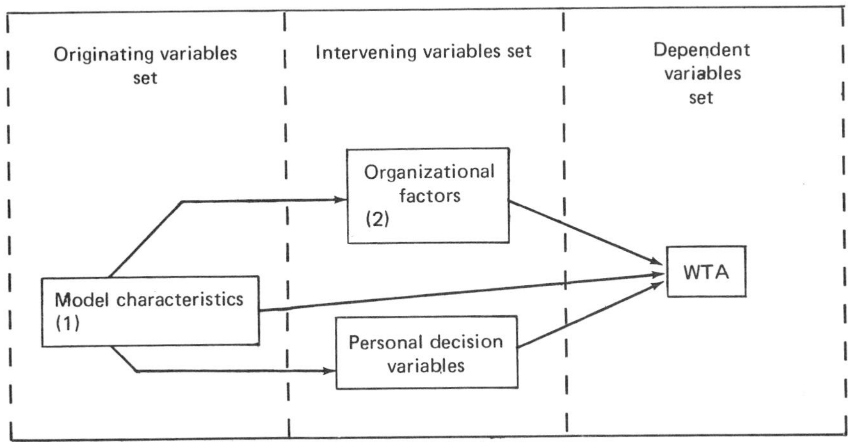

NOTE:"→" represents impact (causal chain)

Fig. 6.1 Basic Adoption-Determining Variables Sets

decision variables. There will be several specific variables within these general, categorical sets of factors and variables. Then, considering these specific variables to be intervening variables in a causal chain, the model builder can adjust his model by manipulating its characteristics (the originating variables). He can watch the impacts of the adjustments on the specific intervening variables, whose further impacts on WTA can then be observed.

Unfortunately, such active research and manipulation is seldom possible in ongoing organizations. Even if managers were willing to turn over their organizations for experimentation, such a simplistic approach would hardly yield useful outcomes in the dynamic and fluid world of real organizations. Instead, a quasi-experimental approach [*21*] has been taken. Specifically, the total procedure consists of two main parts. In the first part, questionnaires are designed and administered to groups of subjects in order to define a statistically significant set of specific variables that influence the group's willingness to adopt a project selection model. These statistically significant specific variables and the WTA variable are then combined in a predictive equation that can be used to measure the acceptability of various models for adoption. In the second part of the procedure the subjects are given formal and informal lectures and are provided the opportunity to use and apply various model forms. Questionnaires are again given to them but this time to collect input data for the predictive equation. The data and the equation can then be used to ascertain the acceptability of particular models for adoption and continued routine use (WTA). The most acceptable model can then be selected.

Specific Variables System

Many different specific variables may be included within the universe of organizational factors, model characteristics, and personal decision variables (Figure 6.1). These specific factors and variables may change with each organization, model, and person. A large number of possibly relevant specific factors and variables is known, having been defined by various researchers [*11, 18*]. Additional possibly relevant specific variables can be solicited by interviews with various persons in the organization under study, by introspection, or by a factor analysis [*11*].

The procedures for identifying the significant specific variables within a universe consist of administering an organizational-personal decision audit to personnel within the organization, and then statistically analyzing the data collected. The major portion of the audit consists of a Likert-type questionnaire [*11*] in which one or more questions are designed around each of the possibly relevant variables in the universe that has been collected.

For example, three items from one such Likert-type questionnaire are shown in Figure 6.2 (slightly abbreviated from those actually used, which may vary from one organization to another). Item 10 in Figure 6.2 measures the respondents' perceptions of the degree to which a project selection model would be compatible with whatever project selection processes are in current use within the organization. Hence, the specific factor being measured here is process compatibility. Item 15 measures the respondents' perceptions of the impacts a project selection model could have for increasing the upward compatibility of

---

Each item in this questionnaire consists of one statement with which you are asked to agree or disagree by placing an "X" along a scale that runs from A to D. The A to D scale indicators represent the following:

A = I strongly agree with this statement
a = I tend to agree with this statement
? = I cannot agree or disagree with this statement
d = I tend to disagree with this statement
D = I strongly disagree with this statement

A a ? d D 10. The manner in which we review and evaluate projects in this organization is not compatible with the use of a quantitative project selection model.

A a ? d D 15. My use of a quantitative project selection model would help to make my budget recommendations more compatible with those of my immediate superior.

A a ? d D 39. I would recommend that a quantitative project selection model be used *on at least 50 percent* of my projects.

Fig. 6.2 Selected Questionnaire Items

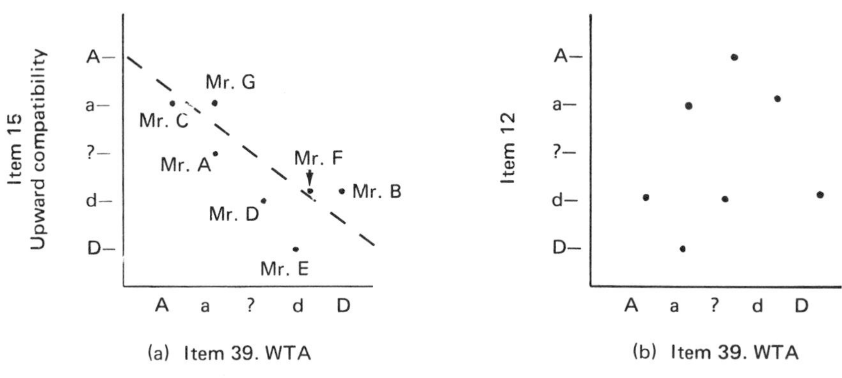

Fig. 6.3 Interitem Relationships

his decisions: the degree to which he and his superiors arrive at similar decisions. Item 39 measures the respondents' willingness to adopt a project selection model. Although Figure 6.2 illustrates cases where one item is used for one factor, many multidimensional types of factors may require multiple items. At one field site, a total of 39 questions were developed around a universe of 27 different specific criteria that were perceived to be possibly relevant [*1*].

Accurate responses to such questionnaires may require the respondents to have certain levels of knowledge about quantitative project selection model forms and their uses. Thus, some standard types of information sessions are normally held with all subjects prior to administering the questionnaires. These sessions permit the subjects to acquire a standard level of knowledge about the forms and types of models available, and also to practice using some of the model forms on their own projects in an informal fashion.

Significant specific variables in the total universe will appear in terms of high interitem correlations. For example, take the scatter diagram for the seven subjects (each point in the diagram represents a different subject's set of responses on two items) shown in Figure 6.3a. Reading from the left side of that plot, these data show that Mr. C responded "a" and "A" to items 15 and 39, respectively. Mr. G gave responses "a" and "a" to items 15 and 39, respectively. Mr. A gave responses "?" and "a." Mr. D gave responses "d" and "?," etc. These responses show a reasonably good linear relationship between "upward compatibility" (item 15) and the subjects' willingness to adopt (item 39). Hence we conclude that upward compatibility is a significant factor relative to the adoption of a quantitative project selection model, for these seven persons as a group. On the other hand, as shown in Figure 6.3b, item 12 is not a significant adoption factor. The actual decision to accept a factor as statistically significant is made on the basis of a consideration of the value of the correlation coefficient τ and standard statistical methods [*11*]. The τ statistic value is near 1.0 for the data in Figure 6.3(a); it is near zero for the data in Figure 6.3b.

As an example of a specific variables system, Figure 6.4 shows the specific factors and variables that were found in one study on the basis of the τ values. Each of the specific factors and variables shown in Figure 6.4 was found to be correlated with willingness to adopt at the .05 level of significance. The organizational factor downward compatibility refers to the degree to which the decision maker views his own decisions as compatible with those of his subordinates. It is reasonable to find that this is a significant factor. An innovation that increases the downward compatibility of one's decisions should be appealing, whereas an innovation that decreases this compatibility would certainly not be highly appealing. Naturally, whether or not this is a significant factor for a particular organization will depend largely on the circumstances. For example, where poor downward compatibility is considered to be a source of current problems it may yield a significant τ statistic. The significance of the factors upward compatibility and process compatibility, as defined above, will similarly be influenced by the circumstances. These three factors are thus categorized as organizational because they are relative to events that arise in the nature of organization structures (or processes therein). They are factors in that they describe elements that influence the conduct and outcome of project selection decisions. It should be noted that these three organizational factors were not found to be significantly interrelated (on the τ statistic).

The four model characteristics shown in Figure 6.4 are relatively self-explanatory and logically important. Communicability refers to the ease with which the subject perceives the project selection model can be communicated to others. Appropriateness of outputs and appropriateness of mathematics refer to the degree to which the subject perceives that the model outputs (data) and the mathematical operations of the model are relevant. For instance, a model that computes a return on investment ratio might exhibit appropriate mathematics in that such ratios may have achieved common use in the decision processes. But, where the model outputs are in the form of future dollar equivalents rather than present worth dollars, then the appropriateness of the outputs may be low. The characteristic availability of inputs—the data to run the model—is not necessarily a model property per se. But models that require generally unavailable data would normally have low potentials. As with the organizational factors, these four model characteristics were orthogonal—not found to be significantly related to each other.

The four personal decision variables shown in Figure 6.4 relate to aspects of the subjects' own decision making. Uncertainty absorption refers to the subjects' perception of the ability of a project selection model to reduce the amount of felt uncertainty surrounding various decision alternatives. Informa-

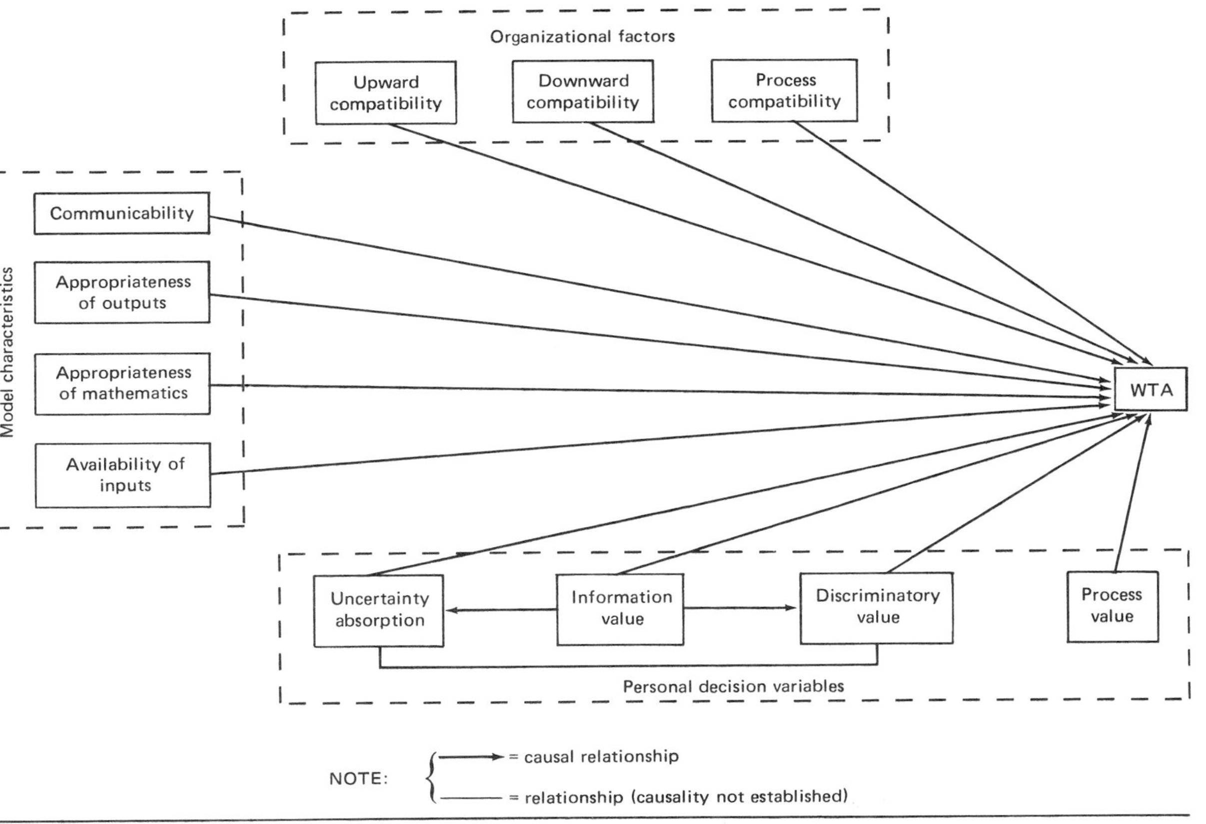

Fig. 6.4 Example of a Specific Variables System

tion value reflects the subjects' perception of the value of both the amount and type of information provided. Note that what is being measured is not information amount and type per se, but the subjects' perceptions of the worth of the amounts and types provided. Discriminatory value refers to the felt contribution that a project selection model might make in distinguishing among the decision alternatives. Process value refers to the cognitive structuring perceived to be provided by a model. It is of interest to note here that information value was found to be closely related with and causal to uncertainty absorption and discriminatory value. This is logical but need not necessarily be true as a general rule. For instance, a model may supply new and valuable information about the risk of each alternative. Even though this information may be of value, the decision alternatives may not be highly distinguishable on this new dimension. Furthermore, the resulting awareness that risk is an important consideration may, in fact, lead to higher rather than lower felt uncertainty. The difference between a simple interrelatedness (correlation) and a directional relationship (causality) is indicated here by a common statistical method known as path analysis [9].

In most instances, interrelationships will exist between the sets of factors, characteristics, and variables, because all the variables constitute an interrelated system of items. Figure 6.5 shows the set interrelationships found in one study. Here, the organizational factor set was closely related to two model characteristics: output and mathematical appropriateness. Similarly, the personal decision variable set was highly interrelated with these same model characteristics.

In general, the originating variables set (model characteristics) have *both* direct and indirect effects on the dependent variable WTA. Changes in the values of the originating variables (model characteristics) will *directly* affect changes in WTA (Figure 6.4). But these changes will also affect the intervening variables sets (organizational factors and personal decision variables), causing changes in them. An example is shown in Figure 6.5. Note that not every variable from Figure 6.4 shows interrelatedness. These changes will, in turn, create changes in the WTA (Figure 6.5). Thus, there is an *indirect* effect (through the intervening variables). This means that a model, which may not be highly appropriate itself, can still have a positive effect on WTA if positive changes are correspondingly made in the organizational factors and/or personal decision variables.

Predictive Equation

The direct and indirect impacts are taken into account in the basic variables weights of the predictive equation, an example of which is shown in Figure 6.6. The predictive equation is developed on the basis of the question-

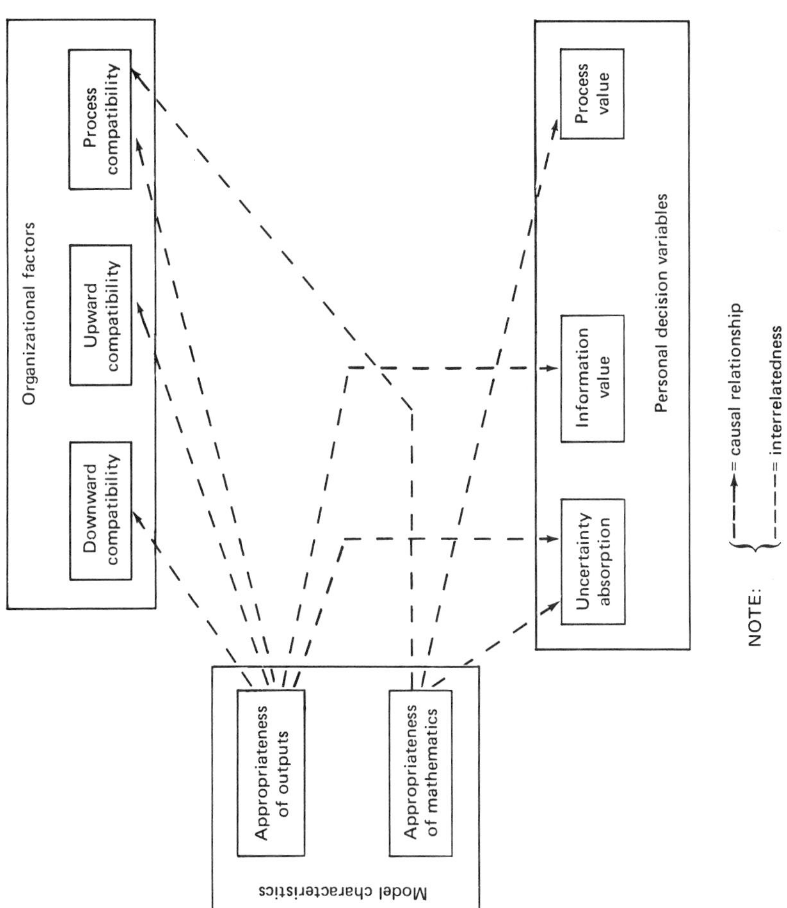

Fig. 6.5 Example of Interrelatedness Between Variables Sets

WTA = −.51 + [.61 × MC] + [.42 × PDV] + [.14 × OF] ± ϵ

where MC = average score, model characteristics
PDV = average score, personal decision variables
OF = average score, organizational factors

MC = communicability score + appropriateness of outputs score
+ availability of inputs score
+ appropriateness of mathematics score ÷ 4

PDV = uncertainty absorption + discriminatory value score + process value score
+ information value score ÷ 4

OF = upward compatibility score + downward compatibility score
+ process compatibility score
÷ 3

± ϵ = error term (range is from −.51 to + .35)

Fig. 6.6 Example of Predictive Equation

naire results and analyses shown in Figures 6.4 and 6.5, using traditional discriminant-regression types of techniques [7]. The weights .61, .42, and .14 reflect the overall relative importance of the three basic variables of model characteristics, personal decision variables, and organizational factors, respectively. Given values for MC, PDV, and OF (scores for the three basic variables) for a particular model, the predictive equation can be used to determine whether or not a group of subjects is willing to adopt that model.

To use the predictive equation for a particular project selection model, the score for that model on each *specific* factor is first obtained by administering questionnaires to persons familiar with that model. Such questionnaires are normally given only after considerable discussions, pilot applications, and familiarization sessions have been completed with a particular model. These questionnaires may be of the same type as those shown in Figure 6.3 in that they yield five-point ("A," "a " "?," "d," "D") response data for each specific variable that has been identified as significant. Note that only the significant specific variables, such as those shown in Figure 6.4, are included in this questionnaire. The questionnaire items are phrased in terms such as "The upward compatibility of my decisions would be enhanced if we routinely used the KZY model." The responses are coded 1, 2, etc., so that a total score over all subjects can be computed for each specific variable (questionnaire item). Thus, there will be an upward compatibility score, a downward compatibility score, etc. These specific variable scores within each of the three basic variables are averaged, as shown in Figure 6.6, to obtain the basic variables scores (input data) for the predictive equation.

The output from the predictive equation will be a value for WTA. Where five-point response scales are used, such as those in Figure 6.2, WTA will range from a value of −.51 to +5.35. The same five-point scale values may be used to translate these numerals into literal terms: a WTA value between −.51 and +1.5 = A, a WTA value between +1.6 and +2.5 = a, etc. An A outcome indicates strong acceptance of the model for adoption, etc.

In reality, predictive equations, such as that shown in Figure 6.6, cannot be used with such high accuracy for two reasons. First of all, there is a known error attached to every WTA value ($-.51 \leqslant \epsilon \leqslant +.35$). Secondly, the averaging of the values for the specific variables (which is done in computing the MC, PDV, and OF scores) imparts a smoothing effect, which also introduces some amount of systematic error. However, there is usually no need to have a predictive equation with great accuracy. In most cases one is only interested in whether the WTA is closer to values of 1 or 2 (A or a) or closer to values of 4 or 5 (d or D). If greater accuracy than this is desired, a predictive equation with the specific factors unaveraged can be developed. That is, one would have an equation with a weight for communicability, a weight for output appropriateness, etc. The simple predictive equation developed here combines ease of use with reasonable accuracy.

APPLICATION I: HIERARCHICAL ORGANIZATION

One application of the design method focused on the resource allocation/budget determination process in a federal agency. As diagrammed in Figure 6.7, the budgetary process at this agency is sequential in nature. Budget guidance is issued from each superordinate level to its immediate subordinate levels, based in turn on the guidance it has received and on its decision as to how the budget should be further apportioned. Thus, guidance information flows from the highest administrative level, through all intermediate levels, and on to the lowest organizational unit. In addition to budget guidance according to organizational entity, guidance is issued according to technical areas. For example, a laboratory might receive guidance regarding its total budget and indicating acceptable budgets for selected programs or groups of projects. The laboratory, in turn, might issue suggestions for its subordinate organizations and for its project subentities.

Once these restrictions reach the lowest organizational level, the information flow is reversed: Each subordinate level transmits a proposed budget allocation to its immediate superordinate level. Each subordinate proposes, to its superordinate, how it would allocate the guidance budgets if they were, in fact, to be authorized. These proposed allocations are integrated at each level and are then communicated to the next higher level. This upward and downward flow cycle may recur many times for more than one set of suggested figures. Ultimately the highest organizational level receives a proposed budget allocation

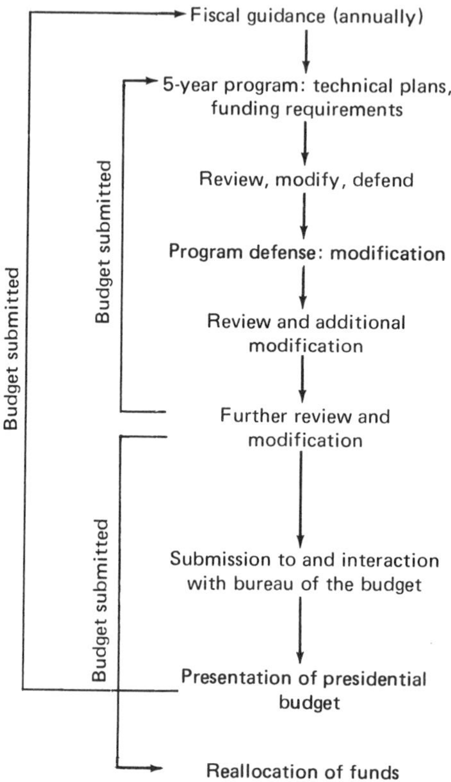

Fig. 6.7 Budgetary Process, Hierarchical Organization

either consistent with the guidance figures it originally issued or otherwise acceptable to it.

Eventually, the highest administrative level determines the total amount of funding that will be appropriated for the entire organization. The appropriated allocations then flow through the organizational hierarchy in a manner analogous to the flow of the guidance information. At this point, each organizational level knows (within limits) the level of funding it can anticipate during the fiscal year and the budgetary constraints that have been imposed on its operation. Specific fiscal year budget plans are then made.

Frequently, these plans must be revised during the year, because the eventual authorizations may deviate from the appropriations. Accordingly, several times during the year each organizational level is faced with a resource allocation decision that is characterized by a large number of budgetary constraints, defined both by organizational entity and activity type [*15*].

Project Selection Model

A specific variables system very much like that shown in Figures 6.4 and 6.5 was defined using the design methodology discussed above. Several resource allocation models were then given trials within the organization. Questionnaires were used to measure the acceptability of each model relative to each of the specific variables that had previously been defined.

A mathematical programming resource allocation model was then developed on the basis of these experiences. As shown by the data in Table 6.1, the questionnaire data indicated that the respondents perceived that this model evidenced high compatibility, appropriateness, and input availability properties. These were the specific characteristics needed to achieve a high adoption potential (WTA) for this model (Figure 6.5).

The mathematical model that was developed is described in considerable detail elsewhere [*2*]. In general, the model determines the allocation of funds among various levels of the organization so as to maxmimze total future expected worth. The input data for the model are: (1) estimates of the values to be received, given various funding levels on the candidate projects, and (2) the various guidance figures. The model was computerized in a time share mode so as to permit a decision maker to enter data at a typewriter-like console and then receive almost immediate printouts of prescribed portfolios and allocations of resources. For example, to initiate a printout, the user supplies the input data and almost immediately receives the following:

```
TO OBTAIN OUTPUT, TYPE IN 5 INTEGERS SEPARATED BY COMMAS
(1=DIRS, 2=ELEMS, 3=PROJS, 4=W UNITS, 5=T GOALS).
THE HIERARCHY OF OUTPUT IS IN THE ORDER OF THE INTEGERS.
FOR LESS THAN COMPLETE HIERARCHY, FILL THE REMAINING INTE-
GERS WITH ZEROS.?
```

Table 6.1
Model Characteristics

Specific characteristics	Frequency of responses per category*		
	A and a	?	d and D
High communicability	15	4	2
High output appropriateness	16	4	1
High mathematical appropriateness	8	10	3
High availability of inputs	11	5	5

*The A and a and the d and D responses are combined to simplify the presentations.

If the user types 1,2,3,4,5, then the full hierarchy is printed out in the order specified. For example:

ENTITY		$(000) ALLOCATION	VALUE
DIRECT	1	100	140
ELEM	1	100	140
PROJ	2	100	140
W UNIT	1	100	140
T GOAL	1	100	140
DIRECT	2	200	421
ELEM	1	100	321
PROJ	2	100	321
W UNIT	1	100	321
T GOAL	2	100	320
ELEM	2	100	100
PROJ	1	100	100
W UNIT	2	100	100
T GOAL	3	100	100
DIRECT	3	150	500
ELEM	1	100	360
PROJ	2	100	360
W UNIT	1	100	360
T GOAL	4	100	360
ELEM	2	50	140
PROJ	1	50	140
W UNIT	2	50	140
T GOAL	5	50	140

TOTAL EXPENDITURES = 450
TOTAL VALUE = 1061

The computer program is a general one that can be run at various levels of the organizational hierarchy, depending on how one defines the entities. Here DIRECT is the directorate (a superordinate) level, ELEM refers to an intermediate level, and PROJ is the project (a subordinate) level. Projects are comprised of subunits called work units (W UNITS). Each work unit may contain work packages oriented to one or more technical goals (T GOAL). In the above printout, the first five lines show that the computer model has allocated $100 thousand to work unit 1 within project 2. Project 2 is housed within ELEM 1, which reports to directorate 1. Of the $100 thousand allocated to work unit 1 in directorate 1, all of it is allocated to work on technical goal 1. The VALUE column lists the corresponding expected worth of the dollar allocations at each organizational entity. The computerized model selects its allocations (ALLOCATION column on printout) such that the total of all these values is maximized. That is, there is no other allocation that can achieve a total value greater than the 1061 shown at the bottom of the printout for a corresponding total expenditure of $450 thousand (shown as 450 in the print-out).

The time share mode of this model permits it to have very high impacts on the process value variable (Figure 6.4). Alternative budget report formats can be readily generated by typing in less than the complete hierarchy code, e.g., one can obtain the following report by typing 0,0,0,0,5:

ENTITY	ALLOCATION	VALUE
T GOAL 1	100	140
~~T GOAL 2~~	~~100~~	~~321~~
T GOAL 3	100	100
T GOAL 4	100	360
~~T GOAL 5~~	~~50~~	~~140~~

Changes in input data are also easily made. At various points the program will inquire:

DO YOU WISH TO CHANGE ANY DATA (1=YES, 0=NO)?

Appropriate printouts of prescribed allocations and budget reports with these new data can then be requested by the user.

The model was generally perceived as having favorable, high impacts on the organizational factors and personal decision variables previously shown in Figure 6.5. These are the intervening variables that our design methodology had shown to have significant relationships with the adoption attitudes (WTA) for this site. As the data in Table 6.2 show, all six of these important intervening variables were perceived to be favorably impacted by the above described project selection model. It may be noted here that it is easy to see how such personal decision variables as the process value and such organizational factors as the upward, downward, and process compatibilities are influenced by the interactive computer program. This new capability to automate the budgeting process, to rapidly examine alternative funding allocations and budgetary figures, and to test the impacts of upward and downward changes in organizational guidance numbers would naturally be expected to have such impacts.

It must be noted that different subjects were included in the groups who supplied data for Tables 6.1 and 6.2. In Table 6.1 the group of 21 subjects included the primary resource allocation decision makers (a high level of the organization), the project and work unit analysts (a low organization level), and a middle organizational level group. Also included were certain persons who primarily serve the organizations as model builders and operations research analysts. Thus, this group is comprised of all those persons who would be direct

Table 6.2
Perceptions of Model Impacts

	Frequency of responses per category†		
	A & a	?	d & D
Organizational factors*			
Improve upward compatibility	6	1	2
Improve downward compatibility	5	3	1
Improve process compatibility	5	1	3
Personal decision variables*			
Increase uncertainty absorption	6	3	2
High process value	9	2	0
High information value	5	4	2

*The respondents were not necessarily the same in these two variables categories because these variables were pertinent to different organizational levels.
†The "A" and "a", the "d" and "D" are combined to simplify the presentation.

users of the model and/or suppliers of inputs to the model, and those persons believed to have some particular knowledge concerning the "goodness" characteristics of models in general. The groups of persons supplying the data in Table 6.2 are subsets of the larger group used in Table 6.1. In particular, only the primary resource allocation decision makers and some of those persons in the middle organizational level were capable of supplying data about the organizational factors. On the other hand, some of the project and work analysts and not all of the primary resource allocation decision makers were relevant subjects for obtaining data about the personal decision variables in Table 6.2.

Impacts of Model on WTA

The impacts of the use of the model are shown in Table 6.3. In general, the data indicate that the respondents were significantly more inclined to perceive a need and utility in the after-use period than in the before-use period. For example, the first line of Table 6.3 shows that only 5 of 21 respondents perceived the model as needed in the before-use period. In contrast, 18 of the 21 respondents perceived the need at the end of a brief period of use.

Perhaps the best indication of impact is shown by the WTA data. In general, these data (last two lines of Table 6.3) show that the organization went from primarily a nonadopter status (only 3 high-adopter persons in the before-use period) to primarily an adopter status organization (16 high-adopter persons,

Table 6.3.
Impacts of Model Use

	Frequency of responses per category††					
	Before use			After use		
Item set*,†	A & a	?	d & D	A & a	?	d & D
High perceived need	5	0	16	18	0	3
High perceived utility	6	0	10	14	1	1
High WTA						
(1) all projects	1	4	5	7	2	1
(2) ⩾ 50% projects	2	2	6	9	1	0

*The need and utility sets contain several questionnaire items. WTA (1) and WTA (2) are single questionnaire items.
†The total numbers of respondents varied from item set to item set because some item sets were not pertinent to persons at some organizational levels.
††The A and a and the d and D responses are combined to simplify the presentation.

of the original 20 persons who could be adopters). Thus, it is clear that the model that was constructed using the design procedure was viewed as highly acceptable.

APPLICATIONS II AND III: LONG-TERM ADOPTION

The study described dealt only with willingness to adopt. The question remains as to whether or not a strong, positive WTA impact is a correlate of actual adoption. Two studies have now been completed on this aspect.

Capital Goods Firm

This study concentrated on the exploratory R&D activities in a large capital goods manufacturer. The exploratory R&D activities included the investigation of new and advanced concepts in fundamental technology of potential value to the company.

The design questionnaires indicated the existence of three specific variables that would have strong positive degrees of association with an individual's willingness to adopt a project selection model. In order of their importance they were: (1) the perceived value to an individual of the data generated by the model; (2) an individual's perception of the appropriateness of the information considered by the organization as a result of using the model; and (3) an individual's perception of the value of changes in projects' research strategies resulting from the use of the model.

Further study indicated that four variables involving the participants' use of new or existing communication channels would be strongly affected by their use of the model. These variables (in the order of the degree to which they were affected) are: (1) an individual's perceived need to develop new communication channels; (2) an individual's perceived need to increase the use of existing communication channels; (3) an individual's perceived use of the new communication channels; and (4) an individual's perceived use of existing communication channels [*11*].

A computer-based project selection model was developed that was a modification of a risk analysis model developed by Hertz [*8*]. The model systematically combines probability estimates associated with possible outcome values for various projects and portfolios of projects. The model was developed to minister to the above three specific variables.

The outcome was that, as predicted, the use of the model caused the individual users to seek out new communications channels (see the above four variables). These channels became permanent interdepartmental bridges within the organization. At the present time, three years after the study was carried out, the organization is still using the original project selection model.

Diversified R&D Department

In this case, the department director needed a means of reducing his uncertainty level and achieving higher degrees of discrimination among his decision alternatives. The R&D work within the department was highly diversified, projects were not readily comparable, and most projects were high-risk type ventures.

The Souder model [*16*] was used with considerable success. The basic function of the model was to provide an environment in which the director could test his ideas in combinations with those of others before actually committing resources to the organizational decision. The model was used to test assumptions, to simulate outcomes, and to determine the sensitivity of profit potentials to proposed alternatives. The use of the model provided insights into such aspects as the effects of changes in department or project budget restrictions, the consistency between intuitive budget restrictions, and the goal of profit maximization. Sensitivity analyses (asking "What if –?" about budgets, and manpower allocations, and running the model to find out) were performed on an interproject basis.

In general this model ministered to the uncertainty absorption and discriminatory value variables. In this case, these variables were found to be direct determinants of WTA. Furthermore, the director adopted and used the model during most of his entire tenure in his job as the R&D director [*20*].

SUMMARY AND CONCLUSIONS

A method for designing organizationally acceptable R&D project selection models has been described. The total design method consists of a two-part sequence. In this first part, significant organizational and personal decision variables systems that influence willingness to adopt are identified. In the second part, a suitable model form is selected from among several candidate forms, on the basis of the models' impacts on these significant variables. A series of questionnaires is given in the first part of the design method in order to define the significant variables systems. Another series of questionnaires is given in the second part to aid in selecting a suitable model from among several potential candidates. This second series of questionnaires may be used to collect input data for a predictive equation that can be used to predict the acceptability of (or the willingness to adopt) particular model forms. The predictive equation serves as a useful quantitative measure of whether or not the model builder is moving in the direction of greater WTA with variations in his project selection model.

The design method has been used in three different field studies. In one, the subjects' (the project selection decision makers') willingness to adopt a project selection model was reversed from negative to positive. In the two other studies, the use of the design method was shown to result in highly useful and effective models, which were adopted for long periods of time.

References

1. Atkinson, A. C., and Bobis, A. H., "A Mathematical Basis for the Selection of Research Projects," *IEEE Transactions on Engineering Management,* **EM-16,** no. 1 (February 1969).
2. Baker, N. R., and Pound, W. H., "R&D Project Selection: Where We Stand," *IEEE Transactions on Engineering Management,* **EM-11,** no. 4, 124–134 (December 1964).
3. Baker, N. R., Souder, Wm. E., Shumway, C. R., Maher, P. M., and Rubenstein, A. H., "A Resource Allocation Model for a Hierarchical Organization," working paper, February 1974.
4. Cetron, M. J., Martino, J., and Roepcke, L. H., "The Selection of R&D Program Content," *IEEE Transactions on Engineering Management,* **EM-14,** no. 4, 4–13 (December 1967).
5. Cochran, M. A., Pyle, E. G., Greene, L. C., Clymer, H. A., and Bender, A. D., "Investment Model for R&D Project Evaluation and Selection," *IEEE Transactions on Engineering Management,* **EM-18**, 89–100 (August 1971).
6. Disman, Saul, "Selecting R&D Projects for Profit," *Chemical Engineering,* **II**, 87–90 (December 1962).

7. Fisher, R. A., "The Use of Multiple Measurements in Taxonomic Problems," *Annals of Eugenics,* **7,** 170–188 (1936).
8. Hertz, David B., "Risk Analysis in Capital Investment," *Harvard Business Review,* **42,** 95–106 (1965).
9. Hilton, Gordon, "Causal Inference Analysis: A Seductive Process," *Administrative Science Quarterly,* 44–57 (March 1972).
10. Maher, P. Michael, "An Experiment with a Computer-Based R&D Project Selection Technique," Program of Research on the Management of Research and Development, Department of Industrial Engineering and Management Sciences, Northwestern University, March 1971.
11. Maher, P. M., "Some Factors Affecting the Adoption of a Management Innovation,' PhD Dissertation, Department of Industrial Engineering and Management Sciences, Northwestern University, Evanston, Illinois, 1970.
12. Pacifico, Carl, "Is It Worth The Risk?," *Chemical Engineering Progress,* **60,** no. 5, 19–21 (May 1964).
13. Rogers, Everett M., *Diffusion of Innovations,* Glencoe, Illinois: The Free Press, 1962.
14. Rubenstein, A. H., et al., "Intergroup Climate Characteristics, Work Related Values and Communication," Program of Research on the Management of R&D (POMRAD) Document 70/48, Northwestern University, Evanston, Illinois, September 1970.
15. Shumway, C. R., Maher, P. M., Baker, N. R., Souder, Wm. E., and Rubenstein, A. H., "Diffuse Decision Making–An Empirical Examination," *Management Science,* in press.
16. Souder, Wm. E., "Selecting and Staffing R&D Projects Via Operations Research," *Chemical Engineering Progress,* **63,** 27–37 (November 1967).
17. Souder, Wm. E., Baker, N. R., Maher, P. M., Shumway, C. R., and Rubenstein, A. H., "Instrument Package At Airlie House," POMRAD document 70/58, Northwestern University, Evanston, Illinois, 1970.
18. Souder, Wm. E., "A Scoring Methodology for Assessing the Suitability for Management Science Models," *Management Science,* **18,** 526–543 (June 1972).
19. Souder, Wm. E., "Comparative Analysis of R&D Investment Models," *AIIE Transactions,* **4,** 47–64 (March 1972).
20. Souder, Wm. E., "An R&D Planning and Control Servosystem," *R&D Management,* **3,** no. 1, 13–21 (October 1972).
21. Souder, Wm. E., Maher, P. M., and Rubenstein, A. H., "Two Successful Experiments in Project Selection," *Research Management,* **15,** 44–54 (September 1972).
22. Souder, Wm. E., "Analytical Effectiveness of Mathematical Models for R&D Project Selection," *Management Science,* **19,** no. 8, 907–923 (April 1973).
23. Souder, Wm. E., "Utility and Perceived Acceptability of Project Selection Models," *Management Science,* **19,** no. 12, 1384–1394 (August 1973).
24. Souder, Wm. E., "Achieving Organizational Consensus in R&D Planning," *Management Science,* in press.

Chapter 7

Implementation and Organizational Validity: An Empirical Investigation*

Randall L. Schultz and Dennis P. Slevin

The study of the implementation of operations research/management science (OR/MS) models and techniques is a relatively new topic in the field of management and behavioral science. Beginning with Churchman and Schainblatt's salient paper in 1965 [*4*], describing a dialectic of implementation, efforts in this area have produced little more than 30 published articles (for an annotated bibliography see Reference *23*). A review of this literature leads to two conclusions. First, there has not been much research on the topic. The total amount of scientific man-hours spent on the implementation problem is but a small fraction of the amount of time and effort spent in the development of new and improved models. Although this trend seems to be changing, it will be some time before a large body of implementation research has been accumulated. Second, much of the research that has been done is of a theoretical as opposed to an empirical nature. For example, besides Churchman and Schainblatt [*4*], work by Argyris [*1*], Bennis [*2*], Hertz [*12*], Little [*16*], and Shakun [*22*] are all of a theoretical nature. Although theoretical discussions are a necessary and integral part of the development of any field of research, at some point in time they must be examined for their conformity with empirical evidence. What appears to be needed now is an orderly way to accumulate such data and to analyze them. This capability, a prerequisite to the testing of general theories, would provide the means for determining key variables in the implementation process, for testing hypotheses, and for providing guidelines for researchers to follow in solving implementation problems.

If we might draw a historical parallel with recent developments in programs of research in the behavioral sciences, it is possible to conclude that one

*Preparation of this paper was supported by a grant from the Ford Foundation to the Graduate School of Business at the University of Pittsburgh and by a grant from the Organizational Effectiveness Research Programs of the Office of Naval Research to the authors. The authors wish to thank Mr. Graham Baxter and Mr. Robert Keim, research assistants in the project, and an unnamed corporation, site of the research, for their help.

way to stimulate the orderly collection of data across a field of research as broad as implementation is to provide a meaningful and easily used *instrument* for data collection. For example, a master's thesis by Stoner in 1961 [*24*] reported that under certain conditions groups made significantly riskier decisions than individuals. This research used the Choice Dilemmas Questionnaire to determine individual and group risk preferences. Although this instrument contained only twelve items and has since been demonstrated to be highly imperfect in its operationalization of risk, the initial risky-shift findings, combined with the availability of this instrument, have stimulated over 100 studies using the questionnaire [*5, 7*].

In a similar vein, Christie in 1955 (cf. Reference *3*) developed the Mach IV and the Mach V instruments, which were designed to measure the individual trait of "Machiavellianism." He showed how high-Machiavellians could be separated from low-Machiavellians and pointed out how differences in their behaviors in laboratory experiments, in the classroom, in the business world, and in other settings could be investigated. The Machiavellian instruments have stimulated a large body of research using them as a basis for data collection.

In a third area, Vroom and Yetton [*25*] have developed an innovative measure of leadership style through the use of scenarios. Their "instrument" is novel, has a high face validity, and will undoubtedly be used in many future research studies in the future on leadership style and participation in decision making.

The point of these three examples is that researchers interested in studying human social behavior are constrained by the availability of data. When an instrument is developed that provides a systematic method for data collection, quantification, and analysis, it tends to stimulate research in the direction of using the instrument and, more importantly, in the direction of solving the research problem. Forrester [*11*], for example, in developing an intuitively pleasing conceptual model and an easily used simulation technique (Dynamo) has stimulated research not only on industrial organizations, but also on urban and, more recently, world problems.

Our intent in this report is to present and evaluate a data collection instrument that can be used by OR/MS researchers implementing management science models in a variety of settings. Although we do not propose to have the same impact as the instruments reported above, it is our goal that this device will stimulate further empirical investigations into the implementation problem.

THE RESEARCH APPROACH

In Chapter 3 we have discussed in some depth the *organizational validity* of OR/MS models [*21*]. The concept of organizational validity implies that for a model to be implementable in a social organization, it must be compatible with, or fit, that organization. This fit must occur at three levels: individual, small group, and organizational. If an OR/MS model requires an extraordinary amount of change in individual attitudes, small group dynamics, or organizational structure, then the probability of successful implementation will be reduced. The first stage in investigating the organizational validity of OR/MS models is an evaluation of individual attitudes toward the OR/MS innovation. The large body of research on individual attitude measurement and change (cf. References *10* and *13*) indicates that human behavior is affected by attitudes, that attitudes can be measured, and that attitudes can be changed with a variety of techniques.

Given this motivation for an interest in implementation attitudes, then there are three basic research questions:

1. What are the key attitudinal dimensions affecting implementation success?
2. How can these attitudes be measured?
3. How do these attitudes affect implementation success?

We set as our objective the development of an attitude scaling instrument for implementation research that has the following traits:

1. general—easy to adapt to a variety of implementation situations
2. easily understood by the user
3. simple to administer
4. capable of being quantitatively scored
5. providing meaningful attitudinal dimensions, i.e., attitudes that the researcher might be able to modify and change through his implementation activities

In investigating the available approaches to attitude measurement, two scaling techniques stand out because they possess many of the traits listed above. The first technique is a Likert instrument that consists of a number of statements to which the respondent indicates how strongly he agrees or disagrees on a five-point or seven-point scale [*15*]. The second technique is that of the semantic differential developed by Osgood, Suci, and Tannenbaum [*18*]. This scale consists of the statement of a concept to which an individual responds by checking a series of bipolar adjectives: good-bad, interesting-uninteresting, etc. Using both the Likert and the semantic differential techniques, an instrument was developed and tested in a field setting.

METHODOLOGY

Because it was decided that the attitude measurement instrument should be designed as generally as possible, and not just for a specific research setting, a

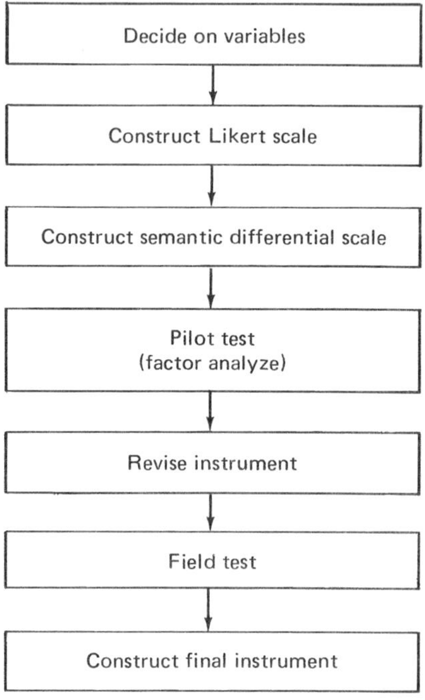

Fig. 7.1 Steps in Instrument Construction

sequence of steps was undertaken in the scale-development process. First, previous research on impelmentation of OR/MS models and research on organizations in general was examined to determine what *variables* should be included in the instrument. Second, the Likert scale section of the instrument was constructed. Third, the semantic differential portion of the instrument was developed. Fourth, the instrument was pilot tested and factor analyzed. Fifth, the instrument was revised in preparation for a field test. These steps are all shown in the flow chart in Figure 7.1 and, along with the industrial sample, will be described in more detail in this section. The final field test, the results, and the form of the final instrument are described in the results section.

Search for Variables

A search for variables was undertaken with special attention directed to the problems of implementation in the organizational environment. First, March and Simon's [*17*] classic volume, *Organizations,* was examined for key organizational variables that might be relevant to the implementation problem. This book lists in an appendix 206 organizational variables of which 57 were judged to be relevant to the implementation of OR/MS models in an organization. These 57 variables were reduced and grouped into 14 general headings: authority, communication, conflict, decision making, interpersonal relationship, leadership, participation, goals, power, satisfaction, structure, supervisory style, and technology.

Second, Radnor, Rubenstein, and Tansik's review [*19*] of the OR/MS and R&D literature was examined for relevant variables. The review isolated 17 factors influencing implementation activites. These factors were included as separate variables or subsumed under another variable in the preeeding list.

Third, the 7 variables described in Manley's (1971) research on the effect of client behavior on implementation were added. These were: support from above, urgency of the project, technical complexity of the project, amount of personal participation required to implement the project, risk, confidence and trust, search drive, and receptiveness. These variables were then used as inputs into the Likert and semantic differential scale development.

Likert Scale

Approximately 100 Likert-type statements were generated based on the 81 input variables. The statements were worded in such a way that they referred to what would happen as the result of the implementation. A statement reflecting expected job satisfaction, for example, would be: "My job will be more satisfying." Each statement was followed by a five-point scale that ranged through strongly disagree, disagree, uncertain, agree, strongly agree. The first draft of the Likert scale was assembled consisting of 81 items. (The correspondence between this number and the 81 initial input variables is purely accidental.)

Semantic Differential Scale

The semantic differential scale was intended to augment the Likert scale in the event that certain factors were omitted and was to be used as somewhat of an exploratory instrument. Eleven concepts were selected for the semantic differential scale. They were selected on the basis of the 14 general headings distilled from March and Simon [*17*], the 17 implementation factors of Radnor, Rubenstein, and Tansik [*19*], and the 7 client-oriented variables of Manley (1971). The concepts were:

1. the chances of success using this technique
2. confidence in the developers of the model

3. changes in executive decision making
4. changes in the communication system
5. the effects of interpersonal relationships
6. the effect of this on subordinates
7. the importance of this project to you
8. the amount of support being given to this project
9. the urgency of this project to the company
10. technical complexity of this project
11. the amount of your personal participation required to implement this project

The original work of Osgood, Suci, and Tannenbaum [*18*] lists 35 adjective pairs that are related to the evaluative dimension. Since implementation likelihood should be a function of a positive or negative evaluation on the part of the user, a subset of these 35 pairs was selected. Of these, 25 adjective pairs were selected based on their relevance to implementation for the initial pilot test version of the instrument.

Pilot Test

Both the Likert and the semantic differential scales were assembled into one questionnaire together with instructions. This questionnaire was administered to a sample of 145 MBA students yielding 136 usable responses. They were given a short description of an advertising budgeting model called ADBUDG developed by Little and described by Kotler [*14*] and were asked to assume that they were a marketing manager who was considering using this model to assist in making advertising budgeting decisions. They were asked to respond to the instrument as they thought they would if they were a real-world marketing manager. This approach, of course, was imperfect, but it gave us a mechanism for pilot testing the instrument.

In order to examine the structure of responses (i.e., the structure of attitudes) a factor analysis was performed on both the Likert and semantic differential scales. Nine, 10 and 11 factors were rotated for the Likert portion of the scale to explore possible bases for defining attitudinal dimensions. The rotation of 10 factors provided the most interpretable results. The factors were interpreted and named as follows:

1. effect on the organization
2. changes occurring after implementation
3. effect on decision making
4. interpersonal relationships
5. degree of acceptance of the model
6. perceived improvement in organizational performance
7. perceived difficulty of implementation

8. top management support
9. importance of project to the user
10. similarity of own and organizational goals

Based on a factor analysis applied to the 25 adjective pairs under each semantic differential concept, 10 adjective pairs were chosen to be used in the fianl questionnaire. The selection process used to determine these adjective pairs consisted of a combination of heuristically evaluating the factor analysis and applying common sense to the appropriateness of these adjectives to the implementation problem.

An Instrument Revision

As a result of the pilot testing, the instrument was revised into the form used in the field test. Approximately half of the original items on the Likert scale were either dropped or modified, and a number of new items were added based upon the factor analysis and comments provided by an operations researcher who was very knowledgeable about the field setting in which the instrument would be tested. The final Likert scale consisted of 67 items.

The total of 11 semantic differential concepts comprised the semantic differential scale and were used in the field version of the instrument. They were:

1. the chance of success using this technique
2. confidence in the developers of the FORECAST*
3. changes in executive decision making
4. changes in the communication system
5. the effects on relationships with others
6. the FORECAST
7. the importance of this project to you
8. the amount of support being given to this project
9. the urgency of this project to the company
10. the technical complexity of this project
11. the amount of your personal participation required to implement this project

Dependent Variables

A number of dependent variables were proposed to determine whether the attitudinal factors would correlate with the stated likelihood of use by the

---

*FORECAST is the name of the sales forecasting model that was to be implemented in the company under study.

client. The relationship between intentions and actual use is not precise and future research, given an implementation attitudes instrument, can focus on *behavioral* and not just *attitudinal* correlates. The following 5 dependent variables were defined (and measured) by these statements:

1. Please circle the number on the scale below that indicates the probability that you will use the FORECAST.

   0 .1 .2 .3 .4 .5 .6 .7 .8 .9 1.0

2. Please circle the number on the scale below that indicates the probability that other managers will use the FORECAST.

   0 .1 .2 .3 .4 .5 .6 .7 .8 .9 1.0

3. Please circle the number on the scale below that indicates the probability that the FORECAST will be a success.

   0 .1 .2 .3 .4 .5 .6 .7 .8 .9 1.0

4. On the 10-point scale below indicate your evaluation of the worth of the FORECAST.

Not useful at all				Moderately useful					Excellent
1	2	3	4	5	6	7	8	9	10

5. Please circle the number on the scale below that indicates what level of accuracy you expect from the FORECAST.

Not accurate at all				Moderately accurate					Extremely accurate
1	2	3	4	5	6	7	8	9	10

The final instrument, then, consisting of 67 Likert items, 11 semantic differential concepts, and 5 dependent variables, was assembled and administered in a field setting.

The Sample

To management personnel in a large, basic metals manufacturing company 106 questionnaires were administered. The sample included district sales managers, assistant district sales managers, district sales administrative managers, industry managers, industry staff assistants, industry division managers, product managers, and two general managers. All of these individuals were asked by the OR staff to use a new computer forecasting model to assist them in short-term forecasts of sales. Ninety-four usable responses were received.

RESULTS

Two key questions were of interest in analyzing the data collected using this questionnaire. First, did conceptually meaningful and understandable attitudinal factors emerge from the questionnaire? Second, were these attitudinal dimensions correlated with the dependent variables having to do with model use and perceptions concerning the model? In order to answer these questions, several factor analyses were run and then a number of correlational analyses were completed examining the relationship between attitudinal dimensions and the dependent variables. The dimensions reveal the attitude structure toward the model.

Factor Analysis

An orthogonal factor analysis was performed on the 67 Likert items to determine the key attitudinal dimensions and to provide appropriate guidelines for scoring the questionnaire.

The factor analysis was made using the Factor Analysis Program (BMD 08M) of BMD Biomedical Computer Programs as implemented in the Digital Equipment Corporation's PDP-10. The varimax orthogonal rotation was used to produce the reported results [*8*].

One of the first decisions in factor analysis is specifying the number of factors to rotate. This is not a straightforward process, and Rummel (1970) has listed three categories of criteria for making this decision: inferential, mathematical, and rules of thumb. Using both inferential criteria (generalizability and meaningfulness) and rules of thumb (scree test, interpretability, and discontinuity), the number of factors was set at 7. This decision was based on analysis of the results produced by rotating 6 through 12 factors, respectively. The final factor solution was based on a rotation of 8 factors. One of these factors consisted of only 6 items that were uninterpretable, and it was discarded, resulting in 7 meaningful attitudinal factors. The summary of the results of this analysis is shown in Table 7.1.

Table 7.1 indicates that a reasonable separation exists on the factors, because only 14 items had a loading of .4 or more on more than 1 factor. In addition, the 7 factors listed accounted for 49 percent of the total variance. To

Table 7.1
Final Factor Loadings Likert Questionnaire Items

	Factors						
Item	I	II	III	IV	V	VI	VII
2	.63		.30				
3	.39			.35			.31
7	.59						.41
11	.44			.32			.48
14	.73						
22	.69						.32
27	.54		.43				
28	.73						
31	.64						.34
49	.47	.37					
59	.53						.55
60	.40		.47				
63	.36			.30		.35	.43
1		.43					
29		.73					
44		.61					
46		.71					
48		.77					
12			.49				
24			.58				
30			−.42			.34	
36		.31	.40				
20			.39	.33			
25			.48	.46			
26				.68			
32				.47			
42			.31	.42			
45				.46			
62	.35			.59			
66	.45			.50			
67			.31	.44			
4					.38		
10					.56		
21					.35		.43
33		.32	.43		−.43		
39		.30			−.59		
40					.67		
41					.45		.53
43					.67		
55				.35	−.52		
64					.36		
65					.67		
13			.33		.33	−.31	

Table 7.1—*Continued*

	Factors						
Item	I	II	III	IV	V	VI	VII
51						.79	
52						.82	
5				−.32			−.39
6							−.42
8				.41			.55
9	.31						.59
15	.56						.61
16	.59						.58
18							.71
23							.57
34							.73
47							.58
56							.80
61				.45			.49

give further interpretability to this factor analysis, the final version of the questionnaire is shown in Appendix I.

Of the initial 67 Likert items used in the field test, 10 were discarded because of low factor loadings or lack of interpretability. The remaining 57 Likert items are shown in Appendix I. In addition, so that the instrument might be readily available to other researchers, the semantic differential concepts are listed along with the ten adjective pairs selected for this portion of the instruments. Some additional information on the scoring of the attitude instrument appears in Appendix II.

Likert Factor Scores vs. Global Likert Score

A Likert factor score is computed by summing the scores for each questionnaire item loading significantly on the factor. For example, Table 7.1 shows that 16 items (item 2, 3, 7, 11, . . .) load significantly on Factor I, 5 items (1, 29, 44, 46 and 48) load significantly on Factor II, 4 items (12, 24, 30, and 36) load significantly on Factor III, and so forth. These results, together with the actual questions, also appear in Appendix I. Each individual, then has a Likert factor score for each of the 7 factors computed in this way. In addition, a global Likert score can be computed by summing across the 7 factor scores. This global score is an overall measure of the respondent's attitude toward the implementation (see Appendix II for details).

Table 7.2
Correlation of Likert Factor Scores with Global Likert Score
(n = 94)

	Likert factors						
	I	II	III	IV	V	VI	VII
Global Likert	.90	.28	.30	.79	.47	.45	.87

Key: Likert factors

I. Performance. Effect of model on manager's job performance.
II. Interpersonal. Interpersonal relations.
III. Changes. Changes resulting from the model.
IV. Goals. Goal achievement and congruence.
V. Support/resistance. Support for the model/lack of resistance.
VI. Client/researcher. Client/researcher interface.
VII. Urgency. Urgency for results.

It should be noted that these computed Likert factor scores are, in general, not equivalent to the "full" factor scores computed in the factor analysis. The latter scores are functions of all 67 items because an extracted factor is, by definition, a linear combination of the full set of items. Thus, the Likert factor scores used below represent, in effect, summary measures of attitude dimensions from a "new," more parsimonious instrument, but one in which the factors are not necessarily orthogonal.

The correlation of Likert factor scores with the global Likert score is an indication of the extent to which, say, an overall positive attitude toward the implementation is related to positive (or negative) attitudes on the individual factors. These correlations are shown in Table 7.2. They are notable in that performance, urgency, and goals are most highly correlated, and interpersonal and changes least highly correlated with the global Likert score. There is some indication from these data that factors II and III may not be reflecting the same "feeling toward the model" that the other factors seem to represent. This point will become more pertinent as we examine the other results.

Likert Factor Scores vs. Semantic Differential Concepts

As noted above, the semantic differential scale was employed in an exploratory fashion to augment the primary Likert scale. It is interesting to compare the two scales through the correlation of Likert factor scores with semantic differential concepts. These correlations are given in Table 7.3.

Table 7.3
Correlation of Likert Factor Scores with Semantic Differential Concepts*

	Semantic differential concepts†										
Likert Factors	**1**	**2**	**3**	**4**	**5**	**6**	**7**	**8**	**9**	**10**	**11**
I	.56	.37	.41	.45	.36	.53	.63	.29	.37	.40	.47
II	−.09	−.14	−.06	−.12	.08	.01	.02	−.10	−.05	.00	.08
III	−.01	.11	.01	.00	.04	−.10	.13	.08	.17	−.02	.14
IV	.51	.41	.45	.48	.39	.52	.45	.36	.38	.37	.38
V	.44	.45	.44	.33	.34	.44	.39	.47	.38	.30	.34
VI	.19	.29	.24	.24	.31	.27	.19	.29	.14	.11	.27
VII	.63	.46	.49	.53	.38	.60	.69	.39	.51	.41	.42
Global Likert	.63	.49	.52	.53	.46	.62	.68	.43	.50	.44	51

*$n = 94$; $r = .20$; $p < .05$
†For definitions of the semantic differential concepts, see page 159.

The correlation of the global Likert score with the 11 concepts is generally high, ranging from $r = .43$ to $r = .68$ and exceeds the .50 level in 7 of 11 cases. Of the individual Likert factors, we note that II and III (again) are very weakly correlated with any semantic differential concepts. There are no significant correlations in rows 2 and 3. Some "direct" comparisons of Likert factors and semantic differential concepts are possible. For example, semantic differential concept 9 is urgency as is Likert factor VII: in column 9, the correlation with row 7 ($r = .51$) is the highest. Similarly, semantic differential concept 8 is support as is Likert factor V: in column 8, the correlation with row 5 ($r = .47$) is the highest. Other comparisons of this sort are less direct, and there appears to be some inconsistency between the scales in measuring changes and interpersonal relations.

There is no relative advantage of the semantic differential scale in this case. In addition, the semantic differential concepts are highly intercorrelated. For these reasons, we continue to regard the Likert factor scores and the global Likert score as the primary measures of implementation attitudes in the subsequent analysis.

Correlation Analysis

Because of our interest in assessing attitudes and in predicting the chances of success of an implementation, we are concerned with the relationships between the attitude dimensions and the dependent variables. Three basic analyses are possible. First, the simple correlations among Likert factor scores, global Likert scores, semantic differntial concepts, and the dependent variables can be examined; second, the multivariate structure of the data can be analyzed through multiple regression analysis; and, third, possible differences (in attitude profiles) between intended users and intended nonusers can be explored with multiple discriminant analysis. The latter two techniques (discriminant analysis is a special case of regression analysis) require some theory of implementation against which the results can be evaluated. In this chapter, our goals are more modest: We are seeking to develop an instrument and to lay the groundwork for future theory building and testing. For this reason, we confine the present discussion of statistical results to the correlation analysis and draw conclusions regarding the potential of the instrument and the nature of subsequent research.

The results of the correlation analysis are shown in Table 7.4. As can be seen from an examination of the results, a substantial number of attitudinal variables correlated significantly with the 5 dependent variables. Of the 95 correlations given in the table, a total of 83 are significant at the .05 level or better. All of the global Likert and semantic differential correlations are significant and 23 of the 35 individual Likert correlations are significant. The important question is: What is the pattern of these correlations?

The first pattern to be noticed is that the correlations are generally higher for the worth-accuracy dependent variables than for the probability of use-success variables. Correlations of Likert factor scores with dependent variables 4 and 5 are uniformly higher than with dependent variables 1 and 2 if Likert factors II and III are excluded. These results suggest that the attitude instrument may have value not only in revealing salient attitude dimensions but also in predicting evaluations of accuracy and worth as well as probability of use.

In the Likert section of Table 4, factors II and III, interpersonal and changes stand out because of their low and insignificant correlations. In some cases the correlations are insignificant and negative. These results suggest that changes and interpersonal relations are not related to measures of intended use or evaluations of accuracy and worth. If they are related, it may be in a negative way such that a status quo effect inhibits implementation. In this case, changes and interpersonal relations are not significant attitudes toward the model, although they may represent significant feelings toward the general (job) situation that were not tested.

The most interesting dependent variable is perhaps the first, representing an individual's *own* intended use. The results indicate that two factors are most important: performance and urgency (r = .60 and r = .59, respectively). These are *personal* factors and suggest that the appeal of a model to a manager may be greatest in terms of "what can the model do for him." Support and goals are also important (r = .30 and r = .26, respectively). These factors seem to be *organizational* and suggest that they augment personal benefits in the manager's mind.

Table 7.4
Correlation Analysis—Likert Factor Scores, Global Likert Score, and Semantic Differential Concepts vs. Dependent Variables*

	Dependent variables†				
Likert Factors	**1**	**2**	**3**	**4**	**5**
I	.60	.45	.51	.59	.61
II	.08	.04	−.04	−.02	.13
III	.01	−.02	.08	.04	.13
IV	.26	.30	.50	.54	.50
V	.30	.30	.43	.35	.31
VI	.10	.12	.36	.20	.29
VII	.59	.54	.56	.69	.60
Global Likert	.56	.49	.62	.66	.66
Semantic differential concepts	**1**	**2**	**3**	**4**	**5**
1	.53	.46	.61	.68	.61
2	.32	.25	.43	.48	.36
3	.34	.36	.52	.44	.51
4	.33	.35	.49	.47	.46
5	.33	.29	.34	.37	.31
6	.47	.42	.57	.61	.55
7	.68	.47	.53	.68	.53
8	.25	.34	.38	.37	.39
9	.33	.36	.39	.50	.35
10	.38	.29	.29	.41	.29
11	.39	.28	.31	.39	.41

*$n = 94$; $r = .20$; $p < .05$

†For a definition of dependent variables, see page 160.

Client/researcher is not significant, but this may be a special case. The model in this study was designed at the corporate staff level without much (if any) interaction with most ultimate users. For this reason, the client/researcher relationship may be interpreted as irrelevant by the manager who is being asked to use the model. Notice that this factor is significant when the respondent assesses the accuracy and worth of the model. As noted above, interpersonal and changes are not significant.

The results for the second dependent variable, the probability of others using the model, are roughly similar. Urgency is the most important in this case;

otherwise the conclusions are identical. For the third dependent variable, the probability that the model will be a success, urgency, performance, goals, and support are most important. Client/researcher is not significant, but interpersonal and change are not. These results imply that a number of factors are related to "total success" of the implementation, among them being the quality of the client/researcher relationship.

For the worth-accuracy evaluations, dependent variables 4 and 5, the results are similar. Urgency, performance, and goals are most important; support and client/researcher are important; interpersonal and change are not significant. It is interesting to note that the client/researcher relationship is more highly correlated with accuracy than with worth (r = .29 and r = .20, respectively). These results again suggest a set of relevant attitude dimensions that may be related to affect variables. From a statistical viewpoint, it is important to note that the "importance" of factors is deduced without regard for the intercorrelations among them. In a multivariate analysis, we would expect (and have found) that a subset of the factors explain most of the variance. Future research should focus on the *relative* importance of the factors.

The global Likert correlations are highest for the worth-accuracy measures, then success, then own intended use, and finally lowest for others' intended use. This sequence is logical (e.g., we expect that it is more straightforward to assess the worth of a model, less to assess own use, least to assess others' use) and shows that the global Likert is an efficient and promising measure for future research.

Given the success of the Likert factors, the semantic differential concepts are relatively less important but nonetheless interesting. For the primary dependent variable, probability of own use, the concepts "the importance of this project to you" and "the chance of success using this technique" are most highly correlated, again suggesting that *personal* factors may be the key to successful implementation.

Finally, this study of attitudes and intended behavior should be put into the broader perspective of previous behavioral work in this and other areas. Our basic conclusion is that, in predicting individual behavior, correlations in the neighborhood of .60 are extremely high and thus the attitude dimensions are salient and, more importantly, the instrument can be used in future research.

CONCLUSIONS

The principal conclusions of this study fall into two categories: research implications and policy implications. In both cases, the results are discussed with a view toward future work.

Research Implications

As we have previously discussed, the organizational validity of an OR/MS model is its compatibility with the user organization. According to this theory, the greater the compatibility or fit between the model and the potential user, the greater the probability of use, other things being equal (namely, the technical validity of the model). We have suggested earlier (cf. Chapter 3) that a quantitative measure of the fit between a model and an organization is the degree of organizational change required to implement the model. This degree of change could be measured by the distance between the initial and final states of each variable, such as

$$\text{Change} = (X_1 - X_0)$$

where

X_1 is the required state of individual variables

X_0 is the actual state of individual variables

In the full theory, small group and organizational variables are considered as well, but here we limit the analysis to individual attitudes (X). The research plan to test this theory involves the following steps:

1. Find dimensions of X.
2. Measure X_0.
3. Measure X_1.
4. Show how $(X_1 - X_0)$ is related to actual use.

The present study aids in defining the dimensions of X and in providing a measure of X_0 (i.e., the attitude instrument). Future work must proceed with measuring X_1 by analyzing dimensions of successful models and then with demonstrating how organizational change affects actual use.

It is important to note that organizational change is defined as an *ex ante* measure because the organization and model developers can and presumably will act to bring the model into conformity with the organization or vice versa. The point is that organizational change is a barrier that, if not overcome, will inhibit successful implementation.

The study presented here has, we think, other important implications for building implementation theory. In Figure 7.2, we suggest schematically how this theory building might proceed. In part (a) we show two relationships explored in this research and one that is currently under investigation. The relationships between the set of attitude factors, $[F]$, and, respectively, worth and intended use, D_4 and D_1, are found to be empirically quite strong. At this point, the relationship between intended use and actual use, D_A, is not known.

(a) attitudes ⟶ worth
[F] $r \geqslant .69$ D_4

attitudes ⟶ intended use
[F] $r \geqslant .60$ D_1

intended use ⟶ actual use
D_1 $r = ?$ D_A

(b) attitudes ⟶ worth ⟶ intended use ⟶ actual use
[F] $r \geqslant .69$ D_4 $r = .61$ D_1 $r = ?$ D_A

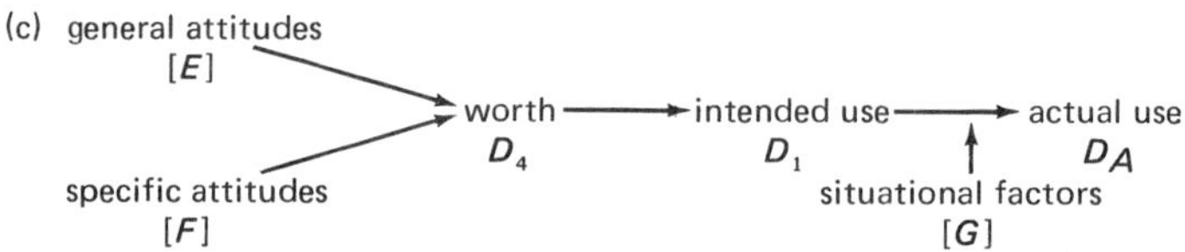

(d) implementation choice model ∩ human choice model

Fig. 7.2 Building Implementation Theory

These relationships are isolated, however, and there is a question of how they fit together. In part (b) of Figure 7.2 we show one possible model of the interrelationship. In this model, we assume that attitudes affect worth, which in turn affects intended use, which is then related to actual use. The relationship of worth and intended use is again quite high (r = .61) as are other correlations between the dependent variables as can be seen in Table 7.5. A further step in theory development may be the model in part (c). Here we include general as

Table 7.5
Correlation Matrix of Dependent Variables*

	Dependent variables				
	1	**2**	**3**	**4**	**5**
1	1.00	.61	.51	.61	.48
2		1.00	.63	.49	.51
3			1.00	.68	.61
4				1.00	.66
5					1.00

*$n = 94; r = .20; p < .05$

well as specific attitudes such that the general attitudes, [*E*], are basically those toward such ideas as performance and models and specific attitudes, [*F*], are those (measured here) toward specific models and toward various *dimensions* of models (cf. Reference *20*). In addition this more complex model includes situational factors, [*G*], which undoubtedly come into play between intended and actual use. In all cases we have used the variable worth to reflect overall value to the manager as well as accuracy. This is consistent with the definition in the attitude instrument.

The final form of an implementation choice model (part d) will intersect with a general model of human choice because the former is just a special case of the latter. This model will be quite complex, recognizing the dynamic nature of the process, feedback links, and simultaneous causality. However, it may be that for practical purposes (as opposed to scientific work) the simpler models can be used with good predictive success. This provides the basis for additional research in real organizations using the current instrument and provisional models.

Before testing theory and building new theories of implementation, it will be useful to gather more data on implementation situations in a variety of organizations. We hope that an attitude instrument, such as the one presented in this chapter, will provide a vehicle for obtaining these data. In a data-rich environment, research on implementation can proceed to realize its scientific objective.

Policy Implications

Despite the preliminary nature of this research, some policy implications emerge that can be considered by those responsible for *managing* implementation. First it may be most useful to emphasize the *personal benefits* of the model or innovation. By stressing how its use will help the manager himself, the likelihood of successful implementation may be increased. Second, by giving *general (top management) support* and by indicating *goal congruence* between organizational tasks and the model, the implementers may facilitate model use. Third, where the potential user is involved with the researcher, or should be involved, *the relationship between the client and the researcher,* is important to implementation success. Finally, *change* and *interpersonal relations* do not seem to be very critical and may be factors to be deemphasized in managing implementation. These prescriptions are tentative, of course, but the careful manager and management scientist can benefit by relating them to his own organization.

Research on implementation is, by definition, management relevant. The interplay between research and management practice is perhaps nowhere more dynamic and is certainly most evident in the nexus of implementation problems. Progress is being made and, in the final analysis, success may turn on the implementation of implementation research itself.

References

1. Argyris, Chris, "Management Information Systems: The Challenge to Rationality and Emotionality," *Management Science,* **17,** no. 6, B275–B292 (February, 1971).
2. Bennis, Warren G., "Commentary on 'The Researcher and the Manager: A Dialectic of Implementation,' " *Management Science,* **12,** no. 2, B13–B16 (October 1965).
3. Christie, Richard, and Geis, Florence L., *Studies in Machiavellianism,* New York: Academic Press, 1970.
4. Churchman, C. W., and Schainblatt, A. H., "An Mutual Understanding," *Management Science,* **12,** no. 2, B40–B42 (October 1965).
5. Clark, R. D., III, "Group Induced Shift Toward Risk: A Critical Appraisal," *Psychological Bulletin,* **76,** 251–270 (1971).
6. Dickson, John W., and Slevin, Dennis P., "The Use of Semantic Differential Scales in Studying the Innovation Boundary," Working Paper #46, Graduate School of Business, University of Pittsburgh, May 1973.
7. Dion, K. L., Baron, R. S., and Miller, N., "Why Do Groups Make Riskier Decisions than Individuals?", in Berkowitz, L. (Ed.), *Advances in Experimental Social Psychology, Vol. 5,* New York: Academic Press, 1970.
8. Dixon, W. J. (Ed.), *BMD Biomedical Computer Programs,* Berkeley: University of California Press, 1973.
9. Fishbein, Martin, and Raven, Bertram H., "The AB Scales: An Operational Definition of Belief and Attitude," *Human Relations,* **15,** 35–44 (1962).
10. Fishbein, Martin (Ed.), *Readings and Attitude Theory and Measurement,* New York: Wiley, 1967.
11. Forrester, Jay W., *Industrial Dynamics,* Cambridge, Mass.: The MIT Press, 1961.
12. Hertz, David B., "Implementing an Operations Research Program," *Banking,* **58,** 47–49 (March 1966).
13. Insko, Chester A., *Theories of Attitude Change,* New York: Appleton-Century-Crofts, 1967.
14. Kotler, Philip, *Marketing Decision Making: A Model Building Approach,* New York: Holt, Rinehart and Winston, 1971.
15. Likert, Rensis, "A Technique for the Measurement of Attitudes," *Archives of Psychology,* no. 140, 44–53 (1932).
16. Little, John D., "Models and Managers: The Concept of a Decision Calculus," *Management Science,* **16,** no. 8, B466–B485 (April 1970).
17. March, James G., and Simon, Herbert A., *Organizations,* New York: Wiley, 1958.
18. Osgood, C. E., Suci, G. J., and Tannenbaum, P. H., *The Measurement of Meaning,* Urbana, Ill.: University of Illinois Press, 1957.
19. Radnor, Michael, and Rubenstein, Albert H., and Tansik, David A., "Implementation in Operations Research and R&D in Government at Business Organizations," *Operations Research,* **18,** 967–991 (November–December 1970).
20. Schultz, Randall L., and Slevin, Dennis P., "Behavioral Considerations in the Implementation of Marketing Decision Models," *Combined Proceedings,* Spring and Fall Conference, American Marketing Association, 1972, pp. 494–498.
21. Schultz, Randall L., and Slevin, Dennis P., "A Program of Research on Implementation," presented at the Conference "The Implementation of OR/MS Models: Theory, Research and Application," Graduate School of Business, University of Pittsburgh, November, 1973.
22. Shakun, Melvin F. "Management Science and Management: Implementing Management

Science Via Situational Normativism," *Management Science,* **18,** no. 8, B367–377 (April 1972).

23. Slevin, Susan M., "An Annotated Bibliography on the Implementation of Operations Research/Management Science Techniques," September 1973, unpublished.
24. Stoner, J. A. F., "A Comparison of Individual and Group Decisions Involving Risk," unpublished Masters thesis, Massachusetts Institute of Technology, Sloan School of Management, 1961.
25. Vroom, Victor and Yetton, Philip, *Leadership and Decision Making,* Pittsburgh: University of Pittsburgh Press, 1973.

Appendix I

COMPLETE DESCRIPTION OF IMPLEMENTATION ATTITUDES QUESTIONNAIRE

This appendix contains a complete description of both the Likert and semantic differential instruments.

LIKERT INSTRUCTIONS

Instructions for Part 1

You are asked to read each statement carefully and to circle one of the words from each following line that describes most clearly how you feel about the statement, e.g.,

I find the FORECAST interesting.

Strongly Disagree	Disagree	Uncertain	(Agree)	Strongly Agree

This would indicate that you agree with the statement.

Please keep in mind that what is important is your own opinion.

The FORECAST is a technique that is presently being considered for implementation. Remember, this questionnaire is asking for *your opinion about the FORECAST.*

Each item implies ". . . after the implementation," that is, this questionnaire is concerned with how you feel about each statement as it applies to the situation *after the FORECAST is operational.*

Each item implies that changes will occur *after the FORECAST* is in use. For example, statement 2

"My job will be more satisfying."

implies

My job will be more satisfying . . . *after the FORECAST is in use.*

IMPLEMENTATION ATTITUDES QUESTIONNAIRE

Factor List

Factor 1.
PERFORMANCE

Effect of Model on Manager's Job Performance and Performance Visibility

Loading	Item	Description
.63	2	My job will be more satisfying.
.39	3	Others will better see the results of my efforts.
.59	7	It will be easier to perform my job well.
.44	11	The accuracy of information I receive will be improved by the FORECAST.
.73	14	I will have more control over my job.
.69	22	I will be able to improve my performance.
.53	27	Others will be more aware of what I am doing.
.73	28	The information I will receive from the FORECAST will make my job easier.
.64	31	I will spend less time looking for information.
.47	49	I will be able to see better the results of my efforts.
.53	59	The accuracy of *my* forecast will improve as the result of using the FORECAST.
.40	60	My performance will be more closely monitored.
.36	63	The division/department will perform better.

Factor 2.
INTERPERSONAL

Interpersonal Relations, Communication, and Increased Interaction and Consultation with Others

Loading	Item	Description
.43	1	I will need to communicate with others more.
.73	29	I will need the help of others more.
.61	44	I will need to consult others more often before making a decision.
.71	46	I will need to talk with other people more.
.77	48	I will need the help of others more.

Factor 3.
CHANGES

Changes Will Occur in Organizational Structure and People I Deal with

Loading	Item	Description
.49	12	The individuals I work with will change.
.58	24	The management structure will be changed.
−.42	30	The FORECAST will not require any changes in division/department structure.
.40	36	I will have to get to know several new people.

Factor 4.
GOALS

Goals Will Be More Clear, More Congruent to Workers, and More Achievable

Loading	Item	Description
.33	20	Individuals will set higher targets for performance.
.46	25	The use of the FORECAST will increase profits.
.68	26	This project is technically sound.
.47	32	Company goals will become more clear.
.42	42	My counterparts in other divisions/departments will identify more with the organization's goals.
.46	45	The patterns of communication will be more simplified.
.59	62	My goals and the company goals will be more similar than they are now.
.50	66	The aims of my counterparts in other divisions/departments will be more easily achieved.
.43	67	My personal goals will be better reconciled with the company goals.

Continued.

Factor 5. SUPPORT/RESISTANCE

Model Has Implementation Support-Adequate Top Management, Technical, and Organizational Support and Does Not Have Undue Resistance

Loading	Item	Description
.38	4	Top management will provide the resources to implement the FORECAST.
.56	10	People will accept the required changes.
.35	21	Top management sees the FORECAST as being important.
−.43	33	Implementing the FORECAST will be difficult.
−.59	39	Top management does not realize how complex this change is.
.67	40	People will be given sufficient training to utilize the FORECAST.
.45	41	This project is important to top management.
.67	43	There will be adequate staff available to successfully implement the FORECAST.
−.52	55	My counterparts in other divisions/departments are generally resistant to changes of this type.
.36	64	Personal conflicts will not increase as a result of the FORECAST.
.67	65	The developers of the FORECAST will provide adequate training to users.

Factor 6. CLIENT/RESEARCHER

Researchers Understand Management Problems and Work Well with Their Clients

Loading	Item	Description
−.21	13	The developers of these techniques don't understand management problems.
.79	51	I enjoy working with those who are implementing the FORECAST.
.81	52	When I talk to those implementing the FORECAST, they respect my opinions.

Factor 7.
URGENCY

Need for Results, Even With Costs Involved; Importance To Me, Boss, Top Management

Loading	Item	Description
−.39	5	The FORECAST costs too much.
−.42	6	I will be supported by my boss if I decide not to use this model.
.55	8	Decisions based on the FORECAST will be better.
.60	9	The results of the FORECAST are needed now.
.61	15	The FORECAST is important to me.
.58	16	I need the FORECAST.
.71	18	It is important that the FORECAST be used soon.
.57	23	This project is important to my boss.
.71	34	The FORECAST should be put into use immediately.
.58	47	It is urgent that the FORECAST be implemented.
.80	56	The sooner the FORECAST is in use the better.
.49	61	Benefits will outweigh the costs.

LIKERT ITEMS THAT DID NOT LOAD SIGNIFICANTLY ON A FACTOR OR WERE NOT INTERPRETABLE

17. The developers of these techniques seldom consult with the people who use them.
19. Implementing the FORECAST will take a lot of my time.
35. I will see less of my friends in the organization.
37. I will report to a different boss.
38. Many other people in the company will be affected.
50. People will realize that the FORECAST is an improvement.
53. I will be in a better position to reach my goals.
54. Others do not see the FORECAST as being important.
57. The FORECAST is worth the time required to implement it.
58. I will play an important role in the implementation of the FORECAST.

DEPENDENT VARIABLES
(Questions 68–72)

1. Please circle the number on the scale below that indicates the probability that you will use the FORECAST.

0 .1 .2 .3 .4 .5 .6 .7 .8 .9 1.0

2. Please circle the number on the scale below that indicates the probability that other managers will use the FORECAST.

0 .1 .2 .3 .4 .5 .6 .7 .8 .9 1.0

3. Please circle the number on the scale below that indicates the probability that the FORECAST will be a success.

0 .1 .2 .3 .4 .5 .6 .7 .8 .9 1.0

4. On the 10-point scale below indicate your evaluation of the worth of the FORECAST.

Not useful at all				Moderately useful					Excellent
1	2	3	4	5	6	7	8	9	10

5. Please circle the number on the scale below that indicates the level of accuracy you expect from the FORECAST.

Not accurate at all				Moderately accurate					Extremely accurate
1	2	3	4	5	6	7	8	9	10

SEMANTIC DIFFERENTIAL INSTRUCTIONS

Instructions for Part 2

The purpose of this study is to measure the *meanings* of certain things to various people by having them judge them against a series of descriptive scales. In taking this test, please make your judgments on the basis of what these things mean *to you.* On each page of this handout you will find a different concept to be judged and beneath it a set of scales. You are to rate the concept on each of these scales in order.

Here is how you are to use these scales:

If you feel that the concept at the top of the page is *very closely related* to one or the other end of the scale, you should place your check mark as follows:

important √ : ____ : ____ : ____ : ____ : ____ : ____ unimportant
important ____ : ____ : ____ : ____ : ____ : ____ : √ unimportant

If you feel that the concept is *quite closely related* to one or the other end of the scale (but not extremely), you should place your check mark as follows:

good ___ : √ : ___ : ___ : ___ : ___ : ___ bad
good ___ : ___ : ___ : ___ : ___ : √ : ___ bad

If the concept seems *only slightly related* to one side as opposed to the other side (but is not really neutral), then you should check as follows:

beneficial ___ : ___ : √ : ___ : ___ : ___ : ___ harmful
beneficial ___ : ___ : ___ : ___ : √ : ___ : ___ harmful

The direction toward which you check, of course, depends upon which of the two ends of the scale seem most characteristic of the thing you're judging. If you consider the concept to be *neutral* on the scale, both sides of the scale *equally associated* with the concept, or if the scale is *completely irrelevant*, unrelated to the concept, then you should place your checkmark in the middle space:

useful ___ : ___ : ___ : √ : ___ : ___ : ___ useless

Important:

(1) Place your check marks in the middle of spaces, not on the boundaries:

correct incorrect
___ : √ : ___ : ___ : √ : ___

(2) Be sure you check every scale for every concept–*do not omit any,*
(3) Never put more than one check mark on a single scale.

Sometimes you may feel as though you've had the same item before on the test. This will not be the case, so *do not look back and forth* through the items. Do not try to remember how you checked similar items earlier in the test. *Make each item a separate and independent judgment.* Work at fairly high speed through this test. Do not worry or puzzle over individual items. It is your first impressions, the immediate "feelings" about the items, that we want. On the other hand, please do not be careless, because we want your true impressions.

Please mark all of the following scales in the same manner as shown in the examples on the previous page. REMEMBER, all concepts listed at the top of the scales refer to the FORECAST.

SEMANTIC DIFFERENTIAL CONCEPTS

1. The chance of success using this technique
2. Confidence in the developers of the FORECAST
3. Changes in executive decision making

4. Changes in the communication system
5. The effects on relationships with others
6. The FORECAST
7. The importance of this project to you
8. The amount of support being given to this project
9. The urgency of this project to the company
10. The technical complexity of this project
11. The amount of your personal participation required to implement this project

SEMANTIC DIFFERENTIAL ADJECTIVE PAIRS

	(7)	(6)	(5)	(4)	(3)	(2)	(1)	
good	___	___	___	___	___	___	___	bad
beneficial	___	___	___	___	___	___	___	harmful
optimistic	___	___	___	___	___	___	___	pessimistic
hopeful	___	___	___	___	___	___	___	hopeless
harmonious	___	___	___	___	___	___	___	dissonant
comfortable	___	___	___	___	___	___	___	uncomfortable
fortunate	___	___	___	___	___	___	___	unfortunate
important	___	___	___	___	___	___	___	unimportant
useful	___	___	___	___	___	___	___	useless
wise	___	___	___	___	___	___	___	foolish

Scoring

The semantic differential is scored by assigning the values shown in parentheses to the locations on the scale. In the list above, the high scoring side of the scale is at all times on the left. The values checked are summed and divided by 10 to compute the final score.

APPENDIX II

LIKERT SCORING NOTES FOR IMPLEMENTATION ATTITUDES QUESTIONNAIRE

Purpose

The purpose of this appendix is to describe the global Likert scoring legend for the Implementation Attitudes Questionnaire. The questionnaire is intended to give factor scores on the 7 attitudinal factors that emerged from the data analysis and also to provide an overall global score that is indicative of how positive the respondents attitude is toward the implementation. The following analysis combines a look at the final factor loading (7 factors), and evaluation of the direction of correlation with each of the 5 dependent variables (items 68–72 on the questionnaire), and a common-sense interpretation of the directionality of the item.

The final column on the table below indicates whether the item is scored in the positive direction, negative direction, or not counted (+, –, 0) in determining the global summated Likert score for the attitude of the respondent. Out of the 67 original items, only the 57 that were kept as the result of the final factor analysis are counted in the final calculation of the global Likert score.

Analysis of Factor Loadings, Correlations with Dependent Variables, and Common-Sense Interpretations of Items to Generate Likert Scoring Legend

			Correlation with dependent variables						
Item	Factor loading	Factor number	1	2	3	4	5	Common-sense interpre-tation	Final scoring direction
1	.43	2						0	+
2	.63	1	.36			.44	.43	+	+
3	.39	1	.24	.26	.36	.31	.48	+	+
4	.38	5						+	+
5	–.39	7		–.26	–.29	–.20	.19	–	–
6	–.42	7	–.34	–.29	–.27	–.32	–.27	–	–
7	.59	1	.63	.38	.44	.54	.42	+	+
8	.55	7	.41	.47	.59	.56	.48	+	+
9	.59	7	.47	.44	.42	.47	.38	+	+
10	.56	5			.29			+	+
11	.44	1	.40	.36	.48	.58	.48	+	+
12	.49	3			.21			0	+
13	–.31	6			–.33	–.25	–.26	–	–
14	.73	1	.35	.32	.27	.38	.40	+	+
15	.61	7	.70	.46	.41	.63	.54	+	+
16	.58	7	.60	.42	.42	.63	.57	+	+
17									0
18	.71	7	.33	.36	.32	.40	.38	+	+
19									0
20	.33	4	.21	.28	.25	.28	.39	+	+
21	.35	5	.29	.37	.30	.32	.36	+	+
22	.69	1	.54	.44	.49	.50	.54	+	+
23	.57	7	.29	.28	.24	.36	.43	+	+
24	.58	3						0	+
25	.46	4			.25	.24	.31	+	+
26	.68	4			.47	.35	.31	+	+
27	.54	1	.27		.22	.33	40	+	+
28	.73	1	.49	.21	.33	.40	.35	+	+
29	.73	2						+	+

Item	Factor loading	Factor number	Correlation with dependent variables 1	2	3	4	5	Common sense interpretation	Final scoring direction
30	−.42	3	.21	.25				−	−
31	.64	1	.45	.38	.47	.46	.50	+	+
32	.47	4			.38	.45	.36	+	+
33	−.43	5	.31	.36	.45	−.46	−.32	−	−
34	.73	7	.46	.49	.43	.51	.41	+	+
35									0
36	.40	3					.23	+	+
37									0
38									0
39	−.59	5	−.24		−.26	−.22		−	−
40	.67	5			.21			+	+
41	.45	5	.30	.34	.24	.30	.36	+	+
42	.31	4			.21	.31	.36	+	+
43	.67	5			.28			+	+
44	.61	2						0	+
45	.46	4		.22	.39	.39	.30	+	+
46	.71	2			.20			+	+
47	.58	7	.27	.25	.33	.52	.32	+	+
48	.77	2						+	+
49	.47	1	.38		.34	.30	.33	+	+
50									0
51	.79	5						+	+
52	.82	5						+	+
53									0
54									0
55	−.52	5	.23		−.22			−	−
56	.80	7	.48	.42	.42	.46	.39	+	+
57									0
58									0
59	.53	1	.70	.42	.42	.48	.41	+	+
60	.40	1					.28	0	+
61	.49	7	.30	.36	.57	.62	.53	+	+
62	.59	4			.25	.29	.21	+	+
63	.36	1	.38	.49	.53	.48	.50	+	+
64	.36	5		.27	.23	.22		+	+
65	.67	5			.35	.26	.22	+	+
66	.50	4	.27	.29	.43	.40	43	+	+
67	.44	4				.29		+	+

Chapter 8

Implementation Attitudes: A Model and a Measurement Methodology

John H. Manley

The success or failure of operations research/management science (OR/MS) models is often dependent upon the attitudes of the people directly affected by them. In this sense, the OR/MS model is an attitude object that can portray a positive, negative, or neutral image to any individual. When its image is positive, it will be supported and probably be implemented successfully, but, when it evokes a negative image, it will be resisted by the organization and implementation will be difficult, if not impossible.

If the operations researcher and manager can somehow measure the attitudes of the people to be affected by a proposed OR/MS product toward that product, it follows that the implementers will be better prepared to select an effective implementation strategy. This approach will help prevent the not infrequent surprises when seemingly utopian OR/MS innovation diffusion projects fail through massive organizational resistance, or even sabotage.

Most recent investigations into methods for improving the management of OR/MS technological change have emphasized the roles of operations researcher/management scientist and manager together with their interpersonal relationships. Little attention has been paid to those persons at the working level whose organizational behavior patterns are directly affected by such change and who, in return, affect the implementation process.*

This chapter focuses on the triad, management scientist-manager-client, where client is defined to be a recipient of an operations research/management science product who does not have any *de jure* authority to decide whether or not to accept or use it. The behavioral response of these individuals to OR/MS innovations can be measured in such a way that the results can be used to predict the probability of success for the innovations. The chapter concludes

*This constitutes the formal feedback loop from the organization in the Behavioral Model Building (BMB) paradigm described in Chapter 3.

with a discussion of the results of experimenting with this new measurement technique in a real-world organization.

RESEARCH METHODOLOGY

The research conducted to develop an implementation attitude measurement model was originally performed as part of the author's doctoral dissertation [*8*]. Specifically, it was directed toward solving the following set of sequential problems:

1. Isolating and precisely defining certain critical factors that signal behavioral response in individuals to external stimuli within the context of OR/MS product implementation.

2. Developing a mathematical scoring model for producing a measure of group "sociological resistance to change." This problem involved mathematically describing the client resistance process in terms of significant variables, which, when properly related, provided a measure of the probability of OR/MS implementation project success due to client behavior.

3. Developing a questionnaire to gather data generated by the defining signaling factors that could be used by the scoring model.*

4. Testing the validity and usefulness of the measurement methodology by performing a field experiment on a real-world organization (a large suburban elementary- and secondary-school district). A hypothetical OR/MS recommendation for change was imposed upon a client group (school teachers) using an appropriate experimental design incorporating the following experimental treatments:

a. Variation in the degree of chief-executive (school district superintendent) support expressed for the OR/MS project.

b. Variation in the level of client involvement required for product implementation.

c. Variation in the degree of relevance of the product to various members of the client group subjected to it.

Completion of this sequence of research activity was used to test the following working, or alternative, hypotheses:

Hypothesis 1

Variations in the behavioral response of clients to an OR/MS product can be measured and used to provide an indicator of the probability of success of implementing that product due to such behavior.

*See Chapter 14 for additional rationale suggesting this approach.

Hypothesis 2

Differences in the level of chief-executive support expressed for an OR/MS product will cause significant variations in client resistance to (or support for) that product.

Hypothesis 3

Differences in the degree to which clients are required to become personally involved in the implementation of a particular OR/MS product will cause significant variations in their support for (or resistance to) such a product.

Hypothesis 4

Differences in the degree of relevance of a particular OR/MS product to a client group will affect the degree to which they support (or resist) such a product.

OR/MS IMPLEMENTATION PROCESS THEORY

Three principal groups of decision makers, i.e., managers, management scientists, and clients, participate in the OR/MS innovation diffusion process through the set of dynamic communication feedback loops illustrated in Figure 8.1. It is shown that each group has the opportunity to impede or even prevent implementation from taking place, as well as to provide support for OR/MS products. The primary consideration that arises from viewing implementation this way is one of trying to determine how management scientist innovators can influence *both* the management and client groups to accept their products.

In addition to the influence the participating groups have upon each other, there are numerous other variables that affect client behavior toward implementation. Figure 8.2 illustrates how some of the various factors that exert pressure upon clients to implement an OR/MS product are counteracted somewhat by still other factors that cause resistance to such change. This conflict normally results in some equilibrium level of resistance for each client affected by the product. Note that this concept also applies to managers and management scientists but the relative effects of the individual factors are not normally the same on these participants. For example, a product that seems highly relevant to the management scientist and manager may not be perceived as relevant by the clients at all. Similarly, the sense of urgency or technical adequacy of the

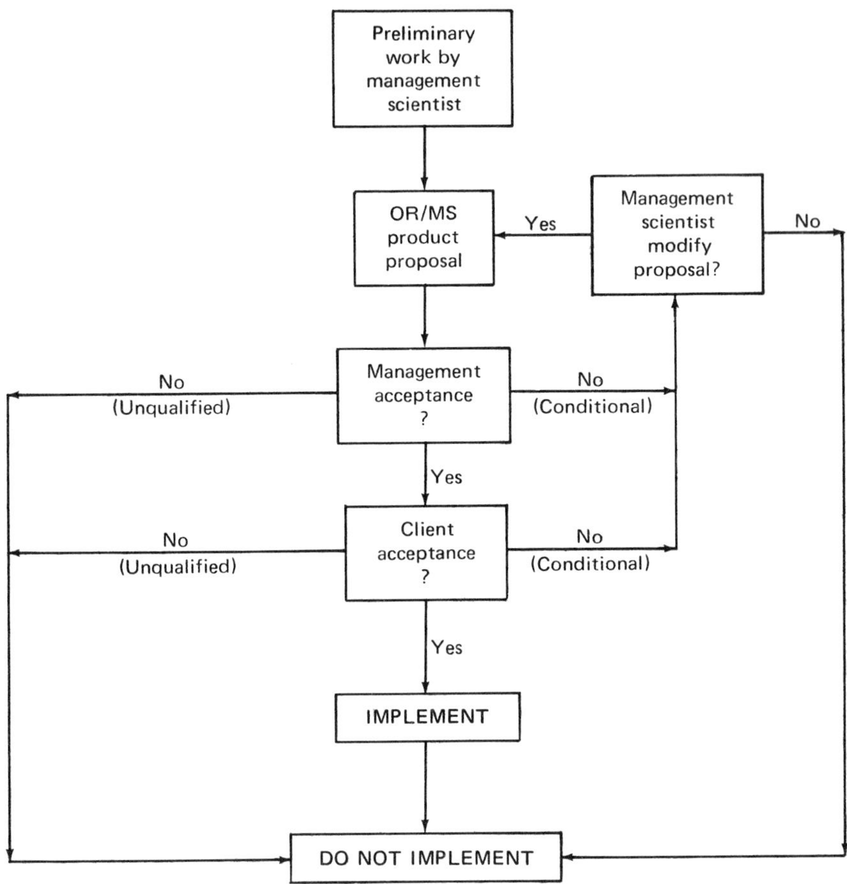

Fig. 8.1 The OR/MS Product Implementation Decision Process

product is almost always perceived differently by each of the three groups involved in the implementation process.

Client Resistance Concepts

Assume a situation in which a single client is faced with a specific OR/MS proposal for technological improvement that requires his personal involvement. Assume further that a single external variable can be isolated that might cause his resistance to the proposed change to either increase or decrease. For purposes of illustration, let such an external variable be the client's perceived degree of

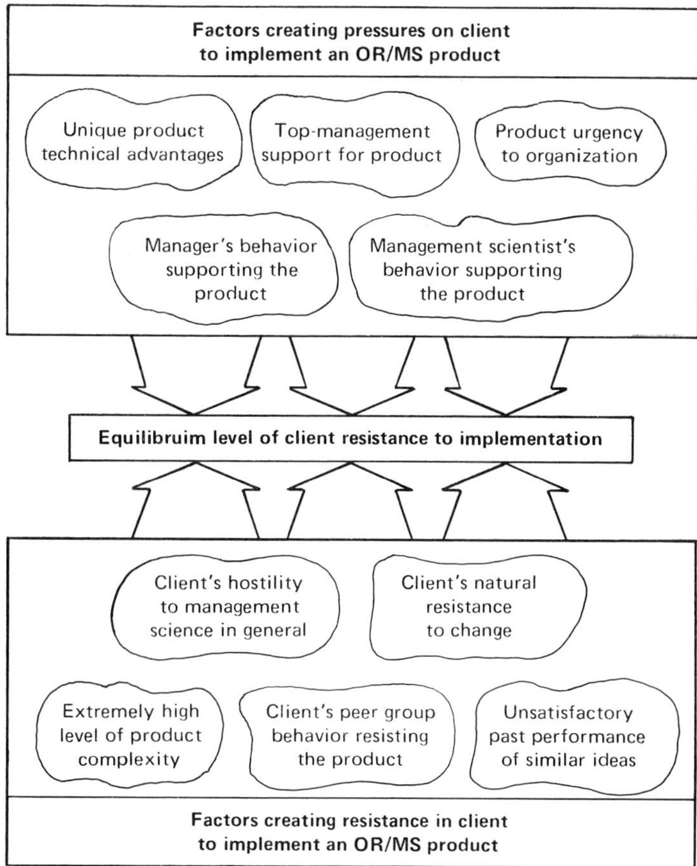

Fig. 8.2 Factors Affecting Client Resistance to the Implementation of OR/MS Products

chief-executive, or top-management, support for the proposal. Also, let an intermediate variable, which will directly interact with this external causal variable, be the client's personal attitude toward the chief executive.

Under these conditions, it is logical to assume that the level of client resistance will be inversely proportional to the degree of support given to the innovation by the chief executive. Note that this is true only if the client is highly supportive to the chief executive's desires. If, on the other hand, the client is extremely hostile toward the chief executive and secretly desires to sabotage any project his superior actively supports, then, in this second case, the client's resistance can be assumed to change in direct proportion to the degree of support given the innovation by the chief executive. These hypothetical examples assume perfect communication of course, as well as no interference from any other interacting variables.

Thus, any client can be either supportive or hostile with respect to most external factors impinging upon him. This concept is of extreme importance to the overall theory of implementation presented here because it underscores one of the fundamental reasons that seemingly well-planned implementation schemes sometimes backfire. Management styles relying on strong central authority and placing a great emphasis on coercion or manipulation do not always take the attitude orientation factor into account. As a result, in some cases the more intensive the pressure placed upon some clients to get them to implement a specific OR/MS project, the *lower* the probability for its success becomes.

The foregoing theoretical development has assumed that clients are naturally hostile toward technological innovations using the general line of reasoning prevalent in the behavioral science literature concerning resistance to change. Looking at the same phenomenon from a positive viewpoint, however, any decrease in client resistance to an OR/MS project can be loosely interpreted as an increase in *support* for the project.

These simple concepts of client attitude orientation toward external factors and the resistance/support relationship provided a basis for developing a mathematical scoring model for predicting OR/MS product implementation success due to client behavior.

IMPLEMENTATION ATTITUDE MEASUREMENT MODEL

The multiplicative scoring model that can be used to predict client resistance to an OR/MS innovation requiring their personal involvement is expressed as follows:

$$L = 0.5 + \Sigma\,(\bar{w}_i\, X_i\, \overline{\sin \phi_i}) \qquad i = 1, \ldots, n \tag{1}$$

The variables making up the scoring model are defined as follows:

1. External variable X_i: This variable represents external and generally controllable factors that stimulate clients to exhibit some behavioral response toward an OR/MS innovation diffusion project. Examples of external variables include the degree of project complexity, amount of management support shown for the project, relative demand of the project for client involvement, and prior history of management scientist success with the client group.

2. Weighting factor w_i: This variable represents individual client value judgments with respect to the relative importance of each external variable in its ability to influence the implementation of OR/MS technological innovations. It distinguishes between those external factors the client considers important from

those he feels are trivial. $\bar{w}_i$ is the expected value of a *group* of individual client's value judgments.

3. Intermediate variable sin ϕ_i: This variable is used to describe an individual client's attitude orientation toward each external factor that pressures him into implementing an OR/MS product. Intermediate variables express the client's degree of support or hostility toward the researcher, manager, level of product complexity, for example, or toward any other tangible external factor about which he can form an opinion. $\overline{\sin \phi_i}$ is a *group* attitude orientation toward external factor i. The sine function was selected to depict client attitude orientation using an angular analogy because attitudes can vary from being highly supportive to totally hostile. The sine function also has the advantage of increasing the sensitivity of attitude measurement scores. For values not equal to 0 on a linear 7-point semantic differential attitude measurement scale (to be described later) the sine function rapidly increases the physical size of client response values in both directions away from the indifference, or zero point. Although the author admits that this does not really change the true values of the attitude scores, he found that client attitude trends were much more readily apparent during the examination of raw data using the sine function than could be distinguished from linear semantic differential scores.

4. Dependent variable L: The dependent variable in the scoring model is defined as a measure of client behavior that can be logically interpreted as an equilibrium level of resistance to (or support for) a specific OR/MS innovation diffusion project. Through the addition of the constant 0.5 and the proper choice of numerical values for w_i, X_i, and sin ϕ_i, a range of possible values for L from 0 to 1 was provided. This permitted the interpretation of L as an indicator of the probability of success for an OR/MS project due to client behavior, that is, an indicator of the *relative level of support* for a project by any selected client group. Note carefully that this "probability" indicator is derived in the sense of a logical probability. It is not claimed to be based upon classical a priori or frequency concepts. It is merely an indicator of probability in the following sense:

a. When the indicator equals 1 it is certain that the clients will fully support a particular OR/MS project due to the factors X_i contained in the model.

b. When the indicator equals 0 it is certain that the clients are totally hostile toward the project due to the X_i factors contained in the model.

c. When the indicator lies between 0 and 1, it provides a rough indication of the degree of support for the project that can be expected from the client group. This implies that the higher the score, the higher the probability for success of the project due to client behavior manifested by their attitudes toward the project.

Table 8.1.
Variables Selected for the Test Model

External variable, X_i	Associated intermediate variable, sin ϕ_i
1 Level of chief-executive support for a specific OR/MS product	Attitude orientation of the client toward what he perceives to be the chief executive's support for the implementation project
2 Priority level assigned to the implementation project by management	Attitude orientation of the client toward his perception of the relative urgency placed upon a particular product by management
3 Degree of product relevancy to client's organizational role	Attitude orientation of the client toward his perceived relevance of the product to him
4 Level of required client involvement to implement the product	Attitude orientation of the client toward his perception of the degree to which he must become involved in the implementation process for a particular product
5 Level of product complexity	Attitude orientation of the client toward his perception of the relative simplicity (or complexity) of a particular product

OPERATIONALIZING THE SCORING MODEL

In order to test the theories presented above, and in particular the usefulness of the scoring model, two major problems required resolution:

1. Specific external variables needed to be precisely defined and quantified so that a viable scoring model could be created for testing in a real-world situation.

2. Methods for measuring the values of the intermediate and weighting factor variables required development.

The first problem was resolved through the derivation of an external variable classification scheme generated subjectively through a critical analysis of 77 different books and articles concerned with OR/MS implementation. This literature was carefully read to isolate statements concerning factors each author considered important to the OR/MS implementation process in general. Some 30-odd typewritten pages of statements were cut and pasted to group similar items together. The general context of each statement group was then condensed into a single factor, defined in terms of the *client's* role in the OR/MS implementation process. Finally, the client-oriented factors were subjectively grouped into logical categories, thus making up the classification scheme. From this scheme, the variables shown in Table 8.1 were selected for inclusion in a test scoring model.*

*See Chapter 6 for another approach toward identifying and classifying significant implementation variables.

The second problem involving data collection and reduction was solved through the use of an attitude questionnaire and the employment of psychometric methods for measuring w_i and sin ϕ_i. The details of these efforts are described below.

Measuring Client Attitude Orientation

The measurement and scaling of client attitude orientations toward external variables was found to be the most difficult step in developing a practical method for researchers and managers to measure client resistance to or support for OR/MS technological innovations. The primary reason for the difficulty in obtaining precise attitude measures within reasonable data collection constraints of time and money required for the process was the necessity for interval-scaled data. This was true because the client attitude orientation variable sin ϕ_i must be measurable on at least an interval scale in order to permit derivation of sociological *group* values of $\overline{\sin\ \phi_i}$, i.e., the expected value of sin ϕ_i, through arithmetic averaging operations.

The attitude measurement literature was found to be inordinately large in describing various techniques for obtaining reliable and valid measures for widely divergent definitions of attitude. The interested reader can verify this for himself by reviewing, for example, Insko [*6*] for a comprehensive survey of attitude theories, Fishbein [*3*] for an excellent treatment of attitude measurement methodology, and Guilford [*4*], Edwards [*2*], or Torgerson [*15*] for mathematical considerations. Because this area of investigation by the author was felt to be the bridge between operations research and the behavioral sciences, considerable time was spent exploring various attitude measurement methods. This effort prompted selection of a psychometric method for measuring sin ϕ_i that was simple enough to be readily useable but yet rigorous enough to provide the desired outcomes of this research—the semantic differential.

The semantic differential attitude measurement form, as originally developed by Osgood [*10*]*, utilizes a set of bipolar adjective scales for each attitude object about which a subject's attitude orientation is desired. The attitude object in this research is the external variable X_i. Each scale on the form has three positive degrees, three negative degrees, and a neutral point for possible scoring by a client. A sample of the semantic differential format that could be used to record client responses in measuring his attitude orientation toward the external factor "project urgency" is shown on page 192.

The linear 7-point semantic differential scale scores were transformed to the required angular basis representing the client attitude orientation described

*See also Osgood and Tannenbaum [*11*] and Osgood, Suci, and Tannenbaum [*12*] for a complete explanation of the semantic differential technique.

Variables Selected for the Test Model

Project urgency

bad	____ :	____ :	____ :	____ :	____ :	____ :	____ good
wise	____ :	____ :	____ :	____ :	____ :	____ :	____ foolish
harmful	____ :	____ :	____ :	____ :	____ :	____ :	____ beneficial
high	____ :	____ :	____ :	____ :	____ :	____ :	____ low
important	____ :	____ :	____ :	____ :	____ :	____ :	____ unimportant
meaningless	____ :	____ :	____ :	____ :	____ :	____ :	____ meaningful
true	____ :	____ :	____ :	____ :	____ :	____ :	____ false

previously. The specific angles used to represent various client attitude scores were as follows:

1. The most negative attitude position on the semantic differential 7-point scale was set equal to an angle of $-\pi/2$.
2. The next most negative position was set equal to $-\pi/3$.
3. The slightly negative position equals $-\pi/6$.
4. The neutral center position on the scale equals zero.
5. The slightly positive position equals $+\pi/6$.
6. The next most positive position equals $+\pi/3$.
7. The most positive position was set equal to $+\pi/2$.

The individual angular scores were transformed into sine values ranging from +1 to −1. Because each concept was eventually scored 10 times by each client, using 10 different adjective pairs, the 10 individual $\sin \phi_i$ values were averaged to produce a single mean attitude score for each client for each concept tested.

Finally, the average scores were themselves averaged over various client groups to obtain a grand average attitude score $\overline{\sin \phi_i}$. This value was used directly in the scoring model:

$$L = .05 + \Sigma\,(\bar{w}_i\, X_i\, \overline{\sin \phi_i}) \qquad i = 1, \ldots, n \tag{1}$$

Determining $\bar{w}_i$ Values

To determine ratio-scaled values for the weights $\bar{w}_i$ assigned to each term in the scoring model above, the author used a particular psychometric method originally proposed by Metfessel [*9*] for the purpose of obtaining psychological values on ratio scales. Metfessel's principles have been elaborated by Comrey [*1*] into a routine procedure for scaling stimuli from constant sum judgments, as described by Guilford [Reference *4*, pp. 214–220]. In this research, the stimuli are represented by X_i factors presented to clients in pairs for individual judgments as to their relative weights. The client responses are manipulated to yield a ratio scale of specific w_i values corresponding to each X_i input. According to Guilford:

> It requires the observer [designated as 0] to report upon observed ratios. Instead of specifying a certain ratio that 0 is to achieve, 0 must name the ratio he thinks exists between two or more stimuli. 0 may be presented with two stimuli at a time or with more than two. The typical judgment is to divide a total of 100 points as he thinks they should be divided to represent the several objects in a set. If 0 states that stimuli A and B should receive 75 and 25 points, respectively, then the ratio of A to B is 3.0 and the ratio of B to A is .33. If 0 divides 100 points among A, B, and C giving them 20, 30 and 50 points, respectively, the ratios are A/B = .67, A/C = .40, and B/C = .60. The reciprocal ratios B/A, C/A and C/B would equal 1.5, 2.5 and 1.67, respectively. Assuming that the observations are correct within sampling errors, the stimuli are thus placed at appropriate distances from the zero point. Letting any one stimulus have the value of unity, we can readily scale the others.

Thus, by administering relatively simple questionnaires to clients following the above procedure, ratio-scaled values of w_i were developed. Given these fairly rigorous scales, it was considered appropriate to use arithmetic to derive the required $\bar{w}_i$ group measures for direct use in the scoring model through a simple averaging process.*

Scaling External Variables

The final scaling problem, creating ordinal scales of X_i values, was solved quite easily by subjectively setting a priori levels of these external variables using written project proposals for OR/MS technological change. The general procedure for setting such X_i levels was accomplished as follows:

1. A one-page written description, or abstract, of a particular OR/MS management improvement project to be proposed to a specific client group (school teachers in this experiment) was prepared to include: (a) a precise statement indicating a specific level of each external variable X_i to be tested, and (b) just enough additional information to provide continuity in writing. The description was kept simple to prevent complicating the experiment through the incorporation of an excessive number of extraneous external variables.

*A computer program was written in FORTRAN to perform these computations. The program listing is available in Manley [*8*].

2. Additional OR/MS project proposals were written in exactly the same format and words as the first, but with one or more of the X_i value statements changed to reflect a different level of pressure for implementation on the client. For example, the last sentence of project description (or "form") number one stated:

> An absolute minimum of personal time will be required from teachers in order to implement this project.

In another version, project form three, the statement was written differently as follows:

> Substantial cooperation and involvement will be required from all teachers in order to provide the data and assistance necessary to successfully implement this project.

These two statements represent two distinctly different levels of the external factor X_4, "level of required client involvement to implement the project."

The above procedure was used to present various X_i values contained in four different implementation project proposals to a client group as test psychological attitude objects. Note carefully that the actual proposals were identical in overall appearance and content with the exception of the manipulated sentences.

It is also important to note that the proposed changes in the client's organizational environment, as suggested by the OR/MS technological innovation verbal descriptions, were not expected to be perceived by each client in exactly the same way. For example, according to Kahn et al. [7] each client's individual role requirements will cause unique coping responses to each change stimulus. However, by using the empirical experimental approach to be discussed later, this problem was not significant as client's differing perceptions of particular X_i values eventually appeared in the error term of an analysis of variance model.

Note also that this methodology will not produce X_i values that can be associated with any scale more rigorous than an ordinal one. This scaling problem limited ultimate model testing to nonparametric methods. If parametric testing is desired, on the other hand, X_i values must be measured on at least an interval scale. The author felt, however, that because the external variable X_i could not be considered as anything but subjective in nature, it was pointless to attempt to develop an interval scale for these variables. Perhaps, future research by other investigators might provide enough empirical data to permit the more rigorous approach. At the present time, however, such a development is not considered feasible.

The main point to consider here is that the primary purpose for going to great lengths to create an interval scale for sin ϕ_i values was to ultimately obtain a sociological group average measure of $\overline{\sin \phi_i}$, using arithmetic. In the case of w_i values, the same purpose underlies the choice of scaling method, i.e., the derivation of an average value $\bar{w}_i$ using arithmetic operations, which is only possible with interval or higher-scaled data. In the case of X_i variables, however, an average value was *not* needed in order to make the model viable. Furthermore, because it was desired to keep the overall measurement methodology as simple as possible, it clearly did not seem appropriate to expend unnecessary effort to develop an a priori interval scale, even if reasonable techniques had been available.

TESTING THE SCORING MODEL

The experimental approach taken to test the scoring model was adapted to those frequently used in the chemical industry. When investigating the operation of certain chemical plants in which various chemical reactions involved are too complex to be economically investigated, researchers sometimes vary the external conditions important to the process and measure their effect on the process output, for example, its yield. Because this research dealt with the *process* of client resistance to OR/MS technological innovation in which the internal interactions are admittedly so poorly known as to prevent rigorous determination of all the underlying causes of the innumerable observed effects, a similar approach was taken.

Specifically, the experimental design provided for treating clients with a written description of a relevant OR/MS project in which two external variables exhibited two different levels of pressure for project implementation, all other X_i variables remaining constant. The client group was divided into fourths and each of the subgroups were treated according to the scheme shown in Figure 8.3.

Actual testing of the scoring model was accomplished through a field experiment. A large suburban school district was used as the test organization with the basic experiment designed as follows:

1. The professional staff of primary and secondary school teachers were treated as clients and were subjected to a proposal for a new OR/MS technological innovation involving a method for optimizing the computation of supplemental pay for extracurricular activities. The school principals and staff administrators were treated as managers, and the superintendent of the school district was cast in the role of the chief executive.

2. The clients (teachers) were provided with a hypothetical, but completely realistic, written proposal for change in payroll methods that had been recommended for implementation by a team of operations researchers and management consultants, including the author. The proposal was submitted to the teachers through their normal organizational chain of command and was

Fig. 8.3 Experimental Design for Field Test of Scoring Model

		X_1	
		High A	Low B
X_4	High C	1 $A \cap C$	2 $B \cap C$
	Low D	3 $A \cap D$	4 $B \cap D$

Forms 1, . . . , 4 = Project description forms submitted to clients
Statements A, . . . , D = Specific statements contained in otherwise identical project forms

A = A tentative project to develop such a system has received the full support of the superintendent.

B = A tentative project to develop such a system is now being examined by the administrative staff to determine if and when it should be implemented.

C = An absolute minimum of personal time will be required from teachers in order to implement this project.

D = Substantial cooperation and involvement will be required from all teachers in order to provide the data and assistance necessary to successfully implement this project.

accompanied by an attitude questionnaire. Plausibility was given to the proposal because the author had actually been conducting separate university-sponsored research within the school district for over a year prior to the experiment. He was well known to all administrators and many of the school principals in his cover role.

3. The questionnaire results were collected and evaluated using standard regression and correlation analyses, as well as nonparametric one-way analysis of variance techniques.

FIELD TEST RESULTS

Respondents to the experimental questionnaire numbered 153 and represented 40 percent of the total client population. Based upon the results using the constant sum technique to measure w_i, the teachers from this particular population perceived the relative importance of the test factors in the following order of decreasing importance:

1. The relative urgency of the requirement for a new OR/MS method to solve a real problem.
2. The relative importance of the new method to those individuals who will be affected by it.
3. The degree of top-level support given to the new method.

4. The relative simplicity of the new method in making it easy to install and use.
5. The amount of personal participation of clients required to implement the new method.

The results obtained using the semantic differential approach to measure client attitude orientations sin ϕ_i were extremely good considering the noisy data involved. The most significant results occurred in the case of varying client attitudes toward the level of chief-executive support indicated for the project as a result of the manipulated forms. Figure 8.4 shows quite clearly that when a high degree of top-level support was communicated to the clients through

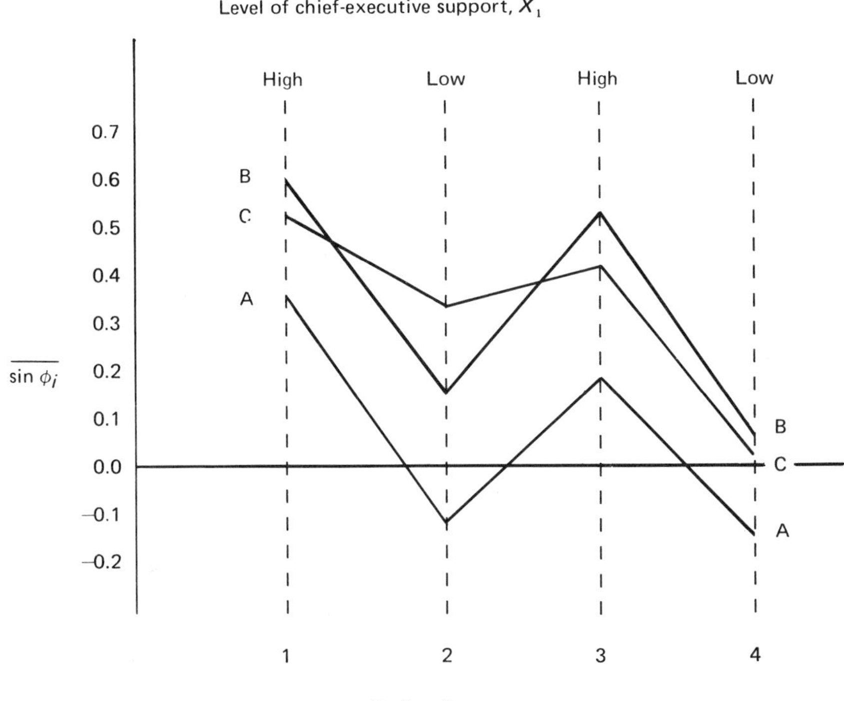

A = Client subgroup that currently receives teacher responsibility pay—directly affected by the OR/MS innovation

B = Client subgroup that expects to receive responsibility pay in the future—indirectly affected by the OR/MS innovation

C = Client subgroup that does not now and never expects to receive responsibility pay—not affected by the OR/MS innovation

Fig. 8.4 Attitude Variations Between Client Subgroups Toward Varying Levels of Chief Executive Support for Project

project forms 1 and 3, their attitudes toward the concept "the amount of support being given to this project by the superintendent" was more positive than when less support was in evidence, as in the statements in project forms 2 and 4 (Figure 8.3).

Less dramatic but clearly significant results were also apparent in the case of the other manipulated variable X_4, as the clients exhibited decreasing attitude scores when they were asked to provide more of their personal time and effort for implementing the new payroll method.

The two control variables, X_2 and X_5, which were the same in all four written communications to the clients, caused erratic client attitude scores and showed no trends of any sort, as was to be expected.

The individual w_i, X_i, and $\sin \phi_i$ values were combined in accordance with the structure of the scoring model to produce values of L. These results were compared with two separate independent measures derived from the same questionnaire administered to the clients:

1. Measured project success indicator P, defined as an independent measure of the probability of success for a specific OR/MS innovation diffusion project, was obtained by asking clients to answer the following direct question:

> What do you think is the chance for success of the proposed teacher responsibility pay project?

2. Measured client support indicator S, defined as an independent measure of client support for a specific OR/MS project, was obtained by asking clients to answer the following direct question:

> What percent of your personal effort would you be willing to expend to support the teacher responsibility pay project?

Because one of the three variables used to derive L was subjectively defined and not measured, the controllable variable X_i, it was excluded from the tests considered most crucial to the research. A modified project success indicator incorporating only w_i and $\sin \phi_i$ called $L1$ was compared with P and S producing the following results:

1. $L1$ correlated positively with P having a correlation coefficient of 0.32.
2. $L1$ correlated positively with S having a correlation coefficient of 0.34.
3. Both correlations were significant to the .005 level.
4. The hypothesis that "there is no difference in the average value of $L1$ (P or S) from subgroups of clients responding to different project form stimuli" was tested using the Kruskal-Wallis nonparametric one-way analysis of variance technique described in Siegel [Reference *14*, pp. 184–194]. The results showed that the hypotheses could be rejected for P, S, and $L1$ with significance levels of .25, .50, and .01, respectively. The same hypothesis applied to the primary indicator L showed that it could be rejected with a significance level of .005.

5. Of the three indicators, P, S, and L, only the derived measure L showed logically consistent results in that both of the following requirements held true:

a. Form 1 client subgroup mean probabilities for project success should be higher than those derived from subgroups having been presented with project forms 2, 3, or 4. This should be true because X_1 and X_4 on project form 1 represented the highest possible pressure on clients to implement the proposed project.

b. Form 4 client subgroup mean probabilities for project success should be lower than those derived from subgroups having been presented with project forms 1, 2, or 3. This should be true because X_1 and X_4 on project form 4 represented the lowest possible pressure on clients to implement the proposed project.

In summary, the results clearly indicated that the derived project success indicator was more sensitive in its ability to detect changes in client behavior toward a particular OR/MS project due to changes in external factors than were the simpler measures P or S. It was not clear, however, whether or not the subjectively derived X_i term is really necessary to provide good results. This question will require a great deal of further research.

LIMITATIONS

It is claimed that the scoring model reported in this chapter is capable of making statistically significant measurements of client resistance to or support for OR/MS technological innovations. Furthermore, it provides a *useful* measure of the probability of OR/MS project success due to client behavior.

Because the research objective was merely to provide researchers and managers with a tool, a numerical measure, that hopefully will permit better planning and controlling OR/MS implementation in general, the model was not intended to precisely duplicate any particular real-world implementation process. This self-imposed constraint on model construction placed the following limitations on the final product:

1. Psychological factors involved in attitude testing cause noise levels that are generally overwhelming in single-person tests. This is evidenced by the degree of sophistication required in psychological testing to derive even the most basic empirical results of any value. Because the psychologist's problem also applies to this research, the scoring model uses expected values of client attitudes derived from a number of individuals in order to reach satisfactory reliability levels. For this reason, the model is not considered to be accurate for measuring *individual* client resistance to or support for OR/MS innovation diffusion projects, i.e., it is not microbehavioral in nature.

2. The most important effect a factor can have upon any individual client

is not what that factor actually is, but what he perceives it is. For this reason, strictly objective measures of factor weights can not be obtained. However, the seriousness of this limitation was reduced considerably through the use of the constant sum psychometric scaling technique.

3. A problem similar to that of obtaining valid measures of factor weights arises in attempting to obtain client attitude or sin ϕ_i values. Even though psychometric methods were relied upon to minimize this problem too, the inherent limitations of such techniques in general must be accepted.

VALIDITY OF THE EXPERIMENTAL RESULTS

With regard to the validity of the experimental results, a great deal of caution must be exercised in making any claims. It must be remembered that this research was merely a first attempt to determine the feasibility of developing a measure for predicting OR/MS product implementation success due to client behavior. The highly subjective nature of the entire research effort makes it most difficult to determine the true validity of the reported experimental results using standard statistical methods.

In view of this major difficulty, the author has followed the lead of Huysmans [Reference 5, p. 72] in adopting a more flexible criterion for validity that is directly applicable to this particular study. According to Huysmans, validity should be based on the usability of the information produced by the experiment for gaining understanding of the processes underlying a real-world situation. Under this criterion, it is claimed that the experimental results reported are valid because they have provided some further insight into the OR/MS implementation process with regard to client behavior. At least this is true within the context of one real-world organization faced with one real OR/MS project.

CONCLUSIONS AND RECOMMENDATIONS

Perhaps the most important contribution of this research is its demonstration that very small changes in written communications to clients concerning an OR/MS innovation diffusion project caused significant variations in their observed attitudes toward the project. The implication is that managers and researchers must be extremely careful in how they present technological innovations to those persons who will be affected by them. It is contended by the author that any approach toward the implementation of operations research/management science innovations must take the client into consideration in order to ensure eventual project success. The strong emphasis placed upon this point is made because the author's definition of success implies that the innovation will not require maintenance by the researcher, that is, the clients will not only adopt the innovation, but also maintain it without further assistance from the researcher. If this type of success is to occur for an OR/MS project, the clients *must* have favorable attitudes toward it or it will eventually fail.

The problem of creating favorable attitudes toward OR/MS projects within client groups is very complex and requires a great deal of further research. Although it was demonstrated that chief-executive support for a project did have a significant influence on client attitudes within the organization tested, it remains to be shown that this is also true in other organizations, within different client groups, and when such clients are confronted with varying OR/MS projects. The same is true for the factors involving project relevance to the client and the degree of involvement required of them to implement a particular project. What did become quite clear, however, is that this research corroborated the relevance of these factors to OR/MS implementation as reported by others, especially in the comprehensive report by Radnor, Rubenstein, and Tansik [*13*].

Another important conclusion is that this research has demonstrated that the measurement of client resistance to OR/MS-induced change is feasible. Even though the scoring model developed herein was only intended to be a simple test instrument, it was shown to be capable of obtaining such measurements in a real-world organization with more accuracy and comprehensiveness than could be obtained from concomitant polling devices. The data collected in the field test revealed that the disperson of P and S values were much larger than for L and $L1$. This meant that the simple "quick and dirty" measures indicating client support S, or client estimates of project success P, may be very misleading to unsuspecting managers who do not take their dispersion into account. The solution to this problem would appear to be the use of more complex but more sensitive measures such as the derived project success indicator L.

It is also concluded that this research represents an important contribution toward building a bridge between operations research/management science and the behavioral sciences. By applying operations research methodology in attacking what is primarily a "people problem," the author has used a variety of techniques that are considered important in themselves. Some of the technical contributions which should be of benefit to other researchers are:

1. A new methodology for using an OR/MS innovation diffusion project proposal as an attitude object in attitude testing.
2. A modification in the employment of the semantic differential attitude measurement technique by incorporating a trigonometric function.
3. The development of a relatively simple method for quantifying factors important to the OR/MS implementation process.
4. A computer program to assist researchers with the calculations inherent in the psychometric constant sum technique.

5. A rather novel combination of the semantic differential attitude measurement technique and the constant sum psychometric scaling method in a multiplicative scoring model.

Finally, it is sincerely hoped that the work reported in this and the other companion studies with regard to the role of the client in the operations research/management science innovation diffusion process will be continued. Because this research has demonstrated that the client does care how his organizational role is affected by technological innovations, it is extremely important that more emphasis be placed upon his group, in addition to studying the effects on the process due to management and researcher behavior.

It is the author's firm belief that it is the triad of researcher-manager-client that is instrumental to the success or failure of OR/MS products.

References

1. Comrey, A. L., "A Proposed Method for Absolute Ratio Scaling," *Psychometrika,* **15,** 317–325 (1950).
2. Edwards, A., *Techniques of Attitude Scale Construction.* New York: Appleton-Century-Crofts, 1957.
3. Fishbein, Martin, Ed., *Readings in Attitude Theory and Measurement,* New York: Wiley, 1967.
4. Guilford, J. P., *Psychometric Methods,* New York: McGraw-Hill, 1954.
5. Huysmans, Jan H. B. M., *The Implementation of Operations Research: An Approach to the Joint Consideration of Social and Technological Aspects,* New York: Wiley, 1970.
6. Insko, Chester A., *Theories of Attitude Change,* New York: Appleton-Century-Crofts, 1967.
7. Kahn, R. L., et al., *Organizational Stress: Studies in Role Conflict and Ambiguity,* New York: Wiley, 1964.
8. Manley, John H., "A Measure of the Probability of Success for OR/MS Projects Due to Client Behavior," Doctoral dissertation, School of Engineering, University of Pittsburgh, 1971.
9. Metfessel, M., "A Proposal for Quantitative Reporting of Comparative Judgments," *Journal of Psychology,* **24,** 229–235 (1947).
10. Osgood, C. E., "The Nature and Measurement of Meaning," *Psychological Bulletin,* **49,** 251–262 (1952).
11. Osgood, C. E., and Tannenbaum, Percy H., "The Principle of Congruity in the Prediction of Attitude Change," *Psychological Review,* **62,** 42–55 (1955).
12. Osgood, C. E., Suci, G. J., and Tannenbaum, P. H., *The Measurement of Meaning,* Urbana, Ill.: University of Illinois Press, 1957.
13. Radnor, Michael, Rubenstein, Albert H., and Tansik, David A., "Implementation in Operations Research and R&D in Government and Business Organizations," *Operations Research,* **18,** 967–991 (1970).
14. Siegel, Sidney, *Nonparametric Statistics for the Behavioral Sciences,* New York: McGraw-Hill, 1956.
15. Torgerson, W. S., *Theory and Methods of Scaling,* New York: Wiley, 1958.

Chapter 9

Behavioral Factors in System Implementation

Henry C. Lucas, Jr.

This volume is an indication of the growing concern over the lack of use of OR/MS models. Can a model be considered successful if it is not implemented? From an aesthetic standpoint a model may be quite elegant and give important results. However, if the results are ignored, as is so often the case, the potential contribution of the model has not been realized, and it cannot be considered a success.

This chapter discusses two empirical studies that identify some of the behavioral factors affecting the use of information systems. An information system can be considered to be a simple management science model; often an information system automates well-understood manual procedures. A model of the procedures is constructed in the form of computer programs and flow diagrams. This model is less sophisticated than many more quantitative operations research models and should be among the easiest models to implement. Yet many of these relatively simple systems have failed.

Another reason for discussing information systems implementation is that many OR/MS models supply information or organize it for decision making; the output of the model is not necessarily "the decision." In fact, one approach to developing more sophisticated models is to begin with a well-understood information system and add models that draw on the data base of the system for input and produce information for a decision maker as output.

In the next section a descriptive model of the classes of variables affecting the use of an information system is presented. An empirical study of the use of a sales information system provides support for the model. The model and results lead to a suggested strategy for implementing information systems and other OR/MS models. The final section presents an example of the development of an information system following the recommended strategy.

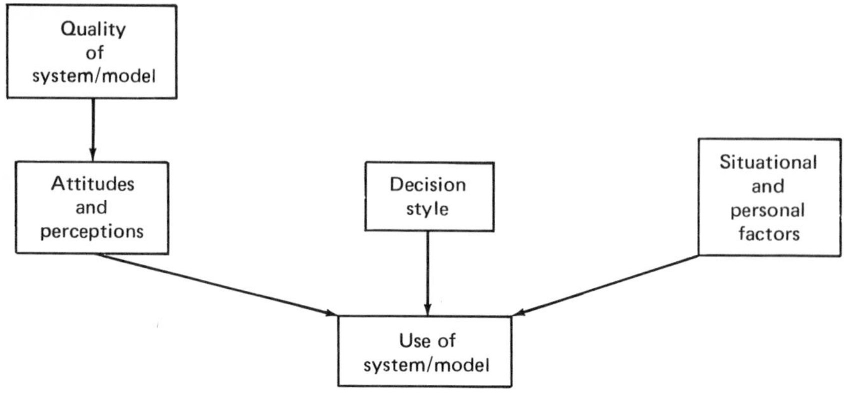

Fig. 9.1 A Descriptive Model of Factors Affecting the Use of a System or Model

DESCRIPTIVE MODEL OF SYSTEM USE

The Model

Figure 9.1 shows a descriptive model of the use of an information system. The model includes four classes of independent variables that influence system use. The quality of a system or model is important in determining a user's experience with it. How easy is it to learn the model; how well does the user understand it [*1*]? The decision maker's use of the system contributes to his formation of attitudes and perceptions about it [*8*]. Attitudes and perceptions are expected to influence the use of a system; attitudes have a behavioral component, and favorable attitudes are consistent with high levels of use of a system [*5, 8, 11*].

Another important variable influencing the use of a model is decision or cognitive style [*2, 10*]. For example, providing highly detailed data to an intuitive decision maker will probably result in little or no use of the information. There is limited research on this class of variables, but it appears important to match models and information with the cognitive style of the decision maker. Finally, situational and personal factors influence the use of information systems and models. These factors include variables such as age, length of service, and education [*12*].

A Research Study

A study was conducted of the use of sales information system by the sales force of a major apparel manufacturing company. This company employs a large group of salesmen selling to retailers, who in turn sell to the buying public. There are three major divisions in the company, and the results for one division are presented here.

The sales informations system maintains detailed data on sales at the buying entity level by product line. (A buying entity is the smallest organizational unit that can order a product, for example, the sportswear section of the men's department.) The system produces a monthly report showing the last twelve month's data on units shipped and canceled and bookings for the next four months. Dollar figures and year-to-date comparisons with the prior year are also provided.

The variables included in this study and their source are shown in Table 9.1. Computer files and a questionnaire administered to salesmen (the response rate was over 90 percent) provided most of the data in the study.* For the purposes of this chapter, the dependent variable is use of the information system. Correlation and factor analytic techniques were used to develop six scales representing the use of the system from items on the questionnaire. See Table 9.1.

Predictor variables in the study include situational and personal factors, decision style, and attitudes and perceptions.† Situational and personal factors describe the unique environment of each salesman, for example, his age, education, and number of accounts. Decision style is measured by two binary variables: whether or not the salesman keeps his own item level records (the information system reports at the product line level) and whether he performs any calculations with the data on the sales report. Attitudes and perceptions of the information systems are measured by three scales from the questionnaire as shown in Table 9.1.

Stepwise multiple regression was used to determine the relationship between the predictor variables and each of the six dependent variables. The repression algorithm was terminated when an incoming variable would no longer be significant at the .10 level (one tailed test). Equations (1) and (2) below show the results of regressing all predictor variables except performance (S_5) on variable U_1 (working with the customer in the store) and U_2 (detailed analysis of buying entity/account).†† For these variables, the use of the system was

---

*Possible responses to questionnaire items range from 1 to 7 or 1 to 5. All results are coded so that higher numerical values are more favorable.

†It was not possible to include variables related to the quality of the system in this research. Another type of study is needed in which several systems are involved and some variance in quality can be measured across systems.

††The numbers in parentheses in row (a) below each of the coefficients are standardized beta weights; they show the relative contribution of each predictor variable independently of the unit measure. The beta weight is particularly important for variables like S_1, S_2, and S_5. For example, the value of S_5 is large relative to the 7-point questionnaire scales and its coefficient is 0; however, the beta weights indicate its contribution to the regression

Table 9.1.
Variables in the Study

Variable class	Variables	Source
Dependent		
Use of system	U_1 Working with customer in store	Questionnaire
	U_2 Detailed analysis of buying entity/account	Questionnaire
	U_3 Overall progress	Questionnaire
	U_4 Summary this year vs. last	Questionnaire
	U_5 Planning	Questionnaire
	U_6 Cancellations	Questionnaire
Predictor		
Situational	S_1 Number of accounts	Computer files
	S_2 Number of buying entities (approximate)	Computer files
	S_3 Length of time in present territory (months)	Questionnaire
	S_4 Length of time in present position (months)	Questionnaire
	S_5 Total dollar bookings 1972 season	Computer files
Personal	I_1 Age	Personnel records
	I_2 Education	Personnel records
Decision style	D_1 Records orientation-keeps own item records	Questionnaire
	D_2 Calculations performed with sales report data	Questionnaire
Attitudes and perception	A_1 Quality of output	Questionnaire
	A_2 Computer potential	Questionnaire
	A_3 Management computer support	Questionnaire

expected to influence performance so performance was not included as a predictor variable [9]. (Table 9.2 presents the statistical results of the regression analysis.)*

---

equation. These weights indicate the change measured in standard deviation units expected from a standardized unit change in a predictor variable. The numbers in row (b) are t statistics for each variable.

*With a large number of independent variables, there is always the possibility of multicollinearity. In this study, the zero-order correlations between dependent and indepen-

$$U_1 = 3.26 - .01S_1 + .59D_1 + .42A_1 \quad (1)$$
(a) (−.23) (.16) (.31)
(b) (2.53) (1.79) (3.46)

$$U_2 = 3.34 - .01S_3 - .07I_2 + .21A_1 + 26.4_2 + .13A_3 \quad (2)$$
(a) (−.38) (−.09) (.25) (.31) (.14)
(b) (5.02) (1.24) (3.08) (4.01) (1.90)

The results of regressing all predictor variables on the last four information-use scales, U_3 to U_6, are presented in equations (3) through (6). Performance (S_5) is included as a predictor variable in these equations because the use of the information included in the scales should be useful in problem finding, which is stimulated by low performance [*9, 13*].

$$U_3 = .33 - .01S_4 - .00S_5 + .02I_1 + .37D_1 + .36A_1 + .16A_2 \quad (3)$$
(a) (+.27) (−.15) (.13) (.14) (.38) (.18)
(b) (2.55) (1.84) (1.25) (1.71) (4.24) (1.96)

$$U_4 = 5.05 - .00S_2 - .01S_3 + .30A_3 \quad (4)$$
(a) (−.20) (−.25) (.22)
(b) (2.21) (2.77) (2.45)

$$U_5 = 2.68 - .01S_1 + .01S_3 - .01S_4 + .48D_2 + .35A_1 + .21A_2 \quad (5)$$
(a) (−.25) (.22) (−.45) (.19) (.34) (.21)
(b) (3.32) (1.63) (3.35) (2.62) (4.25) (2.66)

$$U_6 = .61 - .01S_4 - .00S_5 + .04I_1 + .34A_1 + .27A_3 \quad (6)$$
(a) (−.17) (−.19) (.20) (.24) (.18)
(b) (1.47) (1.94) (1.77) (2.48) (1.85)

Table 9.2.
Statistical Results for Equations

	Equation number					
	1	2	3	4	5	6
R^2 *	.21	.52	.38	.17	.51	.20
F statistic	8.76†	21.33†	10.10†	6.89†	17.28†	4.87†

* R^2 may be interpreted as the percentage of the variance in the dependent variable explained by the independent variables.
† $p < .001$
$n = 104$

dent variables had the same sign as the regression coefficients, which increases confidence in the results.

The results of equations (1) through (6) indicate the importance of all the predictor variables in determining the use of the information system. As predicted by the models there is a strong association between favorable attitudes and the use of the system. However, the impact of personal and situational factors appears to vary widely. Low performance does stimulate the use of summary and cancellation information (U_4 and U_6). Cancellations may be one of the few variables the salesman can influence because cancellations are made by the manufacturer rather than the customer. Keeping item level records is also a predictor of high system use in equations (1) and (3) whereas performing calculations with the sales data is a predictor of high use in equation (5). Possibly the salesman keeps his own item level records for his most important accounts and relies on the information system for his more numerous, less important accounts. Less time in the territory and as a salesman is also associated with greater use of the information system. This finding probably reflects newer salesmen using the report to familiarize themselves with their jobs or territories.

Implications

The results of this study of the use of a sales information system make an important contribution to the development of an implementation strategy for OR/MS models. First, the findings show the importance of attitudes in predicting the use of a system. Attitudes are formed during systems design or model construction; an implementation strategy should consider the process of designing the system or model. Situational factors are also important in determining the use of the system, but there does not appear to be a consistent pattern. An implementation strategy is needed that considers the unique aspects of the intended user, such as his age, length of service, and decision style. Unfortunately, there were no data available to directly examine the quality of system from the study. However, intuitively it seems logical that simple models are preferable during early stages of design; more elaborate models can be developed later when a simple one has been successfully implemented.

AN IMPLEMENTATION STRATEGY

The results discussed above suggest the following strategy for implementing OR/MS and information systems models. First, it is important to consider the process of systems design and to work with the user so that the user actually designs the system or model and develops favorable attitudes toward it. The OR analyst or information systems designer translates user needs into the model; the designer and user work closely enough together so that the decision maker understands the model. Frequent review meetings should be held with all those affected by the system; users should suggest ways to build the model or system to best meet their needs. The reason for this widespread review and participation is that involvement builds understanding and creates commitment to change [*3, 14–16*]. The entire design process should concentrate on helping potential users develop favorable attitudes.

The next major component in the implementation strategy is the consideration of the impact of the model or system on the user as a conscious part of the design effort [*12*]. Work groups and individuals often are affected by a system [*12, 16*]; a system also has an impact on the organization, particularly if the model or system changes power relationships [*6*].

Finally, it is an important part of the implementation strategy to design a simple and easily understandable model. Complexity and additional elegance can be added after an initial success. A simple system is easier to design, increasing the chances for success; it is also easier for the decision maker to understand a simple model [*4*].

AN EXAMPLE

The implementation strategy above guided the development of an information system for the United Farm Workers Organizing Committee. This example is taken from the information systems field, but should apply to other model-building efforts as well [*7*].

Background

The United Farm Workers Organizing Committee was founded to help secure the benefits of higher wages and better working conditions for farm workers. The union, headed by Caesar Chavez, became well known during its grape boycott of the mid- and late-1960s. Union membership includes Mexican-Americans, Mexicans, Anglo-Americans, Philippinos, and blacks. One goal of the union has been the elimination of the migrant labor contractor. All of the union contracts use a union operated hiring hall to assign workers to various ranches. To be dispatched to a ranch a member must show that his dues payments are current. A seniority system has also been established and available jobs are assigned in order of seniority.

The Robert F. Kennedy Memorial Health Plan helps to offset certain medical costs of the worker and his dependents and also provides death benefits. Eligibility for the plan is based upon the number of hours worked during the preceding quarters by the union member. The medical plan is entirely funded by contributions from growers based upon total hours worked during the month by the farm worker.

In order to provide these benefits to members, the union must keep a number of accurate records up to date. The membership office keeps track of dues payments and the Kennedy Plan office maintains records of hours worked reported by growers. Rapid increases in membership threatened these operations and stimulated the union to investigate the possibility of a computerized information system.

Project Approach

A major goal in the process systems design was to obtain the maximum amount of guidance from the union itself. The objective was to develop a system to meet the union's needs not to sell a preconceived system to the union. Frequent review meetings were held with union members, who were encouraged to design as much of the system as possible. Graduate students and research assistants participated with faculty members in the project. An attempt was made to plan for the impact of any system on the union. The union is a flexible and dynamic organization, and the designers wanted to avoid turning it into a rigid bureaucracy. An effort was made to forecast the impact of changes on work groups, the individual, and the union as a whole. A final goal was to design as simple a system as possible that could be programmed successfully.

User Survey

In order to obtain both design data and to assess the organizational readiness for a system, interviews and questionnaires were used to collect information from the union [5]. In the fall of 1970, an initial survey was conducted of 25 union members using questionnaires administered during an interview. The sample included staff members from all levels of the union and from all major departments. Interviews were held with top union officials, departmental supervisors, and clerical personnel in all the areas having some potential for a computer application. Data for designing the system and on user attitudes toward a computer system came from the questionnaire. The questionnaires were coded, and correlation and factor analytic techniques were used to develop scales from these individual variables. There was substantial agreement among those interviewed on the most critical areas for information processing. The concurrence of the Kennedy Plan staff and the union membership office showed a commonly held set of priorities for improving information processing within the union. In addition to the statistical tabulation of potential applications, other design data came from the interviews. Because of the interview format, many of the respondents provided additional information to that requested on the questionnaire.

An analysis of the organizational variables provided useful information about procedures for investigating the feasibility and design of a computer system for the union. Table 9.3 shows the median responses for key attitudinal variables. Union staff members felt there was an overload of paper work and expressed strong needs for information. The staff had very high job satisfaction

Table 9.3.
Median Responses for the First Sample

Variable	Median*	No. responses
Design data		
Computer use on crucial applications	1 2 3 4 5 (X at 5)	23
Computer use on secondary applications	1 2 3 4 5 (X at 4)	22
Paperwork overload	1 2 3 4 5 (X at 4)	24
Need for information	1 2 3 4 5 (X at 4)	23
Time filing	1 2 3 4 5 (X at 3)	25
Time reporting and answering questions	1 2 3 4 5 (X at 3)	25
Attitudinal data		
Identification with union	1 2 3 4 5 (X at 5)	25
Satisfaction with job	1 2 3 4 5 (X at 5)	22
Importance of job to union	1 2 3 4 5 (X at 4)	21
Thoughts of leaving job	1 2 3 4 5 (X at 2)	21
Benefits of computer	1 2 3 4 5 (X at 4)	25
Computer potential	1 2 3 4 5 (X at 4)	23
Negative computer impact	1 2 3 4 5 (X at 2)	24

*Possible responses ranged from 1 to 5, with 1 being low and 5 being high.

and identification with the union. From a computer standpoint there were high expectations, particularly for the use of the computer on crucial applications including those of the Kennedy Plan and membership office. Benefits were seen from using the computer and little negative impact was expected. Correlation analysis showed that position in the union was negatively associated with filing activities; union officials spent more of their time filling out reports and answering questions than in detailed record keeping. In examining computer related attitudes, the position of the union was positively associated with a favorable evaluation of the benefits from a computer system. The position of the union was also positively related to the potential of the computer and negatively associated with fears over its impact.

Different responses were also observed based upon the age of the union member. Older workers tended to be less satisfied with the union, but had fewer thoughts of leaving their jobs than younger workers. Based upon the consensus of a need for computer assistance in the Kennedy Plan and membership office, these departments were combined and compared with all other departments in the union. In these offices, fewer benefits were seen from computerization, and the computer was rated as having less potential than in other departments. Less assistance was also expected from the computer in crucial applications.

Implications

Several of the findings from the questionnaires were important from a systems design standpoint. First, the negative reactions of older workers to computers meant that their anxieties had to be relieved. The union leadership was young and had to be sensitive to the problems of some of the older staff members. The differences between the Kennedy Plan and membership office compared with other departments indicated that it was important to pay special attention to the workers in these departments. It was necessary to carefully prepare the clerical staff for change. The apparent resistance on the part of the Kennedy Plan and membership office contrasted with the general concensus that these areas were in the most need of help from a computer system. (Even though the members of a group agree intellectually that a system is desirable, they may resist a computer on more emotional grounds.) Later, these departments were placed under a common supervisor who was very supportive of computer systems, and this helped to reduce some of the implementation problems. The findings from the questionnaire also point out one possible paradox. Because the union leaders were in favor of a computer and emphasized its positive aspects, they might have been unaware or have underestimated some of the resistance of other union members. If the leadership of an organization tends to be too optimistic, it may not take the necessary steps to reduce the fears and anxieties of other employees when a system is implemented.

Systems Design

Following the completion of the initial questionnaires, the design team conducted interviews in which flow charts of the information flows and decisions within the various departments of the union were prepared. Questionnaire data indicated that the membership and the Kennedy Plan office should have the highest priority, and the first two visits concentrated on these areas. Because of the volunteer status of the union staff (members work for a small allowance plus expenses necessary for subsistence), a normal cost-benefit analysis was not suitable. Rather the feasibility of a proposed computer system had to be considered in light of intangible benefits provided. It was becoming increasingly difficult to find volunteers who would work in some of the posting jobs. Both the volume of information processed and the need for accuracy and timeliness indicated that the use of the computer system could be beneficial to the union. Such a system also offered a major advantage because of its relative insensitivity to fluctuations in the volume of transactions (membership in the union had been increasing rapidly).

After the initial interviews in the various union departments, a preliminary design for a minimum feasible system was developed. Developing a simple system made it possible for the union to process on the largest possible number of existing computer installations. A simple system helped to avoid a lengthy development phase; it was stressed that after an initial success, further use of computer processing for other application would be easier.

User Participation

A systems review meeting was held at a union retreat early 1971 to encourage user participation. The entire staff was invited to discuss the preliminary conclusions from the five months of study. The presentation emphasized that the system was at an early stage of development and the meeting could only be successful if changes were suggested by the staff. The union staff members quickly grasped the objective and intricacies of the proposed system, and a number of extremely worthwhile modifications were made. Changes in planned reports were suggested along with ideas for new reports. The original system dealt with operational control aspects of processing; several suggestions were made for including summary information of interest to union management. Later, several smaller meetings with different union staff members clarified certain design issues, and requests to vendors and software houses to program the system were prepared jointly. After initial investigations, the union decided that the most economical and desirable alternative was to recruit a computer staff as volunteers and obtain as many donated services as possible. The full-time staff gradually assumed responsibility for the system and began to rely on the original design team only for occasional advice.

Follow Up Survey

By the summer of 1971 the union was close to finalizing a systems design and beginning programming. The first steps in the conversion of existing records to a computer readable medium were well underway. This appeared to be an opportune time to collect follow-up data to assess the effects of the systems design on the Union and prepare for implementation. Although not completely conclusive, the data on this follow up study suggested that there were no or few unfavorable changes in attitudes between time 1 and time 2.

However, the data indicated that there was a very low perceived level of involvement in the design of this system by the union staff. Most of the response to the question on the amount of time spent working on design of the project indicated no involvement of less than one day. Because those who attended the review meetings spent a minimum of one day, there is some doubt that staff members perceived as much participation in the effort the project team attempted. The design group within the union discussed these results and tried to develop more involvement and participation as implementation progressed.

Evaluation

An attempt was made to design an information systems in which users developed and understood the system. User attitudes were considered during the process of design and in the specifications for the system. The impact on users and the organization were also considered consciously in the design of the system and a simple system was developed. The results in general were favorable; the follow-up survey showed no adverse effects. A visit to the union also confirmed the success of the system. Clerical personnel through the union leadership were visibly enthusiastic about computer processing and the output of the system was used heavily.

CONCLUSIONS

A descriptive model of the use of an information system or management science model has been described. This model suggests the development of an implementation strategy that consists of three major components. First, it is important to consider the design process and to recognize that design activities influence user attitudes. Second, the impact of the system or model on individuals, work groups, and the organization should be considered. Finally, it is desirable to implement as simple a system or model as possible at first; later refinements are possible after an initial success. An example using the strategy in the design of an information system was presented. The Farm Workers represent only one case, and other studies are required before the value of the implementation strategy can be fully assessed. However, it is hoped that the research and the results to date will convince model builders to consciously consider crucial behavioral factors in implementation.

References

1. Ackoff, R. L., "Management Misinformation Systems," *Management Science,* **14,** no. 4, B147–B156 (December 1967).
2. Doktor, Robert, and Hamilton, W. F., "Cognitive Style and the Acceptance of Management Science Recommendations," *Management Science,* **19,** no. 8, 884–894 (April 1973).
3. Lawler, E. E., and Hackman, R. J., "Impact of Employee Participation in the Development of Pay Incentive Plans: A Field Experiment," *Journal of Applied Psychology,* **53,** no. 6, 467–471 (December 1969).
4. Little, John, "Models and Managers: Concept of a Decision Calculus," *Management Science,* **16,** no. 8, B466–B485 (April 1970).
5. Lucas, H. C., Jr., "A User-Oriented Approach to Systems Design," *Proceedings of the 1971 ACM Annual Conference,* pp. 325–338.
6. Lucas, H. C., Jr., "The Problems and Politics of Change: Power, Conflict and the Information Services Subunit," in F. Gruenberger (Ed.), *Effective vs. Efficient Computing,* Englewood-Cliffs, N.J.: Prentice Hall, 1973.
7. Lucas, H. C., Jr., and R. B. Plimpton, "Technological Consulting in a Grass Roots, Action Oriented Organization," *Sloan Management Review,* **14,** no. 1, 17–36 (Fall 1972).
8. Lucas, H. C., Jr., "User Reaction and the Management of Information Services," *Management Informatics,* in press.
9. Lucas, H. C., Jr., "The Performance and Use of an Information System" *Management Science,* in press.
10. Mason, R. D. and Mitroff, I. I., "A Program for Research on Management Information Systems," *Management Science,* **19,** no. 5, 475–487 (January 1973).
11. Mumford, E. and Banks, O., *The Computer and the Clerk,* London: Routledge & Kegan Paul, 1967.
12. Mumford, E. and Ward, T. B., *Computers: Planning for People,* London: B. T. Batsford, 1968.
13. Pounds, W. F., "The Process of Problem Finding," *Industrial Management Review,* **11,** no. 1, 1–20 (Fall 1969).
14. Proshansky, H. and B. Seidenberg (Eds.), *Basic Studies in Social Psychology,* New York: Holt, Rinehart and Winston, 1965.
15. Scheflen, E., *Organizational Psychology,* Englewood Cliffs, N.J.: Prentice-Hall, Inc., 1965.
16. Trist, E. L., *Organizational Choice,* London: Tavistock Publications, Ltd., 1963.

Chapter 10

Improving the Implementation of OR/MS Models by Applying the Lewin-Schein Theory of Change

Richard E. Sorensen and Dale E. Zand

APPLYING CHANGE THEORY TO OR/MS IMPLEMENTATION

Management scientists are constantly attempting to bring about change in client organizations by applying OR/MS models and techniques to the problems of these client organizations. During an OR/MS project an influence relationship develops between the management scientist and the organization. The ultimate aim of this influence relationship is to cause change in the client organization. Unfortunately, in many cases, even after the expenditure of much effort, the OR/MS models are not implemented and little or no change occurs in the client organization.

This lack of change is not unexpected. There is a natural tendency on the part of organizations to resist change. Individuals within organizations become adjusted to stable situations and over a period of time performances of many tasks becomes routine and habitual. Individuals learn to best satisfy their various needs within this stable environment. Change upsets this stability and is threatening. It introduces uncertainty in organizations and requires adjustment on the part of organizational members. This resistance to change is sometimes beneficial because it provides stability in organizations. When change is necessary, however, this resistance must be overcome.

The Lewin-Schein theory of change emphasizes the various organization forces resisting change [*2, 5*]. In order to overcome this resistance and insure long-term achievement of change, change must be considered a three-step process consisting of unfreezing, changing, and refreezing. Unfreezing refers to overcoming resistance to change by introducing disequilibrium into the present, stable equilibrium. Changing refers to exposure to new information, attitudes, and theories in order to achieve new perception and to learn new behavioral patterns. Refreezing refers to reinforcement, confirmation, and support of new behavior.

This theory stresses the sequential nature of these activities. Unfreezing must be achieved before changing is attempted, or the new information introduced in changing may be rejected. After changing is achieved, a new stability must be insured through refreezing. These new behavioral patterns are unfamiliar to individuals who could easily slip back into old behavior patterns.

If the management scientist is a change agent attempting to influence the client organization, then this influence relationship can be examined using the Lewin-Schein theory of change. The level of success of management scientist-manager influence relationships would be influenced by the elements of the Lewin-Schein theory, and the variability in the level of success of OR/MS influence relationships would be explained by this theory.

Several authors have recognized the need for improved implementation of OR/MS. Malcolm asserts that many management scientists present alternatives to managers with little regard to implementation [*4*]. Such action, he claims, unrealistically assumes that management approval automatically means implementation. This has resulted in the failure to implement many management science projects that were otherwise well thought out.

Huysmans similarly calls for improved implementation of operations research and considers implementation the final criterion for measuring the success of an OR effort [*1*]. He considers the lack of implementation and not the development of an OR/MS model one of the major problems of operations research.

THE LEWIN-SCHEIN THEORY OF CHANGE

In order to better understand the Lewin-Schein theory of change, a more detailed discussion of the elements of this theory is necessary.

> **Unfreezing.** Unfreezing is overcoming resistance to change by encouraging dissatisfaction with current behavior in order to unlearn this current behavior and create a desire to learn new behavior. It involves reducing the defensiveness to learn so the individual will search and explore the environment for new and improved ways of behavior.

Schein considered change a difficult process because of the need to unlearn the old before the new can be learned. Change is also considered giving up something to which the person had previously become committed and that he values [*5*]. Because change tends to be emotionally resisted, something is necessary to alter the current stable equilibrium. In addition, defensive reactions in the change target must be reduced. The act of achieving this is what we call unfreezing.

Unfreezing makes one ready to pay attention to new categories of information as a prelude to redefining one's assumptions, beliefs, and constructs. Unfreezing can be brought about by lack of confirmation or disconfirmation. In lack of confirmation, we no longer receive positive communication concerning present equilibrium, and gradual unlearning occurs. In disconfirmation, we hear and receive cues about our behavior that cause us to question the effectiveness of typical behavioral patterns. Customary ways of doing things are no longer considered adequate. Because this is a more immediate disequilibrium than lack of confirmation, unlearning occurs more rapidly. The induction of guilt or anxiety also acts to unfreeze. In addition to being disconfirming, feelings of shame are induced in the change target. The target feels as if he had not lived up to certain expectations. This could be achieved through contrasting the current performance of an individual or an organization with better performance achieved in other areas. Current performance could also be contrasted to better performance that is theoretically attainable.

Another technique for unfreezing would be to provide psychological safety in new situations in order to reduce fear and anxiety of change. For instance, a trial or break-in period may be used during which an employee would not be evaluated. This would allow the employee to learn how to operate effectively in the new environment before his performance is compared with either the earlier environment or other employees. By reducing the anxiety of change, resistance to change is also reduced.

Unfreezing, however, is difficult. In many cases unfreezing does not occur even when it is attempted because [6]:

1. We tend not to pay attention to disconfirming cues.
2. If cues are the least bit ambiguous, we can easily dismiss them.
3. If cues are too blunt, we can attempt to dismiss the person who provided them.
4. If we cannot evade the message at all, we can still rationalize the behavior that triggered the disconfirmatory cue as not being characteristic of our typical behavior.

Changing. Changing is exposure to new information, attitudes, and theories in order to achieve new perceptions and learn new behavior patterns. It involves gathering new information, considering and interpreting new and existing information, and devleoping alternative courses of action, which could lead to learning new behavior patterns. In this process a method of choosing among alternatives may need to be developed or perhaps modified.

Changing requires that new responses or behavior be learned. Alternative behavioral patterns first must be considered and then a choice made between them. These alternatives may be developed in a number of ways. Information currently possessed by the change target could be reevaluated based upon new or different standards. With a changed frame of reference, the target's perception of certain information may be modified. New information could also be introduced providing additional alternatives for consideration. In addition to reevaluating existing behavioral patterns and introducing new ones, the criteria for choosing between alternatives may be modified.

Change can be considered a three-phase process [*3*]. The initial phase involves clarifying or diagnosing the client's systems problem. This involves information gathering and analysis in the client organization. The second phase involves the examination of alternative routes and goals, and the establishment of specific goals and means of reaching them. Information must be grouped and evaluated, and decisions made using some criteria of selection. The last phase involves transforming these intentions into actual behavior or achievements. It stresses that measurement and feedback are necessary to assess the extent of the change.

Changing can be accomplished by scanning the interpersonal environment for cues drawing different items of information from different people or by emotionally identifying with another person. This change process is difficult because of a pattern of relationships and interlocking expectations in the organization that tend to maintain the status quo.

> **Refreezing.** Refreezing is reinforcement, and confirmation or support of new behavior. It requires integrating new responses into the total personality and attitude systems for the individual and integrating new responses into ongoing significant relationships for the organization. Refreezing can be achieved through positive feedback and is necessary for the resulting stability of the new situation. [see Reference 5].

HYPOTHESES DEVELOPED FROM THE LEWIN-SCHEIN CHANGE THEORY

Hypotheses were developed based upon the Lewin-Schein change theory when applied to the implementation of OR/MS models. In general, high levels of unfreezing, changing, and refreezing are anticipated in high-success influence relationships. Low levels of unfreezing, changing, and refreezing are anticipated in low-success influence relationships. The expected results are shown in Table 10.1.

The specific hypotheses that were tested are:

Table 10.1.
Expected Results

Level of success of influence relationships	Level of unfreezing	Level of changing	Level of refreezing
High	High	High	High
Low	Low	Low	Low

Unfreezing

H–U+: The index of items favorable toward unfreezing, *U+*, will have a high positive correlation with the level of success of influence relationships.

H–U–: The index of items unfavorable toward unfreezing, *U–*, will have a high negative correlation with the level of success of influence relationships.

$$H_0 U+ : \rho\ U+,S \leqslant 0 \qquad H_0 U- : \rho\ U-,S \geqslant 0$$
$$H_1 U+ : 1 \geqslant \rho\ U+,S \geqslant 0 \qquad H_1 U- : -1 \leqslant \rho\ U-,S \leqslant 0$$

Changing

HC+: The index of items favorable toward changing, *C+*, will have a high positive correlation with the level of success of influence relationships.

HC–: The index of items unfavorable toward changing, *C–*, will have a high negative correlation with the level of success of influence relationships.

$$H_0 C+ : \rho\ C+,S \leqslant 0 \qquad H_0 C- : \rho\ C-,S \geqslant 0$$
$$H_1 C+ : 1 \geqslant \rho\ C+,S \geqslant 0 \qquad H_1 C- : -1 \leqslant \rho\ C-,S \leqslant 0$$

Refreezing

HR+: The index of items favorable toward refreezing, *R+*, will have a high positive correlation with the level of success of influence relationships.

HR–: The index of items unfavorable toward refreezing, *R–*, will have a high negative correlation with the level of success of influence relationships.

$$H_0 R+ : \rho\ R+,S \leqslant 0 \qquad H_0 R- : \rho\ R-,S \geqslant 0$$
$$H_1 R+ : 1 \geqslant \rho\ R+,S \geqslant 0 \qquad H_1 R- : -1 \leqslant \rho\ R-,S \leqslant 0$$

AN EMPIRICAL INVESTIGATION OF THE APPLICATION OF CHANGE THEORY

This chapter reports on an empirical investigation in which the Lewin-Schein theory of change was used to explain the variability in the success of 280 OR/MS projects. In this study specific hypotheses were developed from the Lewin-Schein theory of change. A methodology was developed for measuring the variables contained in these hypotheses, and these hypotheses were tested at the .05 level of significance using Pearson product-moment correlation coefficients, Spearman rank-order correlation coefficients, and Kendall rank-order correlation coefficients.

A pilot test was conducted to assist in developing scales that could be used to measure the independent variables, unfreezing, changing, and refreezing (U,C,R), and the dependent variable, the level of success of the OR/MS influence relationship. In the pilot test eight management science consultants were interviewed using a critical incident technique. Each consultant was asked to consider two OR/MS projects, one exceptionally successful and one exceptionally unsuccessful, and discuss each one at length while the interview was being recorded on tape. The interviewer used a series of general questions in order to elicit a full discussion of each project and still not restrict the scope of the response. Because one is dealing with critical or extreme incidents, a wide variability was insured in the projects being reported on.

The researcher separated the taped interview material into individual ideas or thought units using content analysis. Thought units are either groups of words or sentences that are large enough to have meaning, yet small enough not to have many meanings and be easily identifiable. Each thought unit was recorded on an index card. These thought units represented all the incidents and ideas that had been discussed by the eight respondents.

In order to determine which category these thought units represented, they were categorized using the Q-sort technique. Categories were established for unfreezing, changing, and refreezing, and each of these categories was further broken down into seven subcategories. These subcategories indicated whether the items were either favorable or unfavorable toward the particular category they represented. Seven judges familiar with the Lewin-Schein theory of change independently sorted all of the thought units that had been recorded on index cards into these 21 previously established content categories. The judges were assisted in their sorting by having been provided with definitions of unfreezing, changing, and refreezing. The classification of each thought unit was recorded indicating both the category and level of favorableness as indicated by each judge's evaluation.

A comparison of the judges' evaluations was made. Thought units that had not received a high level of agreement among the judges' evaluation of a category classification were eliminated. This was done by keeping only those thought units receiving a similar categorization by a minimum of five of the seven judges. From these remaining thought units, those that were either highly favorable or highly unfavorable toward the agreed upon category were selected for inclusion in the test instrument. Thought units were discarded if they were neutral concerning a particular characteristic could not be used in measuring the level of favorableness or unfavorableness of that characteristic.

A behaviorally anchored scale needed to measure the level of success of the OR/MS projects was also developed in the pilot test. A behaviorally anchored scale provides the respondent with a number of categories that, when summed, are believed to represent the variable being measured. Each category has a scale with behavioral description representing high, intermediate, and low levels of that category. By comparing his actual experience with these behavioral categories, the respondent can locate his experience or incident with respect to all potential projects. This provides the repsondent with a uniform basis for evaluation.

This scale was developed through an interactive process. In the pilot test the respondents were asked to suggest criteria that could be used to measure the level of success of the projects they were discussing. The respondents were also asked to suggest behavioral anchors that could be used for measuring these criteria. These criteria and their behavioral anchors were then reviewed by the judges and grouped into four distinct categories. Each category represented a different aspect of the project's success. Categories included: the development of a solution, the profitability of the project, satisfaction of the client with the project, and the consultant's overall satisfaction with the project. The summed categories represented the overall success of the project.

The preliminary questionnaire was constructed from the behaviorally anchored scale and the thought units that had earlier been developed and categorized in the pilot test. In answering the questionnaire the respondent was asked to consider two projects he had actively engaged in, one successful and one unsuccessful. For each project he was asked to answer a series of 66 questions by indicating on a 5-point scale the degree to which each question represented what had occurred in that project. Specifically, the respondent was asked:

> For each statement below, while considering only the project you have selected, decide which of the following answers best applies. Place the number of the answer in the box at the left of the statement.
>
> 1. accurately depicts what occurred
> 2. less accurately depicts what occurred
> 3. don't know or doesn't apply to this project

4. less accurately depicts the opposite of what occurred
5. accurately depicts the opposite of what occurred

When analyzing the questionnaire, the level of any one characteristic for a particular influence relationship was determined by taking the sum of the responses of all questions representing that given characteristic. This was used as the index for that category.

A pretest was used in order to identify problems with the questionnaire. Here the entire instrument was tested exactly as the final test was to be performed. The questionnaire was mailed to the eight management science consultants who had participated in the pilot test. In addition to being asked to complete the questionnaire, these individuals were also asked to comment on the questionnaire and its instructions. These comments and the pretest results were collected and analyzed, and in order to reduce the questionnaire's length the number of questions in the questionnaire was reduced from 66 to 60. This was the only change made resulting from the pretest.

This final test instrument was mailed to 391 members of the Metropolitan New York Chapter of The Institute of Management Sciences (TIMS). The instructions given in the questionnaire were similar to those discussed earlier in the pretest. A copy of the questionnaire can be found in Appendix I. The test instrument measured three independent variables (unfreezing, changing, and refreezing) and one dependent variable (the level of success of the OR/MS influence relationship) with values for each obtained in both a successful and unsuccessful OR/MS influence relationship for each management scientist.

The data from the test consisted of the individual scores for each question in the questionnaire. To assist in the analysis of the data, a summed scale was constructed for each of the experimental variables for all of the returned questionnaires. These scales were constructed by summing the individual question responses for the various questions that comprised the variables being investigated. There were 193 responses to the questionnaire resulting in a 50.8 percent response rate. These questionnaires provide complete data concerning the levels of unfreezing, changing, and refreezing and the level of success of 280 OR/MS projects. These data were then used to test the hypotheses which had been developed from the Lewin-Schein change theory.

ANALYSIS OF EXPERIMENTAL RESULTS

The hypotheses that had been developed from the Lewin-Schein theory of change were tested using the experimental data obtained from the questionnaires. Pearson product-moment correlation coefficients were calculated between the individual indices of $U+$, $U-$, $C+$, $C-$, $R+$, and $R-$, each of which had been paired with the level of success index (LSI). This was done to test for a linear relationship between these paired values that had been hypothesized from the Lewin-Schein theory. A test of significance utilizing the *t* test and partial R^2's were also computed for these paired variables. Results are shown in Table 10.2.

All correlation coefficients had proper signs and were found to be significant at the .0005 level using a one-tailed *t* test thereby supporting the experimental hypothesis. The indices of refreezing ($R+$, $R-$) had the highest correlation coefficients with 0.85 and −0.62, respectively, therefore rejecting the null hypotheses. This means that those projects with the highest level of refreezing were the more successful projects. The partial R^2 values were particularly significant. $R+$ individually explained 72.5 percent of the variation in the LSI, and $R-$ individually explained 38.5 percent.

One of the critical differences between the Lewin-Schein theory of change and other change theories is the recognition of the need for unfreezing before change can effectively be introduced. In the experimental results the correlation coefficients of unfreezing ($U+$, $U-$) were equally high at 0.45 and −0.46, respectively. Both were significant at the .0005 level, thus rejecting the null hypotheses for unfreezing. The indices of $U+$ and $U-$ respectively explained 20.4 percent and 21 percent of the variation in LSI. This strong linear relationship between unfreezing and the level of success of the project indicated that the projects with the higher levels of unfreezing were also the more successful. This primary hypothesis of the Lewin-Schein change theory was thus supported.

The correlation coefficients of changing ($C+$, $C-$) were also significant at the .0005 level with values of 0.40 and 0.58, respectively, thus rejecting the null hypotheses.

Hopefully, the experimental data conformed to the underlying assump-

Table 10.2.
Experimental Results

Variable	t*,†	Partial R^2	LSI	$U+$	$U-$	$C+$	$C-$	$R+$	$R-$
			Intercorrelation Matrix						
$U+$	8.44	.204	0.45	1.00					
$U-$	−8.76	.217	−0.46	−0.39	1.00				
$C+$	7.30	.161	0.40	0.62	−0.19	1.00			
$C-$	−11.87	.336	−0.58	−0.42	0.61	−0.40	1.00		
$R+$	27.12	.725	0.85	0.53	−0.46	0.47	−0.59	1.00	
$R-$	−13.20	.385	−0.62	−0.41	0.42	−0.37	0.52	−0.64	1.00

*All values were significant at the .0005 level.
†Degrees of freedom equals $N-2 = 278$d.f.

tions, which must be met in order to use Pearson product-moment correlations. The most critical assumptions are: the pairs of observations are independent, the joint distribution is bivariate normal, and variables are measured in an interval scale. In many cases these assumptions are met and, even when they are not met, the data may tend to approximate these assumptions. If these assumptions are met then the Pearson product-moment correlational analysis has a higher power efficiency than other analytical methods with less stringent assumptions; one would prefer to use this method because of the higher power efficiency. The requirement that variables be measured in an interval scale may cause difficulty because the properties of the measuring instrument being developed are not known. The scale may only act to rank the variables, and assumptions concerning an interval scale may not be met.

Spearman rank-order correlational analysis is a nonparametric statistical test requiring only an ordinal scale for measuring. Here the paired values are replaced by ranks in both dependent and independent variables. Ranks are determined by arranging the data points in order of increasing size. The difference in ranks between paired dependent variables are determined and a correlation coefficient is calculated from these rank values. This still requires random sampling from independent bivariate sample populations but interval measurement is not required.

Kendall rank-order correlational analysis is another nonparametric statistical test similar to the Spearman rank-order test. Here the paired values are tested for a monatonic relationship by measuring the difference in the sequence in ordering of the paired dependent and independent variables. Results are similar to Spearman rank-order results.

Nonparametric statistical tests have a lower power efficiency than parametric tests when the stringent assumptions of the parametric tests are met. It was impossible to determine before hand, however, if the data generated by the questionnaire met these stringent restrictions. Only by analyzing the experimental data, using various analytical methods, could the most appropriate analytical method be determined. Before analyzing the data, it was impossible to tell which underlying test assumption would be violated most severely. As a check, rank-order tests were also used. All three methods were therefore used, and a comparison was made of their results.

Both Spearman and Kendall rank-order correlation coefficients were computed from the experimental data. Results, including the Pearson product-moment correlations, are shown in Table 10.3. All values were calculated for each of the six independent variables using the level of success index as the dependent variable. Results using Spearman rank-order coefficients and Kendall rank-order analysis all supported the experimental hypotheses and led to conclusions similar to those reached using Pearson product-moment analysis

Table 10.3.
Experimental Results

Vari-able	Pearson product moment		Spearman rank order		Kendall rank order		
	$\rho_{X,S}$	t^*	ρ_S	t^*	τ	SD	Z^*
$U+$	0.45	8.44	0.46	8.75	0.31	.04	7.86
$U-$	−0.46	−8.76	−0.46	−8.87	−0.31	.04	−7.83
$C+$	0.40	7.30	0.39	7.12	0.28	.04	7.30
$C-$	−0.58	−11.87	−0.57	−11.78	−0.41	.04	−10.42
$R+$	0.85	27.12	0.84	26.30	0.61	.04	15.70
$R-$	−0.62	−13.20	−0.61	−13.15	−0.43	.04	−11.00

*278d.f.; all t and Z values significant at the .0005 level.

RETEST OF THE TEST INSTRUMENT

A retest was used to test the reliability of the test instrument. A sample of 39 individuals who had completed and returned the questionnaire were asked to complete an identical questionnaire dealing with the same project that had been reported on earlier. The time between the original test and retest was less than one month with both tests reporting on the same project. Therefore, no significant change was expected between the two values of the test-retest results. Any such change would have indicated lack of stability of the test instrument with a corresponding lack of reliability.

A total of 22 retests were returned resulting in complete test-retest information on 33 different OR/MS projects. The various indices were computed from the retest information, and correlation coefficients of the paired test-retest values were calculated using Pearson product-moment, Spearman rank-order, and Kendall rank-order correlational techniques for each of the six independent variables and the one dependent variable. These were used to test the reliability of the test instrument.

Results were analyzed and tests of significance were computed and tested using a one-tailed test at the .05 level to determine if change had occurred between the test-retest results. Experimental results are shown in Table 10.4. In all cases the null hypotheses were rejected at a more stringent level of significance than the required .05 level indicating a high level of stability of the test instrument.

The test-retest Pearson product moment correlation coefficients were quite high. The level of success index had the highest correlation coefficient (ρ = .97), whereas $C+$ had the lowest (ρ = .69). All values were significant at the .001

Table 10.4.
Test-Retest Results

	Pearson product moment			Spearman rank order			Kendall rank order			
Variable	r	t	SIG*	ρ_S	t	SIG*	τ	SD	Z	SIG*
$U+$	.75	6.31	.001	.80	7.43	.001	.65	.124	5.22	.001
$U-$	.86	9.39	.001	.80	7.43	.001	.63	.124	5.06	.001
$C+$	.69	5.30	.001	.47	2.96	.005	.46	.124	3.69	.001
$C-$	.91	12.28	.001	.85	9.00	.001	.69	.124	5.55	.001
$R+$	.92	13.22	.001	.83	8.30	.001	.68	.124	5.45	.001
$R-$	.76	6.53	.001	.77	6.69	.001	.57	.124	4.59	.001
LSI	.97	22.01	.001	.96	18.92	.001	.88	.124	7.08	.001

*one-tailed test; d.f. = $N - 2 = 33 - 2 = 31$

level indicating consistent results. The null hypotheses were also rejected using both Spearman rank-order and Kendall rank-order techniques, and, with the exception of ρ_S, $C+$, all results were significant at the .001 level. The test-retest results demonstrated a high level of stability of the test instrument.

FINDINGS AND CONCLUSIONS OF THIS STUDY

Management scientists frequently are employed as change agents attempting to bring about change in client organizations. In many cases desired changes do not occur, and a great many technically well-conceived OR/MS projects fail in implementation. Because there is a natural tendency on the part of organizations to resist change, this failure of implementation is not surprising. The management scientist, however, has the responsibility of overcoming this resistance to change and insuring the implementation of the project.

This study has applied the Lewin-Schein theory of change to the OR/MS influence relationship and has used change theory to help explain the wide variation in the success of implementation of OR/MS projects. All of the hypotheses, which had been developed from the Lewin-Schein theory of change, were supported and the results were found to be quite stable in a test-retest analysis. This research suggests that the success of implementation of OR/MS projects can be significantly improved through the application of Lewin-Schein change theory.

References

1. Huysmans, Jan H. B. M., "The Effectiveness of the Cognitive-Style Constraint in Implementing Operations Research Proposals," *Management Science,* **17**, no. 1, 92–104 (September 1970).
2. Lewin, Kurt, "Group Decision and Social Change," in *Readings in Social Psychology,* Maccoby, Newcomb, and Hartley (Eds.), New York: Holt, Rinehart and Winston, 1947, pp. 197–211.
3. Lippitt, Ronald, Watson, Jeanne, and Westley, Bruce, *The Dynamics of Planned Change,* New York: Harcourt Brace Jovanovich, 1958, pp. 129–140.
4. D. G. Malcolm, "On the Need for Improvement in Implementation of O.R.," *Management Science,* **II**, no. 4, B-48–B-58 (February 1965).
5. Schein, Edgar H., "The Mechanism of Change," in *Interpersonal Dynamics,* Bennis, Schein, Steele, and Berlew (Eds.), Homewood, Ill.: The Dorsey Press, 1964, pp. 362–378.
6. Schein, Edgar H., and Bennis, Warren G., *Personal and Organizational Change Through Group Methods,* New York: Wiley, 1965, p. 278.

Appendix I

Section A

Management scientists are sometimes engaged in projects that have the potential for influencing client organizations.

Think of one project you have participated in where you, as a management scientist, have had either an *exceptionally high* or *exceptionally low* level of influence on the client organization.

Select a nontrivial project, one where you expended a considerable amount of effort and that would have had a significant impact on the client organization. This project may be a recent one or one in which you were engaged in the past, perhaps with a different employer. It should be one that has been concluded.

For each statement below, while considering only the project you have selected, decide which of the following answers best applies. Place the number of the answer in the box at the left of the statement.

1. accurately depicts what occured
2. less accurately depicts what occured
3. don't know or doesn't apply to this project
4. less accurately depicts the opposite of what occured
5. accurately depicts the opposite of what occured

EXAMPLE:

A. Management felt comfortable using the new solution.

If management felt comfortable using the new solution, then indicate #1.

If management did not feel comfortable using the new solution, then indicate #5.

If no new solution was proposed and therefore the statement doesn't apply, then indicate #3.

If the statement applies, but you have absolutely no idea what the answer is, then indicate #3.

There is no *right* response. We are only concerned with what actually occurred. Please answer *all* questions.

The following terminology has been used to better understand these statements:

We, Our, I–The consultant or management scientist conducting the study.
The division–The subsection of the company or organization in which the study was conducted.
The company–The entire organization, usually excluding the division in which the study was conducted.
Top management–President, V.P., Comptroller, or Board of Directors of the company.

☐ 1. We had demonstrated success in similar projects in other divisions.
☐ 2. Top management of the company ignored our solution.
☐ 3. We jointly gathered data with management of the division.
☐ 4. Management of the division did not recognize the need for change.
☐ 5. After the solution was initially implemented, we made sure managers got positive feedback.
☐ 6. The problem was significant to the company's future.
☐ 7. After the solution was initially implemented, we tried to encourage new patterns of relationships between individuals in the company.
☐ 8. Management of the division initially looked upon the project as a chore.
☐ 9. We persuaded management of the division to discuss former assumptions.
☐ 10. The problem lent itself to tools of analysis that we were familiar with.
☐ 11. We didn't try to support and encourage new behavior of the manager after the solution was initially implemented.
☐ 12. We sequentially improved our solution.
☐ 13. Top management of the company was not confident in our ability.
☐ 14. Management examined alternative courses of action.
☐ 15. We weren't experts in the area we were investigating.
☐ 16. The new solution has been shown to be superior to the old through utilization.
☐ 17. Top management of the company was very open with us.
☐ 18. The top management of the company was afraid to get involved in a large-scale project.
☐ 19. The measurement of results in this area is difficult.
☐ 20. We gathered the necessary data ourselves.
☐ 21. Top management was advised of the various options available.
☐ 22. Management of the division initially resented our study.
☐ 23. After an initial successful application we got widespread acceptance of the solution.
☐ 24. There is a lack of standards for evaluating results in this area.
☐ 25. We persuaded management of the division to redefine former assumptions.
☐ 26. Management of the division accepted the superiority of our solution.
☐ 27. The study was concluded too quickly.
☐ 28. Management of the division did not have confidence in us.
☐ 29. We did not have the proper data.
☐ 30. Management of the division did not feel comfortable using the new solution.
☐ 31. Top management of the company became intimately involved.
☐ 32. Management of the division did not provide the requested information.
☐ 33. Top management of the company participated in the development of the solution.
☐ 34. We had earlier completed successful projects for the division.
☐ 35. Management of the division wanted us to use a technique that was improper.

☐ 36. After the solution was initially implemented, we didn't try to reinforce new procedures.
☐ 37. Top management of the company did not encourage other divisions to utilize this solution.
☐ 38. We familiarized ourselves with the operations in this area of the division.
☐ 39. Management of the division initiated the study.
☐ 40. We persuaded management of the division to be dissatisfied with the old solution.
☐ 41. The solution was not compatible with the division's recognized needs.
☐ 42. Because of the study, current performance of the division has now improved.
☐ 43. We persuaded management of the division to open up.
☐ 44. Management of the division now also uses this solution in other areas.
☐ 45. Management of the division developed most of the solution.
☐ 46. The company did not have a high level of need for this solution.
☐ 47. We uncovered alternatives that had not been considered before.
☐ 48. Top management of the company initiated the study.
☐ 49. We did not propose a solution to the problem.
☐ 50. Management of the division thought they could do the job well themselves.
☐ 51. Management of the division is satisfied with the solution.
☐ 52. Top management of the company did not recognize the need for change.
☐ 53. We didn't try to reestablish stability in the company after the solution was initially implemented.
☐ 54. Management of the division utilized the solution.
☐ 55. Management of the division felt threatened by the study.
☐ 56. Management of the division did not understand our solution.
☐ 57. Management of the division recognized the need for change.
☐ 58. Management of the division did not participate in the development of the solution.
☐ 59. When we asked management what they wanted, they couldn't tell us.
☐ 60. We couldn't educate the management of the division.

For the project you have just considered, indicate which one of the following answers best applies for each group below, and place the number of the answer in the box to the left of the group. (If necessary, give what you think it would have been).

A. Development of a solution

☐

1. A solution was not developed.
2. A solution was developed, not implemented.
3. A solution was developed, partially implemented.
4. A solution was developed, fully implemented as intended.
5. A solution was developed, fully implemented here and in other areas.

B. Profitability of the project

☐

1. The project caused a large loss for the company.
2. The project did not cover its cost.
3. The project paid for itself.
4. The project provided an acceptable return on investment.
5. The project provided higher than usual return on investment.

C. Satisfaction of the client with the project

1. The client was highly dissatisfied with the project.
2. The client was dissatisfied with the project.
☐ 3. The client was neutral toward the project.
4. The client was satisfied with the project.
5. The client was highly satisfied with the project.

D. Your overall satisfaction with the project

1. You were highly dissatisfied with the project.
2. You were dissatisfied with the project.
☐ 3. You were neutral toward the project.
4. You were satisfied with the project.
5. You were highly satisfied with the project.

END SECTION

Section B

You have just considered a project in which you had either an *exceptionally high* or *exceptionally low* level of influence on the client organization. Now, please select a different project in which you had the opposite level of influence, that is, exceptionally low now if the first was exceptionally high, or exceptionally high now if the first was exceptionally low.

Again select a nontrivial project, one where you expended a considerable amount of effort and that would have had a significant impact on the client organization. This project may be a recent one or one in which you were engaged in the past, perhaps with a different employer. It should be one that has been concluded.

For those who have difficulty considering a project with an exceptionally low level of influence, consider the project you participated in that had the lowest level of influence on the client.

For each statement below, while considering only the project you have selected, decide which of the following answers best applies. Place the number of the answer in the box at the left of the statement.

1. accurately depicts what occurred
2. less accurately depicts what occurred
3. don't know, or doesn't apply to this project
4. less accurately depicts the opposite of what occurred
5. accurately depicts the opposite of what occurred

There is no *right* response. We are only concerned with what actually occurred. Please answer *all* questions.

The following terminology has been used to better understand these statements:

We Our, I–the consultant or management scientist conducting the study.
The division–The sub section of the company or organization in which the study was conducted.

The company–The entire organization, usually to exclude the division in which the study was conducted.

Top management–President, V.P., Comptroller, or Board of Directors of the Company.

☐ 1. We had demonstrated success in similar projects in other divisions.
☐ 2. Top management of the company ignored our solution.
☐ 3. We jointly gathered data with management of the division.
☐ 4. Management of the division did not recognize the need for change.
☐ 5. After the solution was initially implemented, we made sure managers got positive feedback.
☐ 6. The problem was significant to the company's future.
☐ 7. After the solution was initially implemented, we tried to encourage new patterns of relationships between individuals in the company.
☐ 8. Management of the division initially looked upon the project as a chore.
☐ 9. We persuaded management of the division to discuss former assumptions.
☐ 10. The problem lent itself to tools of analysis that we were familiar with.
☐ 11. We didn't try to support and encourage new behavior of the manager after the solution was initially implemented.
☐ 12. We sequentially improved our solution.
☐ 13. Top management of the company was not confident in our ability.
☐ 14. Management examined alternative courses of action.
☐ 15. We weren't experts in the area we were investigating.
☐ 16. The new solution has been shown to be superior to the old through utilization.
☐ 17. Top management of the company was very open with us.
☐ 18. The top management of the company was afraid to get involved in a large-scale project.
☐ 19. The measurement of results in this area is difficult.
☐ 20. We gathered the necessary data ourselves.
☐ 21. Top management was advised of the various options available.
☐ 22. Management of the division initially resented our study.
☐ 23. After an initial successful application we got widespread acceptance of the solution.
☐ 24. There is a lack of standards for evaluating results in this area.
☐ 25. We persuaded management of the division to redefine former assumptions.
☐ 26. Management of the division accepted the superiority of our solution.
☐ 27. The study was concluded too quickly.
☐ 28. Management of the division did not have confidence in us.
☐ 29. We did not have the proper data.
☐ 30. Management of the division did not feel comfortable using the new solution.
☐ 31. Top management of the company became intimately involved.
☐ 32. Management of the division did not provide the requested information.
☐ 33. Top management of the company participated in the development of the solution.
☐ 34. We had earlier completed successful projects for the division.
☐ 35. Management of the division wanted us to use a technique that was improper.
☐ 36. After the solution was initially implemented, we didn't try to reinforce new procedures.
☐ 37. Top management of the company did not encourage other divisions to utilize this solution.
☐ 38. We familiarized ourselves with the operations in this area of the division.
☐ 39. Management of the division initiated the study.
☐ 40. We persuaded management of the division to be dissatisfied with the old solution.

☐ 41. The solution was not compatible with the division's recognized needs.
☐ 42. Because of the study, current performance of the division has now improved.
☐ 43. We persuaded management of the division to open up.
☐ 44. Management of the division now also uses this solution in other areas.
☐ 45. Management of the division developed most of the solution.
☐ 46. The company did not have a high level of need for this solution.
☐ 47. We uncovered alternatives that had not been considered before.
☐ 48. Top management of the company initiated the study.
☐ 49. We did not propose a solution to the problem.
☐ 50. Management of the division thought they could do the job well themselves.
☐ 51. Management of the division is satisfied with the solution.
☐ 52. Top management of the company did not recognize the need for change.
☐ 53. We didn't try to reestablish stability in the company after the solution was initially implemented.
☐ 54. Management of the division utilized the solution.
☐ 55. Management of the division felt threatened by the study.
☐ 56. Management of the division did not understand our solution.
☐ 57. Management of the division recognized the need for change.
☐ 58. Management of the division did not participate in the development of the solution.
☐ 59. When we asked management what they wanted, they couldn't tell us.
☐ 60. We couldn't educate the management of the division.

For the project you have just considered, indicate which one of the following answers best applies for each group below, and place the number of the answer in the box to the left of the group. (If necessary, give what you think it would have been).

A. Development of a solution

☐

1. A solution was not developed.
2. A solution was developed, not implemented.
3. A solution was developed, partially implemented.
4. A solution was developed, fully implemented as intended.
5. A solution was developed, fully implemented here and in other areas.

B. Profitability of the project

☐

1. The project caused a large loss for the company.
2. The project did not cover its cost.
3. The project paid for itself.
4. The project provided an acceptable return on investment.
5. The project provided higher than usual return on investment.

C. Satisfaction of the client with the project

☐

1. The client was highly dissatisfied with the project.
2. The client was dissatisfied with the project.
3. The client was neutral toward the project.
4. The client was satisfied with the project.
5. The client was highly satisfied with the project.

D. Your overall satisfaction with the project

1. You were highly dissatisfied with the project.
2. You were dissatisfied with the project.

☐ 3. You were neutral toward the project.

4. You were satisfied with the project.
5. You were highly satisfied with the project.

END SECTION

Chapter 11

On Mutual Understanding and the Implementation Problem: A Philosophical Case Study of the Psychology of the *Apollo* Moon Scientists*

Ian I. Mitroff

RATIONAL, *adj.*, Devoid of all delusions save those of observation, experience and reflection.

Ambrose Bierce
The Devil's Dictionary

In their landmark paper [5], Churchman and Schainblatt identified four positions with respect to the problem of implementation: (1) the separate function position, (2) the communication position, (3) the persuasion position, and (4) the mutual understanding position. Each of these positions depended fundamentally on the crucial concept of understanding. The separate function position asserted that in order for implementation to occur it was not necessary for either the manager (M) or the management scientist (MS) to understand one another. Positions (2) and (3), on the other hand, asserted that it was necessary for one of the parties to understand the other but that it was not necessary for both parties to understand each other. Contrary to these positions, the mutual understanding position asserted that it was necessary for both the M and the MS to understand one another if implementation was to occur. Of the commentators who were invited to review the Churchman-Schainblatt paper [7], most were favorably predisposed toward the mutual understanding position. They agreed that implementation demanded mutual understanding. However, once this was granted, agreement was less forthcoming. A number of concerns surfaced regarding the concept of understanding. More specifically, clarification was needed regarding the definition and meaning of the concept of understanding. Even further, a number of the commentators wanted to see in more detail what the mutual understanding position entailed. It was generally felt that Churchman and Schainblatt had done an excellent job in pointing up

*This work was partially supported under NASA grant NGL39011080.

the defects of the separate function, communication, and persuasion positions but that they had not said enough regarding the mutual understanding position. Although this, to be sure, was a valid point, it was not, in my understanding, the basic purpose of their paper. If I understand the spirit of their paper, it was to introduce the crucial concept of understanding and to argue its necessity with regard to the concept of implementation, not to explicate both concepts in all of their fascinating and varied forms.

The purpose of this chapter is to add to our understanding of the concept of mutual understanding, particularly with regard to what the mutual understanding position entails. The basic argument of this chapter is briefly as follows: (1) If in order for implementation to occur it is necessary that the two parties to the implementation (the manager or the client and the scientist) both understand one another, then the most difficult implementation problems may be those wherein the client is also a scientist. That is, as hard as it is for the scientist and the manager to mutually understand one another, there is evidence that it may be even harder (or at the least, just as hard) for scientists of a different kind to mutually understand one another. (2) So put, the problem of implementation is not merely a management science problem, but it is also a problem for the philosophy of science and the social psychology of science [*2, 15*], to mention but two of the many fields having a vital interest in the problem. In other words, one of the fundamental issues underlying the problem of implementation is the fact that different scientists have different concepts (images) of science and of scientists; hence, the problem or difficulty of mutual understanding between fundamentally differing kinds of scientists. In short, before scientists can come to understand the manager (client), they will first have to come to better understand themselves and to develop a deeper understanding of science [*21*]. *Self-reflection is a necessary precondition for implementation.*

DIFFERENT TYPES OF SCIENTISTS AND DIFFERENT CONCEPTS OF SCIENCE

This chapter is primarily based on a philosophical case study of the psychology of the *Apollo* moon scientists. The subjects of the study were over 40 of the scientists who participated in the *Apollo* lunar missions. The basic purpose of the study was to test certain contemporary and critical propositions in the sociology, psychology, and philosophy of science through a combined philosophical and behavioral science investigation into the attitudes, beliefs, and practices of a highly interesting yet specific group of scientists. Each scientist in the study was intensively interviewed on four separate occasions over a span of three years. The scientists were generally interviewed in the time period just after the completion of one *Apollo* mission and before the start of another, thus between *Apollos 11* and *12, 12* and *14, 14* and *15,* and *15* and *16.*

The central question with which the study began and that occupied it throughout was the following: Would it be possible to identify and to study those specific scientists, if any, who exhibited a high degree of *prior* commitment (i.e., before *Apollo 11*) to certain pet hypotheses or theories regarding the nature and origin of the moon and who thus showed as a result a high degree of reluctance to give up their pet hypotheses in the face of or in spite of the data returned subsequently from the moon? In terms of the interviews with the 40 scientists, a small number of scientists were overwhelmingly and consistently nominated by their peers as the ones most likely to hang onto their hypotheses 'til death do them part.' The perceptions of these few key scientists by their peers (the 40 scientists) were repeatedly studied over each interview round for their implications for the sociology, psychology, and philosophy of science.

In general the issues and subsequent topics that were investigated were too numerous for us merely to be able to list them, let alone for us to report the results of them here. However it should at least be mentioned that one of the topics with which the study was concerned was the precise measurement, in theoretical terms, of the change in scientific beliefs of the scientists with respect to certain hypotheses proposed for the origin of the moon. To this end, repeated measurements were taken of each scientist's opinion of the probability of the various scientific hypotheses at various points during the *Apollo* missions. The beliefs and attitudes of the scientists were also studied and measured with respect to certain basic issues in the methodology of science. The reader is referred to *The Subjective Side of Science: A Philosophical Enquiry Into The Psychology of the* Apollo *Moon Scientists* [*21*], for a full description of the study, e.g., a detailed description of the sample of scientists, the study's methodology, its results, and, most of all, its implications.

Very early on during the first round of interviews, a number of the scientists, independently of one another and of their own accord, suggested a typology of different kinds of scientists. In their opinion, their experience suggested that there were very sharp differences between a realtively small number of fundamentally differing kinds of scientists. Indeed, on presenting the typology to the rest of the sample for their reaction and evaluation, a remarkable degree of consensus was obtained as to, first, the validity of the typology, and then, second, the names of those specific scientists who most typified each of the various types. The precision of the typology was continually refined on subsequent interview rounds. In addition the perceptions of those few scientists who were most frequently nominated as best typifying the various types were systematically measured. Each of the 40 scientists in the study reported their perceptions of these few scientists in terms of a variety of attitudinal scales.

Although the differences between the various types cannot be reduced to a single or simple underlying dimension, the most fundamental dimension and the one that originally suggested the typology was that of speculativeness or willingness to extrapolate beyond the available data. In any social grouping, there are always those who prefer to stay close to the facts and those who prefer to venture out beyond them even at the risk of ignoring them. Type I scientists, were distinguished by the essential defining quality that they excelled at extrapolating from data. Although they were often fine, detailed experimenters themselves and even at times enjoyed experimental results or numbers for their own sake, theorizing was obviously their most pleasurable and exalted task. *Type I scientists were willing and even relished the bold intuitive and theoretical leaps always required in making inferences from incomplete data to a comprehensive and encompassing theory.* Type III scientists represented the other end of the spectrum. Here, numbers are often relished primarily for their own sake. There is a preoccupation, even an obsession, with data gathering. There is often an extreme disdain of theorists who deal with highly inferrential and abstract concepts. Speculation or extrapolation from data is valued little, *only* engaged in when the data clearly warrant such extrapolation, and then with extreme cautiousness. Where Type I's more readily tended to see the positive advantages of speculation in science and to speak glowingly of it, Type III's tended to disparage it. They tended to equate speculation with wild theorizing and refer to it as "finger-painting in the sky."

Type III scientists are often seen as brilliant but extremely narrow and specialized experimenters. In some instances, they are regarded as nothing more than "super-technicians with a Ph.D." (In fairness, it was noted that theorists can often be just as narrow. In general though, it was the consensus opinion of the sample that it was much more difficult for a theorist to be a narrow specialist than it was for an experimenter. Theorizing on something so broad as the origin of the moon requires, by its very nature, that a scientist be familiar with, if not competent in, several diverse scientific fields.) Type II scientists represented something in between. Here were to be found scientists who were equally capable of doing competent experimental work as well as engaging in modest theorizing and extrapolating activities. From time to time, they could even rise to bold feats of theorizing and extrapolation, but in general, they represented the middle ground, running to neither of the extremes represented by Types I and III.

The original typology of three types was refined in two ways: (1) each of the I, II, and III types was further subdivided, and the final typology thus contained six types instead of three, and (2) the number of dimensions underlying the typology was expanded, allowing the differences between the types to be drawn more sharply. Although both of these refinements were important,

Table 11.1.
Adjective Profiles for the Different Types of Scientists

Semantic differential scales	TYPES					
	S_I^3	S_I^2	S_I^1	S_{II}	Y	S_{III}
Biased-Impartial 1	Markedly biased	Markedly biased	Moderately biased	Neither or both impartial-biased	Moderately impartial	Neither or both impartial-biased
Brilliant-Dull 2	Extremely brilliant	Markedly brilliant	Markedly brilliant	Markedly brilliant	Neither brilliant nor dull	Neither brilliant nor dull
Theoretical-Practical 3	Markedly theoretical	Markedly theoretical	Moderately theoretical	Both practical and theoretical	Both practical and theoretical	Moderately practical
Generalist-Specialist 4	Markedly generalist	Moderately generalist	Markedly generalist	Moderately generalist	Moderately generalist	Markedly specialist
Creative-Unimaginative 5	Extremely creative	Markedly creative	Markedly creative	Markedly creative	Moderately creative	Neither creative nor unimaginative
Agressive-Retiring 6	Extremely aggressive	Markedly aggressive	Markedly aggressive	Markedly aggressive	Moderately aggressive	Moderately aggressive
Vague-Precise 7	Neither or both vague-precise	Moderately precise	Moderately precise	Markedly precise	Moderately precise	Markedly precise
Rigid-Flexible 8	Moderately rigid	Moderately rigid	Neither or both flexible-rigid	Moderately flexible	Markedly flexible	Moderately rigid
Theoretician-Experimentalist 9	Markedly theoretician	Markedly theoretician	Moderately theoretician	Both experimentalist-theoretician	Both experimentalist-theoretician	Markedly experimentalist
Speculative-Analytical 10	Markedly speculative	Moderately speculative	Moderately speculative	Both speculative-analytical	Moderately speculative	Markedly analytical

KEY: Extremely or significantly = 1.0 to 1.5 or 6.5 to 7.0 scale values on SD's
Markedly = 1.5 to 2.5 or 5.5 to 6.5 scale values on SD's
Moderately = 2.5 to 3.5 or 4.5 to 5.5 scale values on SD's
Neither or both = 3.5 to 4.5 scale values on SD's

only the latter need concern us here. Table 11.1 gives the results of one of the many exercises that were used to measure more precisely the differences between Types I, II, and III.

From the first set of interviews, five specific scientists were identified as significant representatives for each of the three types. The perceptions of each of these specific scientists by the 40 scientists were separately measured in terms of a semantic differential (SD) consisting of 10 scales [*24*]. The perceptions of three Type I scientists, S_I^3, S_I^2, and S_I^1; one Type II scientist, S_{II}; and one Type III scientist, S_{III} were scaled. Finally one general category Y was created, which referred to the designation yourself. That is, in addition to scaling five other scientists, each of the 40 scientists scaled himself so that it could later be determined where the general body of scientists lay in relation to the specific representatives of the various types.

It should be noted that the decision to scale three Type I scientists was made for very specific reasons. In response to the question, "What scientists are, in your opinion, most committed to their pet hypotheses or theories and as a result least likely to shift their commitment as a consequence of the Apollo data?," three scientists were consistently nominated over and over again. These three scientists were also mentioned as the most outstanding examples of Type I scientists. More than any other group of scientists, these scientists excited the envy and hostility of their peers. They also excited the most positive superlatives. They not only dazzled their peers with their spectacular feats of speculative theorizing, but they also offended them with the abrasive, provocative, and often aggressive manner with which they presented and defended their theories. These reasons alone warranted comparing these three Type I scientists among themselves as well as against the other types. In addition it was felt that it was important enough to get a collective portrait of those scientists who were perceived as most committed to their ideas to warrant the study of three Type I's.

Table 11.1 shows that there is a marked and systematic difference between the perceptions of the types as we move across the table from left to right. That is, if we take the means ($\bar{x}$) of the perceptions of each of the five specific scientists, including the general category yourself, Y, and lay them out on ten straight lines (one line for each of the ten scales against which the types are being rated as indicated in Table 11.1) then S_I^3 is generally found at one extreme of the scales, S_{III} at the other. Furthermore, S_I^3, S_I^2, and S_I^1 bunch together; i.e., the differences between S_I^3, S_I^2, and S_I^1 are inconsequential when compared to the differences between themselves as a group and the other types of scientists. Above all it should be noted that the differences between types (S_I, S_{II}, Y, and S_{III}) are highly significant. We are not dealing with borderline or trivial differences. A one-way analysis of variance (ANOVA) reveals that the differences between the mean scores for the types are statistically significant at an α-level of substantially less than 0.001, i.e. $\alpha \ll 0.001$. Furthermore, multidimensional scaling and correlational analyses [*34*] reveal that the ordering pattern, S_I^3, S_I^2, S_I^1, S_{II}, Y, S_{III}, is itself statistically significant. That is, *not only are the differences between the types significant but so is the relative placement (order) of the types with respect to one another.*

The significance of these results is as follows: (1) they add needed support to the validity of the original typology, and (2) , they give us some interesting insights regarding the psychological differences between the great and the normal scientist [*21*]. With regard to the first point, if the specific scientists, S_I^3, S_I^2, S_I^1, S_{II}, and S_{III}, are really representative of the various types, then it is comforting that they at least fell on certain of the scales according to prior expectations. For example, according to the original definitions of the types one would expect that S_I^3, S_I^2, and S_I^1 would tend to fall toward the biased end of the biased-impartial scale, S_{II} in the middle, and S_{III} toward the impartial end. (S_{III} is the only scientist who does not fall as expected on this scale.) The placements follow similarly on scales 3, 9, and 10. Scales 9 and 10 are particularly crucial because they literally feed back the original dimensions on which the typology was initially proposed. It would have been particularly distressing if the placements on these scales turned out to be anything other than as expected. Of course this by itself does not establish either the uniqueness or the ultimate correctness of the typology, but it is reassuring that it has survived the most elemental tests. The full report [*21*] of the study presents an extensive number of validating exercises. The typology survives every one of these critical tests.

With regard to the second point, the differences between the three Type I scientists and the single type III scientist are most instructive. In order to appreciate the significance of these differences it is necessary to point out that throughout the study S_{III} was the particular scientist who was judged most representative of the *average* or *typical scientist* in the lunar program. (It should be emphasized in this regard that throughout the study the scientists talked extremely freely about one another. There were as a result many opportunities to obtain consistent portraits of the various scientists. That is, the descriptions and inferences with respect to the types are not based on isolated, infrequent observations.) The three Type I scientists on the other hand were the ones who were most frequently judged the *outstanding, extraordinary scientists* of the program, the scientists who most consistently stood at the creative apex of the profession. It is thus both interesting and important to compare the adjective profiles between these two rather distinct types, I and III.

If the Type-I scientists most nearly correspond to Kuhn's [*16*] great scientist (as I believe they do), and if the Type III scientist most nearly corresponds to the normal scientist, then the results imply that the great scientist is more likely to be more creative in the production of bold and speculative ideas. They are also most likely to be the kinds of scientists who become most rigidly committed to their ideas. That is, the three Type I's were perceived as extremely creative in the sense of their being able to produce and having produced many original innovative ideas over a long period of time, and in this sense they were regarded as extremely flexible. They possessed the requisite mental agility and nimbleness of mind to see old problems in a new light and to perceive (literally invent) highly imaginative patterns in a complex sets of data; thus, the judgments of brilliant, theoretical, generalist, speculative, and the tendency toward vagueness. On the other hand, they were perceived as extremely attached to their ideas once they were produced; thus, the strong judgments of bias, aggressiveness, and rigidity. Indeed, independent exercises [*21*] establish that over a span of three years, there is virtually *no* perceived shift (according to the 40 scientists) in the positions of each of the three Type I scientists with respect to certain scientific hypotheses with which they have long been associated. This point cannot be overemphasized. Although the psychological differences are interesting and important for their own sake, they are even more important for what they imply for the understanding of the growth and change of scientific ideas. Although it is beyond the scope of this chapter to demonstrate how these psychological differences operate in detail, it can be shown [*21*] what kinds of rationalizations *and* rational arguments the different types use to hang onto, preserve, as well as change their ideas. In other words, under certain circumstances, it is now possible to relate explicitly differences in psychology to the growth of a scientist's ideas.

We shall comment on the implications of these findings with regard to the problem of implementation after we have had the opportunity to review some additional results.

ON THE NATURE AND FUNCTION OF COMMITMENT AND BIAS IN SCIENCE: THE CASE FOR SCIENTISTS AS HIGHLY PARTISAN ADVOCATES

One of the most striking things about the contents of the interviews was the tremendous extent to which the scientists documented the intense emotions that permeate the entire process of science. No matter what the topic that was being discussed—for example, the status of a certain physical theory—the scientists continuously moved the discussion toward a consideration of highly personal matters and social concerns that affected their stance toward the topic. It was fundamentally impossible for them to discuss the status of a physical theory and the evidence for and against that theory without reacting to the proponents of that theory and in the most intense and volatile of terms. It would appear that it is only in idealized accounts of science that scientists are able to keep their personal feelings toward the issues (and particularly their feelings toward those of their peers who are associated with the issues) clearly apart from their abstract, impersonal thoughts about the issues. This is not to say that scientists ought not to keep the two clearly apart. It is to say, however, that the reasons that have been advanced in support of separating the two largely amount to meaningless prescriptions if scientists are psychologically unable to obey them in the heat of practice. If scientists are to keep these two aspects apart then we will have to provide them with far more effective means that will actually allow them to accomplish this. Indeed if it is fundamentally impossible to confine intense emotions in science to a particular area, then the most effective means would actually be a theory about how emotions function in the whole of the scientific process so that we could effectively account for their influence [*6*]. If we could thus account for them, we would not have to worry about eliminating or confining them. Whatever the outcome, mere prescriptions and abstract discourses alone on "good scientific method" do not seem sufficient to do the job (they are necessary, however). Furthermore, it is even debatable whether scientists should always keep the two apart. If there are good reasons for keeping the highly personal and supposedly subjective apart (or at the very least, distinguishable) from the impersonal and supposedly objective, then there are also good reasons for not separating the two. The latter reasons deserve as much serious consideration as the former have received.

From the interviews it is clear that scientific ideas are not only tested against an elaborate background of prior theories and ideas, but they are also tested against an elaborate network of prior social and personal relations. Although theories, ideas, and evidence have an abstract and impersonal side, they also have a strong, concrete, and personal dimension. In many cases this personal dimension actually overwhelms the impersonal. It certainly always influences it.

The interviews also show that theories are associated with particular men who serve and are identified as the personal advocates of those theories. This is particularly true when the theories are bold, provocative, and all encompassing. To disprove or falsify a theory does not merely discredit an abstract entity, but it also discredits the idea and position of a scientist who is personally associated with that idea and who has a stake in it. It was clearly recognized by the respondents that more often than not scientists were ardent, passionate, partisan advocates for their personal theories and that scientists did everything in their power (excluding cheating) to muster every bit of evidence favorable to the theory that they could find. They were not out to falsify their own theories but to confirm them. If they were out to falsify anything, it was the theories of their opponents.

The foregoing remarks do not merely represent my own conclusions and interpretations of the interview materials but they also represent the perceptions of many of the scientists themselves. Indeed, the recognition of the preceding was so strong that time and time again virtually the entire sample of over 40 scientists laughed at, and in the most derisive terms, the notion of the dispassionate, unbiased, objective observer of nature. Not only was it recognized that in point of actual conduct the scientist was more often than not highly committed to a point of view—at the very least to his pet theories and hypotheses—but even more interesting and important, strong reasons were evinced why this *ought* to be the case, i.e., that *ideally* scientists *ought not* to be without strong prior commitments. Now I am perfectly willing to grant that many of these reasons are nothing more than outright rationalizations. Nevertheless even as rationalizations they are still worth considering, because they then represent some of the functional norms and operating rules of practicing scientists. Further they give one reason to pause and consider other models of science that are not dependent on the presumption of untainted, unbiased observers in order for scientific knowledge to result. Because of the importance of these points, it is worthwhile to present some representative excerpts from the interviews:

> SCIENTIST A: Bias has a role to play in science and it serves it well. Part of the business [of science] is to sift the evidence and to come to the right conclusion, and to do this you must have people who argue for both sides of the evidence. This is the only way in which we can straighten the situation out. I wouldn't like scientists to be without bias since a lot of the sides of the argument would never be presented. We must be emotionally committed to the things we do energetically. No one is able to do anything with liberal energy if there is no emotion connected with it.

> SCIENTIST B: The uninvolved, unemotional scientist is just as much a fiction as the mad scientist who will destroy the world for knowledge. Most of the scientists I know have theories and are looking for data to support them; they're not sorting impersonally through the data looking for a theory to fit the data.

> You've got to make a clear distinction between not being objective and cheating. A good scientist will not be above changing his theory if he gets a preponderance of evidence that doesn't support it, but basically he's looking to defend it.

> Without commitment one wouldn't have the energy, the drive to press forward sometimes against extremely difficult odds. Trying to collect data on the moon is not the easiest thing in the world [this may be the biggest understatement of the entire study]. There are not only physical problems but there are bureaucratic problems as well to fight.

> You don't consciously falsify evidence in science, but you put less priority on a piece of data that goes against you. No reputable scientist does this consciously but you do it subconsciously.

> The experimentalist doesn't have to be committed to a theory to do good work, but the theorist does, so the experimentalists can call the theorists metaphysicians. Lunar physics is not typical of science; there have been more theorists than experimentalists. It's a field dominated by theorists; until 2 years ago it was impossible to do experimental work on the moon.

SCIENTIST C: The disinterested scientist is a myth. Even if there were such a being, he probably wouldn't be worth much as a scientist. I still think you can be objective in spite of having strong interests and bias.

If you make neutral statements, nobody really listens to you. You have to stick your neck out. The statements you make in public are actually stronger than those you believe in. You have to get people to remember that you represent a point of view even if for you it's just a possibility.

It takes commitment to be a scientist. One thing that spurs a scientist on is competition, warding off attacks against what you've published.

SCIENTISTS D: In order to be heard you have to overcommit yourself. There's so much stuff if you don't speak out you won't get heard, but you can't be too outrageous or you'll get labeled as a crackpot; you have to be just outrageous enough. If you have an idea, you have to pursue it as hard as you can. You have to ride a horse to the end of the road.[1]

SCIENTIST E: The notion of the disinterested scientist is really a myth that deserves to be put to rest. Those scientists who are committed to the myth have an intensity of commitment which belies the myth.

Those scientists who are the movers are not indifferent. One has to be deeply involved in order to do good work. There *is* the danger that the bolder the scientist is with regard to the nature of his ideas, the more likely he is to become strongly committed to his ideas.

I don't think we have good science because we have adversaries but that it is in the attempt to follow the creed and the ritual of scientific method that the scientist finds himself unconsciously thrust in the role of an adversary.

It should be clearly understood that I am *not* saying that this particular group of scientists did not critically test their theories. They did. Even those scientists who most strongly held onto their theories still tested them. Likewise I am not saying that this particular group of scientists is any less objective than their colleagues in other fields. What I am saying is that the actual process of science is vastly more complicated than its portrayal in the conventional, stereotypical images of science. Indeed, I have argued elsewhere [*21*] that the conventional images of science have actually hindered us from uncovering behavior that would most effectively challenge the conventional images. The fascinating thing about images is that they tend to be self-reinforcing and hence self-perpetuating.

This is not to deny that this conception of science raises as many problems as it promises to solve. For example, it is unfortunately beyond the scope of this chapter to demonstrate in detail how scientific objectivity could still emerge from such a system. In a number of previous papers [*19, 23*] I have tried to lay the foundation for a combined philosophical/behavioral theory of science by outlining various epistemological and behavioral mechanisms whereby a consensually based notion of scientific objectivity could still result even though the starting point was an initial state of strong conflict, i.e., strongly contending adversary positions. The goal (as well as the problem) of such a conception is to show that objectivity is possible, not by excluding strong emotions from science (which is a psychological impossibility), *because* of them, not in spite of them. As Churchman and Ackoff [*3*] have put it:

> Pragmatism does not advocate a scientist who removes all his emotions, sympathies, and the like from his experimental process. This is like asking the scientist to give up being a whole man while he experiments. Perhaps a man's emotion will be the most powerful instrument he has at his disposal in reaching a conclusion. The main task, however, is to enlarge the scope of the scientific model so that we can begin to understand the role of the other types of experience in reaching decisions, and can see how they too can be checked and controlled. The moral, according to the pragmatist, should not be to exclude feeling from scientific method, but to include it in the sense of understanding it better [p. 224].

CONCLUDING REMARKS: SOME IMPLICATIONS FOR MUTUAL UNDERSTANDING

There are a great many implications that could be drawn from the preceding material with regard to the problem of implementation. We have space to draw only a few of the more important of these implications.

Although intense differences between fundamentally differing kinds of scientists create severe strains within the system of science, they also appear to be fundamentally necessary for the advance of science [*14*]. Strangely enough they are also necessary for the mutual understanding between *some* scientists (i.e., for those scientists who can learn from conflict and tolerate differences) and for the ultimate adoption and implementation of *all* scientific ideas [*21*]. For the most part the intense differences between the scientists seemed to make them aware of the necessity for having various types well represented within the system of science. There was a clear recognition that the system would be the worse off if all scientists were of the same kind, if all scientists immediately agreed, or if they immediately gave up their pet hypotheses at the first sign of negative evidence. On the other hand, this is not to say that everybody agreed with this idea. There were more than just a few of the scientists who would be more than happy to see certain of their colleagues disappear from science altogether, particularly those scientists identified as the most extreme of the Type I's. I am thus obviously not contending that intense differences by themselves are sufficient for the occurrence of mutual understanding.

In their paper [*5*], Churchman and Schainblatt defined understanding as follows:

> An individual understands a stimulus if he responds to the stimulus in an efficient manner relative to his ends. For example, the assertion "the manager understands the researcher" means that the manager reacts to what the researcher is trying to do in a manner that improves the manager's chances of attaining a purpose empirically assigned to him [p. B70].

In terms of this concept, I would propose that the highest form of mutual understanding between scientists occurs when:

1. One scientist not only responds positively to the intentions [*1*] of another scientist but is also able to give a sympathetic (yet critical) explication and justification of the psychology of another scientist that differs fundamentally from that of his own.
2. As a necessary corollary to (1), when a scientist can be said to understand his own psychology, i.e., what type he is in relation to the range of other types.

To repeat an earlier point, *self-reflection is a necessary prerequisite to the understanding of others.*

In an age where science is seen as the solution to more and more of our problems and where science is encouraged to study everything under and including the sun, it had better study itself, i.e., it had better examine its own implicit underlying assumptions. If it does not, it will breed a false understanding of itself and of the world around it. We need to better understand the nature of science before we can use science to promote mutual understanding.

References

1. Ackoff, Russell L., and Emery, Fred, *On Purposeful Systems,* Chicago: Aldine, 1972.
2. Churchman, C. West, *The Design of Inquiring Systems,* New York: Basic Books, 1971.
3. Churchman, C. West, and Ackoff, Russell L. *Methods of Inquiry,* Saint Louis: Educational Publishers, 1950.

4. Churchman, C. West, and Schainblatt, A. H., "On Mutual Understanding," *Management Science,* **12,** no. 2, B40–B47 (October 1965).
5. Churchman, C. West, and Schainblatt, A. H., "The Researcher and the Manager: A Dialectic of Implementation," *Management Science,* **11,** no. 4, B69–B87 (February 1966).
6. Churchman, C. West, *Prediction and Optimal Decision, Philosophical Issues of a Science of Values,* Englewood Cliffs, N.J.: Prentice-Hall, 1961.
7. Churchman, C. West, and Schainblatt, A. H., Eds., "Series of Ten Commentaries on 'The Researcher and the Manager: A Dialectic of Implementation'," *Management Science,* **12,** no. 2, B1–B42 (October 1965).
8. Churchman, C. West, *Theory of Experimental Inference,* New York: Macmillan, 1948.
9. Doktor, Robert H., and Hamilton, William F., "The Acceptance of Operations Research Proposals: An Experimental Study," Wharton School of Finance, University of Pennsylvania, 1971.
10. Eiduson, Bernice T., *Scientists: Their Psychological World,* New York: Basic Books, 1962.
11. Hudson, Liam, *Contrary Imaginations,* New York: Schocken Books, 1966.
12. Huysmans, J. H., "The Effectiveness of the Cognitive-Style Constraint in Implementing Operations Research Proposals," *Management Science,* **17,** no. 1, 92–104 (September 1970).
13. Kiesler, Charles A., *The Psychology of Commitment,* New York: Academic Press, 1971.
14. Kuhn, Thomas S., "The Essential Tension: Tradition and Innovation in Scientific Research," in C. W. Taylor and F. Barron, Eds., *Scientific Creativity,* New York: Wiley, 1963, pp. 341–354.
15. Kuhn, Thomas S., "Logic of Discovery or Psychology of Research?," in *Criticism and The Growth of Knowledge,* Imre Lakatos and Alan Musgrave, Eds. Cambridge University Press, 1970, pp. 1–24.
16. Kuhn, Thomas S., *The Structure of Scientific Revolutions,* Second Edition, Chicago: University of Chicago Press, 1970.
17. Maxwell, Nicholas, "A Critique of Popper's Views on Scientific Method," *Philosophy of Science,* **39,** no. 2, 131–152 (June 1972).
18. McClelland, David C., "On the Dynamics of Creative Physical Scientists,' in *The Ecology of Human Intelligence,* Liam Hudson, Ed., Harmondsworth, England: Penguin, 1970, pp. 309–341.
19. Mitroff, Ian I., "Epistemology As General Systems Theory: An Approach to The Conceptualization of Complex Decision-Making Experiments," *Philosophy of The Social Sciences,* in press.
20. Mitroff, Ian I., "The Mythology of Methodology: An Essay on The Nature of a Feeling Science," *Theory and Decision,* **2,** 274–290 (1972).
21. Mitroff, Ian I., *The Subjective Side of Science: A Philosophical Enquiry Into the Psychology of the Apollo Moon Scientists,* Elsevier, in press.
22. Mitroff, Ian I., "Solipsism: An Essay in Psychological Philosophy," *Philosophy of Science,* **38,** no. 3, 376–394 (September 1971).
23. Mitroff, Ian I., "Systems, Inquiry, and the Meanings of Falsification," *Philosophy of Science,* in press.
24. Snider, James, and Osgood, Charles E., Eds., *Semantic Differential Technique,* Chicago: Aldine, 1969.
25. Popper, K. R., *The Logic of Scientific Discovery,* New York: Harper & Row, 1965.
26. Popper, K. R., "Normal Science and Its Dangers," in Imre Lakatos and Alan Musgrave, Eds., *Criticism and The Growth of Knowledge,* Cambridge, 1970, pp. 51–58.

27. Popper, K. R., *The Poverty of Historicism,* New York: Harper & Row, 1964.
28. Roe, Anne, "The Psychology of the Scientist," *Science,* **134,** 456–459 (1961).
29. Roe, Anne, "A Psychological Study of Physical Scientists," *Genet. Psychol. Monograph,* **43,** 121–239 (1949).
30. Scheffler, Israel, *Science and Subjectivity,* Indianapolis: Bobbs-Merrill, 1967.
31. Shapere, Dudley, "Meaning and Scientific Change," in Robert G. Colodny, Ed., *Mind and Cosmos,* Pittsburgh: University of Pittsburgh Press, 1966, pp. 41–85.
32. Shapere, Dudley, "The Paradigm Concept: A Review of 'The Structure of Scientific Revolutions' by Thomas S. Kuhn and 'Criticism and The Growth of Knowledge' by Imre Lakatos and Alan Musgrave, Eds.," *Science,* **172,** no. 3984, 706–709 (1971).
33. Suppe, Frederick, "What's Wrong With The Received View of the Structure of Scientific Theories," *Philosophy of Science,* **39,** no. 1, 1–19 (March 1972).
34. Torgerson, Warren S., *Theory and Methods of Scaling,* New York: Wiley, 1967.
35. Toulmin, Stephen, *Human Understanding, Vol. I,* New Jersey, Princeton University Press, 1972.
36. Walberg, H. J., "A Portrait of the Artist and Scientist as Young Men," *Exceptional Children,* **36,** no. 1, 5–12 (September 1969).

Chapter 12

A Study of OR/MS Implementation as a Social Change Process

Ilan Vertinsky, Richard T. Barth and Vance F. Mitchell

Social change is the process by which alteration occurs in the structure and function of a social system [*20*]. OR/MS in an organization may bring about social change directly and indirectly. OR/MS groups may induce directly a class of behaviors, perceptions, and attitudes on the part of other managers in the organization that increase the likelihood of the acceptance of modes of decision making characterizing management science. OR/MS may indirectly bring about social change through the implementation of particular OR/MS techniques at focal points in the organization's decision structure, which may lead to alteration in both organizational structure and function. For example, implementation of a corporate linear programming decision model in multiproduct industries, such as the forest products industry, has provided industry with a means of dealing with problems of joint costing, thus altering relationships among divisions that previously operated as independent enterprises. Decision algorithms often induce new requirements for information and impose new modes of communications, changes that have secondary impacts on interaction and decision patterns.

This chapter attempts to investigate the processes of both direct and indirect social change induced by OR/MS groups in the organization. Although previous research by the authors [*24, 25*] focused on processes of OR/MS diffusion and legitimization in the organization, this chapter centers upon the dynamics of OR/MS-induced social change, after OR/MS activities in the organization have approached equilibrium. In this phase of the OR/MS life history, modes of OR/MS interactions with other groups in the organization change slowly, if at all. The effects of these patterns of exchange flow between OR/MS groups and the remainder of the organization are the focus here.

ADOPTION OF THE OR/MS MANAGERIAL PARADIGM: SOME BASIC CONCEPTS

It is important to consider operations research and management science not just as a collection of special skills and techniques, but as an expression of the weltanschauung of an organization's management. The OR/MS point of view recognizes the interdependence of organizational activities and decisions, and it treats the organization as a complex system of activities aimed at attaining a set of objectives. OR/MS places emphasis on the utilization of scientific methodology in organizational problem solving. Consequently, emphasis is placed on the systematization of information flows and decision modes and on the introduction of teleological programs for organizational roles. Moreover, a long-run perspective is emphasized instead of the type of crisis-centered decision making described by Cyert and March [*10*]. Burack [7] has pointed out that a long-term perspective incorporating a larger planning horizon is characteristic of the more matured OR/MS activities as opposed to the "quick payoff" stance that characterizes many unsuccessful activities.

The introduction into the organization of these management perspectives (holistic organizational point of view, teleological programming of the organization, and scientific methodology) and their effect on the organization's orientation toward its task environment constitute the essence of the OR/MS objective as a change agent. Thus, if operations research and management science is viewed by members of the organization as merely an inventory of decision techniques advocated and sometimes used in an atomistic fashion, the direct impact of its presence in the organization is minimized. The acceptance of techniques without the acceptance of the scientific paradigm underlying them may lead to social change but not necessarily in the direction planned. The recognition of the gap between the OR/MS managerial paradigm and the present mode of management is a necessary condition for a conflict process that may lead to the desired social change, that is, the dissemination of the OR/MS management style within the organization.

There are at least three levels at which change must take place if the weltanschauung of management science is to be realized. First, individual attitudes and values must undergo a major shift, especially with regard to the disproportionate emphasis placed on functional and jurisdictional interests, personal experience as a basis for decision making, and interpersonal competition. Only when these and other traditional managerial values have changed can modification of managerial behavior be expected that will lead to an holistic outlook toward corporate problems and the use of decision methods based upon scientific principles. Second, major changes must also take place at the level of the organization. Norms and goals must be redefined to emphasize integration and rationality. Clear goals must be established in *operational* terms, and the norm of goal-directed activity implanted. Together with these changes, organizational roles must be redefined to highlight the greater frequency and importance of intraorganizational interactions and interdependencies of interest groups (not functional groups) and decision-making units. As these changes emerge, new patterns must be developed for allocating organizational resources and creating reward structures that reinforce the goal-directed organizational point of view. Finally, new patterns of interaction with the external environment must be established to buffer the effects of value and style differences between members of the organization and suppliers of inputs, client systems, financial institutions, and regulatory agencies [*23*].

There are essentially three ways in which these changes might come about: random, evolutionary, and planned. It is possible but not very likely that a series of random events, either endogenous or exogenous, will bring about the changes that might lead an organization to the state described above. What is more likely is that either an evolutionary or planned program will bring about such changes. It is important to note, however, that neither approach is likely to succeed unless key individuals are highly motivated to bring about such an outcome and are successful in motivating others in the organization to perceive the potential payoff associated with an OR/MS orientation. By evolutionary we mean the set of changes that might result from acquisition through the normal employment process of some personnel with OR/MS knowledge. If these individuals have vision and strategic organizational skills and are sufficiently motivated, they will over time diffuse their OR/MS orientation throughout the organization and its infrastructure [*3*]. Rubenstein *et al.* [*22*], Radnor and White [*19*], Bean [*4*], and others, e.g. [*18*], have described a taxonomy of life history stages characteristic of successful (and unsuccessful) OR/MS activities representing the evolutionary process described here.

Successful planned change requires the conversion of some influential members of top management, who then provide sponsorship for the formal introduction of an OD-like effort. It is important to note here that OD is defined as a planned program, motivated and directed from the top, for the change of an organization through the use of behavioral science techniques [*5*]. We are aware of but few instances [*7, 8*] where this approach has been coupled with attempts to introduce the OR/MS weltanschauung.

Many of the barriers to the type of social change discussed here have been alluded to above. Perceptions of threat to an individual manager's security or territorial jurisdiction are among the most frequently encountered barriers and the most difficult to surmount. Likewise, lack of comprehension of the concepts of OR/MS tends to be a characteristic of older executives. In a very real sense this phenomenon is evidence of managerial obsolescence [*6*]. Finally, the doctrines of neoclassical economics as operationalized through conventional accounting procedures tend to reinforce traditional, intuitive, crisis-centered management [*9*].

In an effort to test these constructs of OR/MS as an agent of social change, a pilot study was conducted in a number of organizations in Western Canada.

METHODOLOGY

The collection of data utilized questionnaires as well as a series of semi-structured interviews with both OR/MS practitioners and client managers in a variety of business organizations. This technique allowed for a complementary approach to examining a relatively broad data base in some depth.

Instrument

In designing the questionnaire and our interviews, we attempted to investigate the following dimensions: (1) management style, especially as it relates to the principles of an OR/MS point of view and the perception of OR/MS as a vehicle for these principles, i.e., (a) holistic perception of the organization, (b) teleological outlook concerning structure, function, and activity, and (c) programmability and systematization of tasks; (2) skill aspects associated with OR/MS techniques; (3) modes of interaction with OR/MS and use of OR/MS; and (4) personal characteristics of clients and OR/MS personnel.

The questionnaire consisted of four parts. Part I contained 17 items presented in Likert-type format with a four-point scale ranging from strongly agree to strongly disagree. Representative of the items used are the following:

> The use of OR/MS forces a group to consider how what it does affects, or is affected by, the activities of *other* groups or departments.
>
> The use of OR/MS does *not* contribute to a more overall viewpoint in planning and decision making.
>
> The use of OR/MS *enhances* communication with *other* departments or groups.
>
> It is impractical to clearly define, in quantitative terms, the *overall* organizational objectives of this organization.
>
> Much of the critical information regarding problems faced by a man in my position is *not* quantifiable.

Part II incorporated six sets of bipolar adjectives (e.g., trusting-not trusting, aimless-goal-directed) in a semantic differential format [*16*] in order to obtain a measure of the quality of the OR/MS unit-client relationship. Two additional items asked for frequency and closeness of interaction with the OR/MS activity; a third item provided data on the percentage of the respondent's decisions that affect decisions of other departments. This latter item can be interpreted as an indicator of a given client unit's interdependence with other units in the organization.

The five items of Part III were directed at assessing the extent to which various forms of quantitative output (e.g., diagrams, charts, statistical summaries, and analyses) facilitated the respondent's thinking with regard to decision problems faced by him and his group. Part IV asked for a number of demographic characteristics such as the respondent's functional area, type and size of company, and type of position (line vs. staff). A total of 115 usable questionnaires were obtained.

Interviews

Interview data were obtained from business organizations in the utility, forest products, and transportation industries. These industries are the major users of OR/MS in Western Canada. The researchers visited each of the firms and met with the senior practitioner managers and separately with a number of managers who had been identified by the OR/MS staff as clients or potential clients.

The format of the interviews was semistructured to ensure that all those interviewed were asked the same basic set of questions. Ample opportunity was afforded, however, for the exploration in depth of their views, impressions of experience within their company, and the relation of illustrative anecdotes. The interviewers focused primarily on the dynamics of experience with OR/MS in the organization and the nature and extent of such experience. Second, attention was directed to the interviewee's attitudes toward OR/MS as measured in the questionnaire and their perception of the attitudes of significant others in the organization.

The practitioners invariably seemed to enjoy the interview sessions, perhaps because, as one manager put it, the meeting provided a welcome opportunity for catharsis. Reactions of the client managers varied over a wide spectrum, as will be related later.

RESULTS AND DISCUSSION

Questionnaire Results

Analysis of individual questionnaire items revealed that the participating managers, especially those from the accounting and finance areas, perceive the organization as a cooperative system. Seventy-five percent disagreed with the statement that the various elements of the organization are basically in competition with each other. Only 24 percent agreed that it is impractical to clearly define overall organizational objectives in quantitative terms. However, less than one-fifth of the sample indicated a preference for the *empirical* identification of objectives.

One dimension of management perception—programmability and systematization of decision planning—was found to be viewed as antithetical to respondents' point of view. For example, 86 percent agreed that most problems faced by them could not be solved through the application of predetermined programs or approaches. Fifty-one percent agreed that organizational realities do indeed significantly limit the effectiveness of organizational planning. A similar percentage indicated experience and intuition as the prime guides for formulating decision premises and in decision making.

These results suggest that there is some congruence to view the organization as a holistic, teleological entity with regard to organizational activities. However, there appears to be a discrepancy between scientific principles (e.g., programming and systematization of activities, including planning) vs. intuitive, experiential, and adaptive norms of management.

The second area of managers' perception investigated was the perception of the OR/MS role in the organization. It was suggested in previous sections that, if OR/MS is perceived only as a particular collection of skills and techniques, its impact in creating conflict in managerial points of view, and subsequently managerial response to this conflict, is minimized. The questionnaire and the interviews indicate that managers perceive OR/MS as a vehicle for management style change, and not only as a collection of techniques and skills. Eighty-two percent of the respondents considered the use of OR/MS a means for organizational coordination. Managers strongly agreed that OR/MS groups increase the awareness of how departments affect or are affected by the activities of other groups or departments. Eighty-six percent indicated that the use of OR/MS contributes to a more overall view point in planning and decision making, and 70 percent considered OR/MS a vehicle for effective joint decision making. Eighty-four percent considered OR/MS as having impact in facilitating communications with other departments or groups. A similar percentage indicated that OR/MS forces establishment of systematic decision procedures. In conclusion, most managers in the sample perceived OR/MS as a vehicle for the diffusion of a management style that incorporates a holistic teleological point of view with systematic planning and decision making.

The intercorrelations of items in Part I were subjected to principal components analysis, with subsequent rotation according to the Varimax criterion. With the exception of two items, this analysis yielded five relatively orthogonal factors that provide additional empirical weight to the constructs suggested above. The five factors were clearly interpretable and can be characterized in terms of the following dimensions:

1. perception of the organization as an entity
2. perception of the organization as a goal-directed system
3. perception of programmability of the manager's role
4. perception of intuition and experience as a basis for managing
5. perception of the role of OR/MS as a vehicle for changing or modifying management style

The items that asked managers to rate their perceived aptitudes and abilities associated with the use of OR/MS techniques (Part III) were subjected to a separate factor analysis. This procedure yielded only one principal component, with factor loadings of the items ranging from .54 to .83. An index score based on the five items indicates that 60 percent of the managers perceived themselves as having quantitative aptitude. However, although analysis of item scores revealed that only 8 percent of the respondents perceived mathematical modeling as an aid to problem formation and solution, the index score was found to be significantly related to both frequency (r = .37, p < .002) and closeness (r = .31, p < .01) of client-OR/MS interaction. This index was also significantly correlated with Dimension 2 (goal directedness, r = .21, p < .10) and Dimension 3 (role programmability, r = .22, p < .10) identified above. Respondents receiving high scores on the index also perceived interactions with OR/MS as relatively supportive (r = .31, p < .01) and goal directed (r = .28, p < .05).

Another area of investigation concerned the quality of OR/MS group interactions with others in the organization. Forty percent of the managers had experienced no contact with OR/MS groups or activities. Thirty-five percent had occasionally used OR/MS services, mainly in solving problems of data processing and for obtaining some preliminary statistical analyses. Nineteen percent reported frequent contact with the OR/MS group and use of OR/MS. Only 6 percent indicated using OR/MS services continuously. The modes of interactions between managers and OR/MS groups were characterized by trust (45 percent of the managers indicated a relationship of trust, 21 percent one of indifference, and only 24 percent reported distrust). Similar percentages indicated warm rather than cold relationships. Fifty-four percent of the respondents rated their relationships with the OR/MS group as supportive, whereas only 14 percent perceived them as competitive. The relationship with OR/MS groups was identified as mainly goal directed. Forty-one percent of the repsondents indicated uninformed modes of utilizing OR/MS services.

Correlational analysis of frequency and closeness of interaction with the quality of interaction revealed the following. Close and continuous interaction with OR/MS was characterized by an intergroup relationship reflecting supportiveness (r = .66, p < .001) and goal directedness (r = .65, p < .001). At the same time, the relationship was perceived as relatively warm ($r = .48, p < .001$) but *un*informed ($r = .49, p < .001$).

Quality of client-OR/MS interaction was found to be significantly correlated with only the dimension based on viewing the entire organization as a goal-directed system ($r = .28$, $p < .05$) and programmability of the manager's role ($r = .26$, $p < .05$). The correlations between interaction and the other three dimensions ranged from .03 for Dimension 5 (OR/MS as a vehicle for changing or modifying management style) to .13 for Dimension 1 (perception of the organization as an entity).

Results and Analysis Based on Interviews

When integrated with the questionnaire data, results from the interviews suggested that an expectancy-instrumentality-valence theory approach [*17*] would provide a coherent framework for developing a model to describe and explain the process of social change in organizations with established OR/MS activites. The motivational model which emerged from the analysis is outlined in Figure 12.1. Following a description of the model, the interview data are described through several case studies which characterize the experience of OR/MS as an agent of social change under alternative circumstances. The model is then used as a basis for the evaluation of alternative strategies of OR/MS implementation.

The motivation model of OR/MS implementation (Figure 12.1) proposed here was adapted from Lawler [*14*] by Barth and Mitchell [*2*]. The model indicates that the motivation to expend effort to use or implement OR/MS is primarily determined by three variables.

The first variable—Type I expectancy (Box 1)—refers to the manager's expectation that the use or implementation of OR/MS will lead to task accomplishment or performance. One can conceive of situations where the manager would have a very low expectation (e.g., even if I use OR/MS in an informed and goal-directed fashion, I would not be able to perform work more effectively) or a very high one (e.g., if I use OR/MS I will certainly perform better than managers of comparable groups that do not utilize OR/MS). Type I expectancy can vary from certainty that use of OR/MS leads to more effective performance to certainty that its use would be nonfunctional or harmful to the manager's position in the organization.

In the model, Type I expectancy is influenced by two factors: (1) the manager's self-esteem (Box 4), that is, his general beliefs about his ability to cope with and control his environment [*1, 21*] and (2) his previous personal or observed experience in similar or identical stimulus situations (Box 3), for example, his perception of OR/MS and OR/MS activities, observed instances of

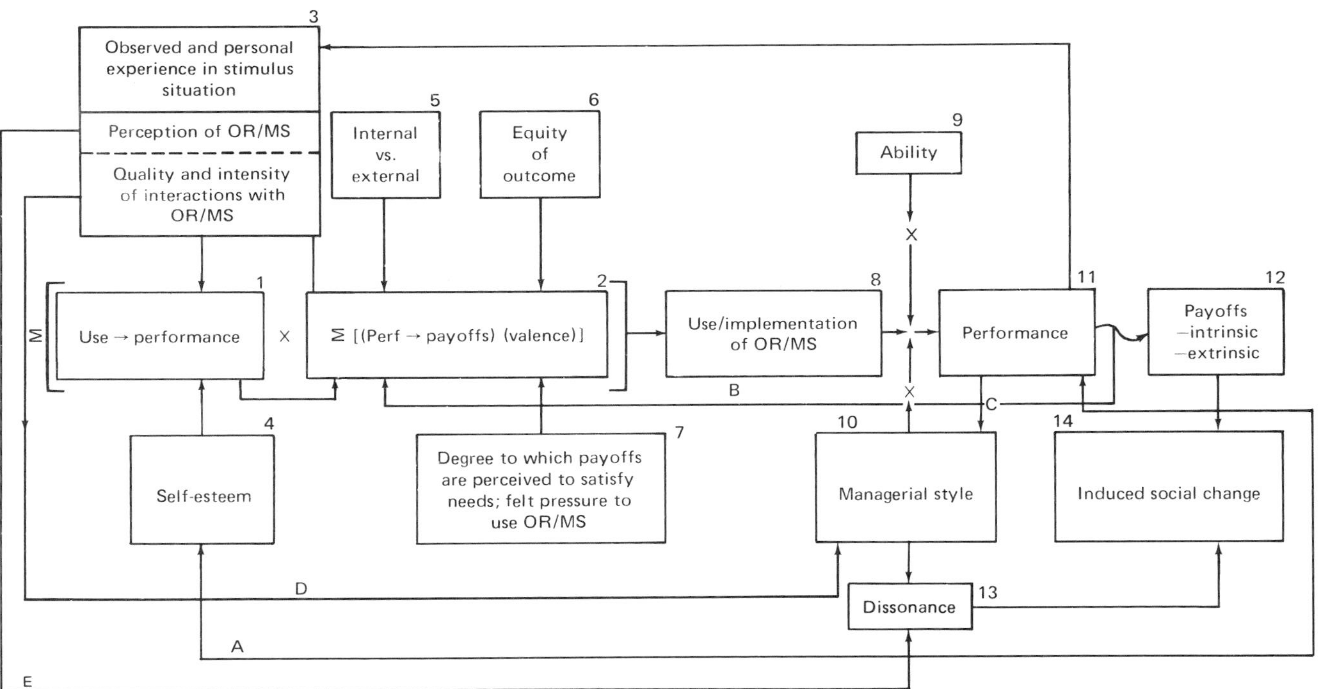

Fig. 12.1 Motivation Model of OR/MS Implementation and Social Change (Adapted by Barth and Mitchell [2] from Lawler [14]).

successful or unsuccessful OR/MS utilization in the same or other organizations, and past modes of interactions with OR/MS groups. The model also indicates that the manager's self-esteem is influenced by his perceived job performance (Loop A). In general, the higher a manager's self-esteem, and the more effective his perceived performance (through the use of OR/MS) in similar stimulus situations, the higher will be his Type I expectancy, and vice versa.

The second main variable–Type II expectancy (Box 2)–refers to the manager's belief that task performance based on the use of OR/MS will lead to desired outcomes or payoffs. Thus, this type of expectancy involves beliefs about reward contingencies and taps his confidence that either he himself will experience some kind of self-satisfaction from performance based on the use of OR/MS, or the organization or other agents will provide payoffs for this performance after its completion.

The third variable–valence (Box 2)–refers to the manager's degree of preference for different kinds of payoffs that can be directly contingent upon performance achieved through the use of OR/MS. As indicated by Box 12, such payoffs can be of two major types: intrinsic, such as, feelings of accomplishment and fulfillment, or feelings of failure and threat; and extrinsic, such as promotion, modification of his pay, reassignment, and other good or bad outcomes that can be determined by the organization in response to successful or unsuccessful performance through OR/MS implementation.

The expectancy theory approach on which the model is based hypothesizes that these three variables (Type I and II expectancies and valence) combine to determine the extent of the manager's use of OR/MS. As protrayed in Figure 12.1, the model suggests that:

1. the manager's subjective probability that performance affected by the use of OR/MS will lead to payoffs is weighted by the valence of the array of relevant payoffs
2. the weighted probability-valence combinations be summed,
3. this weighted sum be combined with Type I expectancy in a functional relationship the exact form of which can vary according to the circumstances [*13*].

Figure 1 further shows that the manager's performance → payoff subjective probability beliefs (Type II expectancies) are influenced by two factors. One of these consists of the individual difference factor which Rotter [*21*] and others have referred to as a belief of internal vs. external control (Box 5). This concept is similar to that of person causation, defined by de Charms [*11*] as "...the initiation by an individual of behavior intended to produce a change in his environment." According to this view, some managers see the world in terms of internal control (i.e., *they* act on the world), whereas others see it in terms of external control (the world acts on *them*). The influence of the second factor, the perceived strength or intensity of the connection between performance and payoffs to the performance payoff probability, is through feedback Loop B.

The model also suggests that the valence of payoffs can be influenced by the perceived equity of the cost-benefit balance (Box 6) and a factor (Box 7) based on the argument that the more an outcome associated with the use of OR/MS is perceived as satisfying one or more needs (such as those contained in Maslow's [*15*] need hierarchy), the more valued it will be by the manager. In addition, felt pressure as a result of organizational directives or informal influence to use OR/MS is included as a second component of this factor.

It is important to reiterate at this point that the two types of expectancies and perceived valence of payoffs are hypothesized as affecting only the manager's level of effort directed at the use of OR/MS. The extent to which such efforts are converted into better performance is shown by the model to be mediated by managerial style (Box 10), which in turn may be modified by results of performance (Loop C) and by learning from previous experience (Loop D). The term managerial style is used here to refer to the degree of congruence between the manager's "how to do it" approach and the point of view underlying OR/MS. The manager's abilities (Box 9), such as his quantitative aptitude, also moderate the relationship between effort and performance. Both of these variables (style and ability) are shown to combine in some functional relationship with effort, stressing the point that lack of ability or inappropriate style will result in poor performance.

The link connecting performance (Box 11) to payoffs (Box 12) is shown as a wavy line to indicate that payoffs do *not always* follow *directly* from better performance due to the use of OR/MS. Whether performance through the use of OR/MS will lead to payoffs depends on a number of aspects of the work situation. For extrinsic rewards, the connection between performance and receipt of these rewards will depend not only on general past organizational practices with regard to rewarding good performance, but strongly on the degree to which the formal reward system is *re*designed to provide specific rewards or payoffs for better performance resulting from the implementation of OR/MS. With respect to intrinsic rewards, much will depend on the existing redesigned structure of the task in light of OR/MS use. If the implementation of OR/MS and subsequent performance carries with it aspects of job enrichment as well as, for example, feelings of accomplishment and recognition, intrinsic rewards may be strongly connected to performance. Again, the converse is also true.

The specific relevance of the model to social change becomes clearer as Boxes 13 and 14 are considered. Box 13 represents the perceived discrepancy, on the part of the manager, between the OR/MS management point of view and the managerial style characterizing OR/MS clients and others in contact with OR/MS in the organization. This discrepancy or perceived gap in styles is a necessary condition providing the impetus for social change. In fact, both questionnaire and interview data revealed that in those cases where OR/MS was used in an uninformed way and was perceived merely as a "bag of techniques (tricks?)," client managers did not perceive any stimuli for change in their management styles, even when in close contact with OR/MS groups.

The direction of change in managerial style depends on the manager's response directed at reducing cognitive dissonance. Various alternative strategies can be suggested for reducing this perceived gap. These include an absolute change in style to make it consonant with OR/MS, total withdrawal from OR/MS if possible, building buffers to minimize OR/MS impact on the manager's unit, overt resistance to OR/MS, plus any number of covert attempts to contain the influence of OR/MS on the unit's activities. The choice of strategy depends on the particular mix of intrinsic and extrinsic features of the payoff environment. As shown in the model, the social change (Box 14) effected is determined by the cumulative influences of the payoff environment and the perceived discrepancy between Box 3 and Box 10.

Overall, the model presented here provides a basis for further theoretical and empirical development of a better understanding of managerial motivation to implement OR/MS.*

OR/MS practitioners interviewed in several companies all indicated that the potential net payoff perceived by the manager as associated with the use of OR/MS is the main factor affecting the patterns and intensity of interactions with the OR/MS group. Identified as foremost on the benefit side of the payoff balance were immediate payoffs resulting from visibly improved performance.

Several of those interviewed pointed out that improved performance was not necessarily defined in terms of organizational objectives. For example, the use of sophisticated decision and analytical techniques improved the image of the manager in some organizations, imputing improved performance through association with an OR/MS style. Similarly, OR/MS practitioners pointed to conspicuous consumption of OR/MS for the purpose of report writing, at times without any impact on decision processes. Other perceived payoffs were associated with the belief that OR/MS may legitimize a particular position a group takes in intraorganizational conflicts.

On the personal level OR/MS practitioners identified intrinsic rewards that some managers, especially those with appropriate abilities, derive from nongoal-

*It should be noted that the logical consistency of the model appears also valid at a level that takes the organization as the unit of analysis. If this were done, the appropriate mapping of the variables of Figure 12.1 to the organizational level of analysis would imply that the internal vs. external variable refers to the organization's perceived influence over its task environment and domain, Type II expectancy would be treated in terms of the organization's beliefs about its understanding of cause/effect relationships with regard to environmental uncertainties (see, for example, Thompson [*23*] and Duncan [*12*] for the importance of this concept), and so on.

directed experimentation with new techniques. These rewards are associated with psychological factors such as self-esteem and self-actualization.

On the cost side the most important factor was identified as territorial threats. Territorial threats were often associated with OR/MS projects originating in staff-corporate levels of the organization and forced upon divisions or departments. Client managers considered some of these activities as threatening the accepted pattern of organizational resource allocation and the independence of their units. Often OR/MS activities were regarded as moves toward a greater centralization. The threats to job security were often associated with an increase in evaluation intensity and not with perceptions of take over of managerial functions. An important factor of costs associated with OR/MS use was the dissonance arising from the difference in approaches and methods between OR/MS practitioners and other managers in the organization. OR/MS practitioners indicated that managers who viewed skeptically the application of scientific methodology in management situations were unlikely to use OR/MS and, if forced to do so, engaged in both overt and covert resistance to all OR/MS activities in the organization. Payoffs from OR/MS use were rarely perceived and an effort was exerted to sabotage the activities. The use of continuous force only led to further polarization of attitudes and approaches.

Another important cost perceived by client managers, which was identified by the OR/MS practitioners, related to an important organizational resource: information. OR/MS was perceived as a threat to what Barth and Vertinsky [*3*] have described as information monopolies. In many of the organizations, some units such as production and marketing were identified as especially reluctant to part with information.

The interviews relating to successful OR/MS uses indicated that these successes often resulted from situations in which OR/MS had led to the solution of a pressing problem, and OR/MS was either perceived as a technical service or the client manager was predisposed to the OR/MS management point of view.

It was pointed out that when warm, trusting relationships emerged between OR/MS groups and user groups, mutual conversion took place in points of view. Through mutual socialization OR/MS personnel tend to identify more with the scientific method of management than with particular tools in their possession. Although managers may accept the validity of scientific principles in management, the environment for mutual socialization depends in part on the maintenance of an appropriate reward system as well as on the interpersonal competence of OR/MS personnel.

This last condition was explicitly recognized in one company that had had longer experience with OR/MS, which was incorporated into recruiting policies for OR/MS personnel by weighting technical abilities equally with social skills. The result was faster and smoother diffusion of OR/MS in the organization.

In the interviews we attempted also to analyze particular experiences in the OR/MS diffusion and implementation processes. We have selected a few case studies involving OR/MS use in various functions of the organization. One of these cases evolved form the experience gained in developing and implementing a linear programming corporate decision model in a multidivision forest products corporation.

The interviews with both OR/MS groups and corporate finance staff indicated agreement in perceptions of the organization and its activities. (Both groups perceived the organization as a goal-directed entity). Finance staffs accepted the principles of role programmability and planning as bases for management. The only perceptual discrepancy between the two groups was with respect to the breadth of organizational objectives. No inclination to monopolize information or threats to job security were perceived by the finance staff. The only perceived cost associated with the use of OR/MS to the finance group was the need to upgrade quantitative abilities.

The use of OR/MS arose initially from the problem of joint costing and financial evaluation confronting the finance staffs. OR/MS personnel were able to help in the solution of this problem through the development of a mathematical programming model of corporate activities (Boxes 11 and 12). Through continuous use of these services, the finance staff gained personal experience with the OR/MS group (Box 3) and OR/MS activities leading from uninformed use of OR/MS to at least some level of informed awareness. Because the programming experience proved effective (Box 12) and provided no threat to finance's jurisdiction (the OR/MS group functioned essentially as service technicians) the net valence of using OR/MS (Box 2) in this instance increased, leading to exploration and implementation of still other uses.

As the two staffs gained further successful experience with this application of OR/MS (Boxes 11 and 12) a congenial, trusting relationship emerged (Box 3) that led to an increase in quantitative abilities (Box 9) on the part of the finance group, as well as to a reduction of cognitive dissonance through adoption of a broader view of organizational goals (Boxes 14 and 10).

In this case only limited social change was possible in the finance group, given the initial congruence between their and the OR/MS points of view. However, the effective solution of the joint costing problem had an important impact on the resource allocation pattern in the organization as well as on the reward system because management now was provided with an effective evaluation tool.

It was this latter use of OR/MS that alienated the line personnel involved in production. Forced to work with OR/MS personnel to provide the essential data for the corporate model (Box 7), the operating managers did not perceive improved performance in their domain. At the same time, they anticipated high costs in terms of added resource control by corporate staff and an increase in accountability for their personal performance.

Some of the line managers (particularly engineers) were especially resistant to parting with the technical information needed for construction of the model. In addition to their low motivation for OR/MS use, the line managers perceived inconsistency between their management style and an OR/MS point of view. Most line managers perceived their unit to be in competition with others in the organization for scarce organizational resources, territory of jurisdiction, and authority. In their opinion, muddling through characterized the desired and the only practical mode of corporate management. Experience and intuition were seen as the prime guides to management. The resolution of dissonance in this case was achieved by minimizing contact with the OR/MS group and its activities, and in a few cases subversive actions were taken to reduce OR/MS impact on the client unit's performance. The confrontation with OR/MS acting as a change agent mobilized antagonistic reactions that had not been overcome at the time of the study.

A similar experience was identified in a large transportation corporation. OR/MS activities were started simultaneously in both corporate staff and line. The line OR/MS group offered immediate payoff by solving some of the pressing scheduling problems encountered by line managers. Line managers maintained strict control over the activities of the group and perceived no threats associated with the employment of OR/MS. The staff OR/MS group, while aiming to reach line units, encountered indifference and distrust with little voluntary use of its services. In a subsequent reorganization of the firm the two groups were merged as a staff group. The strategy that was adopted successfully by this new group was to maintain a mix of activities. Those activities with proven positive effects or payoffs received high visibility, whereas activities that were aimed to introduce new modes of management maintained low profile. Through maintaining a high level of motivation toward OR/MS and establishing a relationship of trust with users, the group succeeded in diffusing OR/MS activities and approaches that had been resisted when initially introduced to the organization by the staff OR/MS group.

Finally, we attempted to investigate some voluntary uses of OR/MS. Here the importance of intrinsic rewards assumed an important role. Those managers with high needs for esteem and/or self-actualization [*15*] often engaged in fishing expeditions with the OR/MS practitioners. In many of these instances managers perceived OR/MS as a set of sophisticated techniques, and little conflict in managerial approaches was perceived by the users. Only when extrinsic rewards led to intensified use of OR/MS did evolutionary changes in management styles occur.

SUMMARY AND CONCLUSION

The principal findings of our study may be summarized as follows:

1. OR/MS solutions leading to significant social change tend to mobilize counter forces aimed at reversing or at least containing these changes.
2. Forced implementation of OR/MS solutions does not necessarily lead to changes in management approaches and may often result in counter-productive long-term consequences.
3. Changes in management approaches depend on the intensity of dissonance stemming from a manager's perceptions of conflict between his management style and OR/MS. The choice of strategy for reducing dissonance is determined by the level of motivation to use OR/MS that exists in the organization.
4. Use of OR/MS when solutions do not significantly affect the function or structure of the organizational unit may lead to long-run social change if the following conditions are met: (a) dissonance is experienced in using OR/MS; (b) use is continuous; (c) modes of interaction with OR/MS are informed and trusting.
5. The establishment of trusting, informed relationships with OR/MS practitioners depends on both the level of motivation for use of OR/MS in the organization and the interpersonal competence of the OR/MS practitioners.
6. The managers' quantitative aptitude increases the likelihood of successful and informed use of OR/MS.

These findings, of course, cannot be generalized from the limited base of the present study. Much more research is needed in a variety of organizational and geographical settings. It is significant, however, that the phenomena encountered in our study are consistent with the broad body of knowledge concerning organizational processes that has emerged from the field of behavioral science.

Further, several implications seem evident for those who are concerned with the future of OR/MS as an agent of social change. First, the mix of OR/MS activities within organizations should be carefully chosen to highlight those activities that will provide positive motivation for further use of OR/MS and the associated weltanschauung. Second, diffusion of OR/MS is significantly related to the interpersonal competence of practitioners. The implications of this for training and recruitment of future practitioners seem obvious. In addition, the successful strategy we encountered where OR/MS practitioners are indoctrinated within a staff OR/MS group and subsequently reassigned to any operating function, deserves wider use. This strategy may become less important as the proportion of managers increases who have been trained in OR/MS techniques and orientation.

Finally, we would urge a much higher level of collaboration between

OR/MS practitioners and behavioral scientists who are concerned with organizational development. Both groups are deeply interested in social change that will lead to the emergence of more effective and rational organizations. Working alone, their successes have been limited. The phenomena we have encountered in the present study strongly suggest that the objectives of both OR/MS and OD practitioners can be advanced more effectively through a combined approach.

References

1. Argyris, Chris. *Integrating the Individual and the Organization,* New York: Wiley, 1964.
2. Barth, Richard T. and Mitchell, Vance F., "Motivation Theory as it Relates to OR/MS Use and Implementation." Working Paper, Faculty of Commerce and Business Administration, University of British Columbia, Vancouver, Canada, 1973.
3. Barth, Richard T. and Vertinsky, Ilan, "Organizational Form and OR/MS Implementation in Colombia," *Quarterly Journal of Management Development,* in press.
4. Bean, Alden S., "Management Science-Client Relationships: Studies of Linking Mechanisms," PhD Dissertation, Northwestern University, Evanston, Ill., 1972.
5. Beckhard, Richard, *Organization Development: Strategies and Models,* Reading, Mass.: Addison-Wesley, 1969.
6. Burack, Elmer H., "Meeting the Threat of Managerial Obsolescence," *California Management Review,* **XV**, 83–90 (1972).
7. Burack, Elmer H., "Organizational Development in Operations Research," *Proceedings of the Academy of Management,* Vance F. Mitchell, Richard T. Barth, and Fran Mitchell (Eds.), 1973.
8. Burack, Elmer H., and Batlivala, Robert B. D., "Operations Research: Recent Changes and Future Expectations in Business Organizations," *Business Perspectives,* in press.
9. Caplan, Edwin H., "Some Behavioral Assumptions of Management Accounting," *The Accounting Review,* July 1966, 496–509.
10. Cyert, Richard M. and March, James G., *A Behavioral Theory of the Firm,* Englewood Cliffs, N.J.: Prentice-Hall, 1963.
11. de Charms, Richard, *Personal Causation,* Reading, Mass.: Addison-Wesley, 1968.
12. Duncan, Robert B., "Toward an Operant Model of Organizational Learning: Adpatation to Environmental Uncertainty," *Proceedings of the Academy of Management,* Vance F. Mitchell, Richard T. Barth, and Fran Mitchell (Eds.), 1973.
13. Ghiselli, Edwin E., "Interaction of Traits and Motivational Factors in the Determination of the Success of Managers," *Journal of Applied Psychology,* **52,** 480–483 (1968).
14. Lawler, E. E., *Pay and Organizational Effectiveness,* New York: McGraw-Hill, 1971.
15. Maslow, A. H., "A Theory of Human Motivation," *Psychological Review,* 370–396 (1943).
16. Osgood, G. E., Suci, G. J., and Tannenbaum, P. H., *The Measurement of Meaning,* Urbana, Ill.: University of Illinois Press, 1957.
17. Porter, Lyman W., and Lawler, Edward E., *Managerial Attitudes and Performance,* Homewood, Ill.: Irwin-Dorsey, 1968.
18. Radnor, Michael, Rubenstein, Albert H., and Tansik, David A., "Implementation in Operations Research and R & D in Government and Business Organizations," *Operations Research,* **18,** 967–991 (1970).
19. Radnor, Michael, and White, Michael J., "Institutionalization of Change," Working Paper, Northwestern University, Evanston, Illinois, 1970.

20. Rogers, Everett, *Modernization Among Peasants,* New York: Holt, Reinhart and Winston, 1969.
21. Rotter, J. B., "Generalized Expectancies for Internal Versus External Control of Reinforcement," *Psychological Monographs,* **80,** 1–28 (1966).
22. Rubenstein, A. H., Radnor, M., Baker, N. R., Heiman, D. R., and McColly, J. B., "Some Organizational Factors Related to the Effectiveness of Management Science Groups in Industry," *Management Science,* **13,** no. 8, 508–518 (April 1967).
23. Thompson, James D., *Organizations in Action,* New York: McGraw-Hill, 1967.
24. Vertinsky, Ilan, and Barth, Richard T., "A Model of Diffusion and Implementation: An Exploratory Study of Managerial Innovation in Colombia," *Socio-Economic Planning Sciences,* **6,** 153–171 (1972).
25. Vertinsky, Ilan, "OR/MS Implementation in Valle, Columbia, S.A.: A Profile of a Developing Region," *Management Science,* **18,** B314–B327 (1972).

PART FOUR

CONSIDERATIONS FOR IMPLEMENTATION MANAGEMENT

Chapter 13

Operations Research Implementation and the Practice of Management

Jan H. Huysmans

Operations research (OR) successes are abundant. OR has been applied successfully to important management decisions such as refining scheduling (LP), planning of large projects (CPM/PERT), and investment decisions (risk analysis). The high quality of OR solutions and their superiority to more traditional approaches have been shown in many instances. For example, demonstrable cost savings of 25 percent from applying inventory control techniques are not uncommon.

Why then do not only OR and behavioral theorists, but also many OR practitioners feel that OR implementation should get more attention? One reason seems to be that we still know relatively little about how OR implementation is achieved and how the implementation process can be controlled. Another more disturbing reason is that the lasting impact of OR on management decision making is still in doubt, in spite of the many success stories that continue to come forward.

The picture one gets when trying to observe and understand the OR implementation process in its real-world management context is in many respects confusing. However, this very confusion also help to identify what must be done to advance our understanding and practical control of OR implementation. As a first step, it seems useful to distinguish between two stages in the design of an OR implementation strategy, dealing with: (1) assessing the implementation problem in a given situation, and (2) gearing the implementation strategy to the specific needs of that situation. The purpose of the first stage is to determine what implementation means, or should mean, in a particular situation and to evaluate the importance of the various factors that may affect it. In the second stage the specific characteristics an implementation strategy should have to maximize its chances of being successful can then be determined.

ASSESSING THE IMPLEMENTATION PROBLEM

Reviewing reports on OR implementation that are published from time to time in OR journals or considering one's personal experience in this matter, one will recognize that many forms and degrees of what can rightfully be called an OR success exist. One will also find that the implementation problems that had to be dealt with in these different situations range from virtually nonexistent to very strong management resistance. But more importantly, these experiences suggest that some advance assessment of the implementation problems that are to be expected in a particular situation is often possible. In fact the magnitude of these problems in part depends on the objectives that one sets out to achieve. Making this advance assessment, therefore, involves (1) defining the objectives of applying OR, and (2) evaluating the relative importance of the factors affecting implementation (as defined by the objectives), and the degree to which these factors are likely to create an implementation problem.

Defining the Objectives of Applying OR

Generally, the ultimate aim of applying OR will be to improve the performance of some system. However, the problems to be overcome to achieve this broad aim may differ sharply, depending on the characteristics of a given situation. As a result, it is by no means obvious that the application of OR to management problems always involves overcoming management resistance to the scientific, teleological, and holistic characteristics of the OR approach. This can best be illustrated by a few examples that, in terms of the ultimate criterion of improved performance, would generally be labeled OR successes:

1. **Resisting an OR solution may be more difficult for management than accepting it.** The computer/OR department of a food retailing chain took the initiative to introduce an inventory control and reordering system to be implemented on the computer. The system was developed in close cooperation with the merchandisers (buyers/product managers) who were responsible for inventory levels: Demand patterns, the calculation of profit contributions, the product cost elements to be included, as well as updating procedures were carefully reviewed with them.

The system, after being put on the computer, ran parallel with the established procedures for some time. One by one, agreement was reached with the merchandisers to adopt the new procedure fully. This relieved them from a considerable amount of routine work. The computer prepared daily, weekly, and monthly stock-status reports (replacing the card systems of each individual merchandiser) and printed automatically the order forms when reorder points were reached.

The system now operates satisfactorily and is a classic example of good

OR work. But who implemented it in this case? Clearly, the initiative and most of the analytical work came from the computer department. For the merchandisers (or management), it probably was more difficult *not* to adopt the new system then to do so. They could retain products with very special features on the manual system (as was agreed with the computer department in some cases); some merchandisers even continued to keep their old card systems, even though they now should be of little use to them. Were they nonimplementers? Certainly, only few of the merchandisers fully understood the mechanics of the inventory model, but they did not seemed alarmed as long as inventories and stockouts remained at reasonable levels.

Thus, *not* to implement would have meant a special initiative and more work for a merchandiser. He also would have had to distinguish himself from his colleagues who went along with the new procedures, which probably also made acceptance more attractive.

2. **The OR model may be so suited to management's desires that it merely confirms its intuitive decisions.** The production manager of a distillery concern invited the OR department to develop a production planning model together with his production planner. The production planner at that time made the production plans for the company's four plants for the next half year by a time-consuming manual procedure that was not too well described; the production plans were generally thought to be good, though.

The OR department developed a LP that, after many revisions, seemed a useful tool for the production planner. The revisions were necessary, because so many constraints had to be discovered by the OR worker because he knew little about the distilling process and because the production planner appeared a strongly intuitive (but not uncooperative) man whose reasons for making certain proposals were by no means obvious.

The production planner now uses the model. That is, in preparing his semiannual plans, he has several computer runs made, apparently until he feels comfortable enough about the plan he will propose. Without any doubt, use of the model has diminished the time he used to spend on calculating alternatives mentally. But, with regard to implementation, several questions remain. Did the model builder include too many constraints that were mostly of the planner's own making? Did the various model runs do more than confirm the planner's intuitive judgments?

3. **The OR model may be adopted for other reasons than to make better decisions.** Each year management of a bank had to determine how much to spend on advertising the bank's services. The amount had only been vaguely related to the profit economics of the business and was difficult to justify.

A computer-based simulation model was developed to determine how large the proposed advertising budget should be to meet the bank's performance goals for each geographical retail service area.

The successful use of the model came about through the enthusiasm of the bank's advertising executive—an enthusiasm due at least partly to the use in model runs of his subjective estimates of market response to advertising. Bank management also liked the model as it gave them an easy to understand and uniform tool to determine advertising expenditures in the different service areas.

The qualities of the OR model as a better decision-making tool were hardly questioned; in any case, they were not of overriding importance to the decision to adopt the model as an ongoing planning tool. How should we consider this case from the OR implementation point of view?

4. **An OR model may be developed and used successfully in one situation, but not even be considered in a similar situation at a later date.** A textiles and carpeting firm was considering the desirability of opening a production facility in a foreign market that had until now been served from home plants. Past problems of delivery delays and capacity limitations at these plants, coupled with indications of competitive threats, called for an especially thorough analysis of the question whether to open this new facility.

A simulation model was developed to calculate overall financial results for a range of assumptions on investment, costs, and demand characteristics. Results showed that the proposed facility should significantly exceed the company's after-tax ROI target of 10 percent, assuming a 20-year life. Moreover, the analysis showed that this ROI target would be satisfied even if no new business in the home market were obtained to replace the demand to be satisfied by the foreign facility. These analyses contributed to management's decision to establish the facility.

Few would doubt the implementation success of this example. However, some doubts about the lasting impact of the OR approach are cast by subsequent events. About one year later, management was again confronted with a facility decision; this time, the opening of a new production facility in the home market was considered. Aside from the business economic aspects, political factors and labor conditions played a major role in this decision. Although management still consisted of the same members, a comprehensive simulation model was not used to help make this decision; the traditional ROI calculations were again used. Apparently, management felt comfortable and knowledgeable enough about its home market to be able to make a decision on the production facility on the basis of these limited calculations and its own evaluation of nonquantifiable factors.

These examples suggest that at least three levels of OR adoption—each of which leading to an OR success in the previously described meaning of this term—might be distinguished, related to the following questions:

1. Does the development of an OR model lead to management *action?* (Is the OR model used at all?)
2. Does the development of an OR model lead to management *change?* (Is full value from the OR model received?)

Table 13.1

Action suggested on the basis of OR model	Underlying change required
1. Cut out technically noble products A and B	1. Eliminate distinction between noble and ignoble products.
2. Absorb subsidiary A	2. Reason in integrated terms
3. Introduce marginal contribution concept	3. Rely on marketing for pricing decisions (abandon secretive approach)

3. Does management's contact with the OR method lead to *recurring use of the OR approach?* (Has the OR approach become an integral part of management thinking?)

The difference in the first two questions between action and change is illustrated by a few examples in Table 13.1. These two types of management response to a specific OR proposal correspond to what has been called acceptance and implementation, respectively [*1, 3*].

The third question is not normally considered part of the implementation problem and is, in fact, of quite a different order than the first two. However, the lasting impact of OR will ultimately be measured by management's willingness and ability to turn to OR whenever its problems call for it. In fact a lot of today's concern about the use of OR seems to result from the apparent problem to give OR its place as management's trusted decision-preparation tool. It is important that this third question be considered in its own right: It would be naive to assume that adoption of the OR approach would come more or less automatically (as some seem to assume), once we have improved our ways to get management action and change vis-à-vis individual OR proposals.

Although the three levels of OR adoption are of an increasing order, achievement of even the lowest level (management action) may be sufficient to call an OR application fully successful. This could therefore be a valid objective of an OR application (as might be the case with, for example, the installation of an inventory model with built-in features to keep the model on track).

I recognize that it will be difficult to distinguish among the three levels of OR adoption in practice. However, it would already be helpful if those who report on the subject of OR implementation would clearly identify which level of success one claims to have achieved or is striving to achieve. At a minimum, this would reduce the amount of misunderstanding that now often exists.* More

*Impreciseness in defining the OR implementation problem and lack of a common language often make it difficult to relate the various efforts, findings, and conclusions in the area of OR implementation. They also may account for some of the contradictions that have been observed in implementation theories. For example, Starr notes that some theories

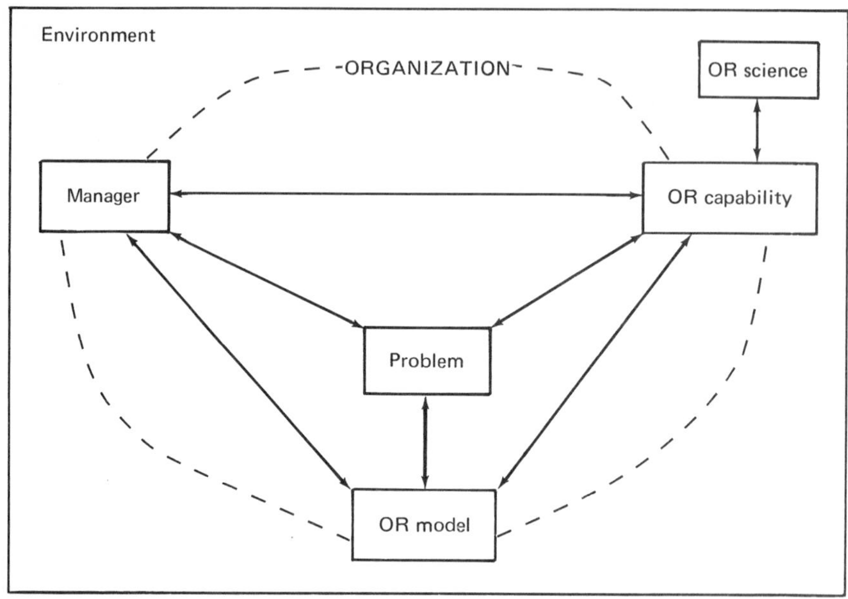

Fig. 13.1

importantly, however, it would be helpful, as will be discussed later, to think through, before applying OR, which level of adoption is feasible and necessary for an OR success in order to design an implementation strategy accordingly.

Evaluating the Relative Importance of Factors Affecting OR Implementation

Practically useful recommendations to achieve OR implementation must consider the whole range of complex factors that may affect it. One can only hope to gain the understanding needed of these factors if, one is able to order them and deal with them consecutively, while one does not lose sight of the interactions among all individual factors that may play a role in a concrete situation. As a starting point for evaluating their relative importance, Figure 13.1

---

of implementation "say that the manager should participate in the entire loop of activities, others that the manager be brought in only at the final phase, the implementation stage, and then only if necessary." [See Reference *10,* p. 108.] A more accurate statement might be that, generally, managerial involvement during the development phases of an OR project will be helpful for its implementation, but that the degree to which this is necessary depends on the circumstances and objectives of the application.

provides a simple framework to discuss the main factors and their interrelationships.

The meanings of the factors shown in Figure 13.1 are briefly discussed below. Each of them can be further described by a series of characteristics, some of which will be quite general, whereas others will be highly specific to a particular situation. A few of the more general characteristics and their meaning for the design of OR implementation strategies are also discussed.

1. **The manager.** The term manager may stand for a group of managers, in which case it also covers a complex set of interpersonal relationships. The manager is responsible for making decisions and initiating actions; he is the one who has to implement the OR recommendations.

Generally, managers have to deal with a large quantity and a great variety of tasks and frequent interruptions and changes of plan, together resulting in high time pressures. As a result, they often tend to prefer easy to understand, often verbal, communications and contacts of short duration that focus on the solutions to their concrete problems rather than approaches or inputs to these solutions. Moreover, there often remains little time for taking some distance from day-to-day operations to focus on the more important strategic issues. When this time *is* taken, many managers tend to continue the described work habit. The advancement of computers and communication technology has increased the pressures; More information is to be processed by the manager and more options (opportunities/problems) have to be considered as the system he perceives is enlarged.* OR implementation efforts generally must begin with adapting the development and presentation of OR proposals to these characteristics.

Because manager's are strongly end product oriented and often try to minimize their risks, they make changes only step-by-step in order to optimally control the change processes. These tendencies appear, at least in part, to result from reward structures that focus on performance measured over a fairly short time period. For operations researchers this poses the problem that management's time horizon may be shorter than the time required for an OR model to demonstrate its value.

2. **The problem.** To achieve organizational objectives, the manager has to define operational goals, to specify ways to achieve them, and to obtain and allocate resources; many issues have to be resolved in the process. The term problem may refer to any combination of these activities.

When we consider the problems to which OR is applied, we find a number of significant developments in several dimensions. Thus, OR applications have

*A further discussion of these general management characteristics is given by Mintzberg [5].

generally shifted from the low-level, routine, operational control decisions (such as production scheduling, distribution, and inventory control) to the higher-level, more sophisticated, and more complex strategic decisions (such as setting corporate policies, increasing advertising effectiveness, planning R&D, measuring management effectiveness and motivation, and evaluating mergers and acquisitions). With these changes, emphasis has tended to shift from the traditional OR areas of production, distribution, and logistics, to R&D, finance, marketing, and personnel. As part of these developments, the problems attacked by OR have evolved from very well structured to more difficult to structure. One important implication of all this is that the manager's role in OR problem formulation is, generally, becoming more important.

3. **The OR capability**. By OR capability I mean the technical capability that is required to formulate and solve OR models for different organization problems. The OR capability may exist within an organization as a separate staff function (centrally or as part of the line organization) or it may even be a direct attribute of line managers. The OR capability may also be accessed externally.

Clear general advantages of one form of access to the OR capability over others are difficult to show. The best form in a particular situation may well depend on the characteristics of the other factors.

4. **The OR model**. The term OR model refers to more or less formalized results of applying the OR capability to an organization problem. It may cover an OR solution/recommendation as well as an analytic method proposed to help make a certain decision.

Related to the developments mentioned under point 2, the clear financial benefits of relatively short-duration OR projects, using relatively simple OR techniques, are being replaced by the less tangible benefits (e.g., better information) obtained from projects of longer duration that involve more complex OR methods. (See, e.g., Turban [*11*].) The implementation problem in the last case will generally be quite different from that in the first: clearly, in the last case, the manager's confidence in OR is taxed more heavily and he will have to understand more of the OR solution in order to benefit from it.

These factors and their characteristics interact within an organization and jointly determine the degree of OR success.* In any specific situation, it will often be possible to identify and evaluate a number of specific characteristics that may strengthen or weaken the impact of the more general characteristics

---

*In Figure 13.1, we also drew the box OR science and the link OR capability-OR science. This was done because much of the concern of OR scientists about implementation seems to result from the very limited practical use of many new OR techniques and refinements, compared to the relatively intensive use of such tested techniques as LP. However, we do not intend to discuss this any further here. That is, we assume that OR approaches and techniques *can* be useful to management decision making–an assumption that is sufficiently supported by OR successes over the past 25 years.

discussed above. This involves the assessment of what Schultz and Slevin call the technical and organizational validity of a model [*8*].

Designing an Implementation Strategy According to Needs

In terms of the framework described in the previous section, implementation strategies can be seen as dealing with the questions of what characteristics OR capability and model should have and how they should relate to manager and problem in order to maximize the probability of OR success; the strategy that is best in any given situation will depend on the characteristics of manager and problem that prevail.

Given the general management characteristics described in the previous section, chances for OR implementation will generally be enhanced if OR models/solutions have the characteristics described by Little [*4*]. These characteristics are simplicity, robustness (i.e., the model does not easily come up with unusual or strange answers), ease of control, adaptiveness, completeness, and ease of communication.

In this section, I would like to review some further implications of the problem and management characteristics and developments thereof for OR implementation strategies. Corresponding to the three levels of adoption that may be attained, these strategies can be divided into three categories focusing on achievement of: (1) management action, (2) management change, or (3) recurring use of the OR approach. In terms of Figure 13.1, these strategies emphasize: (1) the model-problem-manager link, (2) the model-manager link, and (3) the OR capability-manager link, respectively.

Strategies Aiming at Management Action

Adoption of the first type (use of OR without close managerial involvement or understanding) may be sufficient for OR success in situations where the problem attacked by OR is fairly well structured and where the advantages of a model can be clearly established in terms of criteria familiar to the manager (e.g., profits). These situations are characterized by OR applications to relatively low-level, routine, operational control decisions, such as the inventory control example discussed above. The applications usually deal with small, well-defined systems; the financial benefits of the applications are mostly very real and can be reached with virtually no risk to the manager.

Strategies to achieve management action usually emphasize the value of an OR model to provide better problem solutions rather than better ways to approach a problem, for example. This approach directly ties into the manager's end product orientation. It convinces the manager via the model-problem-manager link (Figure 13.1); in many cases organizational control processes can be installed that ensure a more or less automatic execution, control, and updating of the OR model/solution.*

However, as we have seen in the previous section, the OR applications to low-level, routine-type problems are becoming part of the accepted business procedures and are no longer the most important applications that we find today. The strengthening of OR tools might somewhat enlarge the problem area for which comprehensive and self-evident OR solutions can be found, but, as is well known, in many cases the insight obtainable from applying the OR approach will be more important than any specific OR solution.

Strategies Aiming at Management Change

Adoption of the second type (use of an OR model with basic understanding by the manager) is necessary for most of the present OR applications. This conclusion follows from the fact that the value of OR models applied to the higher-level strategic problems lies in their ability to stimulate a manager's thinking by generating many alternative answers to his problems on the basis of various sets of assumptions.

To achieve adoption of the second type, or management change, the OR effort must pay at least as much attention to the needs of the manager as to the needs of the problem. In terms of Figure 13.1, this means that the model-manager link should have a central place in the implementation strategy.† The requirements of this type of a strategy can best be described by some examples.

1. **Gradually developing an asset-management model.** Bank asset-management models are meant to assist bank management in their continuing decisions on the portfolio of uses and sources of funds to maximize the bank's return. These decisions are difficult to make because (a) the timing and maturity of funds purchases cannot and should not exactly match the timing and maturities of loans made by the banks; (b) decisions are strongly interdependent through a complex set of business, governmental, and political constraints; and (c) various sources and uses of funds are unstable and market rates are volatile.

---

*This conclusion may appear in conflict with the position taken by Reisman and de Kluyver, who advocate management involvement from the very start of an OR project to arrive at a solution that is construed as the result of a spiral process in which objective and subjective elements are combined [*6*]. However, this conflict may only be artifical as they do not differentiate, as I do in this paper, among several degrees of management involvement. (See also the footnote on page 277.)

†Of course, the OR solution/recommendation must be relevant and a relatively good answer to the problem studied. This is a prerequisite in any implementation situation and the relevance and high quality of the OR solution will therefore be assumed.

Crucial advantages of the use of a bank asset-management model are that management's assumptions are made explicit, that the model covers a longer time horizon than is usually considered, and that it is possible to evaluate systematically changes in banking policies. To realize these advantages, management's cooperation had to be secured already in the design and development stages. The assumptions underlying management's decisions had to be discovered and the managers had to agree to give estimates on market rates regarding sources and uses of funds that were far beyond their habitual time horizon. (The bankers in this example not surprisingly were rather unwilling to give their estimates.) Use of the model challenged the bankers even further: Sensitivity analyses showed them the cost (lost opportunities) that resulted from banking policies that were to a large extent set by themselves and that were hardly ever questioned before. It is difficult to determine to what extent the managers really were willing to consider changing some policies on the basis of model results. However, the model certainly encouraged them to discuss these policies more frequently and systematically than they ever had done before.

The development of a full-scale, asset-management model, including both liabilities and assets, would probably have gone beyond (a) management's comprehension of what the model could do for them, and (b) management's willingness to cooperate in view of the model's potential threats (described above). Therefore, a series of successive models was developed that overcame these problems. The major steps in these successive developments are given in Table 13.2. The main use of the intermediate models was to maintain management's interest and confidence in the whole modelbuilding effort; it also ensured that the model built truly described the decision-making situation. In this regard, we might speak of a mixed descriptive-normative model—the model was descriptive in that all constraints were accepted without question, and the model (LP) was normative in that it generated an optimal solution within the given set of constraints. Questioning of the constraints themselves through sensitivity analysis came only in a later stage.

The development of this OR application appears to be an illustration of what Shakun means when he proposes the approach of situational normativism to achieve implementation and organizational development [*8*]. In this approach, real-world decisions are described in terms of participants and their values, and decision rules. Subsequently, a mathematical model of the system is developed that is used to search for change by generating prescriptive alternatives satisfying constraint (goal) sets that are evolved in the process of OR and corresponding adaptive system redesign. This search for change is a learning process in which manager and scientist gradually come to mutual understanding, a condition for successful implementation.

2. **Selecting OR techniques to meet current management needs.** The following example even more strongly illustrates the need to adapt OR solu-

Table 13.2
Summary of Key Features of Successive Asset-Management Planning and Analysis Models

General features	Specific items in successive models			Final model including both liabilities and assets
	Initial liquidity model	Full liability model	Liquidity model	
Objective: Minimize net cost on controlled items				
Cost items	Negotiable CD's London balances Net borrowing	Nonnegotiable CD's Central banks		
Revenue items	Liquid assets			Investments
Rates and prices	Representative rates for average maturities	Specific rates for individual maturities	Specific prices for individual assets	Specific prices for individual investments
Constraints: Observe constraints affecting potential values of controlled items	Basic balance sheet policy constraints and accounting relationships Market supply limits Legal relationships	Time-deposit mix and multiperiod relationships Time-deposit supply/rate interrelationships	Liquid asset acquisition and early-sale guidelines	Investment acquisition and early-sale guidelines
Time Deposit Maturities: Specify maturity schedules	Negotiable CD's London balances	Nonnegotiable CD's		

tions/recommendations to the management characteristics of a specific situation. It refers to an operations planning model that was developed for distribution management of a company whose products were mainly exported by sea. Distribution management had no previous experience with models, but sensed the need for a more systematic approach to its operations decisions that had to cope with changes in vessel schedules, variations in plant output, production breakdowns, and strikes. A simulation model of the production, transportation, and stockpile systems–including breakdowns and variations in shipping schedules–was developed to analyze the whole operation from plant to port and to provide a picture of potential bottlenecks and overloads in the system in the period ahead. Distribution management was thus provided with information necessary to reschedule plant production to overcome delays.

Only after distribution management had gained some first-hand experience with the simulation approach to analyze its options, were further modeling steps considered. Drawing on its favorable experience, distribution management decided to build its computer skills, appoint a systems-oriented operations manager, and develop a more comprehensive optimizing model.

An extension of this approach is presented by Souder and his associates who describe a design methodology for R&D project selection models [*9*]. Their approach, however, is much more explicit in that they: (1) identify the organizational and personal variables influencing the willingness to adopt an OR model through sociopsychological analyses, and (2) select an appropriate model form from among several candidate forms on the basis of the model's impact on the variables identified. Although this approach is very appealing, it would be interesting to know how practical it is for the ordinary situation in which OR is applied, given the extra demands it places on time, special skills (which are not usually available), and management cooperation.

3. **Assigning explicit organizational responsibility for model adaptation.** Effective use of an OR model over time requires that the model be adapted to changing circumstances; model adaptiveness is a necessary, but not a sufficient, condition to ensure that the model will actually be adapted when needed. Parameter changes still could be considered part of the regular use of a model and usually do not require special provisions beyond those foreseen in any implementation strategy. However, to ensure that correct structural changes are timely, the OR capability (Figure 13.1) must remain involved.

It may be possible to install the OR capability required for timely and proper model adaptation by assigning explicit organizational responsibility for it when the model is first introduced. Specifically, this was done in the case of a corporate planning model developed for an industrial firm. This model dealt with an extensive system involving many managers, so that it was difficult to determine which manager was to be responsible for it. Therefore, with the introduction of the model, a master of the model was named; this person was made explicitly responsible for updating the model, making model runs, and handling all technical questions that arose. The model has been repeatedly revised since its initial introduction, e.g., to reflect changes in the formal organization structure. The managers appear to be more willing to use the planning model, because this guaranteed service label is attached to it.

4. **Increasing model credibility by gaining support for it in management's traditional reference groups**. Model credibility is seldom the result of the characteristics of an OR model alone, e.g., its ability to generate intuitively reasonable answers to a problem. To increase credibility, and hence the chances of successful implementation, attention might also be focused on organizational and group forces that influence management's behavior.

This is illustrated by the implementation strategy used to convince management of the real estate department of an insurance firm of the validity and usefulness of a set of relatively simple financial models built to evaluate the firm's facility needs. The models incorporated some 50 financial variables, including lease rates, tax rates, mortgage factors, occupancy rates, sublease rates, and construction costs. Making a manual check of all calculations for one model run with a senior officer was only one measure to establish the model's credibility. At least as important to its final adoption by the real estate department was the review of the model logic with the investment department, the audit firm, the law firm, the internal law department, the actuarial department, the accounting department, and selected senior vice-presidents. The real estate department now uses the models as part of ongoing lease-or-buy decision analyses.

In each of the previous examples the OR model had to become an integral part of the internal decision-making processes that management uses to arrive at its decisions. In the first two examples the implementation strategy accomplished this by tailoring the model to the specific managerial needs of the situation. In the last two examples measures were taken to create the most favorable circumstances for a positive management attitude toward the model, which in these cases led to strong adoption and basic change by management.

In the terminology of Schultz and Slevin, the described implementation strategies should be part of a behavioral model building process [*8*]. This means that the user should not only learn about the model's end result but also about the processes that are used to arrive at them. To accomplish this the model builder should study the behavioral characteristics of his user and of the organization so that he can adjust the structure of the model as needed. In contrast to strategies aiming at management action, discussed in the previous section, it will generally not be enough to incorporate the model in the formal organizational procedures to achieve management change.

Strategies Aiming at Recurring Use of the OR Approach

Recurring use of the OR approach by management will be the ultimate test of OR's success. In marketing terms, is the customer repurchasing the product? To my knowledge, little research has been done so far to establish the extent to which managers, who used OR once, have used it again for other problems and for determining the factors that influence repurchase.

Some useful insights are provided by Vertinsky, Barth, and Mitchell who describe and relate the factors affecting management's motivation to use OR/MS [*12*]. The implications for a strategy aiming at recurring use of OR are, of course, that the mix of OR/MS activities within organizations should be carefully chosen to highlight those activities that will provide positive motivation for further use of OR/MS and the associated weltanschauung. They further add that diffusion of OR/MS is significantly related to the interpersonal competence of practitioners, which has obvious implications for training and recruitment of future practitioners. [*12*].

Relating this last observation to the framework presented in Figure 13.1, it is clear that a key link for adoption of the OR approach in general is the relationship manager-OR capability. An important contribution to creating an effective relationship may be supplied by the organization design. This might include, for example, (1) a central OR department able to observe application opportunities (including crossfunctional ones) by overviewing the whole organization as well as external progress of OR (in theory and practice), (2) central or decentral OR function(s) that would evaluate the feasibility of OR applications for the organization and provide the necessary model design and building skills, and (3) an OR implementation capability close to management, such as the master of the model mentioned before. The strategy suggested by Vertinsky et al., in which OR/MS practitioners are indoctrinated within a staff OR/MS group and subsequently reassigned to an operating function, also seems practical and useful.

Finally, I also should mention management training as a means to improve the manager-OR capability relationship. This refers to both formal training before entering business practice as well as management-education programs that are increasingly becoming part of the ongoing business scene. The relative merits of the various forms of management training deserve special attention and will not be commented on here.

The previous discussion has paid little attention to a key question in OR implementation, i.e., how the values are determined that guide any OR effort. With the application of OR to larger and more complex problems, this question becomes more evident; however, even for the smaller systems described in this paper, one might question the true benefits that OR solutions are providing.

The implementation strategies described by Churchman [*2*] address themselves to this much more basic question. His chapter clearly illustrates that implementation strategies, such as the ones discussed above, should be incorporated in a broader strategy that helps establish the objectives of an OR application. Churchman's comments on the value of a computer information system installed by Stafford Beer in Chile indicate the risk that one is running when this basic question is bypassed too easily.

CONCLUSION

In this chapter I have tried to review the problem of OR implementation in the light of management practice. My main conclusions can be summarized as follows:

1. It seems useful to distinguish between two steps in the design of an OR implementation strategy, dealing with: (1) assessing the implementation problem in a given situation, and (2) gearing the implementation strategy to the specific needs of that situation.

2. In the assessment of an implementation problem, one should question: (1) what constitutes a success in the given situation and what type of adoption should therefore be aimed for, and (2) what factors will affect reaching this success. It appears that a more differentiated common language to describe these elements would be useful. I distinguished among three levels of adoption and introduced a simple framework to discuss the factors affecting OR adoption.

3. Adoption of the first type (use of OR models) can be sufficient for OR success in the case of low-level, routine applications in which the model-problem link dominates. It can be achieved by installing the model as part of the ongoing organizational procedures.

4. Adoption of the second type (managerial understanding of OR models) is needed for OR success in the case of the more advanced, strategic applications, in which the model-manager link is essential. Adoption of the second type can be achieved in many different ways; these focus on making the OR solution an integral part of management's internal decision-making process.

5. Adoption of the third type (recurring use of the OR approach) is the ultimate test of OR. Management's propensity to repurchase indicates its willingness to use OR as its trusted, regular decision-preparation tool. Strategies to achieve adoption of the third type include organizational design and management training.

Finally, I would like to draw attention to a special problem that forms a particularly confusing element in the evaluation of OR implementation strategies. This problem stems from the fact that willingness to use OR and ability to make good decisions based on OR analyses do not yet mean improvement of organizational performance. These improvements ultimately depend on management's ability to execute and control its decisions. Therefore, it may be necessary to distinguish between OR implementation in the narrow sense and OR success, referring to successful completion of the chain from problem identification to decision execution and control.

References

1. Churchman, C. West., "Managerial Acceptance of Scientific Recommendations," *California Management Review,* Fall 1964.
2. Churchman, C. West, this volume, Chapter 2.
3. Huysmans, Jan H., *The Implementation of Operations Research,* New York: 1970.
4. Little, J.D.C., "Models and Managers: The Concept of a Decision Calculus," *Management Science,* **16-8** (April 1969).
5. Mintzberg, Henry, "Managerial Work: Analysis from Observation," *Management Science,* **18-2** (October 1971).
6. Reisman, Arnold, and de Kluyver, Cornelis A., this volume, Chapter 14.
7. Shakun, Melvin F., "Implementing Management Science via Situational Normativism," *Management Science,* **18-8** (April 1972).
8. Schultz, Randall L. and Slevin, Dennis P., this volume, Chapter 3.
9. Souder, W.E., Maher, P.B., Baker, N.R., Shumway, C.R., and Rubenstein, A.H., this volume, Chapter 6.
10. Starr, Martin K., *Management: A Modern Approach,* New York, Harcourt Brace Jovanovich, 1971.
11. Turban, Efraim, "A Sample Survey of Operations Research Activities at the Corporate Level," *Operations Research,* **20-3** (May–June 1972).
12. Vertinsky, Ilan, Barth, Richard T., and Mitchell, Vance F., this volume, Chapter 12.

Chapter 14

Strategies for Implementing Systems Studies*

Arnold Reisman
Cornelis A. de Kluyver

In this chapter we will discuss strategical, as opposed to methodological, considerations of systems studies. This approach complements the behavioral emphasis as presented by Vertinsky, Barth, and Mitchell [*25*], Mitroff [*8*], Radnor [*14*], Souder et al. [*24*], and Manley [*6*], in that in this chapter attitudinal and other behavioral issues concerning the implementation of systems studies are translated into strategies. Moreover, these strategies work, and this has been demonstrated in several large-scale studies performed by the authors. The strategies outlined here also reflect the empirical and methodological results as reported on by Schultz and Slevin [*23*], Huysmans [*4*], and others and reflect some of the philosophical observations made by Churchman [*2*]. Thus, our job is to integrate many of these concepts into strategical considerations regarding the implementation of systems studies. The basis for our discussion is the recognition that systems studies should be structured and conducted in such a way that the probability of successful implementation is maximized. Therefore, implementability of methods used and results obtained is imperative. To achieve this, planning for implementation, the design of the task force, the relationship with the user, and the critical evaluation of results are singled out as important factors. The involvement of the ultimate user may well be the most important one. These strategies will be discussed in detail and illustrated with examples from three completed and implemented studies, which were conducted by the authors. We emphasize strategies that have worked rather than those that may be effective but have not been demonstrated as such. The common element underlying all of these strategies is communication, defined in the widest sense. Success is impossible without enlightened users and sponsors who have achieved ownership of the study. Only then will a climate of confidence favor successful implementation.

---

*The authors express their gratitude to Professor H. Emmons and, posthumously to our friend and colleague, Professor M. H. Stern, Department of Operations Research, Case Western Reserve University, for their constructive criticisms.

The Studies

Three studies conducted by the authors will be used to demonstrate the various points made throughout this chapter regarding a strategy for implementation. Each of these studies can be described as being large scale, multidisciplinary, multiobjective, and implemented or in the process of being implemented. The studies are concerned with inventory control of finished goods for a large manufacturer [*15, 9*], the evaluation of output in each of seventeen disparate social agencies associated in a voluntary federation [*18, 16, 7, 17*], and the distribution of materials in a large network of libraries [*19, 1*].

The Inventory Control Study

The first study was done for a large manufacturing company whose products (7000 catalogued items) are sold to industrial customers via a network of 700 distributors supplied by five field warehouses located throughout the nation. These warehouses are, in turn, supplied by the factory warehouse located in the Midwest. The factory warehouse, in addition to serving the backup needs of the field warehouses, is also used as a field warehouse for the midwestern region. The objectives of the study included:

1. Improvement of the decision rules used for replenishment of inventory at both the factory and field warehouses in terms of the level and the mix of finished goods carried at each of the locations.
2. This improvement was to be done in consideration of the various costs associated with inventory, e.g., set-up costs, reorder costs, costs associated with the holding of inventory including the cost of capital and/or the internal rate of return, space costs, handling costs, depreciation, obsolescence costs, taxes and insurance, and the costs associated with being out of stock.

Other objectives of the study were concerned with demonstrating whether or not operations research could productively be used within this company and, if so, training several line managers in the process of operations research.

The Study for Social Agencies

The second study was initiated by the budget committee of the Jewish Community Federation of Cleveland. This committee is made up of lay community leaders who annually face the task of allocating constrained dollar resources to each of seventeen agencies that differ in the scope of services offered and level of activity. This group included agencies primarily concerned with psychosocial counseling, vocational counseling, and providing institutional care for senior citizens. Also included in this set was a parochial educational system ranging from the preschool to college level of instruction and a large community center. The objective here was to obtain some rational and systematic means of evaluating the output of services offered in order to more effectively allocate funds. The methodology had to be flexible enough so that an agency could be evaluated across all of the services offered to all of its client groups and so that each service could be evaluated across all of the agencies where it was being offered to each of the various client groups. Finally, the methodology was to evaluate how well each client group was being served across all of the agencies that serve this group and across all services offered to this group.

The Library Study

The third study was concerned with the cost and effectiveness of a system that distributed library materials to a network of over 700 libraries in the Cleveland metropolitan area. These libraries represent a consortium of many independent library systems including those operated by the county, by the city, and by each of a number of suburban municipalities. University, school, and special libraries were also involved.

Organization of the Chapter

The chapter is divided into three parts. First, project selection will be discussed. In this section factors that should be taken into account in the selection of projects are considered. Second, the design of the task force is discussed in some detail. Finally, factors affecting implementation during the course of the study are identified. In this discussion, a general format for systems studies is used and factors are discussed as they impacted studies performed by the authors. The concepts we will identify were all validated in the studies mentioned above. Moreover, a recent study comparing systems studies substantiates to a large degree the notions set forth in the following sections [*11*].

WHAT PROBLEMS TO SELECT FOR STUDY?

Project selection can be an important variable affecting implementation. In many instances, corporate operations research groups have a certain degree of freedom in selecting and/or soliciting problems for study. No strict rules can be given to guide the decision whether to accept a certain project or not. However, insights into this problem have been provided by Radnor, Rubenstein, and others [*12, 13, 20–22*]. These authors relate the selection of problems to the concept of a life cycle for corporate OR groups. Their ideas center around the degree to which the OR activity is established and commonly accepted within the organization. Specifically, they describe the integration of a systems function into the organization in three phases: the introductory phase, the transitional phase, and the permanent phase.

The Introductory Phase

In this phase the activity is initiated and accepted only on a trial basis. No formal commitments have been made by top management to support the activity in the future. It is apparent that success is a must in this critical phase if the group is to survive. As a result, the authors recommend the selection of projects with a high a priori probability of success. That is, projects that take a relatively short time to complete, are relatively simple in the technical sense, having an interface with the rest of the system that can be easily identified and perhaps decoupled, and will demonstrate high potential cost savings. The primary objective is to impress both top management (the sponsors) and line management (the users) with results that are immediate and highly visible. Another motivation for selecting relatively small problems is that these studies usually require a smaller task force and fewer demands from management, thus facilitating the establishment of initial communications. Once initial efforts have been successful and the results implemented, the OR group may become a more accepted part of the organization. This gain in status is described as the second phase of the integration process.

The Transitional Phase

Based on initial success, the decision has been made to continue the OR activity on a full-time basis. No formal commitments have been made yet, although the attitude toward the activity is somewhat less skeptical than in the previous phase. Again, the group's mission is to impress both users and sponsors. This time, however, the expectations are higher and small results will not be sufficient to provide the necessary push toward the third phase of permanent establishment and recognition. Because somewhat larger and possibly less visible projects are involved, the group must educate both users and sponsors in what to expect. This can be accomplished by involving both line and top management in the study. Specifically, the task force should consist of OR professionals and representatives of both line and top management. This organization benefits the study in more than one way. First, by working together with the group, line and top managers learn different ways of thinking about problems and may begin to appreciate some of the concepts being used. In turn, it benefits the systems professional in assessing management's needs. Moreover, the technical success of the study is increased, because more frequent communications with line management (the user) allows for better model building, improved assessment of data needs, more accurate data collection, and estimation of parameter values. Nothing must be vague about what it is the group does. Detailed systems descriptions, presentations, and reports are recommended to aid the users in their understanding of the group's activities. If significant results are obtained and functional channels of communication have been established, a further gain in status may result. This transition is described as the third phase of the integration process.

The Permanent Phase

The group has survived the tests set by management and is now established as a formal permanent part of the organization. The position of this staff group is now comparable with that of other well-established staff functions, such as marketing research and planning. The immediate pressure to perform is off and more difficult projects for which a good solution may not exist can be tried. However, it is advisable to maintain the portfolio concept as part of the operation. That is, to have a proper balance of projects in difficulty, in time required, in resources required, and in visibility. Only then will the group always have a recent success at hand to justify its existence.

The previous discussion centered around corporate OR groups. What about outside consulting groups? Although these groups are usually faced with a smaller degree of freedom in project selection, a distinct parallel can be drawn. In assessing the a priori probability of success, that is, of successful implementation of results, the previous experiences of the organization with the systems activity in general must be incorporated. Specifically, the following factors should be considered:

1. The organization's experience with the systems activity in general, e.g., how many studies were performed and how many were implemented?
2. Did previous studies have the full support of both users and sponsors? If so, why did some of the previous studies fail?
3. Are sufficient resources available and is enough time available to complete the study and implement the results?
4. Does this project have the full support of both top and line management? Are these groups willing to participate as part of the task force?

It is clear that this list is by no means complete. However, it forces the analyst to think about the organizational setting in which the study is to be performed. This, in turn, gives the systems professional some indications as to management's attitude toward the study and the organization's readiness to absorb the change resulting from implementation. It should be noted that this process may be formalized. A questionnaire could be developed for this purpose where the answers could be scaled and the composite rating could be interpreted as a subjective assessment of the a priori probability of successful implementation. This instrument could be used to aid in project selection as well as in project strategy.

The Design of the Task Force

The design of the task force is crucial for success. We have argued that both users and sponsors must be involved in the study from the beginning until its completion. The analyst must realize that it is line management (the user) who will have to live with the results of the study on a day-to-day basis. Preferably, representatives of top management and/or lay leadership* are also part of the task force. This ensures that the sponsors are continually aware of the group's activities thus favoring the chances for successful implementation as well as securing cooperation for initiating future projects. It can be stated safely that unless this active participation of top and line management is secured, the likelihood that the study will be a success and the results implemented will sharply decrease. Many reasons can be given for this. First, there is what we label the NIH (not invented here) effect. A study done in isolation of the ultimate user (and the sponsor) generally meets a great amount of resistance in the implementation phase. Moreover, the technical success of the study may be jeopardized. The analyst is dependent on line management for data used in building the model, data used to test the model, and other data needed in the systems description, model building, and validation phases. Secondly, communication problems may arise when the user is not intimately familiar with the study. The analyst may have the wrong perception of the manager's needs and solve, albeit correctly, the wrong problem. Finally, the failure to involve the user may lead to suboptimization, or the optimization of one organizational unit or process at the expense of another. In discussions with line management it may become apparent that several other subsystems within the organization will be affected by the study. A study done in isolation of management may not uncover this and will almost surely fail to get implemented. The communications with the user on the task force may also affect the selection of the methodology for the study. For example, in the finished goods inventory study [*15, 9*], dynamic programming and integer programming methods might have been used; in fact, they may have yielded mathematically better results. However, they

*For nonprofit organizations lay leadership is as important as the top administration.

were discarded in favor of improved min-max and reorder point-E.O.Q. policies as these were in principle what the company used traditionally, and hence, were more easily implemented. Moreover, the other methods would have presented additional computational problems. The key is that management must understand what it is the OR people are doing *with* and not for them. As a result, we postulate that the involvement of management throughout the course of the study as part of the project task force is a necessary condition for successful implementation.

In the study performed for the federation of social agencies [*7, 16–18*], the task force included faculty and graduate students of the School of Applied Social Sciences and of the Department of Operations Research,* while the federation was represented by the Director of Research and Planning, a budget specialist, and a social researcher.

The team as a whole met once a week, and, before long, a learning process on the part of the participants began to develop. The members began to appreciate each other's ways of thinking about the problem and became familiar with each other's jargon. The development of this understanding must not be underestimated. The close interaction patterns favored a detailed concise problem statement that, in turn, led to the development of a good, mutually understood and agreed upon approach to solve the problem at hand. This climate of understanding proved indispensible in later phases of the study when data were collected and preparations made for the implementation of results. In this setting, the reversal of roles within the group was fairly common. For example, this manifested itself when social workers argued for rigor and logic while OR professionals argued against things that would dehumanize the resulting process. Moreover, the OR task force periodically (once every other month) met with a committee of community lay leaders. This committee consisted of a subset of the Federation's Board of Trustees, and it included the current and immediate past chairman of the federation's budget and community service planning committees. These two committees were the most powerful committees of the board, having within their jurisdiction the power of recommendations regarding resource allocation. This committee reviewed and evaluated all progress presented by the task force and was used as a resource for certain information required by the study. Members of this committee played a very valuable role in getting the board to approve the study recommendations and in obtaining acceptance of the methods by the agency executives.

In the case of the industrial inventory control study, the task force consisted of faculty and graduate students from the Department of Operations Research and, on a part time basis, the corporate managers of the market research, quality assurance, and the electronic data processing departments. This

*Case Western Reserve University, Cleveland, Ohio.

task force met once a week both on and off site. This body developed all aspects of the study with the exception of the theoretical developments of the recommended decision rules. However, the entire task force was involved in the systems description, data (both hard and soft) collection, model testing, etc. The task force once a month reported to the company's executive committee, which included the president, all vice presidents, and division heads. As in the above case, these meetings were also used for review and evaluation purposes as well as sources of information and for decision making. In some aspects of the study, several alternative approaches and their respective attributes were delineated. A choice was then requested and obtained from the executive committee.

In the case of the library study, the task force was made up of members of the faculty of the School of Library Science and the Department of Operations Research. It included graduate students from the latter department and, in addition, it included four directors of libraries representing a suburban public library, a special (industrial) library, and two university libraries. The task force also included an executive of the municipal library. As in the previous study, this task force met in working session once a week. The entire group was involved in all aspects of planning and conducting the study and in evaluating the work done by subgroups. The results were reviewed by a watch-dog committee, this time consisting of the directors of all participating libraries. Over a dozen independent library systems were thus represented.

In summary, the involvement of the ultimate user and preferably, the sponsor is a necessary condition for success. Unless this is done, the user will feel uneasy about the presence of the OR group, and the analysts will have a hard time defining the problem, collecting the data, and implementing the results. The key is to motivate management to identify problems and solve them *with* the OR group. The involvement of the user, then, transfers the ownership of the study directly where it belongs, to line management.

HOW IS IMPLEMENTATION AFFECTED BY THE STUDY ITSELF?

In this part of the discussion, we turn to the problem-solving process itself. We examine its steps and the factors that may increase or decrease the probability of success at each step. For ease of exposition we illustrate the problem solving process* in a spiral representation (see Figures 14.1 and 14.2). Each loop describes one iteration in the process, its stages are described as the identification of the problem (need), the problem statement, the development of a model, analysis and testing, the evaluation of the results, and the decision whether to iterate (i.e., to modify the problem statement or the model) or to stop the

*See Chapter 1 in Reisman and Kiley [*17*].

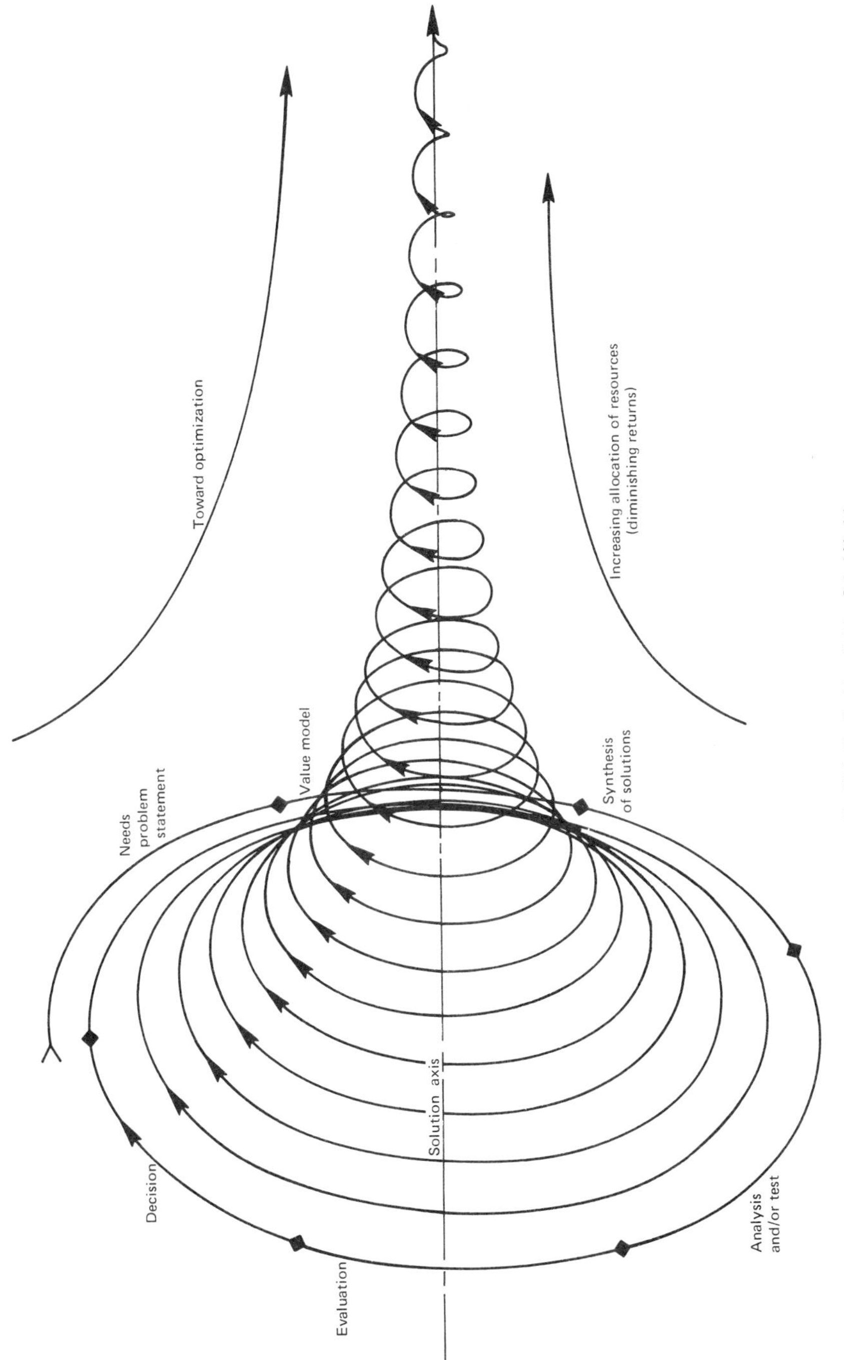

Fig. 14.1 The Problem-Solving Spiral Model

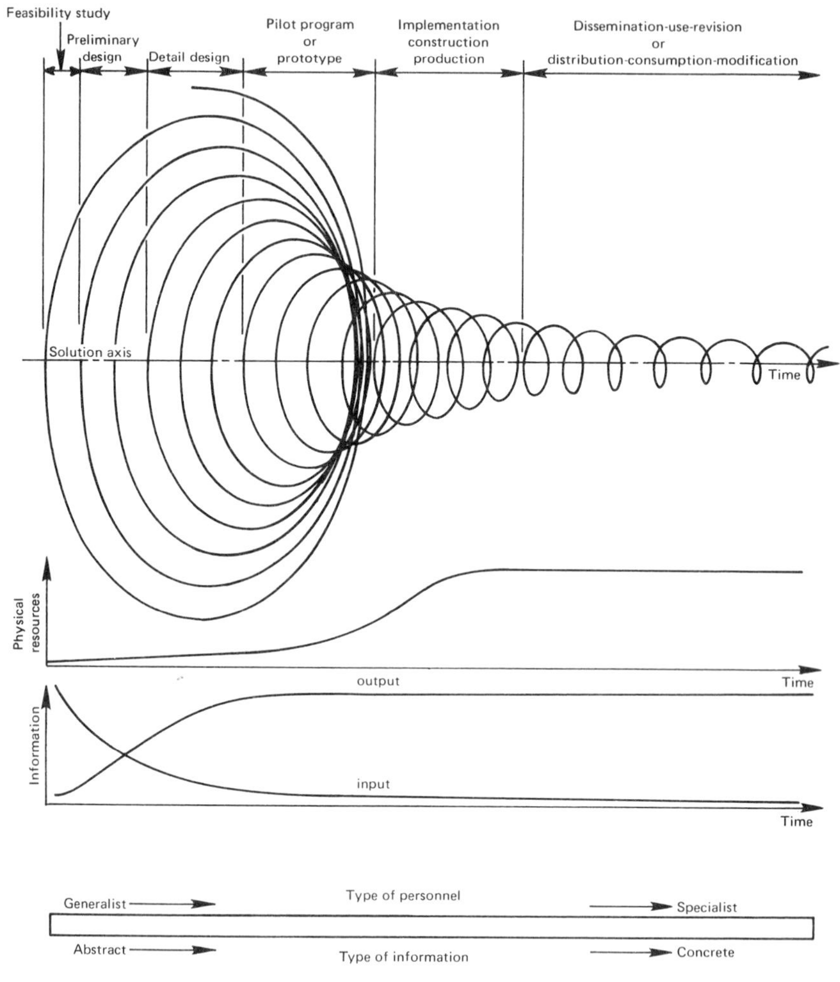

Fig. 14.2

process. Before relating implementation to each of these stages, we examine the spiral a little closer and note the following. First, this representation suggests the iterative nature of the process, converging over time to the desired solution. This, in turn, indicates the need for continuous involvement and assistance of line management in the process to affect the convergence. Second, as with most converging processes, we need criteria to decide when to stop the process. Since it is line management who will have to work with the results on a daily basis, their satisfaction with the solution is the desired criterion. Third, the spiral illustrates the effect of law of diminishing returns on problem solving. In the initial phases of the process, a relatively large amount of progress is made with a relatively small amount of inputs (resources), whereas in later iterations more information, time, and other resources are invested to affect what we might call adjustments to the current model. This is another important reason for management's involvement *from the beginning.* The continuity of the process is greatly enhanced if these resource allocations can be anticipated by management and the OR professionals. Moreover, important adjustments of the model may be overlooked if line management has not been involved in its initial formulation. In addition to the amount of resources invested at each phase, we can say something about the nature of the resources needed. At the outset of the study, the professional seeks general information. Company and study objectives must be stated, the nature of the constraints on the problem determined, etc. The OR group takes a generalist's point of view trying to uncover the governing relations between subsystems as a whole. The information needed might be labeled general, in that no numbers are required–rather, an insight into the existing managerial process is sought. The task force at this stage must be able to abstract from the complexities of the real world that which is germane. The latter, moreover, must be documented in understandable yet operationally useful terms. In later phases of the study, once the model has been formulated in its crude form, attention must be paid to the subsystems themselves. As a result, line management and the analysts take a specialist point of view, trying to collect data, write computer codes for data analysis, and develop and test mathematical and/or computer solutions, or in other words, analyze more detailed aspects of the model.

In summary, the nature of the problem solving process itself indicates the need for line management's continuous involvement from the beginning of the study until its completion. The process also indicates the nature of the resources needed at each phase, thus allowing for better planning, continuity in the study, and hence favoring the chances for successful implementation. In particular, the analyst should take a generalist's point of view at the outset of the study. In later phases more details should be considered. Thus, he adopts a specialist's viewpoint. We now examine the factors affecting the process.

The Problem Definition Stage

Most problems are ill defined at the time the systems professional enters the picture. Line management might have a "feeling in their bones" that something is wrong, they may have identified the right problem but attributed it to the wrong causes, or it may happen that they have identified a problem that on closer scrutiny appears to be a part of a much larger problem. The task of the analyst is how to identify and define the correct problem. This is more simply stated than done. At the outset of the study, the analyst needs all the help he can get from line management in drawing up a functional systems description and securing the relevant information. Specifically, he needs information from top management on organizational and study objectives, constraints affecting the problem, and criteria of effectiveness. The line management, aided by the analyst, will have to provide the precise problem definition, as well as descriptions of variables and parameters involved and other subsystems affected by the solution. Again we emphasize that this may best be accomplished by having representatives of both top and line management on the project task force.

One may ask why a systems description is necessary in the first place and how this may affect implementation of the results? Several justifications can be given for its use. First, we emphasized that the systems analyst must make an effort to educate the manager in different ways of looking at a problem. A carefully prepared systems description can be of great help in this respect. It helps the line manager to understand the kind of approach used by the OR specialist at an early stage in the game. Moreover, it helps the professional to understand the functional relationships between organizational subsystems and their interdependencies. In addition, the preparation of the systems description itself actually involves the line manager right from the beginning. He has to supply the relevant information and has the chance to become thoroughly familiar with the requirements of the study. As a result his confidence will increase and he will have the feeling that the group is working with and not for him.

Most importantly, however, a good systems description will indicate the possibilities for conflict and suboptimization. In particular, the analyst can guard himself against building a model that will lead to the optimization of part of the system at the expense of other parts or of the system as a whole. For example, in the case of the industrial inventory control study, it was found that it was necessary to structure the recommended policies for finished goods inventory in such a way that efficiency in production, marketing, and the company as a whole did not suffer.

Another distinct advantage in preparing a detailed systems description is that many erroneous assumptions made by management are uncovered. For example, in the finished goods inventory study, management held the following beliefs:

1. Goods must be shipped within 24 hours following receipt of the order. (An investigation proved that the distributors never expected better than a two-week delivery as they kept their own stock for the replacement parts market; the original equipment manufacturers, on the other hand, were annoyed at early deliveries, because they affected the cash flow balance and created storage problems.)
2. More inventory on hand means increased sales. (As the company sold

strictly to industrial customers, the amount of impulse buying was negligible. Demand was fairly predictable and inventory beyond the incipient stockout level did not motivate anyone to sell or buy more.)

3. The turns-ratio is a good criterion for judging how well field warehouses manage their inventory. (It was shown that at least in one instance this criterion proved counterproductive because it encouraged the warehouse manager to behave like a broker at the expense of customer service and production schedules for the factory.)

A good systems description very often gives line managers a better understanding of their own systems. Since a systems description is done early in the course of a study, it is a tangible and useful result that motivates management toward proceeding further with the study. For instance, in the social welfare study, a simple incidence matrix having as rows different services and as columns the various agencies, very quickly and clearly established the extent of overlap in services provided among the agencies. In the case of the library study, the systems description pointed out that trucks from the county system and those from the city library system called, on a scheduled basis, to several libraries that were geographically extremely close to each other. Most enlightening was the fact that such instances were not at all rare.

Therefore, a good systems description aids both the analyst and the user in their understanding of the problem. In addition, the early involvement of line management is a favorable factor not to be underestimated. The earlier the task force begins to operate as a team, the better are chances for successful implementation.

The Model Building Stage

Many failures can be attributed to poor modeling. Often models are too complex, or are perceived as such. Even though it is true that the user does not have to understand all technical details, the model must make sense to him; it must agree with his experience and knowledge about the problem. At the same time many models appear to lack sensitivity. The user must be able to vary all parameters and variables of interest to him. Moreover, it must be easy for him to do so. As a result, a model should be plausible and easily manipulated. To formalize this concept, we use the criteria proposed by Little [5]. The author suggests that a model should be:

Simple. Here we refer to ease of understanding and manipulation. A good systems description will differentiate between important and unimportant variables. Those that are unimportant should be left out or be summarized and included as one composite factor.

Robust. This refers to the sensitivity of the model. It should be difficult to force the model to produce meaningless answers. To prevent this, the model should be able to handle all meaningful ranges of values of parameters and variables.

Easy to control. The user should be able to manipulate the model in any way he wants. This does not only refer to inputs to the model. The user must be able to come up with any set of outputs he desires, not for the purpose of fudging, but rather to make sure he understands all relationships between the model components.

Adaptive. Updating of parameters and other model components should be relatively simple.

Complete on important issues. This seems to contradict simplicity. Here, the problem is to decide what level of detail to include in the overall model and what quantities to approximate and incorporate as aggregate components. We encounter a trade off between manageability and descriptiveness. Specifically, in order to be complete, one needs to formulate the model to be as detailed as possible. This, however, tends to make the models large and complex. We have to remember that the model must be implementable, i.e., it must be a good representation of the situation at hand and be communicable at the same time to enhance the chances for successful implementation. We emphasize the term representation because this incorporates the notion of approximation. No model will be 100 percent accurate. However, the difference between a large, complex, 90 percent accurate model and a more simple, 80 percent accurate model may be large in terms of implementability. Experience indicates that in successful studies, one should err during the earlier phases of the study on the side of descriptiveness. However, it is often necessary in later phases to combine variables and aggregate parameters to make models manageable and, therefore, more implementable. This aggregation process should not be viewed as a compromise action. On the contrary, it requires a high level of competence on the part of the team. Moreover, the study's cost-benefit ratio is improved. This aggregation process often takes place as a result of data collection attempts. The latter must not only be interpreted to mean that the data are not available. It may well be that it proves too costly to collect certain data or that earlier tests indicate that the model is insensitive to such data.

For instance, in the early phases of the federation study we worked with seven client groups. However, after preliminary data collection it was discovered that the differences between both the values and the evaluations of the services offered to high school and to junior high school groups were not great enough to justify the separation of these two age groups. Consequently, the two age groups were combined. Similarly, it was found that one of the agencies operated on a minimal budget as compared to others. It was therefore decided to eliminate this particular agency from the systems study.

Easy to communicate with. Conversational I/O becomes more and more popular to computer-implemented models. The on-line mode offers unique advantages over batch processing, with ease of access being important for implementation. The user must have the feeling that he controls the model, not the fear that the model will control him.

In summary, the level of aggregation employed in the model-building phase may well be a decisive factor in the success of the study. Simpler models are more easily managed, communicated, and understood. As a result, the user will feel more at ease with the resulting model and solutions, thus favoring the chances for successful implementation.

Collecting Data and Testing the Model

Data collection is an important part of any study. The kinds of data used, the way they are collected, and their timeliness may well affect the ultimate success of the study. In particular, data used to validate the model and/or particular decision rules have a great impact on implementation, because the validation is a measure of confidence in the results. Here we will not digress into an elaborate discussion of different kinds of data, methods of collecting these data, and their use. However, one comment seems appropriate. Our experience indicates that data too often are interpreted to mean hard (objective) data. Very often key (hard) data are either uncollectable, unavailable, or too costly to collect. In those instances, subjective estimates must be used as a substitute for, or as an enrichment to, hard data. It is often best to get such subjective estimates from panels of line and/or staff people representing the organization. This procedure is significantly facilitated by having some of these people on the project task force with others organized in a guiding committee to which regular reports on progress are submitted. A consensus on these subjective estimates is, of course, desirable. We have found the Delphi method [*3, 10*] very effective in achieving this. This method was used in industrial, governmental [7], health care [*3*], and social welfare studies [*17*] and is found particularly useful in securing three types of information: inputs to forecasts and/or projections, subjective estimates on the values of parameters, and information used in the evaluation of alternative courses of action.

In the case of the inventory control study, it was not a simple matter to decide what method to use to calculate the corporate cost of capital and the cost of holding inventory. After several methods were considered, the executive committee was asked to decide among the alternatives based on the recommendations made by the task force. Moreover, the method for calculating the cost of capital, which was eventually found acceptable, required a judgment as to what the cost of capital might be like in the future as compared to what it was currently. A factor representing management's judgment on this issue was in fact established and used. In the process of computing the expected stockout or shortage cost, subjective information gathered by a questionnaire submitted to a stratified random sample of distributors was used to establish the probabilities of various customer reactions to stockout and subsequent actions by the company. These probabilities then were used in conjunction with estimates of costs associated with each customer reaction to a stockout in order to calculate an expected shortage cost [*9*].

In the case of the federation study, the guiding committee was asked to estimate the relative weight for each of seven factors which together comprised an evaluation of the quality of service. Moreover, a rather diverse panel of lay leaders representing all community interests was asked in a Delphi [*16, 18*] session to establish the value of each of some 250 client service packages in terms of a written statement of the community's goals and objectives. The executive directors of each of the agencies were asked in a Delphi session to provide utility curves for each of the seven elements of quality mentioned above. Outside experts and clients were consulted to evaluate the services offered and received by each of the agencies.

In the case of the library study, a Delphi panel representing the various libraries [*18*] was formed to establish the hierarchy of values for each of the eleven library materials. The same panel produced a set of utility curves that describe the sensitivity of users to the timeliness of delivery for each of eleven material types.

Another benefit of using this approach needs to be underscored. By expanding the involvement of line management and other experts, a large number of people become familiar with the study—a fact not to be considered lightly.

Thus, the kinds of data collected, how they are collected, and how they are used is another factor in the success of the study. The collection of soft data may not only be necessary, but better in the long run because the base of support for the study has been broadened, thus increasing the probability of successful implementation.

Validating and Demonstrating the Results

Before the decision to implement is made, the results should be carefully examined. This validation process can take many forms. Experience indicates that simulation can be an extremely powerful tool in this process. With this technique, it is possible to show management, using the same set of data, how the present system operates, how management thought the present system was operating, and how the new system might have operated had the new decision rules been used. This approach allows for a sensitivity analysis as well. In addition, it implicitly demonstrates the results of the study and generally makes a strong impression on management. This kind of reporting and validation is easily understood by and communicated to management and thus favors the chances for implementation.

In both the inventory control and library distribution studies, computer simulation was used to emulate the system as it operated at the time the study was initiated. The results of this emulation were then used in a comparison with the operation of the system using the new or recommended decision rules based on the same data. In the case of the inventory study, a stratified random sample of 90 out of the 7000 line items was used for the testing phase. Specifically, over a 100,000 transactions involving these 90 items over a 12-month period were used to emulate the system as it existed, to simulate the system had the company followed its own stated policy, and to simulate this system had the company followed the recommended policy. The results of this comparison were dramatic, and, because they were based on hard as well as soft data, management decided to implement the study.

The Final Phase: Implementation

The implementation phase itself is the most crucial one. Here the success or the failure of the study is determined. We have argued for a deep involvement of management in the study to reduce resistance to the changes made. If management has the feeling something has been accomplished with and not for them the climate favors success. However, additional factors come to play. The amount of planning done for this phase is the most important one. Many systems have failed because of lack of planning. The training of personnel, informing other personnel of the coming changes by line management, making resources available for the transfer, and many other factors should be planned for. The old system should be continued until all bugs have been eliminated in the new system. Even then the old system might be maintained operative for some time as a backup system until all people involved are thoroughly familiar with the new procedure. The OR group should aid in this process, be available for consultations and the training of personnel, and be prepared to handle all possible emergencies that could arise. When the system is installed and the problems have been worked out, the task has been completed. Periodic post-audits by the team are advisable to make sure their success is indeed a success. An informed and excited user is the key to this success.

CONCLUDING REMARKS

In this chapter we emphasized strategies for implementing systems studies rather than theoretical considerations underlying the implementation process.

Several large-scale studies were used to illustrate how these strategies may be used. We do not claim to have all the answers. However, experience indicates that the strategies presented are effective. The involvement of the user is essential. This can best be accomplished by having the user participate on the project task force. A guiding committee made up of top management and sponsors is often an effective instrument to affect implementation. Unless the user becomes familiar with the approach and accepts it as at least partially his, a great amount of resistance will be found in the implementation phase. Moreover, if the user is not intimately involved in the study, the chances for technical success become smaller. In particular, the problem of suboptimization must be avoided if the system is to be improved. Validation of results and models is an important factor affecting technical success. Simulation, using operating data when, if, and to the extent possible has been described as a powerful tool in demonstrating to management the impact of the various models and decision rules. In contrasting the results of descriptive vs. the prescriptive uses of simulation cost savings and increased efficiency can be demonstrated. Such uses of simulation tend to increase the chances of successful implementation. Continuous reporting, the utilization of all data sources, and the continuous planning for implementation during all phases of the study have been emphasized as other important determinants of success. A postaudit by the systems group after implementation and the elimination of initial bugs in the new system is advisable. Communications between the systems group and the users are particularly important in the initial phases of the study when the project is planned, the problems defined, and the methodology selected. An excited user is the key to success. They must be involved from the outset—the deeper the better.

References

1. Fancher Beeler, M.G., Reisman, A., Dean, B.V., and Herling, J., "A Multi-Library System Distribution Network Design," presented at the XX International Conference, TIMS, Tel Aviv, June 1973.
2. Churchman, C. West, this volume, Chapter 2.
3. Dalkey, C. "Long Range Forecasting Methodology." A symposium held at Alomogordo, New Mexico, 1967, pp. 1–12; Air Force Office of Scientific Research, Office of Aerospace Research, USAF, Arlington, Virginia.
4. Huysmans, Jan H.B.M., this volume, Chapter 13.
5. Little, John D. C., "Models and Managers: The Concept of a Decision Calculus," *Management Science,* **16,** no. 8 (April 1970).
6. Manley, John H., this volume, Chapter 8.
7. Mesarovic, M.D., and Reisman, A., (Eds.), *Systems Approach and the City,* Amsterdam: North Holland Publ. Co., 1972.
8. Mitroff, Ian I., this volume, Chapter 11.
9. Oral, Muhittin, Salvador, M., Reisman, A., and Dean, B.V., "On the Evaluation of Shortage Costs for Determining Inventory Control Policies," *Management Science,* **18,** no. 6 (February 1972) B334–351.

10. Pill, Juri, "The Delphi Method: Substance, Content, A Critique and Annotated Bibliography," *Socio-Economic Planning Sciences,* **5**, 57–71, (1971).
11. Pill, Juri, "Technical Management and Control of Large-Scale Urban Studies: A Comparative Analysis of Two Cases," Technical Memorandum No. 222, Department of Operations Research, Case Western Reserve University, March 1971.
12. Radnor, M., Rubenstein, H., and Bean, A., "Integration and Utilization of Management Science Activities in Organizations," revised version of a paper presented at the 1966 Conference of the Operational Research Society, *Operational Research Quarterly,* New York: Pergamon Press, vol. 19, pp. 117–141.
13. Radnor, M., Rubenstein, A.H., and Tansik, D. A., "Implementation in Operations Research and R and D in Government and Business Organization," *Operations Research,* **18,** no. 6 (November-December 1970).
14. Radnor, M., "Implementation Across Organizations," *Proceedings,* Invited Paper, Conference on the Implementation of OR/MS Models, University of Pittsburgh, November 1973.
15. Reisman, A., Dean, B. V., Oral, M., and Salvador, M. *Industrial Inventory Control,* New York: Gordon and Breach, 1972.
16. Reisman, A., Mantel, S., Dean, B. V., Service, A. L., Markus, E., and Eisenberg, C., "Measurement of Output in a System of Social Agencies," presented at the XVII International Conference of TIMS, London, England, July 1970. Technical Memorandum No. 188, Department of Operations Research, Case Western Reserve University, June 1970.
17. Reisman, A., and Kiley, M. L., (Eds.), *Health Care Delivery Planning,* New York: Gordon and Breach, 1973.
18. Reisman, A., et al., "The Application of Operations Research to Community Planning," a series of papers presented at the Annual Meeting of the National Conference of Jewish Communal Service, New York, New York, May 29, 1969. *Journal of Jewish Communal Service,* Vol. XLVI, no. 1, pp. 70–92, Fall 1969.
19. Reisman, A., Herling, J., Beeler, M.G., Kaminski, G., and Srinivasan, S., "Timeliness of Library Materials Delivery: A Set of Priorities," *Socio-Economic Planning Sciences,* **6**, 145–152 (1972).
20. Rubenstein, A. H., "Integration of Operations Research into the Firm," *The Journal of Industrial Engineering,* (September-October, 1960).
21. Rubenstein, A. H., Radnor, M., Baker, N. R., Heiman, D. R., and McColly, J.B., "Some Organizational Factors Related to the Effectiveness of Management Science Groups in Industry," Program of Research on the Management of Research and Development, presented at the 12th International Meeting of TIMS, Vienna, September 1965.
22. Rubenstein, Albert H., and McColly, J. B., "Phases in the Life-Cycle of Industrial Operations Research Groups," presented at TIMS-ORSA in San Francisco, 1961.
23. Schultz, R. L., and Slevin, D. P., this volume, Chapter 3.
24. Souder, W. E., Maher, P. M., Baker, N. R., Shumway, C. R., and Rubinstein, A. H., this volume, Chapter 6.
25. Vertinsky, I., Barth, R. T., Mitchell, V. F., this volume, Chapter 13.

Chapter 15

Ethical and Value Dilemmas in Implementation*

Robert B. Duncan and Gerald Zaltman

The issue of ethics and values in professional life is a significant philosophical problem. Few professional associations, which have put forth ethical guidelines for professional practice, have escaped that action without provoking considerable response from substantial numbers of their membership. The American Psychological Association [*1, 5, 6*] and the Operations Research Society of America [*12*] are perhaps the two associations that have precipitated the strongest and most sustained reactions, both positive and negative, among their membership with the issuance of professional practice guidelines. For example, some psychologists challenge the view that the subject should be informed of the nature and purpose of the experiment in which he is participating. Resnick and Schwartz [*14*] found that subjects who were informed of the purpose of an experiment behaved much differently than those subjects who were unaware of the true purpose of the experiment. Mitroff [*9*] has challenged the operations researcher's objectivity and emphasizes that scientists are often biased and partisan to their own theories.

Thus, although ethical standards exist for practitioners, it becomes important to ascertain the extent to which the practitioner abides by these standards. For example, Menges [*8*] examined all articles published in six psychological journals to indicate what effect new standards regarding informing subjects of the purpose of experiments had on actual practice. Menges concluded:

> The author finds no evidence to indicate that . . . the use of deception will decline, even though they seem inherently incompatible with APA's (1973) call for "openness and honesty" as "essential

*Preparation of this chapter was supported by a grant to the authors from the Organizational Effectiveness Research Programs of the Office of Naval Research.

> characteristics of the relationship between the investigator and research participant" (p. 1034).

In this chapter a number of ethical issues are discussed concerning the implementation of applied social change. Special emphasis is placed on issues involving the relationship between the interventionist and the client. An *interventionist* is defined here as any person or agency making a deliberate and invited or solicited effort ultimately intended to induce change in the structure and/or function of a social system. It is recognized that such a person may also be active in resisting change and maintaining the status quo. We are not concerned here, however, with this aspect of the role. The interventionist may or may not be a formal member of the social system involved. A client broadly defined is the social unit that solicits assistance from an interventionist. The client, however, is generally operationalized in the form of a particular person who is authorized by the social system to seek advice. In this chapter the term *client system* will be used to refer to the larger social system and the term client will be used to refer to a particular individual with authorization to act on behalf of the client system in matters involving change within that system.

This chapter is divided into two parts. Part I identifies some of the ethical and value dilemmas an interventionist might encounter. Part II presents the results of a preliminary survey of 323 members of The Institute of Management Sciences. These interventionists were asked to indicate their agreement with the issues identified in Part I, how important they believed the issues to be, and how often they encountered the issues as interventionists. These issues were cast in normative terms in a one-page questionnaire.

The reader should be made aware that we are challenging the issue of scholarly neutrality. All interventionists or change agents are advocates of some position or technique. Therefore, the notion of a value-free applied social change is a myth. The OR/MS interventionist is certainly not value free. He or she strongly believes in the overall rationality of this technology and its potential for improving the effectiveness of the adopting system. The same holds true for the organizational development interventionist. Here the expressed values are that clients should be a participative process, etc.

In studying the scientist's role, Mitroff [*9*] indicates that the objectivity stance of the scientists is unrealistic and " . . . if the scientist *qua scientists* is not a staunch partisan *advocate* for his theories, hypotheses, and positions they may be too readily ignored or not taken seriously by the surrounding scientific community." In a study of the psychology of over 40 *Apollo* moon scientists, Mitroff [*10*] concludes

> that scientists did everything in their power (excluding cheating) to muster every bit of evidence favorable to the theory that they could find. They were not out to falsify their own theories but to confirm

them. If they were out to falsify anything, it was the theories of their opponents (p. 15).

The critical question then becomes not one of value vs. value-free orientation of the interventionist but rather, "what are the values of the interventionist?" The values of the interventionist are critical because they have an important impact on how a problem is defined, diagnosed, and solutions and strategies selected [*7*]. The key issue may thus move from the value vs. value-free issue to the one of "whose side is the interventionist on?" and "does he know it?" For example, the OR/MS interventionist may identify or take sides consciously or unconsciously with the advocates of his position in the organization. This partisanship could lead to certain second-order or unanticipated or unintended consequences such as manipulation or coercion of those individuals not sympathetic to the advocated change. Argyris' study [*3*] of an OR/MS team in a large organization pointed out how these specialists became aggressive and competitive with clients as they tried to get their techniques adopted.

The more appropriate strategy might be for interventionists to be more aware of their values and deal with them openly with the client system. In this chapter we have attempted to cull from the literature various value-ethical issues affecting the interaction of an interventionist with his client or client system.

PART I: VALUE-ETHICAL ISSUES

Compatibility of Interventionist and Client System Goals

The goals of the interventionist and the client system may or may not coincide. This depends in part upon the level of goals under discussion. For example, a management consultant may be concerned with maximizing his financial gain derived from serving as a consultant. This goal or concern may not be compatible with the client system's desires to limit the outflow of financial resources in all areas of activity. At the same time both a consultant and client system place high value on improving the financial performance of the organization in one or more areas. For the consultant this increases the likelihood of being rehired in the future.

The issue involved here is quite complex and several questions can be raised. Must the client or client system disclose to the consultant the nature of the goals that the consultant's advice is intended to further? Must a consultant be told that his services will be used to secure a contract or the passage of legislation relevant to a military system that the consultant opposes? Should a management specialist be informed that a family planning clinic or health delivery system he is helping to design is going to emphasize a birth control technique that he is opposes by virtue of his religion or other value consideration? Similarly, should the client be fully informed of the values of the consultant? This is particularly important if there is any danger that the means for furthering goals can alter those goals and that the consultant or interventionist, with values at variance with those of the client system, may unwittingly make recommendations that would tend to subvert those goals.

Imposition of the Interventionist's Values

One of the first questions an interventionist must be aware of is whether he is acting on the basis of certain values and whether he is not engaging in an activity in a value-free way. We have challenged this value-free position above as being a myth. The interventionist does in fact have values as pointed out earlier in this discussion.

Thus the issue becomes what values and therefore whose values are to be served by an intervention. There is a natural tendency for the change agent or interventionist to promulgate his values, and in such circumstances we must ask whether these values are representative of those possessed by the client. Often the answer is yes because client systems or at least client system representatives tend to seek out interventionists with like value schemes. However, sometimes the interventionist may discover only belatedly a discrepancy in values between himself and the client or client system. In a specific situation the client system representative who selects an interventionist may not always share the values of the larger system or of key colleagues and may call in an interventionist known by the client to be sympathetic to his view. The interventionist is used selectively and possibly unknowingly by the client, whereas the interventionist may be assuming the client is representative of the larger social system.

For example, a manager who is an advocate of the implementation of a computer-based management information system might select an interventionist favorably disposed to the development of an MIS to do a systems analysis to determine the organization's need for this technology. The manager might use this interventionist as an advocate of this new technology to sell it to the resistant members of the organization. It would be important for the interventionist to be aware of the fact that the manager who contracted him was more favorably disposed to an MIS than others in the system. Being aware of the fact that there are some who resist the innovation would provide the interventionist with the knowledge that his first issue would be to reduce resistance or potential for resistance and open up the system to considering this change.

It is also both appropriate and necessary for the client to seek clarification from the interventionist about the latter's values, because they may affect the client or the system the client represents. Seeking such clarification forces the interventionist subscribing to the value-free myth to identify his values in an explicit way. Psychotherapists, for example, must undergo therapy as a part of their training. The rationale for this is that it sensitizes the trainee to his own biases that may act as moderators in his dealings with patients. For example, a therapist who has experienced rather traumatic experiences with his father might perceive all psychological problems as an indicator of the patient having experienced the same traumatic experience.

Whether psychotherapy is the mechanism or not, it might be constructive for interventionists in general to become more aware of their values and motives. Is the interventionist really concerned about the welfare of the client system, or does intervention activity satisfy his needs for power and control? If the latter motives are operating, this might cause the interventionist to be more manipulative in dealing with the client system [*2*]. If the interventionist is too eager to show the client system how good he is, he may not allow the client system to develop its own capabilities for dealing with the problem situation. As a result, the client system becomes overly dependent on the interventionist. For example, an OR/MS interventionist might be so concerned about proving the usefulness of his techniques that he does not allow the clients to develop those skills through trial and error that would enable them to effectively implement this innovation when the interventionist is no longer on site.

In general, questions should also be raised as to what the values of the interventionist are that are most relevant to the activities he is to perform. These activities may include problem definition, program planning, implementation, evaluation, and control. It is likely that different values are differentially relevant to different activities. For example, values concerning participatory decision making may be most relevant for program-planning problems, whereas values concerning the rights of human subjects may be most relevant when the interventionist is conducting research as part of the problem diagnosis process.

Selection of Client Systems

Is a professional interventionist obligated to provide assistance to anyone who requests it? Should a professional interventionist refuse his services to clients whose values are not compatible with his own? In the legal and medical professions the answer to this is fairly simple: Mechanisms do exist for providing these services to persons or groups who can demonstrate a need for legal and medical services and the inability to satisfy their need in conventional ways. It is also clear that vendors of restaurant services, real estate, and other commodities and services cannot refuse clients on the basis of certain values, such as those associated with the desire or preference not to have Blacks as neighbors or customers. Recently an interesting and as yet unsettled legal case in Great

Britain was brought to our attention where a manufacturer of industrial goods brought suit against a management consulting group that refused to provide consulting services because the manufacturer refused to hire immigrant Pakistanis for any position but menial, unskilled tasks. Although many details of the case are unknown, it is known that one argument put forth by the complainant is that the consulting agency withheld needed services, which it alone was best able to provide, and that this was done on the basis of a company (complainant) policy of no relevance to the consulting agency. The consulting agency contended that the hiring policy at issue was symptomatic of the inability of the manufacturer to act reasonably and to make effective use of any advice it might receive. One case in Great Britain is not necessarily an indicator of a trend. But perhaps it is not too soon to begin considering criteria or guidelines for use by an interventionist in deciding whether to refuse its publicly offered services to a potential customer. Argyris [*2*], for example, suggests that an interventionist should work only with client systems that permit free choice, the generation of valid information, and an internal commitment to solve the problem at hand. Argyris' assumption here is that a system can not really effectively create enduring change unless these three criteria exist.

Nature of Interventionist Contract

The contract established between the client system and interventionist can be complex, and there may be several key issues that may not be addressed in the contract. Who is the client? Is it the manager that brought the interventionist into the particular organizational unit of the client system organization or is it the organization as a whole? Does the unit to be most directly affected by the interventionist's efforts act as a group in seeking his help or are there just certain key members of that group who seek his help? How are conflicts in values and approaches to the problem to be solved? Is the interventionist free to opt out when he feels an unsolvable conflict exists? How responsible is the interventionist for dysfunction effects of his efforts? Should he make his services available to dealing with unforeseen problems of a solution after its implementation or does his responsibility simply end after a solution is implemented?

Type of Intervention

The choice of means to implement change represents another very important area where value and ethical dilemmas are likely to arise for interventionists. Closely related to the kind of manipulation selected is the issue of degree of manipulation.

There is a wide array of strategies or types of intervention. These have been classified as coercive, persuasive, educative, and facilitative. Manipulation is defined as "... (the) deliberate act of changing either the structure of the alternatives in the environment ... or personal qualities affecting choice without the knowledge of the person involved. ... [*16*]." If manipulation is defined in this fashion then all strategies involve manipulation to some extent. An interventionist is always related to manipulation whether directly in that he may, e.g., as a manager, reorganize a company division or indirectly as a consultant, e.g., in providing information for others to use in deciding where, when, and how to reorganize a firm. Just selectively providing information on the positive aspects of a given change reduces the alternatives a potential adopter has to choose from. This is more likely to manipulate a positive attitude on his part toward the given change.

Thus, manipulation is not a phenomenon that can be side-stepped either by the interventionist, who may claim that he only provided information or advice, or by the client, who may claim that it was the interventionist who by word or deed produced some change. The former case assumes a value-free activity in presenting particular information or recommendations to the client when in fact the interventionist is an advocate. The latter case, at the very least, assumes no value bias in the selection of an interventionist and in the cooperation provided him. Neither assumption seems to avoid manipulation.

The basic question here would seem to be "under what conditions are particular forms of manipulation warranted?" The alternative question suggested by others is "under what conditions is any manipulation warranted?" It is interesting to note that our colleagues, with whom we have discussed this, typically posed the alternative question just presented as the most important issue. This implies something negative about the concept of manipulation. Why isn't the alternative question ever phrased in the following manner: "Under what conditions is manipulation *not* warranted?"

It is difficult to arrive at any universalistic criteria as to when coercion is to be preferred over facilitation, education over persuasion, and so forth. The answers seem to be more context bound.

We certainly agree with the Population Task Force of the Institute of Society, Ethics and the Life Sciences [*13*] that core values such as *freedom* (the capacity, opportunity, and incentive to make and act on reflective choices), *justice* (equitable distribution rewards and punishments), and *welfare* (maintenance and improvement of vital interests of society) should be preserved. Inevitably, however, matters of interpretation arise. Consider the sales manager whose own position would be enhanced if a particular redesign of sales territories were put into effect producing more revenue for the firm and certain salesmen, yet less income for other salesmen. The redesign and reallocation of sales territories—say, giving more effective salesmen more or better territory—is consistent with the welfare of the manager, the firm, and certain salesmen. At the same time it is not to the welfare of still other salesmen who lose by the change. It can be argued that it is only justice being done in giving rewards to those who sell more effectively and giving punishments to those who do not. But this is a value position unique to few cultures.

Responsibility for Change Outcomes

Responsibility for Diagnosing the Problem

Before discussing some of the issues involved in the responsibility for the outcome of change efforts, it is necessary to pause and consider the diagnosis of the problem. In many ways, the diagnosis of the problem determines the general outline of the solution(s), and in this indirect way it is related to the change outcome. For example, diagnosing an organizational problem as simply not having enough information might oversimplify the apparent solution of just providing more information to decision makers. It may be that the problem is somewhat more complex in that organizational decision makers do not trust one another. Thus simply providing more information without dealing with the cause of this mistrust is unlikely to improve decision making.

We feel then that an interventionist's responsibilities for the change outcome vary as partial functions of his involvement in the problem definition. The exact same reasoning is applicable to the involvement of the interventionist in the various activities related to the implementation of change strategies. In the above example, the choice of the strategy selected for dealing with the "information problem" will affect the outcome. A purely technological strategy of generating more information for the decision maker will not resolve the mistrust that underlies his failure to interact cooperatively in decision making. A broader strategy might be required that focuses not only on the technological needs of greater information but also on organizational development in some form of team building that has the additional objective of reducing mistrust and conflict.

There seems to be little in the literature discussing how an individual's values affect his diagnosis of social problems [7]. In general, values influence both the stimuli to which one responds and the interpretation and weighting of the corresponding data. An interventionist who places high value on participatory democracy in formal organizations in particularly likely to look for and notice the extent to which collective decision making is engaged in relative to authority decision making. He is more apt to be critical of a perceived deemphasis of collective decision making and to rate this perceived deemphasis as an important factor contributing to a problem. It is our feeling that the client in his own self-interests should attempt to determine how the interventionist's values are operating and that the interventionist should cooperate with the client in clarifying this. Exactly how the client can do this is unclear and warrants considerable attention.

The client or client system is also a value-laden social unit. Values of the client for example may bias the selection of information to be given to the interventionist to evaluate. Moreover, client values may cause a particular structuring of information that presents a biased view of the nature and source of problems. This raises the general issue of how much freedom the interventionist has in discovering the real problem. The withholding of information from an interventionist restricts the number of alternative problems he is able to identify and choose from. In this special sense his freedom of choice has been narrowed. His freedom of choice is further narrowed if the data provided him are highly structured in a certain way so that certain interpretations are unlikely. Thus an important operating strategy for the interventionist is to consider the client system's definition, if any, of the problem as a hypothesis. The interventionist's first task then is to collect his own data in the system to then determine if in fact the client's definition of the problem is in fact correct. Of critical importance here, then, is the access of information to the interventionist. The interventionist must be allowed to gather the information he feels is needed.

Implementation of Change Program

The unavoidability of manipulation has been mentioned earlier. It would seem generally that manipulation, say in the form of a strategy of persuasion, is *less onerous* when the following techniques are utilized: (1) Getting and keeping attention focused on a particular problem or bottleneck–this is the indispensible first step. The quality of the attention must be active and alert; therefore the focal issue presented must have high interest potential and ego involvement. (2) Getting and keeping rapport with clients–credibility is essential in establishing rapport. (3) Building credibility–besides implementing basic methods, such as truthfulness and accuracy, credibility is often enhanced by utilizing the two-sided approach, sometimes referred to as the "yes, but" technique. (4) Appealing to strong motives–including emotions. It is acceptable to appeal to people's emotions as long as the appeal is presented rationally. There is often a practical necessity to appeal to strong motives if people's actions are to be changed. (5) Action involvement–it is often necessary in implementing attitude change, for example, to actively involve people in the change process.

The classic Coch and French [*4*] study of reducing resistance to change characterizes the above techniques. The complete participation group in implementing the change that demonstrated the least resistance to the seasonal job reassignments in their decision making with management (1) focused on the specific problems of how to more effectively implement the seasonal job transfers, (2) saw management as being credible in getting them (the workers) involved in the change process, and (3) was appealed to by management because the organization's survival and thus everyone's job relied on these changes. (See Reference [*11*].)

It would also seem that manipulation via a persuasive strategy approach is *more onerous* when the following techniques are employed: (1) Lying. (2) Innuendo–implying an accusation without risking an argument by actually saying it. This technique is often used when an accusation lacks sufficient evidence. The use of innuendos is often more harmful to one's own credibility than to that of its victim. (3) Presenting opinion as fact–that is perhaps the most common of all the questionable techniques of manipulation. Obviously this technique is counterproductive when one talks to those who know that other interpretations exist. (4) Deliberate omission–one particularly dangerous and common form of deliberate omission is the deliberate refusal to discuss the other side's point of view in a group-conflict situation. (5) Implied obviousness–this technique implies that a certain point of view is the only reality and that no further argument or evidence in support of it is needed. Utilization of the above techniques may cause the interventionist to appear biased and partisan with the result that he is likely to be credible in his attempts at persuasion.

The interventionist can avoid the above problems best when he is informed of all parties both within and without the client system who might reasonably be expected to be affected significantly by the intervention. This might well be information the interventionist could insist on having. At the same time, in providing solutions the interventionist might be expected to provide members of the client system with as many realistic alternatives as possible to choose from. By realistic alternative we mean simply alternatives with similar likelihoods of having similar results. The client system can then select that course of action it considers to have the smallest number of undesirable consequences for itself or some subsystems. It also seems important to us that the client or client system be provided with the rationale for both the advocated solution to a problem as well as the suggested means for implementing that solution. It can be expected that such demands, particularly after the intervention, will be made by persons in the client system who would be affected by any dysfunctional consequences of the intervention. This suggests one issue not mentioned thus far. The issue concerns value conflicts between the interventionist and client in determining the means of implementing a solution. Our own position is that the interventionist is obligated to discuss such conflict with the client. The rationale is simply that if these conflicts are shared openly, the client has an opportunity to more directly affect the decision process and thus the chance for manipulation of the client by the interventionist is reduced. We feel it entirely appropriate, however, for the interventionist to be as partisan and persuasive as he chooses. It should be noted, however, that the interventionist, particularly if he is outside the client system, cannot be expected to know a priori how his values may differ from those of the client or those of the system the client represents. If the client or some third party initiates the contact leading to, say, a consulting relationship, the interventionist may mistakenly assume that there is compatibility in basic values.

Once a problem solution or change is implemented, the issue of responsibility for its impact becomes important. With respect to the interventionist and client system there are several important issues here. Once a change has been implemented what responsibility does the interventionist have for the unintended dysfunctional consequences that might result? Is the interventionist required to provide services to the client system to help resolve these dysfunctional consequences or is it no longer the interventionist's responsibility? For example, the introduction of a management information system may pose a threat to some managers in the system with the result that they are very resistant to its use. Should the interventionists who introduced this MIS be required to come back and help the client system reduce this resistance or is this someone else's responsibility? One might make the case that if the interventionists in this case were more sensitive to resistance to change, they might have introduced the MIS in a way that might reduce the resistance of those affected.

The issue of responsibility also applies to the client system. In the above MIS example, the same issue of responsibility can be raised. What responsibility does the client system have in helping people deal with the psychological impact of change? Should the client system be sensitive and supportive of those affected by the change? Beyond helping people deal with the psychological impact of change, what responsibility does the client system have for relocating personnel who might be displaced as a result of the introduction of some new technological change?

PART II: SURVEY RESULTS

Nineteen value-ethical issues were developed from the review in Part I of this study. These nineteen statements (Table 15.1) are a first attempt to empirically identify to what extent practicing interventionists (1) agree with the issues as stated; (2) feel the issues are important or not; and (3) encounter the issues.

Nature of the Sample

A mailing list of members of several chapters of The Institute for Management Sciences was obtained. From this list a random sample of 754 individuals

Table 15.1
Value-Ethical Issues

1. If the interventionist perceives a conflict between his values and the client's values in defining the problem he is obligated to discuss this with the client.
2. Interventionists should be completely free in their selection of strategies for problem diagnosis.
3. The interventionist should communicate his value orientation to the client system.
4. The interventionist is obligated to perform services even for those client systems with whom he does not share the same values.
5. The client system has an obligation to inform the interventionist of all parties to be affected by the interventionist's activity.
6. In the absence of a written contract covering termination of an interventionist/client relationship the interventionist is obligated to work with the client system as long as the client system requests his services.
7. In implementing a solution to a problem, the interventionist should provide members of the client system several options to chose from.
8. Those affected by a given solution have a right to be informed of the rationale for that solution.
9. Those affected by a given solution have a right to have access to the evidence supporting a solution.
10. The interventionist is responsible for making services available for dealing with dysfunctional consequences of his activities.
11. The interventionist is obligated to inform members of the client system as to the goals and objectives of the interventionist's activities.
12. A client hiring an interventionist should make known to others in the client system what the interventionist is doing in the system.
13. The client system should provide any information the interventionist feels he needs to perform his task.
14. If the interventionist perceives a conflict between his values and the client's values in defining the goals and objectives of his activities he is obligated to discuss this with the client.
15. If the interventionist perceives a conflict between his values and the client's values in determining the means of implementing a solution, he is obligated to discuss this with the client.
16. If the interventionist perceives a conflict between his values and the client's values in determining the means of evaluating a solution, he is obligated to discuss this with the client.
17. Interventionists should be completely free in their selection of strategies for implementing a solution.
18. Interventionists should be completely free in their choice of criteria for selecting a solution.
19. Interventionists should be completely free in their selection of strategies for evaluating a solution.

Table 15.2
Characteristics of Individuals Returning Questionnaire (n=323)

Type of interventionist	
Outside	44.4%
Inside	55.6%
Area of specialization	
OR/MS	67.2%
Organization change-development	9.1%
Other	23.7%
Employed by	
Government	18.0%
Consulting organization	30.0%
Commercial organization other than consulting	35.9%
Nonprofit other than government	7.7%
Other	8.4%

were chosen to be sent the one-page questionnaire. A response rate of 43 percent (n = 323) was obtained. No follow-up letter was used for nonrespondents. The characteristics of the sample are presented in Table 15.2.

Limitations of the Study

There are several limitations to the study that the reader should be made aware of in interpreting those data presented: (1) The list of issues presented here is not meant to be exhaustive, rather this is a preliminary attempt to ascertain how practitioners view value and ethical dilemmas. (2) The sample is biased in that participants are likely to have a more professional orientation given that they are TIMS members. (3) The normative wording of the items is likely to create a more favorable response. (4) A survey may oversimplify the issues because there is no opportunity for the respondent to discuss and perhaps clarify his or her answer. An interview strategy might be more useful in that it provides for this elaboration.

Importance of Issues

In general all nineteen issues were considered important. The rank order of these issues by importance is presented in Table 15.3. The item (8 in Table 15.1) ranking highest on ascribed importance was considered to be mildly important to very important by approximately 95 percent of the respondents. This item was the statement that "those affected by a given solution have a right to be

Table 15.3
Rank Order of Items on Important Response

Rank	% important	Item	Median	Mean	N
1	94.7	8	5.39	5.19	319
2	92.8	15	5.24	5.07	320
3	92.8	14	5.30	5.08	320
4	90.5	13	5.17	4.98	316
5	90.1	17	4.86	4.74	313
6	89.7	9	4.90	4.81	319
7	88.3	18	4.86	4.74	317
8	88.2	12	5.14	4.91	313
9	88.0	1	5.09	4.84	320
10	87.7	16	5.06	4.87	318
11	87.6	19	4.84	4.71	316
12	86.9	7	4.91	4.73	321
13	86	2	4.69	4.52	319
14	81.7	11	4.95	4.68	317
15	80.7	4	4.58	4.42	316
16	79.2	10	4.94	4.36	307
17	77.0	6	4.39	4.22	314
18	76.8	5	4.70	4.46	314
19	76.0	3	4.43	4.29	317

Range 94.7–76

informed of the rationale for that solution." The item (3 in Table 15.1) having the least ascribed importance was considered important by 76 percent of the respondents. This item read "the interventionist should communicate his value orientation to the client system." The median ranked item was considered important by approximately 88 percent of the respondents. Table 15.3 shows the overall ranking of each item along the importance dimension. In nearly all cases the percentage differences between adjacent ranks were extremely small.

Agreement with Issues

There was considerably more variation in agreement with the issues compared to ascribed importance. The three highest ranking items in importance (Table 15.4) were also the three highest in expressed agreement. This will be commented on below. While 95 percent of the respondents agreed with Item 8 only 32 percent agreed with Item 18, the least agreed with statement. This latter item was stated in the following way: "Interventionists should be completely free in their choice of criteria for selecting a solution." It can be seen in Table 15.4 that the median item was supported by 82 percent of the respondents. Between 90 percent and 95 percent of the respondents were in general agree-

Table 15.4
Rank Order of Items on Agree Response

Rank	% agree	Item	Median	Mean	N
1	94.7	8	1.39	1.67	320
2	94.4	15	1.56	1.79	320
3	93.4	14	1.45	1.75	320
4	91.8	16	1.82	1.99	318
5	90.0	1	1.60	1.90	319
6	87.7	12	1.75	2.04	317
7	87.1	13	1.76	2.06	317
8	84.8	7	2.06	2.30	322
9	83.1	9	1.92	2.26	320
10	81.8	11	1.93	2.30	319
11	79.2	3	2.24	2.51	318
12	76.9	5	2.11	2.48	316
13	72.6	10	2.48	2.79	310
14	62.4	2	2.83	3.12	319
15	60.4	4	2.78	3.28	318
16	46.7	19	3.72	3.61	317
17	40.2	6	4.36	3.92	316
18	37.6	17	4.30	4.01	314
19	31.8	18	4.58	4.19	318

Range 94.7–31.8

ment with five items. Another five items were supported by 82 percent to 88 percent of the respondents and an additional five items were supported by between 60 percent and 79 percent of the respondents. In general a substantial number of the items was supported by a large percentage of the respondents.

Commonalities in Issue Agreement and Ascribed Importance

It was noted earlier that the three items receiving the strongest agreement or support were also the three items receiving the highest ratings on importance. It might be useful to comment further about these items. The three items are:

1. If the interventionist perceives a conflict between his values and the client's values in defining the goals and objectives of his activities, he is obligated to discuss this with the client.
2. Those affected by a given solution have a right to be informed of the rationale for that solution.
3. If the interventionist perceives a conflict between his values and the client's values in determining the means of implementing a solution, he is obligated to discuss this with the client.

We suggest that these three items are three of the most central norms involving the interventionist-client relationship. There is also a linearity of sorts to the separate norms. One concerns the desirability of openness at the start of the relationship and avoidance of conflict. Another concerns openness in an activity further along in the relationship, namely the presentation of the justification for an advocated solution to a problem. The third concerns openness with regard to the next step, which is the implementation of a solution.

One of the key questions that should be raised in any study of norms is, "Why are particular norms supported?" Alternatively, "Why are they maintained?" What function do they perform for the individual who participates in them? The intent and design of the questionnaire did not permit exploring such a question although it will be of central concern in our larger project. Still, some observations might be made. First, interventionist initiated discussion of value-related information as a means of identifying the value positions the client or client system maintains on a particular issue and of how committed he is to that position. This is very useful information for all aspects of the interventionists' activity and most especially in diagnosing problems. Second, open discussion, particularly of problem solutions and their implementation, is a way of co-opting a client in the problem solution and implementation process thus enhancing acceptance of particular solutions and implementation techniques. Third, interventionist initiated discussion is a way of clarifying for the client what his values are and how those values relate to the problem at hand. Yet another set of reasons are somewhat the reciprocal of those mentioned. Open discussion keeps the interventionist more constantly aware of his own value positions, their relevance, and their effect on his involvement with the client problem.

We realize, of course, that value and other differences are not necessarily dysfunctional. Some differences may be very desirable. As Rogers and Bowmik [*15*] have indicated, homophily-heterophily is concerned with the relationship between source and receiver in a communication exchange. They have indicated that when communicators are homophilous, i.e., they share common meanings, attitudes, beliefs, and so forth, communication is likely to be more effective. In heterophilous relationships, the interaction is likely to cause some message distortion, some restriction of communication channels, and so forth. These findings provide the manager with a dilemma in that often the interventionist is seen as somewhat different from the client system, which can lead to a heterophilous type of relationship.

With respect to acknowledgement and being seen as legitimate in this interventionist role, it may be that the heterophilous interventionist has the advantage. This is likely if he is perceived as different, because he is seen as being an expert in the particular area in which the organization is considering some changes. It may be that the change-agent can be most influential here if he is perceived as heterophilous in the sense of being an expert, although at the same time he is seen as sharing many of the same attitudes, values, and beliefs of the client system.

The heterophilous interventionist might be more successful in communicating his views to the client if he is seen as an expert. Again, he is likely to be seen as more legitimate in this role than just another member of the client system. This same argument holds in explaining why the heterophilous interventionist might get a more open sharing of the client's expectations regarding the change.

Encountering the Issues

Another dimension of concern focuses on the frequency with which given issues are encountered. Responses to this question were categorized as very frequently, occasionally, and very infrequently. The percentage range for persons encountering particular items frequently was 49.1 percent to 10.5 percent; for persons encountering an item occasionally it was 55.6 percent to 36.3 percent, and for persons encountering an item very infrequently it was 52.4 percent to 12.3 percent. This is shown in Table 15.5. Items 13, 8, and 7 in Table 15.1 are the most frequently encountered value-ethical dilemmas. Respectively, these items are: "The client system should provide any information the interven-

Table 15.5
Encountering the Issues

Item	Very frequently	Occasionally	Very infrequently
13	49.1	37.3	13.7
8	48.1	39.3	12.7
7	45.3	42.5	12.3
11	40.5	40.6	19.0
12	39.3	43.1	17.6
9	32.9	40.2	26.9
5	26.9	44.5	28.5
3	26.3	44.4	29.2
2	25.7	43.8	30.5
19	22.9	44.3	32.8
18	22.2	47.6	30.2
17	21.2	46.8	32.1
1	19.6	55.6	25.0
15	17.9	48.9	33.2
14	16.6	51.0	32.6
16	13.0	46.3	40.6
6	11.6	36.3	52.2
10	11.5	36.8	51.6
4	10.5	39.9	49.4
Range	49.1–10.5	55.6–36.3	12.3–52.4

Table 15.6
Differences between External and Internal Interventionists on Value Issues

Agree			Important			Encounter		
Item 4: Interventionist perform services for those he does not share values.			*Item 2:* Interventionist free in selecting strategies for problem diagnosis.			*Item 1:* Interventionist-discuss value conflicts in problem definition with client.		
$\bar{X}$	*t*-Value	Significance	$\bar{X}$	*t*-Value	Significance	$\bar{X}$	*t*-Value	Significance
Ext. 3.68 Int. 2.98	3.42	$p<.001$	Ext. 4.40 Int. 4.65	−1.88	$p<.06$	Ext. 3.20 Int. 3.50	−2.14	$p<.03$
Item 5: Client has obligation to inform interventionist of all parties affected.			*Item 3:* Interventionist communicate value orientation to client system.			*Item 14:* Interventionist discuss goal conflict with client.		
$\bar{X}$	*t*-Value	Significance	$\bar{X}$	*t*-Value	Significance	$\bar{X}$	*t*-Value	Significance
Ext. 2.69 Int. 2.34	2.00	$p<.05$	Ext. 4.06 Int. 4.45	−2.49	$p<.01$	Ext. 3.04 Int. 3.42	−2.45	$p<.01$
Item 10: Interventionist make services available for dealing with dysfunctional consequences.			*Item 9:* Those affected by solution have right to evidence supporting solution.					
$\bar{X}$	*t*-Value	Significance	$\bar{X}$	*t*-Value	Significance			
Ext. 3.01 Int. 2.62	2.30	$p<.02$	Ext. 4.69 Int. 4.94	−2.03	$p<.04$			

Item 16: Interventionist discuss conflict in values on evaluation with client.

$\bar{X}$	t-Value	Significance
Ext. 1.81 Int. 2.17	−2.85	$p < .005$

Item 10: Interventionist services available for dealing with dysfunctional consequences.

$\bar{X}$	t-Value	Significance
Ext. 4.10 Int. 5.54	−3.10	$p < .002$

Item 11: Interventionist obligated to inform members of client system as to his goals-objectives.

$\bar{X}$	t-Value	Significance
Ext. 4.42 Int. 4.79	−2.45	$p < .01$

tionist feels he needs to perform his task"; "Those affected by a given solution have a right to be informed of the rationale for that solution"; and "In implementing a solution to a problem, the interventionist should provide members of the client system several options to choose from." Items 4, 10, and 6 in Table 15.1 are the least frequently encountered value-ethical dilemmas. Each of these items concerns obligations the interventionist may have in working with a client or potential client who demands the interventionist's services.

Differences between Internal and External Interventionists

It was expected that there might be some differences on the value issues between those interventionists who are members of the client organization and those who are not. The internal interventionist, by virtue of being a member of the system, is likely to experience the following: (1) As a member of the organization more pressure can be put on him to take on certain problems he might not normally choose; (2) he might have less freedom of operation as more informal pressures can be placed on him to not disrupt the system and to meet the more personal needs of the client system; (3) he may have to be more aware of the dysfunctional consequences of his activities because he is going to remain a member of the system even after this particular task is done. If the intervention is not successful it is going to be easier for the system to request he deal with dysfunctional consequences.

Table 15.6 presents a list of the issues on which there was a significant difference between the external and internal interventionists on the agree, important, and encounter dimensions. Table 15.6 indicates relatively few differences between internal and external interventionists. It should also be pointed out that the mean differences reported, although statistically significant, are not very large. On a scale that ranges from 1 to 6 the mean differences reported are less than 1. Their statistical significance may then be an artifact of the large sample size (external, $n = 125$, internal, $n = 165$).

Perhaps the most interesting result in Table 15.6 is that there are only 2 out of the 19 issues on which there is a difference in *encounter* for the two types of interventionists. Internal interventionists encounter *more* value conflict between themselves and the client system in both problem definition (Item 1) and in defining goals and objectives (Item 14). It may be that the internal interventionist by virtue of being a member of the organization has more independent information about the particular situation and is then in a better position to challenge the clients problem definition and selection of objectives.

As indicated above, we had expected to find more differences especially in the encountering of issues by internal and external interventionists given the assumption that the internal interventionist may have more constraints placed on his activity. The data here seem to indicate that this simply is not the case. The main differences were in the level of agreement and importance.

Internal interventionists *agree* more than external interventionists that the interventionist should perform services even for those with whom he did not share the same values (Item 4), that the client should inform the interventionist of all parties affected (Item 5), and that the interventionist should make his services available for dealing with the dysfunctional aspects of his intervention. The external interventionist agreed more that the interventionist should discuss conflict in values over evaluation with the client system.

On the *importance* dimension, the internal interventionist felt that it was more important that the interventionist be free in selecting strategies for problem diagnosis (Item 2), that he communicate his value orientation to the client (Item 3), that he inform client of his goals and objectives (Item 11), that those affected by a solution have the right to evidence supporting a solution (Item 9), and that the interventionist make his services available for dealing with dysfunctional consequences of the intervention. These differences might be a reflection of being a member of the system. The internal interventionist may have to develop a broader base of influence to gain acceptance of his solution. He is seen as a member of the organization and thus members of the client system may not view him as an objective expert but rather as an advocate of a particular organizational perspective. Thus it may be necessary for the internal interventionist to be more open in communicating his objectives to the client system and more direct in attempting to maintain control over the situation.

CONCLUSION

A relatively large number of value-ethical issues have been identified as important among OR/MS interventionists. These issues, as articulated in a survey, received varying degrees of agreement and varying degrees of encounter. Overall several issues stand out as important and widely held norms. These are put forward here as a subject for further analysis. For example, why do individual interventionists participate in these norms? Some answers were put forward very tentatively. Much closer scrutiny is needed based on additional empirical research to address this question fully. A more intriguing question, which should also be addressed at the same time, is how positions taken with regard to the various value-ethical dilemmas discussed in this chapter affect the ways in which an interventionist behaves. We feel that issues such as those identified in this chapter are confronted at one time or another by an interventionist in his career (particularly early in his career and training). The resolution of this confrontation provides the personality to his professional behavior. This personality is anything but neutral and value free. It is highly partisan, which we feel is a very healthy state. What is not healthy for the interventionist, his profession, or client is the denial of this state and the refusal to assess its practical impact on the helping relationship.

References

1. American Psychological Association, "Ethical Standards of Psychologists," *American Psychologist,* **18,** 56–60 (1963).
2. Argyris, C., *Intervention Theory and Method,* Reading Mass: Addison-Wesley, 1970.
3. Argyris, C., "Management Information Systems: The Challenge to Rationality and Emotionality," *Managment Science,* **17,** no. 6, B275–B292 (1971).
4. Coch, L., and French, Jr., J.R.P., "Overcoming Resistance to Change," *Human Relations,* **1,** 512–533 (1948).
5. Cook, S., Kimble, L.A., Hicks, L.M., McGuire, W.J., Schoggen, P.H., and Smith, M.B., "Ethical Standards for Psychological Research," *APA Monitor,* **2,** no. 7, 9–28 (1971).
6. Cook, S., Hicks, L.M., Kimble, G.A., McGuire, W.J., Schoggen, P.H., and Smith, M.B., "Ethical Standards for Research with Human Subjects," *APA Monitor,* **3,** no. 5, **I-XIX** (1972).
7. Guskin, A., and Chesler, M., "Partisan Diagnosis of Social Problems," in Gerald Zaltman (Ed.), *Processes and Phenomena of Social Change,* New York: Wiley-Interscience, 1973, pp. 353–376.
8. Menges, R.J., "Openness and Honesty Versus Coercion and Deception in Psychological Research," *American Psychologist,* **28,** no. 12, 1030–1034 (1973).
9. Mitroff, I., "The Myth of Objectivity or Why Science Needs a New Psychology of Science," *Management Science* **18,** no. 10 (June 1972), pp. B-613–618.
10. Mitroff, I. this volume, Chapter 11.
11. Marrow, A., Bowers, D., and Seashore, S., *Management by Participation,* New York: Harper & Row, 1967.
12. Operations Research Society of America. "Guidelines for the Practice of Operations Research," *Operations Research,* **19,** no. 5. 1971.
13. Population Task Force of the Institute of Society, Ethics and the Life Sciences, *Ethics, Population and the American Tradition.* A Study prepared for the Commission on Population Growth and the American Future by the Institute of Society, Ethics and the Life Sciences, Hastings-on-Hudson, New York, 1970.
14. Resnick, J.H., and Schwartz, T., "Ethical Standards as an Independent Variable in Psychological Research," *American Psychologist,* **28,** no. 2, pp. 134–139 (1973).
15. Rogers, E., and Bomik, D.K., "Homophily-Heterophily: Relational Concepts for Communication Research," *Public Opinion Quarterly,* **34,** 523–538 (1971).
16. Warwick, D., and Kelman, H., "Ethical Issues in Social Intervention," in *Processes and Phenomena of Social Change,* Gerald Zaltman (Ed.), New York: Wiley-Interscience, 1973, pp. 377–418.

Index

La Salle University
3 5006 00184 8916